ONE GRAND NOISE

CARIBBEAN
STUDIES
SERIES

Anton L. Allahar and Natasha Barnes
Series Editors

ONE GRAND NOISE

Boxing Day in the Anglicized Caribbean World

Jerrilyn McGregory

University Press of Mississippi / Jackson

The University Press of Mississippi is the scholarly publishing agency of
the Mississippi Institutions of Higher Learning: Alcorn State University,
Delta State University, Jackson State University, Mississippi State University,
Mississippi University for Women, Mississippi Valley State University,
University of Mississippi, and University of Southern Mississippi.

www.upress.state.ms.us

The University Press of Mississippi is a member
of the Association of University Presses.

First printing 2021
∞

All photographs are courtesy of the author.

Library of Congress Cataloging-in-Publication Data

Names: McGregory, Jerrilyn, author.
Title: One grand noise : Boxing Day in the Anglicized Caribbean world /
Jerrilyn McGregory.
Other titles: Caribbean studies series (Jackson, Miss.)
Description: Jackson : University Press of Mississippi, [2021] | Series:
Caribbean studies series | Includes bibliographical references and
index.
Identifiers: LCCN 2021010549 (print) | LCCN 2021010550 (ebook) | ISBN
9781496834775 (hardback) | ISBN 9781496834768 (trade paperback) | ISBN
9781496834782 (epub) | ISBN 9781496834799 (epub) | ISBN 9781496834805
(pdf) | ISBN 9781496834751 (pdf)
Subjects: LCSH: Holidays—Caribbean Area. | Jonkonnu (Festival) | Boxing
Day.
Classification: LCC F2130 .M34 2021 (print) | LCC F2130 (ebook) | DDC
394.261—dc23
LC record available at https://lccn.loc.gov/2021010549
LC ebook record available at https://lccn.loc.gov/2021010550

British Library Cataloging-in-Publication Data available

CONTENTS

ONE GRAND NOISE

Transmigration of the Spirit

This book is about Boxing Day, a transnational cultural holiday, as it is commemorated in the Anglicized Caribbean World. Celebrated on December 26, Boxing Day is a long-standing bank holiday for members of the Commonwealth of Nations, currently comprising fifty-three members that were formerly part of the British Empire. Prior scholarship has tended to subsume Boxing Day under the larger Christmas holiday season and discuss it in merely a few paragraphs or a footnote or to examine it as solely a UK holiday, ignoring its distinctive celebrations in the Caribbean where the people "play Carnival at Christmas."[1] Under the auspices of documenting Christmas, scholars have been inclined to elide Boxing Day from the totality of the onetime British Empire, instead privileging its celebration in the UK, Australia, New Zealand, and Canada.

This book issues a corrective to those limitations, being a multisited ethnographic interrogation of Boxing Day in the Anglicized Caribbean World (ACW), chiefly defined as The Bahamas, Belize, Bermuda, St. Croix, and St. Kitts. In these countries, December 26 is more than the day after one of the holiest of Christian holidays. In actuality, many view Christmas Day more as Boxing Day Eve, whether or not celebrants know or care about the holiday's origin. Nassauvian Arlene Nash Ferguson describes the buoyant seasonal spirit in The Bahamas as follows: "As the feasting and sharing, the exchange of gifts and the intoxication of Christmas Day draw to a close, Bahamians from all walks of life prepare for the crowning event of the season: this is Junkanoo" (xi). Whatever the name associated with these cultural productions—Junkanoo, J'ouvert, or Gombeys—this bevy of aesthetic performances and public display events may be little known outside the Protestant ACW, other than in places like Florida's panhandle, which retained many British customs from its own colonial experience. In this book, in addition to describing these cultural events, I intend to theorize about how a certain festal moment is expressed audibly, temporally, and spatially, in a disparate historical, cultural, and political dynamic.

The Bahamas, Belize, Bermuda, St. Croix, and St. Kitts all support masking traditions, much like that of the better-known Carnival or Mardi Gras.[2] However, the *sound* of Boxing Day in the ACW and north Florida is an even more significant characteristic. This book's title, "One Grand Noise," reclaims the phrase by countering centuries of ethnocentric dismissal of these grand translocal celebrations as mere "noise," while honoring the survival mechanisms deployed for generations to resist their deracination. In my attempt to document these practices and improve our understanding of them, I have observed Boxing Day cultural performances on all of the specified Caribbean islands and Belize. To lay the groundwork for my study, in December 2005, I began my preliminary ethnographic fieldwork. That year, on Christmas Day, I traveled to Nassau in The Bahamas to observe the traditional Junkanoo Parade; "rushin" was scheduled to start at 2 a.m., but the weather required that it be postponed by a day.[3] The next year, I arrived in Hamilton, Bermuda (still a British territory and considered the most British of the isles) to connect with that country's Gombeys (pronounced gum-bays). The following year, I went to St. Croix (in the US Virgin Islands) to witness the opening ceremony of the Crucian Christmas Festival Village, which nightly would regal lively crowds on its carnival grounds. Instead of the traditional January 1st parade elsewhere, the Crucian festival is expanded to include the Feast of the Three Kings, which can extend it until January 7, as I observed in 2012. In 2008, I visited St. Kitts to witness its Boxing Day J'ouvert in the predawn morning, with fetes galore continuing until Las' Lap on January 2. I completed my initial ethnographic survey in Belize documenting the Garifuna—or more correctly, Garinagu—who sustain a rich Jankunú tradition as well. I have since returned to all locations for Boxing Day and other events to conduct more in-depth research for comparison.

The initial inspiration for this book was a north Florida family's century-old December 26th "Shooting Match" event. After attending this event for a couple of years, I broke a promise to myself to never again conduct fieldwork where I slept, as I did when researching urban folklore in Philadelphia. The opportunities to take a respite from writing, enjoy family, and indulge living traditions for once as an insider were compelling rationales for experiencing the event simply as a participant, rather than a researcher. Nevertheless, I couldn't avoid becoming curious about this event on a family's property where a Mississippi Blues Trail marker commemorates a historic juke joint that was part of the Gulf Coast "chitlin circuit." Currently, on December 26, that juke joint remains shuttered, with the only music echoing across this family's compound created by military-style bass and snare drums. I was already cognizant of the National Heritage Award winner Otha Turner from Mississippi, renowned for his fife and drum musicianship at his Labor Day picnics.[4] Then, I found a picture of the same military-style drums in *Christmas Sports in St. Kitts-Nevis: Our Neglected*

Cultural Tradition, awakening my curiosity about the reach of this remnant of the fife and drum tradition. At the time, I did not intend for my search to connect this music to the north Florida Shooting Match or even the southern John Canoe; my fascination centered on the military drums, seeking to contextualize them in the ACW. However, after finding little scholarly research on the subject and limited useful information on the internet, I decided to conduct interviews with the Henry family and some of the other drummers and to interact with these individuals again at the annual Martin Luther King Jr. holiday gathering on the property of another landowner, Nazareth Harris. From there, my interests grew, and my research expanded.

This resulting book provides a critical interrogation of Boxing Day as a cultural holiday with a long-standing genealogy in the ACW by focusing on transnational cultural flow in the circum-Caribbean. In the attempt to assess musical and other shared values, my intent is not to position what Tallahasseeans simply call "The 26th" as an example of Boxing Day fetes. Rather, in looking at The 26th, I seek to link equivalencies, in spirit with the ACW's cultural imaginary, aesthetics, and conduct. When I interviewed Virginia Henry Barnes, one of the oldest surviving Henry family members, she recalled, "They had a big day after Christmas." According to her, the event, dating back to circa 1911, was then called George Henry and Brothers's 26th, which they advertised by distributing flyers that attracted hundreds of African Americans to the site. The flyer simply asked, "Are you coming Dec. 26th to George Henry and Bubba's place?"[5] Regarding the origination of this gathering, Barnes admitted, "I don't know why. I just know my father having it and continued it. I say, maybe to find something to do the day after Christmas that was enjoyable to the people." Similarly, Rosita Sands reported that a participant described what Boxing Day Junkanoo meant to him as "something to do, somewhere to go, and the spirit of it" ("Conversation" 104). To expand our understanding of the origins and meaning of these celebrations, this book seeks to define the cultural formations underlying these ludic genres in the ACW.

Festive events are typically expressions of collective spirit, which reflect an intergenerational disposition toward communally participating in a multiplicity of transcendent ludic ideations; I refer to that process here as "transmigration of the spirit." Similarly, an important New Orleans journalist, Robert Tallant, in his introduction to *Mardi Gras* asserts: "Mardi Gras is a Spirit. I believe it is an immortal one. It is certain that it is at least as immortal as Man's ability to make believe, to escape the dreariness of the everyday life that is most men's portion, to have fun, to laugh, and to play" (xi). In New Orleans, historian Sam Kinser says that until the 1840s the Mardi Gras spirit was ensconced within the convivial Christmas season, "not Carnival" (207). Historical conditions led these religious and cultural commemorations to, at times, become associated with each other and, at others, to become distinct. As the next chapter shows, the roots of Boxing Day extend back as far as those of events marking the birth and crucifixion of Christ. In essence, according to Kenneth Bilby, the Black Atlantic supports two Christian-derived festal rites: the pre-Lenten Catholic Carnivals of Trinidad and Tobago, Brazil, and New Orleans are well acknowledged, while the Christmastide Boxing Day ACW festivities are less widely known because, unlike the pre-Lenten carnivalesque merrymaking, the Boxing Day traditions of danced processionals emanated from and were first executed by enslaved Africans ("Surviving Seculization" 179).[6] For instance, explorer Sir Richard Burton noted that, although Trinidad's Carnival resulted from European influence, most other aspects of these types of celebrations are "without doubt African . . . developed without significant interference from European influence" (65). These traditions draw on a distinctly Africanized spirit of ritualistic play as public communication, distinct from European forms of performativity.[7]

In the context of Boxing Day, the term "spirit" refers colloquially to a force that generates inner energy, personal power, and even a more affective life. Consider, for instance, Anthony (Tony) Carroll, who holds bodybuilding titles such as Mr. Universe and Mr. World, but also possesses a more than sixty-year history as a trailblazing Junkanoo artist. In his self-published autobiography, entitled *The History of Junkanoo: My Way All the Way,* Carroll says he valued earning recognition as Mr. Junkanoo even more than his other honors. In his book, he explores and explicates both the spiritual and somatic forces that inspirit Bahamians' preparations for Junkanoo in general and those of his neighborhood and immediate family in particular. He shares an insider's emic perspective about Junkanoo's all-encompassing, infectious, and evolving affect. For fifteen years, when Carroll reigned as "King of the Individual Junkanoo," his fame accrued from donning, for the duration of a parade, the biggest and heaviest headpiece of all those worn that day, such as that of an enormous King Kong character (111). His remarkable physique translated into a powerful somatic representation and performance in the spirit of "rushin'" (dancing to Junkanoo music). He sometimes laments the demise of the "freer spirit" that sustained past celebrations, from 1946 to 1950; but his recounting of a freer spirit is not just nostalgia speaking. Instead, he is bemoaning the loss of individual spontaneity due to institutionalized norms—constrictions that disallow a more carnivalesque extemporaneity. Additionally, he recalls that a large number of individuals became spirit-filled throughout the preparation process during Junkanoo, but now, sadly, many of them are sidelined.

The concept of transmigration also speaks to the movement of spirit into physical embodiments, rendering participants more alive, what we might call "high-spirited." Appearing at the 2001 Smithsonian Folklife Festival, featuring Bermuda, on the National Mall in Washington, DC, Gombey elite member

Allan Warner explained: "I feel that the spirit is what is most important—more important than the headdress, more important than the costume, more important than the drummers. The spirit of the Gombey . . . is the core of one's soul. Acknowledging that claim is the pride that you achieve, working towards elevating that." In the ACW, each contact zone synthesizes a transmigratory spirit in keeping with its own creolized arc in the spirit of embracing its own *particular* cultural production.[8] Creolization, as a key process resulting from intercultural contact, primarily between Africans and Europeans, only partially explains this diasporic complex.[9] A creole society is one in which, historically, a variety of cultures and ideas commingled.[10] Historians of the Atlantic world commend Ira Berlin for capturing the essence of what he called "Atlantic Creoles," who synthesized "the icons and ideologies of the Atlantic World into a new way of life" (255). The result within the Americas was a synchronicity, in which heterogeneous cultures, linked to the institutionalization of the trans-atlantic slave trade and colonialism, exchanged many knowledge fields. Dutch Caribbeanist Alex Van Stipriaan proposes a dynamic theory of creolization, in which "nothing stays exactly the same, while much remains unchanged" (525). In the course of rethinking creolization, folklorist Roger Abrahams defined it as a "cultural archive without walls" ("About Face" 285). The creolization process includes a decolonizing move perpetuated by a revitalization of African esthetics, mobilized through cultural productions that sustain how Atlantic Creoles self-identify. This book can be thought of as exploring Boxing Day as part of a vibrant, dynamic, inspirited creolizing process from slavery into the twenty-first century.

As with the contemporary pre-Lenten Carnival, many former ACW residents who now live elsewhere fill airline flights back to the islands to observe the Christmas holiday as well as Boxing Day festivities with family and friends. Roger Abrahams notes, "These festivities have been translated into homecoming events for those from the community who have emigrated" ("Questions" 77). Returnees contribute to the creation of transnational social fields that stimulate continuity, change, and the economy. In effect, push and pull factors negate the impulse for everyone to emigrate away and stimulate global as well as interisland travel. This seasonal period gives holiday visitants the opportunity to reassert their sense of cultural identity because the holiday is not the same anyplace else.[11] Anthropologist Philip Scher defines this form of transnationalism as "a group in diaspora" who share a homeland or "imagined community" (*Carnival* 2–3). Boxing Day becomes the vehicle to invoke utterly new emergent structures to induce greater revelry, splendor, and creativity. Abrahams explains how these forms of music "travel well, especially if they found their most masterful form through a singing, dancing, even stylized fighting format" ("Afro-Caribbean" 100). In my study, I also privilege the role of transnational cultural flows, as a topic popularized in present-day globalization discourse. In other words, there is a transmigration of the spirit: literally and vernacularly speaking, "The spirit moves."

The expression "transmigration of spirit" also implies a level of revelry consistent with ecstatic, sacred experiences that signify being touched by a transcendent force, in the way that West African–based sensibilities embrace both sacred and secular realms as one spiritual unit. Thus, speaking ritualistically, Bilby defines Boxing Day as a "powerful symbol of a surviving African spirit" that moves throughout the ACW ("Masking" 5). This spirit emerges in ritual art traditions such as drumming, singing, chanting, dancing, "and—most conspicuously—spirit possession and ritual sacrifice" (T. Smith 37). While ritual acts abound, Smith notes that they are not keyed exclusively as religious performances (57), and he links this transformative process with Victor Turner's *communitas*, a communitarian outlook in which a community intentionally "dissolve[s] class distinctions and conventional constraints" (57). Abrahams, too, magnifies "the *call* of the *spirit*," italicizing words to accentuate a "potential flashpoint" from which a renewed sense of communality emerges ("Afro-Caribbean" 97; his emphasis). In this way, festal rites translate into a universal spirit—a sacred and secular holiday mode in which all can participate. Whether called rushin', playing mas, or Jump Up, as celebrants masquerade and parade through town, they perform expressions of subversive, antistructural ideas (if only symbolically).[12] Carnivalesque moments prevail as most famously theorized by Mikhail Bakhtin in *Rabelais and His World* regarding how European carnivals in the Middle Ages embodied a spirit of revelry, mockery, and defiance. In the same festival arc, the carnivalesque gives way to the ritualesque by deploying an "esthetic of resistance," a more serious purpose.

These indigenized modes of cultural production encourage a collective spirit, granting them continuity. In his essay "A Presentation Distant in Space and Time," Édouard Glissant defines the collective spirit as "the common will that alone allows a people to survive as a people" (Glissant and Dash 5). In another essay, he equates survival with maintaining one's identity, generationally, even in the face of conquest and stupefying oppression ("Creolization" 84). Speaking politically and socially as a form of resilience and resistance, a repertoire of cultural knowledge becomes a symbolic or practical survival mechanism. For many islanders, a common history of colonialism drives a collective spirit of resistance for their own avowed personal renewal. In that way, it is via the cultural performances on Boxing Day that a prioritizing of personal and collective survival is achieved, translating into a celebration of life. Darren Bastian characterizes this sensibility best: "[It] brings what is deep in our bellies out for the world to see. It 'brings out a spirit of passion that is deeply embedded and instinctive and allows us to drop whatever social inhibitions we have'" (42).

Drawing other linkages, Virgil Storr equates a spirit of enterprise with Bahamian Junkanoo (300); similarly, Jocelyne Guilbault lauds Trinidadian cultural entrepreneurship (8). Employing Max Weber's Protestant work ethic discourse, Storr fashions a rich connection between Junkanoo and the kind of work ethic conducive to future achievement (301). Adherents, accordingly, value competition and the staggering creative energies it unleashes, while elsewhere the Christian world tends to commodify the Christmas spirit, conflating it into what he calls a "holy day of consumerism." Moreover, Storr assesses how the spirit of enterprise also infuses local economic acumen, with Junkanoo "cementing the belief that enterprise could lead to economic success" (304). Via the festival art, the same spirit of enterprise he outlines resounds throughout the carnivalesque Caribbean, especially by way of seasonal Boxing Day celebrations. Each festal moment supports networks of "glocal" (global-influenced local) entrepreneurial initiatives; as Alleyne-Dettmers explains, "Thus, within the realms of these populist centers carnival is an economic enterprise" or "marginal play, as an adjunct to the survival imperative" ("Jump!" 101). In turn, the autochthonous sounds of Gombeys, Junkanoos, and Carnival troupes depend on new media to capitalize and promote cultural production.

Reflecting a global–local dialectic, historically rife with interconnectivity, the heart and soul of cultural celebrations in the ACW cannot be separated from the African diaspora. Global–local discourse tends to position the two conceptual theaters of globalism and localism in bipolar opposition, with global capitalism leading to ill effects worthy of widespread condemnation due to fear of a global culture. The colonization of the New World witnessed numerous regime changes that resulted in political resistance as well as reverse cultural flows. For my project, I found Ulf Hannerz's reinterpretation of what anthropologist Alfred Kroeber called the "global ecumene" useful. Hannerz resuscitated the construct "to allude to the interconnectedness of the world, by way of interactions, exchanges and related developments, affecting not least the organization of culture" ("Nigerian" 239). I, like other scholars, gravitate to the understanding that transnationalism is not a new process, nor is globalization especially new to the Caribbean (F. Harrison; Matory; Brereton; Kearney). My study raises issues related to the modern world, migratory subjectivities, and even the translocal and glocal within transcultural communities bounded by identity formations that often transcend nation-state boundaries.

Still, many consider globalization to be a process of homogenization/Americanization by which the world becomes increasingly uniform.[13] In past scholarship, the same presupposition accompanied discourse related to the very survival of folklore and folklife—due to urbanization.[14] Only a couple of scholars speak to how heterogeneity is built into particularization throughout the African diaspora by conceding space for the reinterpretation of homogenizing Anglicized/

Americanized moves (Stewart, "Syncretism"; Ritzer). The following questions arise: What does it mean to postcolonial subjects in The Bahamas, Bermuda, St. Croix, St. Kitts, Belize, and even in the United States to celebrate traditions informed by past domination? How does discourse regarding transnational cultural flows complicate past theorizing of creolization? I support Charles Stewart's exploration of cultural mixture in which he states, "People across the world may be linked by their common access to similar goods and ideas, but they make very different sense of them" ("Syncretism" 41). Regarding Junkanoo, E. Clement Bethel wrote, "It is clear that John Canoe cannot be viewed as a single phenomenon transported intact to the New World, but rather as an amalgam of diverse West African elements, that emerged as a distinctive creative expression of New World peoples" (14). Even prior to reifying the globalization process as unidirectional, people of African descent commonly received and interpreted Western cultural imperatives variously, reshaping them in light of local circumstances. Moreover, the idea of creolization and hybridity hazards becoming an overvaluation if used to mask intracultural complexities (Birth 2).

My study seeks to be among the first to address the global economy in the context of the ACW, in conjunction with how regional festal calendars are purposed. As Hannerz asserts, "It can be argued that the center-periphery relationships of culture are not, at least at any particular point in time, a mere reflection of political and economic power"; accordingly, we live in a creolizing world, that is, "a world of movement and mixture" ("The World" 551). Melville Herskovits's 1952 assessment regarding African American influence on mainstream American popular culture still attracts reproach (as in Roach 22). The same opposition might arise within the ACW when Trinidadian Carnival is called "the mecca, or mother, of all carnivals in the Caribbean diaspora" and beyond (S. Burke 113). US hip hop culture exists globally as a somewhat secondary export that is not just musical, but includes appropriation of its faddish apparel. As a considerable turn, the music of the ACW carries more sway by way of the popularizing of world music, especially reggae, dancehall, and soca music. Representative of some of the newest music in the world, these forms communicate a transcendent spirit mobilized by the centrality of impulsive dancing.

Ironically, in the ACW, contemporary governments use Boxing Day fetes to highlight their distinct national cultures by capturing the spirit of these once-maligned traditions. Conceding the political intricacies of postcolonialism, the celebratory activities of the masses, once viewed with disdain by journalists, government officials, and the social elite, have become mechanisms for nation-building. Then, too, cultural tourism elevated a demand for iconic visual representations, and local folklife traditions did not disappoint with their picturesque masqueraders, Mocko Jumbies, and Gombeys to exploit. After centuries, these traditions have now gained a tenuous respectability. On Christmas

Day 2018, *The Bermudian* noted that the "original purpose" of Gombeys was "an expression of humanity and freedom of spirit in the face of unfathomable cruelty and indignation."[15] As a phenomenon, however, Boxing Day fails to impress or attract the casual global traveler for whom these cultural displays register subliminally as only fleeting examples of local color. The invincible spirit of vernacular culture, nonetheless, stimulates its own local economy with a transnational flare. In "The Local and the Global: The Anthropology of Globalization and Transnationalism," anthropologist M. Kearney specifies that "the 'nation' in transnational usually refers to the territorial, social, and cultural aspects of the nations concerned" (548). In this book, I show the extent to which, historically, Caribbean emigrants traversed multiple geopolitical spheres and transformed each emergent sociocultural landscape as well.

Of course, I could visit only one site on Boxing Day, December 26. Therefore, I conducted multiple site visits consecutively from 2005 to 2009, making secondary visits to all beginning in 2010. To generate a comparative analysis, during the summer months of 2009 and 2010, an additional university research grant permitted me to visit all the sites again, except Belize. These site visits were scheduled to coincide with other festive observances such as Heritage Day in Bermuda, Independence Day in The Bahamas, Harbor Night in St. Croix, and Emancipation Day (Culturama) in Nevis. Ultimately, my research data derive from multisited ethnography and formal and informal interviews as well as archival and secondary research. During the yuletide holiday season, governmental offices, libraries, and other agencies are often closed. The follow-up fieldwork enabled me to maximize my travel by conducting archival research and interviews at other times. Thus, I established contacts with archivists, cultural affairs administrators, and practitioners. Eventually, in 2012, I extended my fieldwork stay in St. Croix for the entire twelve-day duration; and in 2013, I witnessed *Wanaragua* and *Charikanari* in Dangriga, Belize, on Christmas Day and Boxing Day, respectively.

Although Jamaica, St. Vincent, Barbados, and Trinidad were not part of this study, I want to mention some similar holidays in those countries for comparison. According to the historical evidence, Jamaica's Jonkonnu tradition was the most legendary of those celebrations, being the site of the earliest recorded Jonkonnu galas by the nineteenth century. In 2003, my conversation with a Jamaican student, Glen Hurd, revealed her remembrances of Boxing Day growing up in Spanish Town, Jamaica, but, regrettably, traditional masquerading is no longer practiced there. In 2000, a *Jamaica Gleaner* columnist lamented the waning tradition: "In years past, the days of Christmas were enlivened by the appearance of the John Canoe bands as they danced and frolicked to the cheerful music of fife and drum. They, too, are almost a distant memory, a casualty of the passage of time and of the grim reality that is life in Jamaica today" ("Origins"). Hurd also supplied me with the central trope I use as my title, "one grand noise." When I first mentioned Boxing Day to her, her immediate response was "It's one grand noise!" Traditionally, Boxing Day commenced early in the morning with revelry by the Jonkonnus. Hurd remembers vividly how the sights, sounds, and images were frightening to her as a child. For instance, as a part of the mass dancing, "Jumping Jonkonnu" masqueraders would intentionally perform menacing gestures to frighten children. Furthermore, Hurd recalled that they would "dance-dance," entertaining any spectators who dropped money in the performers' collection pans. In 1872, a Jamaican observer described "groups of twenty, thirty, or even more, [that] passed through the streets, singing and dancing as they went. Each party had its queen, dressed far more gorgeously than the rest" (Beckwith, "Jamaica" 2).

In Jamaica, Brian Moore and Michele Johnson, privileging British Victorian Christmas symbolism, describe a "civilizing" agenda with a mission: "to purge the people's Christmas celebration of their old-time 'excesses,'" prompting the passing of laws to clamp down on Jonkonnu revelers (157). Instead of a robust Boxing Day Jonkonnu mumming tradition, such masquerading—if it appears at all—now occurs on August 1, which is Emancipation Day throughout the British Caribbean.[16] Nowadays, Jamaicans celebrate Carnival, taking to Kingston's streets annually from Ash Wednesday to the Sunday after Easter. Byron Lee organized Bacchanal Carnival events in the 1960s, appropriating the Trinidadian mas (a derivation of "masquerade") tradition. Yet, when comparisons are made, even Jamaicans call their Carnival "weaksauce" vis-à-vis Trinidad and Tobago's (Magnus). By happenstance, in the ACW, preparations for most pre-Lenten Carnival cycles materialize just as the last of the Boxing Day cycle of public display events terminates on New Year's Day until Ash Wednesday at midnight (Edmonson and Mason).

At the other end of the spectrum, St. Vincentians have a unique seasonal observance called Nine Mornings, which begins prior to Christmas for nine days. Featuring daily community sea baths, street concerts, and fetes before daybreak, the celebration concludes with a Jump Up. Its origin is generally believed to be connected to the novena of the Catholic Church, which occurs on the nine days before Christmas. In 2013, islanders celebrated a century of Nine Mornings fetes, commencing with a street parade showcasing lit flambeaus. Consistent with a foreday morning celebratory preference, in the capital city, Kingstown, the predawn street concert included caroling contests. There is also a lighting competition in which a Nine Mornings committee judges community lights, lit gardens, and individual homes, and nearby islands (counting the Grenadines) compete by zone.[17] Interestingly, though, the Garifuna in Belize are exiles from this isle and, through surrogacy, celebrate Jankunú at the end of the year as in most of the ACW.

Barbados, heavily influenced by its proximity to Latin America and that area's traditions during the Christmas season, is known for its Christmas parade that features Santa Claus and locals who decorate their trucks with colorful lights and rove about the city. There, annually, what is known as Crop Over takes center stage and is of historical importance with references dating from 1787. This premier harvest festival, originating on colonial sugar plantations, signified the end of the sugar season.[18] Dissolved due to a decline in sugar cane production in 1940, Crop Over was later revitalized, and the national celebration enjoyed its fortieth anniversary in 2014. Now, in the guise of an emancipation celebration, Crop Over concludes the Black Atlantic world's Carnival festive cycle. The festivity's latest incarnation spans a five-week period culminating on August 1 with what is called the Grand Kadooment day road march. In Bridgetown, an elaborate calendar of events regales revelers with a variety of expos, including the pageantry called the Ceremonial Delivery of the Last Canes, a decorative Cart Parade, Culture Village, the touristy Bridgetown Market, an extravagant Opening Gala, Calypso Tents, and numerous Finals Contests showcasing singing and dancing by young and old alike. As those festivities wane, more vernacular ones ensue such as Kiddies Kadooment, Cohobblopot, and the Grand Kadooment, culminating the Crop Over's festal season. As with most Boxing Day masking traditions, competition emboldens the heart and soul of nearly all of these cultural productions.

I have found no prior academic study or popular assessment devoted exclusively and specifically to the Boxing Day holiday as it relates to the Caribbean. Therefore, to historicize the event, this book will begin (chapter 1) by colligating this cultural holiday with its ancient origins. Whereas the Roman Saturnalia is widely recognized as a predecessor to Christmas, I note the holiday's connection to the Egyptian Sun King, Akhenaten, along with some particularities about the Greek Bramalia or birthday of the new sun, as another transmission route leading up to the Christian era. As with Christmas, Boxing Day owes its existence to Catholicism, which associated December 26 with St. Stephen, the first Christian martyr. I provide an additional consideration by way of the medieval crusades, a lengthy series of Holy Wars and an apposite site for cultural amalgamation and the introduction of baksheesh (an Arabic word for a gratuity and possible homonym for "boxing"). I note Britain's prolonged initial resistance to Christianity and the role of a missionary named Augustine in the syncretic conversion of Celts from paganism. I also historicize the evolution of masquerades and Christmas mumming into the Victorian period, including a selective summary of the growing resentment of wealthier classes for the working class's demand for Christmas baksheesh (gratuities) for their labor. Then, I present a nuanced argument historicizing the invention of distinctive Boxing Day traditions that led, in 1871, to the Bank Holiday Act, which established the public holiday throughout the British Empire and eventually took a syncretic turn pertaining to the Protestant ACW.

Introducing two principal (and interrelated) festal folk traditions that speak to the Caribbean as "gumbe complex," chapter 2 interrogates the ACW's most illuminating, time-honored, and dynamic Boxing Day customs: Gombeys and John Canoe. I also rejoin the ACW's global ecumene in the circum-Caribbean Basin and suggest a remapping of the Caribbean archipelago, extending it into an area of the American South. The aim is to contextualize and analogize Bermuda's Gombeys to a north Florida performance community, a possible "cousin" based on their shared loyalty to military-style drumming and other proclivities. On December 26 in Tallahassee, locals celebrate a century-old gathering with a Shooting Match that replicates many generic tropes corresponding to Boxing Day in the ACW. While in no way insisting the Floridians' December 26th revelry is a direct descendant of this cultural holiday, I use this ideation to delineate further the reach of the gumbe complex and to speculate about transculturalism in the circum-Caribbean Basin.

In chapter 3, I historicize and present Junkanoo and Jankunú in The Bahamas and Belize, respectively. Junkanoo, as Bahamians express it, is "The Greatest Show on Earth." Based on thick description and overwhelming past research, readers should, ultimately, see that the Bahamian Boxing Day Junkanoo has developed into a fully blown spectacle. Today, it is a competitive parade with massive costumes and huge musical bands, easily comprising upwards of a thousand members. Concurrently, in Belize, the Boxing Day Jankunú season takes place in Dangriga, the home and cultural center of the Garifuna people. Their ancestors faced deportation from St. Vincent island to this Central American coastal area. On this cultural holiday, adherents celebrate what they call *Charikanari*, with men and boys dressed as women and girls, but far removed from Western charivari. This festive art's functions and transitions deserve a full interrogation, chronicling the Garifuna people in a comparative analysis as part of the Boxing Day festal arc.

Chapter 4 situates J'ouvert (pronounced joo-vay) with Carnival in Trinidad. In that country, J'ouvert inaugurates the Lenten season as Carnival, a rite of spring. St. Kitts and St. Croix have their own long-standing masquerade and Christmas holiday traditions although celebrants now appropriate much of the festival culture of their island neighbor, including the celebratory name for their Boxing Day–related Carnival, J'ouvert. Located in the eastern Caribbean, these island chains may offer the most interesting and paradoxical cultural and historical connections. For instance, St. Croix is one of the US Virgin Islands; and while not unusual for Caribbean islands, over the centuries, six nations have ruled it. In addition, locals identify St. Kitts as Ground Zero because, initially named St. Christopher by Christopher Columbus, it bears the weight of the site from which chattel slavery spread. On both Lesser Antilles isles, Boxing Day morning's J'ouvert personifies Caribbean transcultural globalization.

The three subsequent chapters delineate three metaphors—"one grand noise" and "foreday morning" emanating from the "back o' town"—expressions submerged in centuries of temporal and spatialized racism.[19] As discussed in chapter 5, the first of these phrases relates to the tropological energy inherent in soundscapes inspired by an alternative aesthetic model, issuing forth "one grand noise." This phrase underscores centuries of dismissively linking African-style drumming and celebrations with disorder and mere noise. Historically, the region's festal rites produced an aural vibrancy that was perceived as abhorrent and loathsome in Western aesthetic judgment. Such noisemaking, which the ruling class sought to suppress, becomes further complicated when racialized. In this chapter, I will offer insiders' perspectives on evolving efforts to resist authorities using such rites as a survival mechanism. The subjugated strategically retained and deployed alternative modes of musicality to stave off any Western "civilizing" mission. While African-influenced music was often stigmatized as noise or unwanted sound, it signified a strategic act of perseverance and memory and a subversive remedy for those dispossessed. Moreover, today's panoramic soundscapes are rife with postmodern noise; it is an important component of the modern everyday with new technologies and amplified rhythms, especially on Boxing Day in the ACW.

Entitled "Foreday Morning," chapter 6 discusses the nocturnal orientation of Boxing Day in the ACW. While, on the surface, fear of the dark appears to be general, this chapter analyzes the cultural proclivity to celebrate in the wee hours throughout the region. It will trace the multiple cultural, historical, and political subtexts for the darkness trope. As with Boxing Day, the entire holiday season in the ACW stimulates a multiplicity of nightly ludic events, contests, and pageantry taking place in total darkness. Metaphorically, occurring on the cusp of the off-season, darkness alludes to the lack of knowledge most tourists bring about these early morning fetes. As a play on the Enlightenment, I use the term "endarkened" to convey the collective joy of revelers who engage in traditions enjoyed by their ancestors as a way of memorializing them and their bold insistence on upholding free subjectivities despite the imperialistic master plan to deny them humanity.

My fieldwork in the ACW unveiled the ubiquity of temporal and spatial divides that go beyond hegemonic racism and symbolically revealed unresolved political tensions, with Boxing Day as the vehicle for transgressive release. As discussed in chapter 7, parades and procession routes speak multivocally about the symbolic reclamation of seats of power. As a theater of the street, movement from "back o' town" through the center of commerce functions as a reenactment of persistence and resistance along with a sense of triumph over relentless obstruction. The creolized expression "back o' town" pinpoints the localities customarily allocated to the workforce within proximity of rich landowners and merchants. Each Boxing Day site offers its own centuries-old, particularized realpolitik. While not explicitly waging political or class warfare, the masses contest colonial control as a subaltern group of people that openly challenge authoritarian hegemony of space and problematize time through their exercise of antithetical power. As the saying goes, "We just play, you play pon de street."

Finally, my study endorses folklorist Jack Santino's distinction of the ritu-alesque from the carnivalesque. Just as his ethnographic examples cite parades and demonstrations intended "to effect social change," Boxing Day revels have a similar function. The nature of these island communities suggests fragmenta-tion, meaning practitioners no longer seek just the carnivalesque psychic release but support obligatory rituals, directed at enculturating their young in the face of injustice and oppression. Although vital and even revitalized, the rituals were already moving at the time of my research toward the ritualesque ambition to negotiate cultural tourism in the process. Unlike in Western societies, global Boxing Day masquerades do not appear to be endangered due to "guardians of the culture," whereby the festival art is generationally ritualized against the threat of regulations that would lead to greater restraint and bowdlerization. Cultural tourism may induce some locales to bring these fetes out of the dark into the daylight hours and to tune down the noise. Of course, past evidence indicates centuries of attempts from outside, but what if this time the move-ment for change comes from within, a grassroots product of ritual aficionados trying to ensure the perpetuation of age-old cultural performances?

This book is designed to facilitate insight into the polysemic meanings built into festive Boxing Day gatherings, temporally and spatially. In them, adherents surrender to a quality time, when revelers can attain a sense of renewal, recon-ciling physically and spiritually with an invincible life force, which is addictive in its own right. Trinidadian photographer Jeffery Chock explained full partici-pation in repetitive ritualized acts as follows: "It may be to show one's self off, to have a good time with friends to get away from the mundane, to try to fulfil a fantasy, to be able to compete within a category, or, overall, to be judged as the best" (94). This exploration of Boxing Day festive observances articulates a "spirit-touching experience" in the Anglicized Caribbean World.[20]

CHAPTER ONE

Christmas: Boxing Day Eve

The establishment of Boxing Day in the ACW is a long-distance outcome of the Christianizing of Europe, and the lesser known holiday remains most asso-ciated with Christmas, one of the world's most celebrated holy observances. Therefore, this chapter provides a comprehensive description of Christianity's lineage in order to scrutinize Boxing Day's consanguineous relationship to the rise of what Weightman and Humphries call the "Christmas Empire" (16).

Christianity as a religion was a millennium in the making before the adop-tion of widespread celebration of Jesus Christ's birth, established via historical transactions in a syncretic process that commingled with obscure European pagan practices (Miles 19). Although the particulars are abhorrent to many present-day Christians, Clement Miles documents the extensive amount of dis-information in circulation regarding the origins of Christmas and of Boxing Day as well. On the one hand, the historical interconnectivity of Christmas with the Roman Saturnalia festival seldom goes unremarked.[1] On the other hand, scholars rarely acknowledge ancient Egypt as also core to the nascent prom-ulgation of modern Christmas. It is exceptional, then, that Grant Showerman argues in *Rome and the Romans: A Survey and Interpretation* that "Egypt was the bridge to which all the ways of the old pagan times converged, and from which diverged all the ways of Christian times" (36).[2] If mentioned at all, Boxing Day is most often subsumed under Christmas; this chapter intends to provide a nuanced corrective by addressing Boxing Day's genesis and transnational flows.

I would be remiss not to mention Pharaoh Akhenaten first because of his monotheism and worship of a "universal god," circa 1350 BCE, as a precursor to Judaism, Christianity, and Islam. American Egyptologist James Henry Breasted explains that Akhenaten's reign served as a monotheistic revolution. Beginning his rule as Amenhotep IV, the pharaoh invented his new name to reflect his interest in Aten (the Sun God). Silverman describes the ruler as possessing a distinctive personality and warns us not to underestimate the role Akhenaten personally played in imposing his will on religious changes (75). Although this pharaoh's original, persistent belief in one god was short-lived after his demise, few contest Akhenaten's influence on Judeo–Christian cosmogony, which was characterized as "emphasiz[ing] life, daily cyclical rebirth, goodness, order, and the sun" (Silverman 86). Guyanese scholar Kimani Nehusi hypothesizes that the pharaoh's erasure from Christian history was because of his failure to institutionalize festivals to Aten to satisfy Ancient Egyptians' desire for regular celebrations; instead, he emphasized himself ("Origins" 81).

Ancient Egyptian cosmology and iconography were often adopted and adapted during the pre-Christian and early Christian eras. For example, archaeologist Kevin McGeough reports, "Some scholars believe that images of Isis [an Egyptian goddess of fertility and motherhood] holding Horus as an infant were influential in early Christian images of Mary holding the infant Jesus" (189).[3] It was the ancient Greeks that first appropriated the Osiris myth, conflating him with Dionysus, another deity who fits within the pre-Christian resurrection theme. According to tradition, Dionysus died each winter—the day after the winter solstice, on December 21, when days noticeably lengthened—and was reborn in the spring. When Isiac (relating to Isis) rituals filtered into the Roman world and began to become popular, they were suppressed as a "harmful influence on the Republic, and consequently on the Empire when Antony and Cleopatra were connected with it" (E. James 192). Cleopatra's connection to Egypt caused this ancient worship to be perceived as undermining the Roman Empire.

A Greek masking tradition, nevertheless, continued unabated on the Roman calendar, then celebrated on December 25.[4] J. C. Lawson explains, "The most prominent feature of these celebrations was that men masqueraded as various characters, to represent women, soldiers, or animals, and thus disguised gave themselves up to the wildest orgies" (222). In Greek mythology, Bacchus represents raucous and ribald celebratory behavior, currently associated not with Christmas but with rites of spring and worldwide Mardi Gras and pre-Lenten Carnival. Historian Park McGinty explains that "the function of the Bacchic cult was primarily cathartic; it purged infectious irrational drives by allowing the individual to satisfy the impulse to reject responsibility" (184). Today, in Trinidad and Tobago, the term "bacchanal" is a synonym for the carnivalesque. Also, Bacchus syncretized well with the Roman Saturnalia.

Occurring from December 17 to 23 and infused with inversion and hedonism, the Roman Saturnalia achieved greater notoriety than Bacchic celebrations as harbinger of the modern Christmas (Rigoglioso 17). Showerman explains the Saturnalia's evolution: "Originally one day only, December 17, but grown by Cicero's time to seven, the Saturnalia was celebrated by calls on friends, the giving of presents, including wax candles and pastry images, and the treatment of slaves as equals" (301). Historians often rely on accounts by the

Romans Cicero and Virgil to reconstruct ludic and other festive holiday rites. These accounts position the Saturnalia particularly as a period of unrestrained merrymaking and festal license. Historian J. P. Toner's in-depth study *Leisure and Ancient Rome* characterizes the liberatory spirit of such license as follows: "the Saturnalia when the tunic replaced the toga, extra wine was allotted for the household, and gambling was permitted" (69).[5] However, such leisure time created tension and social class conflict as the moralizing elites came to associate such popular activity with the lower class plebeians, eventually placing formidable restrictions on such celebrations. Toner addressed the intermediate stage in this dichotomy: "The dominant view of leisure changed in this transformation from a harmless recreation which supported the system, to an increasingly menacing and perverting danger which had to be mobilized to maintain order," only to be negated as part of the European "civilizing process" during the late republic (115).

In a world initially intolerant of Christianity, it took the Roman Catholic Church three centuries to become fully established and expand across Europe and an additional century to fully gain ascendancy (Showerman 579). Historians credit Roman Emperor Constantine I with merging the rigid organization of Christianity with local paganism to increase its acceptance. Historian Stefan Heir states that Constantine "introduced the celebration of Christmas with this intention" (417). Until then, Christians suffered much persecution and constituted only a small religious population; but after four centuries, Christianity finally gained primacy as a world religion. Constantine aspired to create a universal religion to unite a diversity of religious practices into one church, under his control.[6] In 325 CE, he called and presided over the first Council of Nicaea, a gathering of Christian bishops with the intent to eliminate confusion, controversy, and contention within the Christian church.

The turn toward Christianity stimulated a repressive reaction against the Bacchic cult, long considered to be too Greek (Orlin 64).[7] Documenting attitudes of Christian emperors in the first half of the fourth century, historian Michele Salzman explains that the growth of social class distinctions boosted a conversion by educated elites from paganism to monotheism (113). Interrogating this "clash of faiths," Ronald Hutton (a leading authority on the history of the British Isles) concludes that Christianity "owed its triumph to the fact that it was adopted by the rulers of the Roman Empire, by far the most powerful, admired and respected state in Europe" (248). Even more opportune for my study, British folklorist Ronald Hutton relates how the British church's repudiation of novel doctrines permitted "English paganism to survive as long as it did" (279).[8] Summarizing Pope Gregory's famed letter to Augustine, historian Michael Harrison writes that directions were given to the esteemed missionary to "accommodate the ceremonies of the Christian worship as much as possible to those of the heathen, that the people might not be much startled at the change" (28). Consequently, Augustine did not destroy the pagan temples and eventually converted adherents into the Catholic Church. In the "Christianity Comes to Britain" chapter of his book, Harrison presents, as common knowledge, the trajectory of the rise of the church on the island before the presence of Anglo-Saxons, delineating its lack of "strong appeal to the British Celts" (26). He conjectures that the Celts observed a form of Christianity derived from the Roman conquest (27).⁹ Therefore, the resulting syncretism fused British and Roman practices with much older ancient traditions (28). This hypothesis meshes well with Boxing Day celebrations and cultural flows in the ACW, including "surrogation," a process of substitution to address the recycling of ideations from one cultural group to another (Roach).

Muir's *Ritual in Early Modern Europe*, the first comprehensive study of rituals during that era, describes how the Christian liturgical calendar had been established by the second half of the fourth century. In that process, the Christian calendar syncretized "the pre-agrarian lunar calendar of the Hebrews onto the solar calendar of the Romans" (65). The outcome resulted in two distinct cycles: the Easter cycle of movable feasts and the Nativity cycle of fixed feasts. Strictly speaking, movable feasts, like Easter, occur annually on different dates, whereas fixed feast days, such as Christmas, are liturgical events occurring on a certain set date annually. In accord with this theory of time reckoning, present-day carnivalesque festal rites conform to the same demarcation in the Catholicized and Anglicized West Indies. Michael Harrison credits the word "Christmas" as being "derived from 'Christ' and 'mas'—an old English word, meaning feast or festival" (16).¹⁰ Connecting Christ's Passion to Christ's conception, occurring March 25, John and Miles Hadfield write, "Go forward nine months, and we come to 25 December as His birthday" (15). Whether premised on tradition, chronology, or astronomy, December 25 became the countenanced date for the "Festival of the Savior's birth" although the actual birth date remains unknown (R. Campbell 19).

Subsequently, the Catholic Church assigned December 26 to St. Stephen, described as the protomartyr of Christianity, who sacrificed himself as a true believer in Christ. Stephen is also associated with distributing alms to the poor, with Offering Day as a forerunner to Boxing Day. Catholics in many countries commemorate the life of St. Stephen, but the British Commonwealth's Boxing Day now dominates as a widespread transnational holiday.¹¹ The Irish still refer to December 26 as St. Stephen's Day and traditionally observe it with some reverence as well as revelry. In spite of numerous attempts to define the holiday's origin, there is no consensus. The website "Snopes.com" sardonically asks: "Does the name of Boxing Day come from the need to rid the house of empty boxes on the day after Christmas?" The conventional tendency is to objectify the name, equating Boxing Day with the "church alms-box, the contents of which were not dispensed until the day after Christmas" (Crippen 159). Almsgiving functioned as a category of penance, to gain forgiveness for one's sins often along with fasting as another form of propitiation. St. Stephen's is a feast day; but when abstinence days fall on a feast day, the requirements are abrogated, so there is no need for moderation. Emptying the alms-box, then, led to mutually funded, intoxicating celebratory events.[12]

The Roman Saturnalia was extensively appropriated and survived, as evident in certain English Christmas traditions. In Britain, when the Lord of Misrule, as this character's name implies, "went forth with his band of merry men, they got into trouble" (W. Dawson 198; also reported in Hervey as well as Dyer). During his rule, likened to that of a king, this "master of merry disports" planned all the details that gave meaning to the notion of Christmas sports, organizing a series of masques and masquerades as well as dances (W. Dawson 74). The masque genre thrived during the reigns of the Tudor and Stuart monarchs with the household of every nobleman appointing a Lord of Misrule (called Abbots in Scotland) "or, as we should say at the present day, to act as Master of the Ceremonies" (W. Chambers). Even in the countryside, households competed annually with the metropole to host the most extravagant Christmastide amusements (W. Dawson 112). Concomitant with the Saturnalia, their mock king's reign usually overlapped with the Twelve Days of Christmas, and it was not unusual for his governance to commence on All Hallow's Eve, October 31.

Despite Henry VIII's fondness for the misrule ritual, during his reign some attempts began to regulate and suppress these grand Christmases (W. Dawson 125; Hadfield). Predictably, the rise of Puritanism resulted in even greater denunciation of the practices. Similar to elite Romans' contempt for the Saturnalia, prominent Puritan William Prynne maligned these fetes:

"If," says the author of the *Histrio-Mastix*, "we compare our Bacchanalian Christmasses and New-year's Tides with these Saturnalia and Feasts of Janus, we shall find such near affinitye betweene them both in regard of time (they being both in the end of December and on the first of January) and in their manner of solemnising (both of them being spent in revelling, epicurisme, wantonesse, idlenesse, dancing, drinking, stage-plaies, masques, and carnall pompe and jollity), that we must needes conclude the one to be but the very ape or issue of the other. Hence Polydore Virgil affirms in express tearmes that our Christmas Lords of Misrule (which custom, saith he, is chiefly observed in England), together with dancing, masques, mummeries, stageplayes, and such other Christmass disorders now in use with Christians, were derived from these Roman Saturnalia and Bacchanalian festivals; which (concludes he) should cause all pious Christians eternally to abominate them." (W. Chambers)

In the early days of the Reformation, Protestants jettisoned all Catholic Church traditions, while England's first Protestant queen, Elizabeth I, took an undogmatic approach. In 1561, four years into Elizabeth I's rule, the appointed Constable Marshal "entered the hall in gilt armour, with a nest of feathers of all colours on his helm, and a gilt pole-axe in his hand; with him sixteen trumpeters, four drums and fifes, and four men armed from the middle upwards. Those all marched three times about the hearth, and the Constable Marshal, then kneeling to the Lord Chancellor" (W. Dawson 125). It was not until after dinner that the Lord of Misrule appeared to assist the Constable Marshal with the evening revelry. In this manner, as John and Miles Hadfield report, "The Martyr's Day [became] the mundane Boxing Day" (118).

Mumming is the aesthetic cultural production most affiliated with the Caribbean Boxing Day masquerade traditions. The word "mumming" is derived from the Danish *mumme* or Dutch *momme*: "disguised in a mask—were originally given in dumb-show; but at some time within the latter fifteenth century words had come to attach themselves to the mumming" (M. Harrison 73). In his exhaustive historical account of old English Christmas customs, Thomas Hervey suggests mumming derived from court masques (65). Mumming involved elaborate costumes, overly comic performances, and allegorical plays and speeches, nearly always performed in rhyme. The themes of such dramas gained leverage by way of "the return of the Crusaders" (Hervey 258). First appearing in the Middle Ages, popular heroes in mumming included Robin Hood and St. George, the crusaders' saint. Throughout the United Kingdom, mummers traditionally dramatized old Christmas folk dramas such as "St. George and the Dragon," which featured the King of Egypt. This drama commemorated the legend of the flight by Joseph, Mary, and baby Jesus into Egypt, which figured heavily in the story of Christmas (R. Campbell 46–49).

Hervey's *The Book of Christmas* in 1888 is the earliest study to conflate Boxing Day and St. Stephen's Day, identifying the former as the popularized name for the saint's day (302).[13] Hervey also proposed new hypotheses regarding the derivation of Boxing Day and of Christmas as well. According to his theory, Boxing Day results from a box placed aboard ships making distant voyages; donations placed there were given to the priest at a special mass after a safe expedition. Furthermore, he proposes, "This box was not to be opened till the return of the vessel; and we can conceive that, in cases where the mariners had had a perilous time of it, this casket would be found to enclose a tolerable offering" (303). Therefore, the ship's log would mirror the box's content. Focusing on the special nature of this post-voyage mass, Hervey proposes that "Christmass," which the offering from the boxes funded, is the true origin of the word "Christmas."[14] Interestingly, Hervey condemns the later distribution of a Christmasbox to servants and tradesmen: "The practice, besides opening a door to great extortion, is one in every way of considerable annoyance, and is on the decline" (304). Hervey's dismissal of this practice from his position of privilege may anticipate the adoption of Boxing Day as a site of protest and resistance in the ACW.

In my research for this study, I was particularly struck by the idea that the Crusades may be the source of the holiday's otherwise enigmatic name. Could "boxing" be a kind of homonym for the Arabic word "baksheesh"? According to Atiya, "Arabic has left its impression on Western languages in many fields" (239–40).[15] Although the word dates back to medieval times, more than eight hundred years ago, some scholars have been unwilling to consider etymologies from intellectual traditions with which they are unfamiliar, in an exhibition of modern ethnocentricity. For instance, Rabbi Rudolph Brasch condescendingly notes, "A far-fetched interpretation of the Christmas box sees in it a survival, etymologically as much as practically, of the Oriental *baksheesh*. During the Crusades, this theory alleges, Knights brought back from the East both the word and the tipping practice" (302).[16] In contrast, T. G. Crippen affirmed the Crusades theory, saying, "every person who had or was supposed to have rendered any service to another during the year looked for backsheesh (sic) at Christmas, indeed regarded it as a right" (159). In addition, Crippen furnished examples of those recipients likely and unlikely to expect a gratuity: "No one unless it were Mr. Scrooge before his conversion, would grudge a Christmas box to the postman, the lamplighter, or the dust man; but it is a different matter when servants claim backsheesh (sic) from tradesmen who supply their masters, or clerks and managers of retail traders expect presents from the wholesale dealers" (160). Even today, travelers to the Middle East are cautioned about baksheesh, a centuries-old system of protocol fundamental to the local culture, giving evidence of its globalizing range vis-à-vis the Crusades.[17]

Another outgrowth of the Crusades is the British morris dancing tradition, evincing a sense of the people's preoccupation with the campaigns. Some authorities say this dancing spectacle's name is a linguistic corruption of "Moorish" since it originated when some crusaders transported captive Moors with them back from the Holy Land. The morris dance was famously documented by folklorist Cecil Sharp and speaks to another example of transnational cultural flows. In *Seasonal Feasts and Festivals*, anthropologist E. O. James captures the intense experience of Sharp upon witnessing this dancing for the first time on Boxing Day 1899 and being "so impressed that he was led to devote the rest of his life to the collection, study and revival of the art" (286). James endorses a possible Spanish provenance for the dance since that culture is known for its Moors and Christians Festivals depicting mock battles and the driving out of the Moors in the twelfth century (287). Historically, it has been reported that some morris dancers belonged to a secret society and that originally the dancers blackened their faces.[18]

Later deconstructionists of the Crusades assisted in authenticating connections with the Boxing Day holiday to come, leaving little doubt about the magnitude of centuries of cultural contact on impoverished European commoners,
resulting in a practical consequence—the annual giving of baksheesh.[19] Due to
the brevity of any Western occupation of the Holy Land and Westerners' propensity to return to Europe thereafter, however, the Crusaders had no permanent impact on the Middle East,[20] whereas the Middle East had multiple effects
on the European economy and the desire to mechanize. In *The Invention of the
Crusades*, Christopher Tyerman challenged assumptions about the twelfth century as the golden age of pilgrimage to the Holy Land, including his comment
that "the distinction between a pilgrim and a crusader is often hard to detect,
an uncertainty which reflected reality" (20). Rather than an overarching cause,
the Crusades symbolized change, introducing new ideas that would eventually
hasten the Enlightenment, also known as the Age of Reason.

I posit that the exacting of payment and fees experienced in the Middle
East, coupled with dissatisfaction by the peasantry and the creation of trade
guilds, led to another custom associated with Boxing Day in which Yuletide
tipping became de rigueur. Some resisted; John and Miles Hadfield noted that
"So long ago as 1419 a regulation was made that the Serjeants and other officers
of the Mayor Sheriffs or City (of London) should not beg for Christmas gifts"
(119). Ostensibly, by 1737, the Duke of Chandos, James Brydges, had devised a
payment scale from five shillings to a guinea each for services rendered (119).
A century later, an 1837 New Year's Day article in *John Bull*, a London Sunday
newspaper, reported that the Foreign Office abolished the custom in embassies
by forbidding "the customary Christmas boxes to the messengers of the Foreign
Department, domestic servants of Viscount Palmerston, foreign postmen, etc.,
much to the chagrin of the latter" (Hole 24–25). This article provides not only
another perspective about the ambiguity surrounding the cultural holiday, but
it suggests the breadth of its obligatory gifting ritual and how it rankled those
in authority.

Because household servants frequently labored on Christmas Day, they
expected the next day off along with boxed gifts.[21] These boxes customarily
contained food, fruit, and monetary gifts. "The reliance of middle- and upper-
class families on domestic service meant that large numbers of people were
employed in the Christmas economy," reports Neil Armstrong, which "plac[ed]
particular restrictions on their own ability to celebrate Christmas in a familial
context" (61). Sometimes called "Christmas-boxophobia" in Victorian England,
the bestowal of such gifts also extended to bellmen, streetsweepers, postmen,
and numerous other tradesmen, though it waned as unions sought to abolish
their corrupting, abusive power, according to Armstrong. Unions opted for
higher wages, and the holiday began to lose its raison d'être: boxes. The disinte-

gration of household solicitation for gratuities led to the demise of another tradition: printed vernacular poetry that flaunted the obligation. Hervey describes how the distribution of written broadsides called "Bellman's Verses" resulted in resentment and cynicism by elite families, who equated them with "actual doggerel-poets" such as Warton and Cowper (306–307). Eventually, the dustmen's union issued printed messages instead, such as the following: "The United Association of Dustmen and Scavengers, of the Parish of _____ have the honor to pay their humble duty and respects to the good [Master or Mistress] of this house, and to solicit a Christmas mark of approbation of their unwaried exertions, which they flatter themselves conduce so eminently to the comfort and salubrity of the greatest metropolitan city of civilized Europe" (qtd. in Hervey 308). Kerry Segrave, in *Tipping: An American Social History of Gratuities*, quotes a source that emphasized, "vast sums are levied as Christmas *baksheesh* by housekeepers, butlers and other servants," and called it a "loathsome and corrupting form of roguery" (21). Considered extortion by the wealthier classes, the working class's receipt of gratuities came to be seen as ill-gotten gain. Victorian travelers crossing the British Empire habitually lambasted baksheesh as a "Hated word" (Kennedy-Fraser 332).

By the nineteenth century, the masses preferred to spend their discretionary time visiting attractions and pantomimes, forsaking vernacular traditions.[22] Accordingly, a split occurred: "As the Victorian middle-class Christmas developed, it concentrated the festival into two days—Christmas Day and Boxing Day" (Weightman and Humphries 21). In the same vein, Jim Davis's "Boxing Day" explains, "Traditionally, the Christmas festivities spill over into Boxing Day on 26 December, the day on which tradesmen and servants received their Christmas boxes, a seasonal gift of money from employers or customers, and so had an unaccustomed amount to spend" (13). Davis augments our understanding about the growing popularity of pantomimes (staged musical comedies) by acquainting us also with the disdain shown toward audiences who created their own spectacle by repurposing their rowdiness, brawls, and even throwing orange peels indoors (14). In all respects, the audience functioned as the main attraction, not the staged music, dancing, or humor (16). Therefore, even during the Victorian era, generally known for prosperity and refinement, celebratory disorder was associated with the masses on Boxing Day, in contrast to a formal, well-controlled Christmas for the elite (Connelly 15). In her novel *Abeng*, the Jamaican fiction writer Michelle Cliff illustrates this dynamic: "Like one of the family was a reality they lived with—taking Christmas with their employer and saving Boxing Day for their own" (17).[23]

It is within these historical contexts that Boxing Day came to flourish in the ACW. Because its observance there first expanded through the institution of slavery and British colonialism, those limited by dualistic thinking may resist the idea that Boxing Day dominates Christmas as a beloved holiday tradition.[24] Historically, on Anglophone Caribbean plantations, Christmas was the occasion when masters would "box" up their leftovers for distribution to enslaved persons, a carryover from the English custom. Historian Robert Dirks defines the Christmas season in the British West Indies as the Black Saturnalia. His and others' studies map the entry of enslaved Africans into a significant season of revelry of their own making, often as a hard-won concession (Dirks; Genovese; Joyner; Roach; Bettelheim; Nissenbaum).[25] Dirks notes that, "By the latter half of the eighteenth century, every British Caribbean colony celebrated the season with two or three days of recess, affording the slaves incredible license" ("Black" 2). Thus, common discourse posited it as enslaved persons' Christmas.

Rather than receiving real boxes, it was customary on plantations for enslaved persons to compete to be the first to shout "Christmas gif!" with a hint of a subversive demand.[26] Harnett Kane reports these words of surprise in the early morning were nearly sacrosanct for hundreds of thousands who relished the obligation to receive a gift, signaling that "Christmas was launched in the right way" (64). As supposed acts of noblesse oblige, the following thick description is quite revealing: "The gifts received were usually gay head-cloths for the women and 'hands of tobacco' for the men, plus barbequed pork, molasses and weakened liquor. The Negroes (in Edenton) arose early Christmas morning, singing their John Canoe songs and shouting 'Chris'mus gif' at their masters' doors. With liquor on their breaths and money in their pockets, they spent today in one long jubilee."[27] Although the provisions differed from plantation to plantation, the practices described were customary. These Pan-Caribbean cultural patterns included evidence of not just mumming-style masquerades but of enslaved persons being finely adorned—"Putting on airs"—wearing "cocked hats, cloth coats, silk stockings, white waistcoats, Holland shirts, and pumps" (Marsden 33). Marsden also mentions the degree of social commentary ruefully performed as dancers satirically imitated the motion and steps of the planters to render these elites laughable and ridiculous.

Nineteenth-century Scottish novelist Michael Scott based *Tom Cringle's Log* on his sojourn in Jamaica. In the novel, he declares Christmas time to be "the grand negro carnival," further explaining, "They don't confine their practical jokes to their own colour, but take all manner of comical liberties with the whites equally with their fellow-bondsmen" (227). Even in the Danish colonies such as St. Croix, the same festal traditions prevailed. Correspondingly, Tyson and Highfield record: "Village culture also penetrated in the planter's greathouse . . . most openly, in such institutionalized activities as the Christmas and New Year's festivities, when the field hands entertained their masters and their families with their music and dance, after which the masters recognized them and reciprocated with presents" (xiii). By the late eighteenth century, then, playing mas, or masquerading, became conventionalized throughout the ACW.

Britain's imperialist past means that the countries of the Commonwealth of Nations share a language, a common legal and political system, and regulated bank holidays. In 1871, the British Empire superinduced December 26 as an observance under the Bank Holiday Act, which formalized the practice of extending the holiday season to include Boxing Day. *The Times* noted that "Boxing Day was 'the Saturnalia' of our people secured to it now by Act of Parliament" (Pimlott 95). Pimlott provides the most precise information about the succession of bills that extended the holiday beyond the banking industry. The Holidays Extension Act of 1875 affected government employees, with the private sector following suit by the end of the century. Apparently, laborers in manufacturing companies required more government intervention, with the passage of the Factory Act of 1901. Therefore, the institutionalizing of the holiday was a process. Now, it is customary that, when Boxing Day falls on a weekend, a three- and sometimes four-day holiday ensues (as happened in 2009 when Christmas occurred on a Saturday) with this eventuality being enacted under the Banking and Financial Dealing Act of 1971 (Pimlott 167). Pimlott views the counting of New Year's Day as a bank holiday to be a concession to "widespread absenteeism" by workers. Regardless of having gained additional holiday time, in the ACW, seldom are festival rites curtailed on December 26, unless by the local governments or in accordance with a local idiosyncrasy.

Subsequently, outside of the ACW, by the mid-twentieth century, scholars disparaged the practice of mummers carousing from house-to-houseas "unbidden house visits," equivalent to the appearance of unwelcome strangers (Firestone 97). In the UK, according to one website, "Boxing Day has evolved from a charitable day to an extended Christmas afternoon. It's a holiday with presents that have already been opened and a dinner that has been eaten. It's a holiday best spent lounging around in brightly colored sweaters, wondering, lazily and lethargically, what to do next."[28] Additionally, that website laments that "there isn't anything left to do on Boxing Day except eat leftovers, drink and watch TV. Just as Americans watch football on Thanksgiving, the Brits have Boxing Day soccer matches and horse races. If they're particularly wealthy or live in the country, they might even participate in a fox hunt." With the rise of the internet, Cyber Boxing Day is now a widespread shopping day comparable to Black Friday in the US after Thanksgiving. Ironically, the geographical locales most identified with the Boxing Day holiday are now nearly devoid of any vestiges of an active carnivalesque season. In the UK, Canada, and Australia, Boxing Day is now just another day, except for the numerous Christmas sports events.

In contrast, the ACW constitutes a masking region in which masquerade bands survive generally without experiencing a gap indicative of revitalization.

Most ACW countries eventually followed the trajectory of the Bahamas where, in 1938, religious leaders finally prevailed in transitioning Junkanoo from Christmas Day to Boxing Day, making it another public holiday (Ferguson 12). To my way of thinking, it is this transition that also facilitated the conversion of Christmas into Boxing Day Eve, as described by Ferguson:

> My family gathered to celebrate the Savior's birth in our traditional way, and the air is rich with Christmas greetings and gurgling laughter. And throughout the day, there is a peculiar feeling that one has in the pit of one's stomach only on Christmas Day. It is the anticipation that hangs over everything as heavy as morning dew. There is this thought constantly in one's mind that come 1:00 in the morning, the moment you waited for all year will be here. (49–50)

There is a certain irony regarding the bifurcation created by the Christian leadership to compartmentalize the sacred and the profane. Although few celebrants are knowledgeable about Boxing Day's origin, their main intent is to indulge in festive foods, relax after partaking in the early morning fetes, and party from house to house, also in keeping with past tradition.

Celebrants concede that Boxing Day is a time for "different strokes." Cultural maven Mosimba defines "Old Time Christmas Sports" as "the name given to folklore groups in St. Kitts and Nevis that perform during Christmas time." Traditionally, Christmas Sports, as it is widely known, begins on Boxing Day and culminates with more of the carnivalesque to welcome the New Year.[29] On Boxing Day, festival art comprises only one platform for Christmas Sports; outdoor sporting events abound as well—from horse races to soccer matches—especially as seen in the UK. In Bermuda, an annual bowling tournament functions as a recurring fundraising event. While Jankunú still fascinates residents of Dangriga, a soccer match in Belize City electrifies spectators as the only game in town. In St. Croix, depending on the calendar of events, if scheduled to coincide with the Opening Ceremony at the Carnival Village, the road tramp to the village site may be delayed until festivalgoers arrive from the horse races at Mannings Bay Race Track or Flamboyant Park. St. Kittitians' early morning J'ouvert is entertainment enough, leaving behind only vacated streets as proof of the inauguration of a celebratory spirit that reigns supreme nightly until Las Lap, a week away.

I would be remiss not to also mention the coexistence of Kwanzaa, an African American cultural holiday established in 1966. Although I am not suggesting any inherent connection between the two, Boxing Day is coterminous with Kwanzaa, which emerged to fill a ritualistic void for African Americans during the Christmas holiday season. According to its founder, Maulana Karenga, Kwanzaa "allowed us to capitalize on the holiday spirit and orientation already in existence which facilitated the acceptance of a more meaningful holiday" (21). Karal Marling explains how Kwanzaa addresses ongoing tensions between Christmas and ethnicity: "At the very least, the dilemma of black theorists like Karenga in the face of a pervasively White Christmas demonstrates the immense power of Christmas ideology and symbolism" (279). On the seven days of Kwanzaa, adherents symbolically endorse seven different principles. For its duration, a candle is lit to commemorate the ideology of the day. This time-frame duplicates the period of celebration throughout the ACW but may occur there as well. For instance, in the US Virgin Islands of St. Thomas and St. John, the week-long holiday is observed with daily community-wide events, featuring live music, shows, local foods, arts and crafts, and occasionally a bonfire. On the last night, Imani, the Kwanzaa *zawadi* (gifts) are exchanged. Nissenbaum calls Kwanzaa an "invented tradition" like Thanksgiving for the Pilgrims and Hanukkah for JewishAmericans as opportunities for festive gatherings (313).

During the Victorian period, commentators developed qualms about English Christmas and its excesses, particularly mumming. In 1849, the *Illustrated London News* expressly championed its demise: "Christmas has outlived all antique mummery, and is all the better for having shaken off his ancient and faded trappings" (qtd. in Connelly 31). To its credit, the ACW's Carnival at Christmas, on Boxing Day, survives via Gombeys, Junkanoo, and J'ouvert although not without critics who, as in the past, wish to uphold the sanctity of the season. There is a blurring of Boxing Day fetes, based on national calendars and attempts to adopt a utilitarian scheduling of activities. In the ACW, the holiday's durability acknowledges the social construction of a place identity. At its ludic core, Boxing Day is a cultural holiday that unleashes a collective joy in commemoration of a shared past and a hope for future betterment of celebrants' lives. Deploying a tropological approach, I have sought to disentangle centuries of ostracism and defamation caused by the colonizers' lack of perspicuousness about an incisive rejection of the respectability politics, which they assigned to noise, darkness, and a differing temporal consciousness among their so-called Other. Considering past British colonial rule and postcolonial hybrid spaces, the Boxing Day holiday period transmogrifies, giving sway to both cultural homogeneity and heterogeneity.

CHAPTER TWO

"Military Drums Remain": Gombeys, John Canoe, and The 26th

In this chapter, I consider the distinctive role of drumming in Boxing Day customs in the ACW and north Florida, deconstructing the history of Boxing Day within transnational and transcultural flows as it relates to what Kenneth Bilby designates a "gumbe complex" ("Africa's Creole Drum" 163).[1] Throughout the African diaspora, West African drumming surfaced historically as a conduit for transmission of the festival art, diffused via the rhythm of goatskin drums played solely by hand, identified with an array of localized morphological spellings: gombey, goombay, gumbe, gumbie, gimbay, and so on. These terms are all allied with drumming, but linguistically specify rhythm, thought of synonymously with the beat. Often other idiophones were substituted, perpetuating the deployment of rhythmic sounds and undeterred by the edicts imposed by the authorities, which did not stop their ancestors from improvising and creating beats and resistance art.[2] Nonetheless, the gumbe complex under consideration here elucidates the broader transatlantic system formulated during the British Empire-building era. This focus argues for an expansive view of the long-standing effect of British colonization upon the ACW, "strung out over a length of more than 4,500 miles" (Cassidy, "'Hipsaw'" 45). Opening with Bermuda provides an opportunity to raise awareness about a geopolitical mapping that stretches into the American South, its nearest neighbor. Geographically, the circum-Caribbean Atlantic encompasses the totality of the region germane to Boxing Day in the ACW.[3]

This design calls for a broad interrogation of the historical conditions that enabled Bermuda's traditionalizing of its Gombey dance tradition. Constituting a mere speck in the Atlantic Ocean and once uninhabited, Bermuda remains a site cloaked in legendary mystery. I will historicize the intriguing anomalies representative of its colonization that, for once, did not entail Christopher Columbus. The atoll derived its name from Juan de Bermudez, a Spaniard who in 1515 anchored there while transporting a historian, Oviedo, who published the oldest extant account of his stopover. Therefore, about a hundred years before the island was inhabited, Spaniards knew of Bermuda's existence. Its Gombey tradition, too, stands alone in its unrelenting dedication to its forbears, except for the turn toward adoption of military-style bass and snare drums to be explained regarding the West Indies. More importantly, I will describe the costuming and the intricacies of other idiosyncrasies engineered by Gombey dance troupes to fulfill their objective.

In the folk cultural imaginary, numerous theories circulate about the origin of the festal art form of John Canoe; furthermore, the term appears in an array of orthographic spellings to prioritize sanctioned local pronunciations: Johnkankus, Jonkunu, Jonkonnu, Jonkanoo, Jankunu, Jankunú, etc. The term "John Canoe" is the Anglicized variant from the profusion of orthographies pertaining to pan-Caribbean seasonal holiday fetes (R. Sands; Bettelheim; Alleyne-Dettmers). In the tidewater region of the South, enslaved Africans performed this cultural practice, which was also called John Kunering or John Koonering. I will begin with a diachronic approach to interpolate multiple conjectures about John Canoe's origin and historical contexts, building up to the heyday of this cultural production.

In this chapter, I also transport military-style drumming dependent on the bass and snare drums to Tallahassee, Florida, where one family hosts a longtime December 26th Shooting Match. Although unrelated to the authenticated Boxing Day fetes in the ACW, the focus here takes the form of speculation due to the codification of numerous festal principles in common. As should be clear by now, transculturation engages the amount of reinvention and reinterpretation that intersect, creating new heterogeneities. In the South, shooting matches functioned as a significant custom during the Christmas holiday season. However, the appearance of a drumming style consistent with the instrumentation in the ACW's festal arc provides evidence of the transculturation process. This chapter outlines other particulars that sustain my argument when theorizing the foundational tropological metaphors to follow.

To begin, folklorist Roger Abrahams's territorial mapping assists in the construction of the ACW's geopolitical boundaries and the subsequent commingling of cultural performances. He notes, "It is a region which not only includes the Caribbean and the U.S. South, but many coastal outposts in South America on both the north, east, and west coasts, and many areas of the latifundium of Central America, including Mexico, Belize, and Costa Rica" ("Afro-Caribbean Culture" 100).[4] Bermuda comprises its own subregion in the expanse alternately known as the Greater Caribbean. Despite its isolated location, Bermuda is a subregion that is a significant locus in the formulation of important historical and cultural alignments in the ACW. For some, Bermuda's geographical placement problematizes a dynamic zone of sociocultural exchange. When early cartographers mapped the Caribbean, they often classified it as the "West Indies and Bermuda," which is inset on many maps—premodern and contemporary. That move positioned Bermuda as an outlier based on the latitudes and longitudes delineating the suboceanic basin of the Atlantic Ocean. A crescent-shaped oceanic system of over 150 islands and islets, it is situated in the northwestern Atlantic as close as 570 miles from Cape Hatteras, North Carolina. Its proximity to the US may suggest that it is a territory of that country, whereas, in fact, Bermuda is the longest surviving overseas territory of the British Empire. Even so, a circum-Caribbean imaginary solidifies and dynamically influences the cultural traditions of the West Indies as well as its rim.

Bermuda is also Britain's oldest Caribbean colony, and a persistent enchantment enfolds its "discovery." In 1603, Venturilla, the first individual of African descent to visit the Western Hemisphere, voyaged there on a ship commanded by a Spaniard (Packwood 1). Calling it a "tiny dot in the Atlantic," historian Terry Tucker also referred to Bermuda as "The Shunned and Dreaded Coast."[5] Perceived as too small and being uninhabited, the island was shunned by the Spanish; and it remained unpopulated until the English colonized it, making it their second permanent colony in the Western Hemisphere. Perhaps, with the same awe generated centuries later by space travel, Bermuda's detection captured the imagination of prominent English writers and their readers. Most famously, William Shakespeare was among the first public figures to allude to Bermuda; he "made the 'far Bermoothes'—only recently discovered in his day—the scene of 'The Tempest'" (Strode vii). Strode further attests to Bermudians' indubitable claim of being Prospero's original island (175). In early June 1609, the *Sea Venture* was the flagship of an armada of nine ships headed to Jamestown, Virginia. Caught in a hurricane, instead of sinking, survivors floated ashore to Bermuda. Within a year, one of the *Sea Venture*'s survivors, William Strachey, docked in Virginia and wrote a letter to the Countess of Bedford in London. The published letter serves as proof of the isle's influence on Shakespeare, with the bard borrowing some of the letter's language for his own creative imagination (Tucker 35).

In addition, the Bermuda Triangle legend has stimulated many prose narratives about the coral islands, officially called the Bermudas.[6] Another fact distinguishes Bermuda: its being the northernmost of coral islands in the world and the largest (John Jackson 9). Because it is prone to shipwrecks, sailor yarns abound, "enshroud[ing] the islands" (Hayward 8). John Jackson enumerates the following rationales propagated over the centuries to explain macabre disappearances: "seaquakes, waterspouts, tidal waves, freak seas, death rays from Atlantis, black holes in space, underwater signaling devices which guided invaders from other planets, UFOs collecting earthlings, time warps, reverse gravity fields, and witchcraft!" (17). Despite portents of danger, newcomers continued to colonize Bermuda at a disproportionate rate. In *Vexed and Troubled Englishmen*, historian Carl Bridenbaugh insightfully suggests that swarm behavior led to the out migration of 2 percent of the British population across the Atlantic Ocean. He estimates that, from 1620 to 1642, "Those on the continent of North America numbered perhaps 3,300; and Bermuda had 'above 2000' more" (410). To these seagoers, Bermuda's climate, native foods, and size translated into Edenic.

Unlike elsewhere, on this smallest British colony, Bermuda emerged as a "society with slaves," rather than a plantocracy. Virginia Bernhard's meticulous recuperative study reveals multiple findings related to Bermuda's unique racialized history; for example, "While Bermuda and Virginia had markedly different demographic histories, the two colonies were similar in one important aspect: the ambiguous status of blacks in the early years of settlement. In Bermuda, as in Virginia, it appears that for a brief time at least, while blacks were still few in number, some of them enjoyed a measure of freedom and a status similar to that of white laborers" (27). In 1669, enslaved Africans petitioned Bermuda's new governor for their freedom, based on their having been baptized Christians (138). The governor later ruled that Christian baptism did not equate to liberty. In addition, Bernhard astutely notes the following significant details: "the governor carefully avoided using the words slave or slavery," and "some of Bermuda's blacks were literate and, moreover, were learned enough to put their demands into written form" (139). Indubitably, these particulars established a pre-racial countenance on the cusp of the ascendancy of structural racism as a means to justify the predominance of chattel slavery to come.

Bernhard methodically assessed the island's racial history and confirms, "While Bermuda's whites still avoided using the word slave until the 1670s and seemed reluctant to admit that servitude for blacks was developing into full-fledged slavery, it is clear that the colony's blacks were all too aware of their condition. By the 1640s some were trying to run away" (82). Seemingly, then, racial strife emerged in conjunction with the historical occurrence of conspiracies that involved two horrific components: poisoning and the involvement of French privateers. Sarah (or Sally) Bassett warrants recognition because, on a "broiling June day" in 1730, she committed the capital crime of aspiring to poison her granddaughter's owners, Mr. and Mrs. Thomas Fostera, along with their servants (Tucker 89). A constant fear of being subjected to such poisoning by "trusted" servants existed among slaveholders everywhere. In his travel book, *Bermuda Journey*, William Zuill mused, "It is curious, that while so many punishments have been forgotten, the burning of Sally Bassett should have made such a deep impression that it became a Bermuda legend" (133). In the oral tradition, she survives, blamed for the rare heat wave during the summer months. Significantly, the Bermuda Conspiracy of 1761 is set apart from other islands in the region because those implicated were enslaved, but also included entrepreneurs and merchant marines (Maxwell, "Enslaved"). While most of the conspirators were mariners and/or pilots, the one female named Nanny allegedly possessed links to obeah as a gifted rootworker. This insurgency "remained a watershed event: the last time enslaved peoples on the island would seek to subvert, by any means, the colonial government on the island" (Maxwell, "Enslaved" 178).

Gombeys exist today despite attempts to suppress the tradition "as shown by the banning of their festivities after the trouble of 1761" (Zuill, "Story" 237). Bernhard also helps date the Gombeys by citing laws passed in the late 1720s to limit "Dancing of Nights" (211). The letters of Harriet Suzette Lloyd establish textual evidence that demarcates the revitalization of the Gombeys. Ergo, Zuill writes, "before the end of slavery they were once again an exciting part of the Bermuda scene" ("Story" 237). Visiting Bermuda for two years, Lloyd detailed Bermuda's flora and agriculture as well as its enslaved people. Bermudian historian Cyril Packwood relies on Lloyd's *Sketches* to affirm the existence of enslaved pure Africans, including a man known to Lloyd as "a member of a Gombay troupe" (69).[7] In 1830, according to the *Royal Gazette*, two enslaved Africans, Ajax and Mentor, "mixed in the large crowd" and escaped. Their owner, John Walker, advertised for their return in a local newspaper: "The deluded creatures are advised to come home to avoid expense and punishment, as they went off without a cause at Christmas, following that idolatrous procession the Gumba" (95). Such premeditated acts of flight constitute a form of day-to-day resistance certifying a deep-seated resentment of physical exploitation along with the constancy of a desire to be self-emancipated; thereby, behind the Gombey mask, sedition could arise to fruition. After emancipation, in 1837, the *Bermuda Gazette* railed against the island's Gombey dancers: "We fully agree with our correspondent that the savage and nonsensical exhibition of the Gumba, practiced here by the idle, should be done away with, as a thing not suited to a civilised Community, and highly dangerous to passengers on horses or in carriages."[8]

After Bermuda's complicity with the South during the Civil War, tourism developed into an industry, and "old-fashioned little Bermuda gained the appellative of 'The Riviera of the Western Hemisphere'" (Strode 71). John Jackson reported in 1988 that tourism plays a principal role in Bermuda's economy along with international business, which consistently provides more revenue than tourism (116). In the capital city, "Hamilton's first hotel opened in 1863 but it was not until the 1880s that Bermuda's reputation as a refuge from the North American winter became more established" (131). Unlike the US winter season, Bermuda offers a year-round resort without a rainy season and a climate that allows for year-round enjoyment of outdoor activities (150–51). For a century, however, Bermuda's Gombeys were in no way associated with the isle's tourism;

nowadays, they constitute its most iconic resource in terms of merchandizing and marketing.

Nonetheless, many chroniclers (similar to Margaret Newton in *Glimpses of Life in Bermuda and the Tropics)* were oblivious to the Gombey tradition, preferring to note Bermuda's similarity to British culture. While some travelers delighted in the Gombeys' appearances, others like Newton expressed disdain, stereotyping the Black Bermudians' propensity for everyday self-adornment. For example, the opulence of a bride's wedding caught Newton's attention: "on that occasion [she] wore a cream coloured silk dress with a train, tulle veil, wreathe, etc., and had six bridesmaids dressed similarly, and two little girls to hold up the train" (177). As to be expected, Bermuda attracted countless visiting authors, with the most enduring and exalted being Mark Twain, who dubbed it "the tidiest place in the world" (Packwood 129). Scouring Twain's latest published letters, unfortunately, yielded no mention of Gombeys.

The Honorable Louise Jackson, an educator, was a member of Bermuda's Parliament whom I interviewed in 2009, prior to her death. She published one of the first books about the Gombeys, ostensibly for children but providing a very insightful, endogenous perspective. Pointedly subtitled *Bermuda's Unique Dance Heritage,* the book provides particular descriptions of the Gombeys: their influences, music, and revitalization, as well as the composition of the dance groups. She reports, "There are about 25 to 30 dancers, 5–7 musicians, and two or three money pickers" (1). In keeping with the Christmas mumming tradition, the tossing of money at the dancers' feet is mandated: "After singing a while [the troupe] claim small gratuities and pass along" (Bolton 223). Tucker notes that, if no coins or gifts are offered, then troupes might sing, "Sail away— no money here," and he consigns their performance "to the traditional dance mime of Africa" (88).⁹ Apparently, along their evolutionary path, the Gombeys enacted rhymes, chants, or folk dramas representative of British mumming, but those are no longer performed. Instead, well-rehearsed traditionalized dance moves orchestrated by the crack of a whip or a whistle blast result in a kind of kinetic pantomime.

Louise Jackson, furthermore, documents European influences upon Bermuda's Gombey: "The Christmas Mummers of England had a tradition of going from door to door with their Christmas act. This tradition standard was adapted by the Gombey and use songs that often made social comment on the occupants of the houses or the parish. Every parish had its own band of Gombeys with songs usually ridiculing other parishes or people" (15). To her credit, she supplies lyrical samplings of Gombey songs, as well as alludes to the significance of folk dramas such as "The Giant Despair." Also, from the British mumming tradition, she highlights biblical "playlets such as 'David and Goliath,'" describing them as conforming to basic facial masking, as well as describing a stiltwalker with the nickname "Nine eggs" (17). Today, there is no indication of this figure (related to the Mocko Jumbies); and she describes the simultaneous existence of Gombeys that approximate current dancers although "perhaps not as gaudy, performing a more ritual tribal dance" (17). Unless pantomimed, no documented proof survives of the earlier dramatization.

Like the Black Indians of New Orleans, Bermudian Gombeys today celebrate a close affinity with the early indigenized population, respectfully called Wild Indians (hooks; Kinser; Roach). Historically, "The first slaves in Bermuda are reported to have been one Indian and one Negro, who were brought there in 1616 to dive for pearls" (John Jackson 35).[10] Between 1630 and 1640, Native peoples captured in New England and Virginia were dispatched to be auctioned off in Bermuda (56). Bernhard's investigation of wills and inventories establishes that "by the early 1700s a number of Indians, both slave and free, lived in the capital, St. George's, and on St. David's Island, a narrow 500-acre strip at the easternmost end of Bermuda. . . . Many of [St. David's] present residents claim Indian ancestry" (62). Similarly, Mardi Gras Indians in New Orleans maintain they have "actual Indian ancestors, while others emphasize a psychological identification of blacks with Native Americans who made war on European Americans."[11] Of significance, today's Gombeys are officially recognized descendants of the Mashantucket Pequot and the Eastern Pequot/Wampanoag/Narragansett American Indian tribes in the US, and Bermuda's St. David's Island Pequot Indians have reconnected with the Americans, interculturally.

The annual powwow now held by St. David's islanders serves to authenticate their historical pan-Indian intersectionality. Although the word "tribe" is viewed by some as having a negative connotation when referring to African and American Indian ethnic groups, interestingly, in 1617, Bermuda was divided into tribes named for its "investors" (slaveholders). When it came to land distribution, "Norwood divided Bermuda's lands outside the Company's property in St. George's into eight areas called 'tribes,' each containing approximately 1,250 acres" (Bernhard 7). Today, they are called parishes. In focusing on only their dance vocabulary, some Gombeys view their dance steps and rhythmic drumming as evidence that justifies claiming Pequot heritage. In practice, Gombeys deploy a wider hermeneutic loop to explain their intercultural relationship. For instance, they interpret their freedom dances as celebrating the breaking of shackles and chains from their hands and feet. Since both West African and American Indian cultures honored warriors, a practice that syncretizes well, they insist that the appropriation of Native indigenous garb functioned as another subversive act to mask the African nature of their ancestors' cultural performance.[12]

Most published descriptions of Gombeys emphasize the variegated costumes of the dancers by simply describing them as "colorful" and "gaudy."

Packwood supplements the usual exoteric accounts with a thick description derived prior to Emancipation: "Black men and women, with their faces colored by red and yellow paints, clothed in scarlet and other bright colors wearing flowers and ribbons, and high fanciful headdress, went from house to house singing, dancing, and playing on musical instruments. During some periods masks were worn" (95).[13] In an 1890 essay in the *Journal of American Folklore*, Carrington Bolton observed: "The men wear their ordinary garments, but are masked, bearing on their heads the heads and horns of hideous-looking beasts (formidable only to an uncultured mind), as well as beautifully made imitations of houses and ships, both lighted as candles" (223). His description is similar to that of headgear reported in early Jamaican accounts. The houses and ships were called "gombay houses," which Bolton described as follows: "[They] are large enough to admit the head of the bearer inserted through a hole below, the building resting on his shoulders; these are more common than the ships, which are full rigged" (223). As described by Theodore L. Godet, writing in *Bermuda*, "The dancer's dress is very fantastic; he is ornamented about the head with a miniature chateau, and his face is enveloped in a hideous mask" (151). According to Zuill, "At one time the Gombeys danced with high head-dresses made in many forms—a Noah's Ark, a house, a boat, an aeroplane—but more recently the height has been gained by using peacock feathers" (9). Also, this aesthetic model metaphorically embraces peacocks as the proudest birds in the world, thus equating the dancers with royalty although, formerly, turkey feathers adorned their headdresses.

There was an abundance of identifiable handcrafted objects, which Bolton enumerates: "All are carefully constructed of wood, cardboard, colored papers, string, etc." (223). Typically, contemporary Gombeys' costumes sport plain white sweatshirts and often Converse Chuck Taylor shoes, with multicolored fringe on pant legs, tasseled skirts cinched by decorative aprons, and artistically embellished designs on usually black velvet capes. Zuill notes, "Costumes are still as colourful as they were when Harriet Lloyd saw them, and nowadays are often decorated with large numbers of small mirrors" ("Story" 238). Everything is representative of something; for instance, the colorfully painted-face mesh masks function to discourage evil spirits. The capes are covered with intricate embroidery, ribbons, and tiny mirrors that symbolize conduits to the spirit world. These decorations and the rows of fringe on dancers' pant legs also acknowledge rank as well as serve as an homage to Native peoples; additionally, the multiple rows of fringe augment dancers' dazzling appearance in motion to the jingle of bells strapped to their wrists.

In this performance art, therefore, rank is illustriously displayed in several formal roles. Each troupe boasts a Captain, who wears the most elaborate costume and the longest cape and carries a whip to symbolize his leadership while issuing commands via a shrill, keening whistle. He also functions as a sort of griot, overseeing the transmission of dance techniques and musical history to the younger neophytes. Fundamentally, the whip constitutes "an awe-inspiring symbol," conveying leadership and possessing its own magical aura when twirled during the dance (Fabre 62). Of additional significance, other props include hatchets, tomahawks, and bow and arrows. The Bowman carries a bow and arrow and is also known as the Wild Indian, who leads the snake-like line along the road, while the Trapper totes a rope. The Chiefs carry shields and tomahawks while also assisting in instructing the youngsters about their role as Warriors, bearing hatchets. The tomahawk, if thrown down before them, means they have to demonstrate dance movements competitively. Most paramount, hand painted face masks serve to disguise their individual identities for purposes consistent with ancestral practices to elude recognition by the authorities. Forming an elongated, staged line and bowing from the waist, dancers signal the denouement of their street performance before resuming their road march to the next destination, sometimes singing, "Ayo, here we go!"

Singing once comprised another alluring aspect of Bermudian cultural performances. Related to the gumbe complex, in "Dance Songs and Tales from the Bahamas," Zora Neale Hurston speaks to another variant of the term "Gombey" in situ: "The drummer cries, 'Gimbay!' (a corruption of the African word gumbay, a large drum) and begins the song" (294). Bolton's thick description also mentions the custom, occurring in neighbors' yards: "As the men approach the houses, the group, sometimes twenty in number, dance a breakdown, and shout":

Gombay, ra-lay
Gombay, ra-lay (223)

Apparently, as a part of the mumming masquerade custom, these chants varied over time and space. Lloyd's *Sketches*, too, appraised the Gombeys' musicality, noting their capacity to play instruments without "technical training" (L. Jackson 27). Later, Terry Tucker reports, "Whether they sang the old Bermuda doggerel or not, ancient Bermuda jingles have survived. Such couplets as 'All the way to Mangrove Bay/There the old maids go to stay' or 'All the way to Spanish Point/There the times are out of joint' were used derisively of the different parishes but are not properly Calypso which was never a Bermuda word, being used for the work-rhythm song of the cane-fields—non-existent locally" (88). Furthermore, Tucker attributes their songs with "giving full play to their love of making fun of people" (116). Also, his "dance mime" assessment is still a staple when, in essence, the dancers narrate a story about resistance to European colonial states in the Caribbean via pantomime and instrumental music, dramatizing acts of combative rebellion.[14]

Early on, the kettle drums (known as gombey drums) were constructed from potato barrels and goatskin, with the identifying marker for Bermuda's Gombeys being the constancy of their association with a rapid drumbeat. The hand drum is so privileged in African musicology that the prevalence of drumsticks tends to be muted. Subsequently, the use of military-style drums in Bermuda and north Florida became habitually and simplistically associated with Western musical instrumentation. Affiliated with military marching bands, the ascendancy of the two basic drum types—bass and snare—encompasses novel extratextual meanings and rhythms within a range of possible multivocality. A circuitous history led to the preeminence of these military-style drums due to a precipitous transference attuned to centuries of musicians playing ancillary roles in the West India Regiment and other musical engagements during wartime even in the United States, so that by the late nineteenth century, through a cultural reinterpretation, the instruments accompanied their masquerades and other festivities. According to Zuill, "Although marching bands no longer accompany the Gombeys, the military drums remain" ("Story" 238).¹⁵ Packwood acknowledges the dynamism of Gombey troupes over time and space, writing, "They were led by a band whose players wore white uniforms with scarlet facings. The musicians were all self-taught and played the popular airs of the day. The performance of the Gombays has changed through different periods of time. Alterations have taken place in the dances, music, and costumes, but the Gombays with their drums still perform in Bermuda today—a lasting vestige of Black Culture!" (96). Over temporal-spatial historical moments, honored Gombey musician Dennis Place maintains, "It's all about masquerade music and masquerade music is based on snares" (qtd. in Kawaley-Lathan).

In keeping with the transnational cultural flows associated with Caribbean Carnival fetes, the Gombeys also experienced a degree of revitalization by way of the migration of St. Kittitian workers to Bermuda. In the *Bermudian*, a magazine published in 1946, Charles Norford, the leader of one of the most prominent Gombey groups, revealed that he came from St. Kitts in 1922: "He said that in his native St. Kitts it is called 'Wild Indian' dancing, demonstrating its close connection to the dances of the Caribbean Indian tribes" (R. Smith). Migrant laborers imported from St. Kitts and Nevis worked at the Dockyard; and not only are they credited with revitalizing aspects of the tradition, but the descendants of this migrant population remain as active tradition-bearers.¹⁶ In 2007, the cultural ties between Bermuda and St. Kitts and Nevis were strengthened when a contingent of masquerade and Mocko Jumbie dancers (stilt walkers) visited to perform at the Gombey Festival, reestablishing a historical connection.

The Gombey tradition, according to most experts, is passed down from father to son (who, at a tender age, as soon as he learned to walk also danced); in many families, involvement persists for generations as young descendants wait their turn. The learning process begins as early as three years of age, with the youngsters donning their first regalia by age five. The training usually occurs with formal tutelage twice weekly since performing requires endurance due to the expectation of dancing nonstop for over an hour at a time, stopping only when the drumming halts. On Boxing Day, traversing the island, troupes perform practically the whole daylong (with a cornucopia of food arranged in one spot to sustain them until well into the night). At the time of his writing, Packwood remarked that "the best Gombay Companies hailed from Hamilton and Warwick, two locations with the highest Black population" (96). Although troupes are customarily built around extended familial relationships, the preservation of Gombey troupes depends also on some recruitment from outside. In another example, the Warrick Gombeys is a community troupe designated by locality (parish).

Gender parity is one of the latest innovations in the tradition. In the past, based on Lloyd's early observation, women did participate: "during the Gombey revelry, [they] move in the dance on the lawn with an ease which really surprised me" (170–71). Her surprise at the women dancers, however, arose from the fluidity of their dance movements, not their gender. Most descriptions thereafter portrayed the Gombeys as exclusively male with a transgenerational continuity Bolton's description illustrates the gender normativity: "At this time groups of men and boys (women seldom take part) parade about the country, going from house to house singing, dancing, and playing on rude musical instruments, among which the triangle and tambourine are prominent, penny whistles and concertinas being also called to their aid" (223). A future chapter will further address the status of women, but let me note here that an all-female troupe led by Algina Warner—Alisa Kani Girl Gombeys (Alisa Kani meaning "a dance with energy")—for a short time took the opportunity to display their own competence in performance.[17]

Presently, there are at least six main Gombey troupes, also known as "crowds": Warner Gombey Troupe, Warwick Gombeys, The New Generation Places Gombeys, H & H Gombeys, Gombey Warriors, and Richardson Gombeys. There is always the possibility of more as it is common for a troupe member to branch off and become the founder and managing director of a new crowd with its own fandom. Each troupe makes its separate rounds on Boxing Day, starting in the morning with the beat of a bass drum keeping time and a battery of snares playing a complex of rhythms along with the whistle blown by the Captain to inform the dance troupe's movements. The troupes are known for their distinctive 2/4 marching cadence called "Road Beat." When two groups converge, they may clash, a possibility that Kinser documents as a salient feature of Carnival: "the presence of male competition rivalry, and violence."[18] Troupes span the island from neighborhood to neighborhood, reclaiming Bermuda's roadways in day-long outings and attracting many followers of all ages along the way. There is no current evidence of the European custom of entering private homes to partake of refreshments and dramatic folk cultural displays. Instead, in keeping with local tradition, residents gather outside gateways and home entranceways, often still wearing pajamas (no matter the time of day), to dispense money (collected as a sort of maintenance fee to ensure the preservation of the group) and to watch the thrilling kinetic dance formations. Moreover, the "house visits" include a community service component—visits to hospitals, senior citizen buildings, and other rehabilitation facilities.

Although not registering any claim to the Boxing Day holiday, African Americans in Tallahassee, Florida, still participate in a century-old Shooting Match on December 26, at which celebrants annually perform spectacular sounds, tropes, and merrymaking similar to that seen in the ACW's festival arc. In north Florida, a group of local families' percussive musical tradition signifies a glorified sense of their history and pride of place, with military-style drums as their only form of musicality. Writing about Jamaican Jonkonnu, Bettelheim noted that, at one time, "Jonkonnu music [was] known as fife and drum music" ("Jonkonnu Festival" 21). In their celebration, which those north Floridians call "The 26th," the instruments used are two drums (bass/big drum and snare/ kettle) and occasionally the fife depending on the accessibility of that musician. Although the fife may be nearing extinction in north Florida, the drums and a stylistic manner of playing them resemble those of the Bermuda Gombeys and St. Kittitian Masqueraders. As in the ACW, it is customary for these north Floridians' drums to reappear on New Year's Day and other holidays like their Emancipation Day (May 20) and, with growing inclusivity, the Martin Luther King Jr. national holiday. In my analysis, the bonds that connect this north Florida tradition are the distinctive cadence of the drums and their performance at meaningful holiday gatherings along with the rudimentary tropological components seen throughout the West Indies, as will be discussed later.

Since its earliest colonization, Bermuda had a relationship with the other British permanent colonies in Virginia and New England. However, a shift southward occurred as an economic relationship developed with the loyalists during the American Revolution and later the Confederacy. Writing in 1932 and based on his own experience, Hudson Strode declared that white Bermudians were "somewhat like English; somewhat like Americans; a great deal like Southerners" (118). Yet, he goes on to note that, because of the quality of their soil, trade rather than "great plantations" typified them. Strode's travelogue also typifies the racially charged discursive insults of his time, so that he stigmatized Black Bermudians: "Many delightful old darkies with the manners of 'quality Negroes' of the South still exist" (138). While speculative in nature, his sentiments serve to connect the isle regionally with the southern

United States as well as The Bahamas nearby.[19] Although British rule lasted only twenty years in Florida (1763–1783), via loyalist refugees during the Revolutionary War their cultural hegemony "would long outlast [their] political control" (Turner 2).

Another example of the role of transnational cultural flow can be seen in the US National Park Service's inauguration and elongation of the Gullah/Geechee Cultural Heritage Corridor from Wilmington, North Carolina, to St. Augustine, Florida. Designated by an act of the US Congress, the boundaries extend to St. Augustine because "Florida's tie-in is that King Charles I of Spain issued an edict of 1600 that allowed any African who made their way to Spanish Florida would be granted their freedom."[20] St. Augustine's neighboring Fort Mose (pronounced mo-say) was a maroon community, founded in 1738 and sanctioned by the Spanish government, which quartered the first free Africans. The occupants forged a cultural crossroad where self-liberated Africans preserved a collective consciousness. One Tallahassee family's history shows roots connecting them to the Spaniards in St. Augustine. Evidence indicates that Africa–descended peoples traveled extensively, whether enslaved or free.[21] For example, Toney Proctor (originally named Antonio Propinos) was born about 1743 in then–Santo Domingo. Known as a soldier attached to a British officer, he fought at the Battle of Quebec and during the Revolutionary War. Eventually, in St. Augustine, he obtained his freedom and was awarded 185 acres of land, recognizing him for his "considerable service to the Americans during the Seminole wars as an interpreter, scout, and guide" (Warner 19). An esteemed Indian interpreter for the first governor of Florida, by 1830, he had relocated and prospered in Tallahassee, which is now Florida's capital city. This family's history intimates the mobility of those once enslaved and the complexity of sociocultural contact zones seldom fathomed.

Like the Gombeys, the John Canoe tradition has a long history, evolving from colonial roots into varied contemporary practices in the ACW and the US. (The related tradition of Junkanoo/Jankunú will be discussed at length in chapter 3.) Many, usually reductive theories about John Canoe's origin can be found on the internet. Although usually erroneous, like urban legends, those theories gain widespread circulation. In one example, "John Canoe, a beneficent plantation owner, allowed his slaves time off to celebrate on Christmas Day."[22]

Gaining a more evidence-based understanding of the history of John Canoe requires beginning with the surge in transnationalism that stimulated the Atlantic slave trade and that primarily involved the Dutch and Prussians, with the Dutch owning 60 percent of the ships navigating the Caribbean in the seventeenth century (Noel 31). One of the most intriguing and possibly definitive versions of this history is provided by Pieter Emmer, an expert on the Dutch slave trade:

One of the most colourful figures in this group of slaving "tycoons" was Jan Conny, the "Black Prussian." Conny traded at the German fort of Grossfriedrichsburg, which the Dutch government bought from the Prussians in 1715. However, the WIC [West India Company] commander at Elmina was unable to take possession of the fort because Jan Conny broke into it when the Germans moved out and used his private army to defend it very effectively against every assault. The Dutch commander even went so far as to make an alliance with the English—just for the one occasion—in order to drive out the Black Prussian, but their combined attack was still unsuccessful and at least 36 Europeans were killed. This was a huge loss when one considers that there were no more than about 200 Dutch and English stationed on the coast.... A full nine years after purchasing the Prussian fort, in 1724, the WIC finally succeeded in driving out Conny and taking possession of Grossfriedrichsburg. (47)

In contrast, Fabre theorizes that two spiritual forces, Jannanin and Canno, entrusted the "Last Prussian Negro King" with his power (57).

Migrating West Indian planters and their Africa-born labor force also played a key role in the dissemination of festival customs. Bernhard's historical comparison with Virginia, from 1616 to 1782, provides an opening for tidewater regional connection. As noted by Tucker, the history of Bermuda and that of Virginia have been "deeply intertwined" (33). In Virginia and North Carolina, enslaved Africans also sustained a history of John Canoe (E. Bethel; Bettelheim; Fabre; Piersen; Moore; Reid).[23] According to the Henry family's oral history, Florence and George Henry walked all the way to Tallahassee from Virginia, a popular emigration route into the region. In this light, I suggest that the Henry family's December 26th event aligns with another long-standing masquerade tradition: John Canoe. Most scholars now credit English visitor Sir Hans Sloane with the first descriptive account of the Jamaican festivities in 1688 (Rashford; Kerns and Dirks). Edward Long, author of the 1774 *History of Jamaica*, is recognized for the first-recorded usage of a variant of the term, describing

> several tall robust fellows dressed up in grotesque habits, and a pair of oxhorns on their heads, sprouting from the top of a horrid sort of vizor, or mask, which about the mouth is rendered very terrific with large boar-tusks. The masquerader, carrying a wooden sword in his hand, is followed with a numerous crowd of drunken women, who refresh him frequently with a cup of aniseed-water, whilst he dances at every door, bellowing out John Connu![24]

Enslaved Africans, documented primarily in North Carolina, also traditionalized the public display event, calling it "John Kunering" or "John Canoeing." The festive garb of the all-male assemblages conformed to the transcultural description of masquerade troupes and mummers. James Sprung listed the following instruments: banjo, accordion, tambourine, bones, and cow's horn. Additionally, while dancing, the groups chanted:

Hah! Low! Here we go!
Hah! Low! Here we go!
Hah! Low! Here we go!
Kuners come from Denby![25]

Elizabeth Fenn's account references a source that substantiates a percussive presence: "The musicians beat their gumba boxes" (133). This account institutes a musical vocabulary inclusive of terminology associated with the Caribbean landscapes' cultural articulation. Stephen Nissenbaum found an account published in *The Liberator* (an abolitionist magazine) by a Northern woman who took offense to the John Cooner's "unabashed begging" (286–87).

Most famously, hailing from Edenton, North Carolina, Harriet Jacobs included in her slave narrative, *Incidents in the Life of a Slave Girl* (first published under the pseudonym Linda Brent), a chapter entitled "Christmas Festivities," which includes a comprehensive description of the "companies," their songs, and the gumbo box:

Every child rises early on Christmas morning to see the Johnkannaus. Without them, Christmas would be shorn of its greatest attraction. They consist of companies of slaves from the plantations, generally of the lower class. Two athletic men, in calico wrappers, have a net thrown over them, covered with all manner of bright-colored stripes. Cows' tails are fastened to their backs, and their heads are decorated with horns. A box, covered with sheepskin, is called the gumbo box. A dozen beat on this, while others strike triangles and jawbones, to which bands of dancers keep time. For a month previous they are composing songs, which are sung on this occasion. These companies, of a hundred each, turn out early in the morning, and are allowed to go round till twelve o'clock, begging for contributions. Not a door is left unvisited where there is the least chance of obtaining a penny or a glass of rum. They do not drink while they are out, but carry the rum home in jugs, to have a carousel. These Christmas donations frequently amount to twenty or thirty dollars. It is seldom that any white man or child refuses to give them a trifle. If he does, they regale his ears with the following song: —

Poor massa, so dey say;
Down in de heel, so dey say;
Got no money, so dey say;
Not one shillin, so dey say;
God A'mighty bress you, so dey say. (179–80)

Ultimately, Jacobs's narrative humanizes enslaved persons as more than chattel property; and by mentioning the "gumbo box," she centers her observation in the ACW.[26] Ehrenreich's assessment also has application here: "Thus a moment of white weakness—Christmas—was transformed into black opportunity" (165). The enslaved exploited this opportunity to express themselves artistically and convivially as a bold move in transgressing boundaries. Moreover, their sociality seemingly influenced white youths to expropriate "John Coonering," too. An eyewitness account by a white participant, Henry McKoy, refers derogatively to a similar late nineteenth-century custom as "coonering," as in his title: "DO YOU REMEMBER WHEN we went 'Coonering'"?[27] Annually, late on Christmas Day, to overcome any holiday disappointments and tedium, he and his young neighbors would decide to go "Coonering." He describes how a motley crew of five to ten boys from age nine to sixteen created "cooner-faces" (blackface) and other disguises. Then, they gathered in the twilight and roamed to selected houses in the neighborhood, where they would gain entry. Those "house visits" differed from that of the originators, who instead (perhaps in keeping with local mores) "would stop in front of the different handsome homes, or pass into the gardens and spacious yards of the stately houses," expecting a "Christmas gif'" or refreshments (Louis Moore). After gaining admission, those Coonering did not abide to the British mumming tradition either. McKoy reports, "We did not sing and we had no particular program to follow. We did not try to say or do something funny, but just fitted ourselves into the mood of the home we were in." What he discloses conforms more to present-day Halloween than mumming in certain regards since the boys usually collected a treasure of candy and fruit. McKoy interprets his ritualized act as being transgenerational, as perhaps his father had participated with the Black revelers. McKoy confesses that, upon reading the historical account by Louis Moore, he only then fathomed the "Coonering" tradition's Black origin and "that it was supposed to be 'Koonering.'" Their misspelling may suggest derision of people of African descent.[28] It is estimated that, by 1900, the Wilmington, North Carolina, John Canoe festivities ceased (Reid; MacMillan).[29] However, William Piersen suggests that these forms of John Canoe activity were probably more commonplace than has been recorded ("Festive Style and Creation" 258).[30] Bahamian immigrants once comprised 75 percent of the Key West Florida population and sustained a Junkanoo musical tradition there as well (R. Sands, "Conversation" 102).[31]

To further situate the American South's linkage with the Caribbean gumbe complex, it is useful to remember that the United States is also a postcolonial society (Coronil 201–202), retaining many British customs from its own past. In *The Englishman's Christmas*, Pimlott conjectures that, as early as the thirteenth century, "work in the fields seems to have been virtually suspended throughout the whole of the Twelve Days" (19). Into the twentieth century, Twelfth Night or

Old Christmas remained intact in the Florida Panhandle with January 6 being observed as "Old Christmas." Lay historian E. W. Carswell recalled the practice of Old Christmas, concluding, "They never explained, at least to my satisfaction, the background of the 'Old Christmas' tradition'" (qtd. in McGregory 95). Often quoted, the travelogue of Philip Vickers Fithian testifies to his experience on a wealthy Tidewater Virginia plantation: "Guns are fired this Evening in the Neighborhood [Westmoreland County, Virginia], and the Negroes seem to be inspired with new Life" (39). In passing, he also mentioned schools being closed until January 6 and the prevalence of "Christmas boxes."[32]

At Christmas, the ritual firing of guns was considered a "proper noise" as part of a southern holiday tradition.[33] As historian James Barnett puts it, "The modern Southern custom of setting off firecrackers and shooting guns at Christmas is foreshadowed in a passage from the North Carolina *Wilmington Daily Journal* for December 23, 1851: John Barleycorn retained his usual spirit . . . and our town authorities on Christmas generally let the boys have their way so far as mere noise is concerned" (12). For southern males, clamorous sound translated into jubilation, as they "learned early to be loud and competitive during the holiday season, drawing attention to their presence by firing guns and more often, by setting off fireworks" (Ownby 45–46).[34] None other than Booker T. Washington registered his disdain for the tradition over his first yuletide period in Tuskegee, Alabama, reporting being harangued for "Chris'mus gifts!" first "between the hours of two o'clock and five o'clock in the morning," followed by "free use of guns, pistols, and gunpowder generally" (Nissenbaum 301). Washington also foreshadowed his subsequent puritanical stance regarding "lounging about," by commenting on a household with five children who divided among themselves "a single bunch of firecrackers" (302). Washington's commentary underscores his political agenda geared toward racial uplift, social respectability, and what he considered the proper enculturation of children.

Regardless, firecrackers add another sonic layer that introduces an antithetical component of child's play not available to them in the everyday, commonsensical world. In Tallahassee, on the one hand, although firecrackers are no longer in evidence, several local women recalled to me how rambunctious young boys' mishandling firecrackers was the reason they stopped attending The 26th. On the other hand, Nassauvian George Roberts gleefully described the general kinds of mayhem and violence associated with firecrackers as a significant part of the holiday. In hindsight, he admits the amount of danger entailed, reporting, "But everyone had firecrackers. They throw them at you, everything, but most nobody got hurt [laughter]" (Jenkins 91). Jamaicans once reserved firecrackers for Boxing Day as well according to Hurd: "And my young brothers would put these Thunderbolts under open tin cans and watch them explode and send the cans reeling high or flying high in the air. Of course, dogs were not happy on that day because of the firecrackers. You couldn't find your dog at dinnertime to feed them, or anything. They just disappeared." Likewise, in Dangriga, firecrackers invigorate holiday festivities by bringing closure to Christmas Day and feature nightly thereafter. In the Dutch West Indies, Neville Hall translated the following passage, apparently racializing firecrackers: "the throwing of fire-crackers was reckoned to be one of those innocent pleasures wherewith one distinguished special from ordinary days, and *even whites themselves participated*" (117; his emphasis).

The following inferences are not intended to position The 26th as having a direct genealogy with Boxing Day in the ACW, but to contextualize it as a hybrid in a range of similar seasonal customs relevant to the north Florida Shooting Match. For example, instead of ringing bells, "in Virginia they turned to firearms to provide a proper noise for the holidays. Whereas other parts of the country were to take the Fourth of July as the time for noisemaking and the tossing of firecrackers, for southerners today, as of earlier days, the day for shooting is Christmas" (Kane 15). In another British context, John and Miles Hadfield pose a similar inquiry: "Has this custom some remote link with two sporting occasions now well established on Boxing Day?" (121). The two events they mentioned were the foxhunt and "the Boxing Day shoot." In addition, Karal Marling notes that the oldest general-interest monthly in America, *Harper's*, often published pictorials of "Black Xmas," with most portrayals being racially stereotypical and with several showing hunting events including one with the caption "Another 'comic' Christmas hunting scene" (1888). Piersen recognized the degree to which "similarities among black celebrations across the Americas suggest that the generalized aesthetic of African cultural expression was as important in shaping these celebrations as the particular Euro-American occasions that served as their pretexts" ("Festive Style and Creation" 255).

Therefore, turkey shoots also reverberate, cross-culturally, throughout the US, although generally associated with Thanksgiving. Southern local colorist A. B. Longstreet, in a short story, "The Shooting Match," wrote that "Shooting matches are probably nearly coeval with the colonization of Georgia. They are still common throughout the Southern States; though they are not as common as they were 25 or 30 years ago" (197). Although Longstreet's story was published in 1835, African Americans in north Florida still hold these ballistic competitions, according to one descendant, George Henry: "Today, we call it the Shooting Match because guys come out there. You'd be amazed to know that they like to compete against each other; and I find this seems to be the case with the young people. Who can shoot the best? So what we do we get a target, and then we set that target on a post." As part of their socio-musical everyday existence, this deeply ingrained spirit of competition enriches this African American cultural production. Whether labeled a turkey shoot or Shooting Match, these competitions remain relatively segregated affairs; nevertheless, as historian and folklorist Charles Joyner attests, "Folk culture simply refuse[s] to abide by any color line, however rigidly it may have been drawn" (25); and African Americans have adapted Shooting Matches to fit their own specifications.[35]

Of course, the Shooting Match is only a tangential part of The 26th as a north Florida event, and I intend to propose how the event as a whole relates to Boxing Day celebrations in the ACW. The literature tends to position hybridity, syncretism, and creolization squarely and interchangeably within globalization trends that influence the transnational flow of ideas (Brathwaite; Glissant; Knepper; Nettleford). Folklorists and anthropologists were among the first to theorize cultural mixture; however, I located a gap in recent studies in relation to homogeneity and heterogeneity within the African diaspora.[36] At this historical moment, globalization is popularly considered to be a process of homogenization by which the world becomes increasingly uniform. In past scholarship, due to urbanization, the same presupposition accompanied discourse related to the very survival of African American folk culture at the turn of the last century.[37] Along the globalization/homogenization/heterogenization axis, the concept of heterogenization now predominates in studies of the African diasporic experience within a global ecumene.[38] Traditionally, in the ACW, though generally ignored by scholars, local participants reinterpreted and reappropriated an array of Eurocentric festal practices such as the greasy pole and maypole dance in their public display events (McGregory 2011). Roach posits the idea of surrogation, or substitution, as a mechanism to address the propriety of intercultural genealogies. For example, historically, in Britain, the Christmas holiday season was an occasion for hunting, and African Americans adapted Shooting Matches to suit their own culturally nuanced collective behavioral vortex. Nearly all whom I interviewed decentered the Shooting Match in the day's festivities, as in these comments by Wilbur Barnes:

> The Shooting Match is almost like a sideshow. I was more interested in hearing the drums. It wouldn't be a Shooting Match, if you didn't have no drums. . . . It's just a part of it. That's just part of it. To me, the drumming was the main thing. It was a tradition that you know was ours. I haven't heard no drumming like that nowhere. The only time I heard anything similar to it was maybe with some of these marching bands, where I think they picked up something from country people wherever they were. I don't think that it was just unique to The 26th. That sounds funny, but I know that it was unique to Black folks.

Similarly, Harold Willocks describes another Crucian musical tradition, quelbe, and its syncretic fife and drum origin: "It should be remembered that the slave owners had prohibited the slaves from continuing many of their traditions and rituals, therefore, the slaves had to adapt those European traditions and practices that resembled theirs. Accordingly, when the slaves saw the fife and drum corps, they were eager to adopt it since it resembled theirs in Africa" (18).[39] The development of quelbe (scratch) bands in the Virgin Islands resulted from the addition of song, guitars, flutes, and banjo and the reinterpretive use of an unusual array of objects such car mufflers and alternative percussive instruments.

For African Americans, fife and drum bands have a legacy dating back to British colonialism as well. Evans quotes musicologist Eileen Southern saying that "as early as the seventeen century blacks may have 'picked up' the skills of fife or drum playing from the militia units in New England and the Middle Colonies, since all slaves were compelled to undergo military training until the 1650's" (95).[40] Regardless of the instrument's origin, many Tallahasseeans told me, "If you don't have the drums, you don't think it's 'The 26th.'" The drumming is of major importance because both parents of the event's originators played them: Virginia Barnes's father, George Henry, would beat the big bass drum, while her mother, Pearl, would beat the snare. Notably, women traditionally participated along with men, performing among their community's musicians. During one of his southern field trips in the 1940s, Alan Lomax reported Jessie Mae Hemphill's comment that "I don't look like I could, but I used to carry that big drum all around the picnics and play it" (337). In Mississippi, Sid Hemphill's Band was the most revered in the fife and drum tradition until the arrival of Otha Turner, for whom Jessie Hemphill played backup drums. Ironically, Turner and his daughter (Bernice Turner Pratcher), a renowned drummer in his Rising Star Fife and Drum Band, died the same day, February 26, 2003. In the US, it was not unusual for women to play African polyrhythms on European-style martial drums. On Boxing Day in the Caribbean, however, Bettelheim reports that women typically played more conventional roles: dancing from house to house and providing the chorus to the beat of the snare and bass drums ("Jonkonnu" 69).

The fife and drum tradition is emblematic of the cultural heterogeneity and surrogation typifying African American artistic expression. As local drummer Hunter Hill summarized it:

> Most of our things were from colonial times. If you look at colonial times, they had the drums and the fife. The drums and the fife went hand in hand. So when we got the drum, when our ancestors got the drum, years ago, they had the drums and the fife; and they could really blow the fife. I seen women blow fifes just as good as men down at the Henry's. The only thing different is that Blacks created their own beat.

Dating back to at least 1911, The 26th probably eclipsed even the late Otha Turner's annual picnic.[41] The Hill brothers are knowledgeable of Turner's musicianship, but take pride in their community's distinction from his north Mississippi picnics because they also featured blues performances while, in Tallahassee, drum playing offers the only musical interlude. Since the fife normally is played in conjunction with drums, it is interesting that Turner's aerophonic performances gained the fuller attention. True, with his demise, the playing of this musical instrument is possibly nearer to extinction. In an interview, however, his daughter revealed that, while she was growing up, her father did play the snare drum (Steber 135). Furthermore, folklorist David Evans noted, "One group [he] recorded consisted of simply a bass and snare drum without any fife" (95).

In the past, other musical accompaniments included blowing a bottle and playing washboards and tubs. Hurd observed an array of instrumentation and gave me a vivid description of Jonkonnu in Spanish Town, Jamaica:

> Depending on the size of the group, one person would beat the drum and the others would just jump around and dance around to the drumbeat. One would blow a fife. It's amazing how these things are coming back to me. The drum would be hanging around his neck, a handmade goatskin stretched over bamboo. The length of the cord would allow it to drop about waist length, and he would be banging on it with two sticks. Someone else would be blowing a fife. And there was a time when somebody might have maracas made out of calabash and that would give the rattle effect.

The local Tallahassee musicians whom I interviewed said they lost interest in playing the fife, but not to the detriment of The 26th's popularity. As daylight wanes, the bass and snare drums resound as the final echoes of shotguns being discharged echo from the field. The attention of most of the crowd centers on the rhythmic drumming of men like the Hill brothers, whom participants say have great competence in performance. Hunter Hill explained: "The person who beats the snare leads, and the bass follows him. You have a rap and you have a double rap. As you rap, you follow him, then you can beat straight, but you have to come up with that double rap. And the double rap makes the drums sound good." Evans also highlights the fondness shown the large bass drum usually appearing only in marching bands (97).

In Tallahassee, out of a multitude of homegrown drummers, none have garnered the attention of folklorists or musicologists prior to my interest in them. By the 1950s, Lomax noted the extent to which "The African American tradition, then, always seems to evolve specialized and rather complex orchestras to provide music for community dances" (339). The 26th in Tallahassee offers a lively ludic space for individual drummers to demonstrate their mastery and achieve approval from their peers. Major Anderson, a descendant of the founding family, played a significant role in sustaining the essence of this public display event. George Henry told me that Anderson was also an accomplished drummer:

> That special day is when you hear special music. And I know, when Major was
> alive, he didn't allow anybody to come up and touch his drums. It was like they
> were sacred drums or something like in African tradition certain drums are really
> sacred. You would put him in that category as a master drummer because, as long
> as I remember coming, he was always there playing until older and arthritis got
> into his hands.[42]

Now, Major's descendant, Roscoe Anderson, sets out the family's bass and snare drums early in the day, and the music usually begins in earnest a few hours before twilight, when the majority of celebrants arrive and begin to converge around the bonfire for warmth.

Unlike songs, drum music may draw largely on spontaneous syncopation and sustained polyrhythms, rather than a formal repertoire. As Otis Hill said in an interview: "We don't have the singers like they did, now. The person who was beating the drum would look in the other person's eyes to make him miss the beat." Those with the knack "bunch up" (Evans 99), taking turns beating the drums in a competitive, stylized fashion. Another local drummer, Freddie McGhee, with his jaunty performance style and flamboyant kinetic abilities, usually sparks the crowd to interact with enormous enthusiasm, enticing onlookers to step lively or gyrate their hips to the beat. Although singing is not a fundamental part of the drumming, as Evans documented, spirituals are a mainstay of fife and drum bands (102). Participants enjoy singing religious songs such as "Mary, Don't You Weep" behind the drum. In 2004, John Bailey, the area's only verifiable living fife player, was on hand and performed also as a song leader on a variant of common meter sacred music for "A Charge to Keep I Have." However, occasionally secular songs appear as well. One of Otha Turner's most revered tunes was "Shimmie She Wobble," a popular dance of the 1920s (Evans 102). Among Tallahasseeans, Otis Hill remembered a variant lyric: "And they had the songs they sing like 'Mama, If You Can't Shimmie, You Can't Hold Your Man.'"

Genealogies of performance thus connect Bermudian Gombeys with the drumming in North Florida, presenting multiple signifiers that confirm what Roach calls "the historical transmission and dissemination of cultural practices through collective representation" (25). Roach argues that a "kinesthetic imagination" transmits a repertoire of expressive movements disseminated from "a mental space where imagination and memory converge" (27). Without the strictness of a parade or procession along with the lack of a formal structure, prescribed speeches, or any stringent governance, the Shooting Match on The 26th exists within a specialized sociability. It invokes a kinesthetic remembrance that contributes to the social capital to entice family and friends to gather outdoors into the dark of night even while winter temperatures dip. Publicly

enacted by their bodies, the production of living memory stimulates an enduring kinesthetic vocabulary, without the intentionality of commodifying the cultural practice or the show of any anxiety about the threat of future containment
on this, their ceremonial ground.

The connection of The 26th in north Florida with John Canoe in the ACW
will become clearer in the next chapters, beginning with Junkanoo in The Bahamas and Jankunú in Belize. The sharing of nomenclature alone connects the
two very distinctive variations in festal practices due to their unique economic,
political, and sociohistorical contexts (R. Sands, "Musical Culture" 143). I show
how the different forms of chattel slavery and British colonial experiences perpetuate and even key each idiosyncratic cultural production. Stylistically, they
diverge, with the Bahamian Junkanoo being competitive and showcasing flashy
costumes designed by thousands while visually similar to those affiliated with
"pretty mas" during Carnival in Trinidad and Tobago. In contrast, on Boxing
Day in Dangriga, Belizeans participate in a more traditional mas, wearing signature costumes with a transgenerational flare publicly displayed in a small
group from house-to-house. It is the continuity of the goatskin drums played
on this cultural holiday that chiefly reconcile the two sonorous communities
within the ACW's gumbe complex.

CHAPTER THREE

Junkanoo/Jankunú

This chapter fully interrogates the genesis of Boxing Day masquerades in The Bahamas and Belize by contextualizing each of their proprietary social histories. On the one hand, diachronically and synchronically, the Bahamian celebratory processional path diverges the most from Junkanoo's other West Indian counterparts. Comparatively speaking, in Nassau, Junkanoo art evolved the most from even its late twentieth-century conceptual forms. Winston Saunders's assessment of the spectacle as "gargantuan" only intimates the magnitude attained in the twenty-first century (245). In The Bahamas, the consensus is that the celebration is "The Greatest Show on Earth." This chapter chronicles Junkanoo's autonomous leap from "the early 'grotesque masqueraders' appearances on Christmas Day in cheap materials such as crocus sacks and banana leaves" to appearances morphing into a "breathtaking art" (D. McCartney 5–6).[1] On the other hand, the Belizean Jankunú season principally preserves its traditional root heritage without many signs of revitalization while certainly not fossilized. *Wanaragua* and *Charikanari* dancing persist in Dangriga, extolled as the cultural center of Belize, although the Garifuna people long experienced extensive discrimination. They also live along the Caribbean coast in Spanish-speaking Guatemala, Honduras, and Nicaragua. Within the circum-Caribbean, the Garifuna present an inimitable historical, cultural, and linguistic heritage because British colonizers forced the deportation of their ancestors from St. Vincent Island to Central America (Ward et al.). While presenting a précis of the considerable research already conducted by scholars, this chapter also fills several residual ethnographic gaps and absences to highlight the dynamics of folklore and folklife in the ACW.

First, to dramatically introduce Nassauvian Junkanoo, Frederick Ober described the history of The Bahamas as being "writ in water," alluding to the seafaring mariners who colonized it as their own possession (69). In 1648, nearly twenty years after the British formally claimed the archipelago, a Puritan and former governor of Bermuda, William Sayles, reached Eleuthera Island seeking religious freedom and resulting in Bermuda's claim to being "the birthplace" of The Bahamas.[2] Tellingly, soon after being colonized by the so-called Eleuthera Adventurers, it became the repository for freed slaves, obstinate slaves, and white offenders banished from Bermuda.[3] For example, Bermudians banished to The Bahamas seven "intractable slaves" who were accused of leading a notorious rebellion in 1656 (D. McCartney 41). Thus, regarding transcultural flow and the process of repurposing and the coproduction of culture, ideas about Bahamian and Bermudian intersectionality imply another bond within the gumbe cultural arc.

In the past, while Bermuda was uninhabited, the Lucayan Arawak people populated The Bahamas with connections to what is now Cuba. Columbus occupied the future Bahamian isles for a mere fifteen days (Craton, "History" 37). By all indications, inhabiting the northwestern fringe of the Arawak world, the Lucayans and other Arawaks were the least warlike of all Amerindians. Excerpted from an internet article by Ro Ho, Columbus's diary shamelessly reports, "These people have little knowledge of fighting, as Your Majesties will see from the seven I have had captured to take away with us so as to teach them our language and return them our language and return them, unless Your Majesties' orders are that they all be taken to Spain or held captive on the island itself, for with fifty men one could keep the whole population in subjection and make them do whatever one wanted."[4] Within twenty years, the Spanish conquistadors managed to depopulate The Bahamas with an estimated 20,000 Lucayan being enslaved, "to satisfy [Spaniards'] unquenchable appetite for gold" (E. Bethel 39).[5] Ironically named after the islands' original inhabitants in Nassau, Arawak Cay is now known as the "Home of Fish Fry." Locally owned by Black Bahamians—whose open-air, homey restaurants invoke another indigenous cultural presence—the cay figures prominently in local sociocultural politics by catering to the island's working class, not tourists.[6]

Historian Michael Craton reports that, by 1831, "there were 12,259 Negroes in the Bahamas, outnumbering the white inhabitants by three to one. Of this majority, 2,991 were free; a sixfold increase over the total of barely 500 in 1789" ("A History" 187).[7] Craton and Saunders conjectured that this increase in African bodies is due to what is called the Loyalist slavery era (233). After 1783, this elite class of planters, who were loyal to the British, flooded The Bahamas with those they enslaved only to discover the unsustainability of a true plantation colony; therefore, they sought alternative crops and enterprises. Even before the American Revolution, Bermudians in The Bahamas worked in the grueling salt industry. Enslaved Africans labored as salt rakers, an onerous task that their Bermudian descendants still recall. The Bahamas possessed natural salt ponds defined as "shallow lagoons where sea water evaporated rapidly and formed chunks of salt crystals" (G. Saunders, "Bahamian Loyalists" 41).[8] The mineral sector was an early mainstay of the Bahamian economy; productivity required the salt to crystalize and then be broken up and raked to shore. Historical accounts indicate each laborer raked "from forty to sixty bushels of salt in a day" (McKinnen, qtd. in Saunders 120). Harvesting was also debilitating because the white salt caused the reflection of sunlight to impact the eyes (120). Nonetheless, historians often quote a British abolitionist, James Stephen, who compared the enslavement of Bahamians with others in the West Indies and judged theirs as one of "ease, plenty, health and . . . an increase of their numbers" (Albury 126).

Unlike the situation in other Caribbean isles, sugar plantations never flourished in The Bahamas; nevertheless, the political economy of slavery formed the social context for what came to be known as Junkanoo, "a Pan-African celebration" (G. Saunders, "A Family" 11). Gail Saunders also contextualizes the fete as "a 'grand dance,' or Nassau's biggest party, over a three-day holiday season (10). Scholar Whittington Johnson provides a more comprehensive explanation:

> Celebration of Christmas was one of those practices which did take hold among the slaves. The Consolidated Slave Act (1797) mandated a three-day holiday for slaves during Christmastide; this probably came after the fact because slaves may have been enjoying this privilege before the act was passed. Instead of enjoying it as a privilege, as they formerly did, after 1797 slaves enjoyed the three-day holiday as a right. The time was right for this celebration because the favorite food crops, maize, yams, plantains, bananas and sweet potatoes, were harvested and cattle were slaughtered in the late fall. Several pounds of meats were given to each adult slave and large shipments of foodstuff arrived from abroad, ensuring that more food was available at Christmas than at any other time of the year. Slaves prepared tasty meals, engaged in frolicking and merriment, including performing "rushin," a celebration similar to the ring shout in America. ("Race Relations" 48–49)

Performed on Christmas Day and New Years' Eve at the time, a rushin' meeting referred to a special fundraiser to benefit the church, in which congregants danced counterclockwise en route to deposit their donations in a collection plate (Parsons 456).[9] In addition, the Consolidated Slave Act, enacted in response to the heightened abolitionist movement in 1807, eventually led to the cessation of the slave trade in the UK as well as the US. Serving as a palliative to uphold the status quo, the Consolidated Act still required slave owners to provide suitable clothing and provisions for the slave communities as well as limiting the degree of punishment that could be inflicted on them. Christmas Day and the two following working days were declared holidays, leading to the secularization of rushin', with Boxing Day and New Year's Day nationalized as the holidays on which Junkanoos rushed (elsewhere, jump up, play mas, or tramp).

In its modern incarnation, "rushin'" is the term used for fully participating in the parade competition, which differentiates Junkanoos from the clamorous spectators, who are not only separated by steel barriers but also their fan base who often still tramp alongside them on the sidelines. Groups commonly display four lead costumes and fifty off-shoulders pieces, along with a full complement of other choreographed dancers. Several hundred musicians with bugles, whistles, horns, and cowbells lead the floats, while dancers in bright fringed costumes wind between them, moving with intricate steps to the gombay (goat-skin drum) beat. From an exogenous perspective, the utter scope of this competitive phenomenon connotes arrant chaos and mayhem; however, for those with something like "island-centricity," instead of being pejorative, this "jam up" epitomizes the ACW's Carnival. Behind closed doors, months in advance, group leaders oversee the building of colorful floats made of papier-mâché. Another common behind-the-scenes action is the search for moles, who are competitors' spies usually among the builders and costume designers.

Of all contemporary incarnations of Boxing Day festivities in the ACW, the Bahamian Junkanoo tradition currently gives the impression of being the best documented.[10] For instance, although Whittington Johnson's publication is on race relations in The Bahamas, he interrogates the cultural holiday and organizes a credible timeline for the holiday's enduring transformation.[11] Besides, he not only authenticates evidence of the 1830s as the earliest recorded documentation; he also hypothesizes that a "celebration which the Methodist reverend W. Dawson, a missionary, observed among blacks on Turks Islands in 1811 could also have been a Junkanoo. The blacks were said to have beaten tambourines and danced for a whole day" (49). Others grant equal credence to Junkanoo's evolution from West African festival performance genres; however, Johnson pinpoints with greater specificity the different potential locales with similar particularized festive gatherings. Among those mentioned are the Ibo "Yam Festival," the Yoruba Egungun Secret Society, and the Ga Peoples' *Homowo* harvest festival; he also affirms that the diversity of fetes throughout the West Indies depended on African points of origination. Johnson's chief example affiliates the phonetic derivation of Junkanoo with "the *dzonkonu* from the Ewe people of eastern Ghana and Togo" (49).[12]

Another of Whittingham Johnson's texts is about race relations postemancipation and extends the timeline further into the nineteenth century:

> Little work was done between Christmas and New Year. Nonwhites roamed residential and commercial streets in Nassau playing loud music with drums, conch shells, bugles, and beaten pieces of iron and solicited money, food, and liquor. In the 1850s, band sizes increased, costumes became more elaborate and themes were introduced. Maritime motifs were a crowd favorite, Junkanoo bands varied from

the large, formal, and staid processions that friendly societies organized and which their brass bands led, to the small, ragged, and frequently rowdy "scrap gangs," which improvised their music. Junkanoo celebrations would not become a formal regulated parade, however, until the tourism era of the twentieth century. ("Post-Emancipation" 57)

Because of the disorder and threats of violence associated with its revelers, Junkanoo lacked respectability; and its participants were considered to be mere gangs (Bastian 36). "In those days, being called a Junkanoo," Bastian notes, "was not a complimentary term. In fact, if you were called a Junkanoo you were relegated to the ranks of the uncouth, uneducated, undisciplined and wild, lacking strong social and moral fibre and were considered among the 'dreg' of society who sat (not even stood) at the bottom of the socio-economic ladder. Junkanoo was more of a nuisance than a jewel in our cultural crown" (37). Not exclusive to masquerades in the Caribbean, revelers from behind their masks of anonymity disrupted parade routes by engaging in minor skirmishes out of retaliation for earlier acts of personal retribution, which contributed to public derision and scrutiny.

Bahamian scholar Keith Wisdom undertook the first and most detailed analytical study of Junkanoo.[13] While his dissertation slavishly supports Victor Turner's social drama paradigm, it furnishes an in-depth commentary: tracing the evolution, new trends, and other basic fundamental alterations. Most important, Wisdom periodizes Junkanoo's history: Period One (1800–1899), Period Two (1900–1919), Period Three (1920–1947), and Period Four (1948–1984). Relying on newspaper accounts, Wisdom reports several early references to Bahamian Junkanoo, with one journalist substantiating that, by 1815, Christmas jubilations were well established in New Providence, including the "day next," now Boxing Day. He also presents information about key settlements of freed Africans such as Grant's Town. Quoting from the *Bahama Herald* of October 9, 1845, he describes a Grant's Town Bazaar in which "small boys dressed in costumes and adorned with garlands and ribbons displayed a type of Junkanoo, while singing a Bazaar song" (28).

To be discussed in greater detail later, the largest concentration of Africans lived in the then "Over-the-Hill" suburbs of Grant's Town and Bain Town to the south of the city of Nassau. Whittington Johnson in *Post-Emancipation* confirms: "Residents of Grant's Town and Bains' Town created a way of life distinctly different from that of whites in Nassau, one that was vibrant and self-sufficient, with stores, schools, churches, and places of amusement" (125). During the era of enslavement through postemancipation, Junkanoos from "Over-the-Hill" ambled through downtown Nassau on Bay Street. In 1899, the passage of the Street Nuisance Prohibition Act 1899 (lasting until 1954) was intended not to terminate but to curtail much of the seasonal mirth by imposing an injunction prohibiting Junkanoo between the hours of 4 a.m. and 9:00 a.m.[14] Wisdom notes that, after nearly a century of public displays, this proclamation was the first official attempt to impose public restraints (33–34).

Wisdom's Second Period coincides with World War I when Bay Street served as an important locus for combative public displays. He concentrates on the actions of conflicting Junkanoo bands in a depressed economy: "The gangs would move down Bay Street 'rushing' past each other in opposite directions. This would sometimes result in collisions, some of which were not accidental, between groups" (35). He also chronicles the ephemeral materials on public display, "like sponge, newspaper, tissue paper, banana leaves and a sacking material used for imported foodstuffs, 'crocus sack'" (35). Drawing from a 1916 eyewitness report that focused on the masqueraders' disguises as "an imitation of white people," Wisdom notes its similarity to Orlando Patterson's description of a West African festival of the Ga people: "the improvised masks seen in this section [of the procession] are often native caricatures of local European officials" (36). An actual eyewitness, Valeria Mosely Moss, offers further confirmation of the clashing bands, their wire mesh masks, and their musicality (24). Musically, the songs reflected the kind of social commentary and joviality integral to calypso.[15] As Olga Jenkins gleans from a host of Bahamian interviewees:

> Any effort to describe the Bahamas must include Goombay music. Although Calypso is considered to have its roots in Trinidad, the Bahamas have a unique form of this genre, referred to as Goombay. Reading Goombay folk songs as text is not totally effective because three important elements are missing—the intricate harmonies, the Bahamian accents and the beat of the music. . . . The songs are witty, humorous and/or full of double entendre. (103)

Wisdom concludes this period by noting the pranks and tricks incidental to Junkanoo such as removing gates, fences, carts, and drainage coverings as well as obstructing streets, linking these acts to forms of political resistance (36).

The Third Period developed during US Prohibition, when bootlegging surfaced as a virtual Bahamian national industry. Due to the new "liquor prosperity," The Bahamas grew into an open market known for its rum-running—the last boon in such profits to the island economy occurred during the US Civil War. The profitable local economy trickled down and resulted in a transformation period for Junkanoo as well. Junkanoos created more elaborate costumes and made improvements to the headpieces. According to Wisdom, "The new headdress was now adorned with very elaborate figures, various animals, birds, flowers, and ships as well as inanimate objects, made of cardboard and covered in sheared tissue paper, 'fringe'" (38). Previously designed out of newspaper, sponge, and crocus sacking, tissue paper fringes enhanced the costumes' aesthetics.[16] The period also saw an increased number of participants eager to rush, as well as greater spectatorship; accordingly, E. Clement Bethel emphasizes a shift in musical instrument construction and consumption commensurate with the newfound prosperity. He elaborates:

> Drums once fashioned from empty pork barrels and round cheese containers were now built out of old rum kegs. The conch shells and fog-horns of a simpler, seafaring life were replaced by horns which could be bought in stores—toy horns, bicycle horns, and, for those with enough money, bugles. And no instruments spoke so eloquently of the new age than the "scrapers," which provided a rhythmic accompaniment to the drums. Traditionally made from anything which, when scraped, would make a satisfactory sound—washboards and spoons, the jawbones of animals and sticks—they were symbols of their times. (50)

Symbolically, the totality of these innovations within the tradition denotes a monumental move towards modernity sustained by a new prosperity and unparalleled challenges to Junkanoo's autonomy.

In 1923, labor disputes over the use of Cuban workers to rebuild a prominent hotel destroyed by fire provoked the government to continue the Street Nuisance Rules and to consider abolishing Junkanoo. A local paper gloated about how welcome this would be "by those who have long wished for the abolition of this extraordinary manner of celebrating Christmas" (qtd. in E. Bethel 51). That year, undeterred, revelers faced off with police and fire hoses intended to disrupt their activities. Admirably, over subsequent holidays, Junkanoos boycotted the downtown and refused the bribes of shopkeepers. A sterling editorial praised their resolve, commenting, "it marks a distinct development in the people and reveals a spirit of democracy and unity that has been unknown in The Bahamas formerly" (E. Bethel 53). At best, Junkanoos gained "tolerance," which Wisdom attributes to a superciliousness that impugned their lack of respectability; authorities had, nonetheless, grown accustomed to the disorder (42).

After the lifting of the ban, Wisdom describes the rise of a community resolve to "boycott" Bay Street for two years, while masqueraders conducted their merrymaking "Over the Hill" in its stead. Returning in large numbers to Bay Street in 1924 nonetheless, according to one report, "The participants all wore white face masks or whitened their faces" like an Englishman in the Boutique; another in red velvet Shakespearean costume; another wore a clown's cap on his head and was dressed in flour bags. Other notables included three Highlanders and a group of men dressed as women in the latest Paris fashions" (qtd. in Wisdom

39). By 1925, Junkanoos faced another calculated maneuver: the development board along with private donors offered cash prizes to participants as a means to organize and encourage order on the main streets of Nassau.

In the 1930s, changes in the global economy and local politics affected the aesthetics and the mood of this era's parades. Beginning in 1933, an arm of The Bahamas Development Board, the Citizen's Masquerade Committee, arranged for a cash prize for the "best original costumes." The underlying intent was to regulate the "unofficial" Junkanoo parade system by relegating rushin' to New Year's Day only. Of most relevance to my study, in 1938, when the next Christmas Day occurred on a Sunday, authorities declared Boxing Day an official public holiday, assigning this date for all future Junkanoo fetes (Wisdom 43). The formation of an actual Junkanoo Committee, outside the purview of the development board, affirmed the popularity of Junkanoo as a public display event. By 1939, when only a few hundred were expected, an estimated crowd of 5,000 populated the main thoroughfare.

Due to the Burma Road riot in 1942, which erupted when striking workers who were underpaid (compared to American laborers) for constructing an airfield, officials banned Junkanoo for five years.[17] Regardless, during World War II, illegal parades persisted within neighborhoods (Wisdom; Wood). The ban was lifted in 1947, initiating the Fourth Period (Wisdom 45). With its reinstatement, the committee moved to promote organized groups and control individual participation to stem spontaneous "rushin'." Journalistic reports continued to note resistance to the new restrictions. For example, in 1951, although enjoined against doing so, the masses refused to be constrained. The *Nassau Guardian* denounced this insolence: "As usual, a large number of men and women, who were not attired in costumes, were 'rushing' up and down Bay Street ringing cowbells, blowing horns and beating native-made drums" (qtd. in Wood 78). Eventually, the willpower of these nonconformists succeeded, and they were sanctioned to compete as groups (79). This difference—between "groupers" and "scrappers"—persisted for about thirty years, until the 1980s (Wisdom 47).[18] The groupers (the first ones masking as Mexicans) exerted "massive amounts of time . . . creating their costumes," compared to the scrappers, who spent a minimal amount of time (48). The scrappers (and the community groups) represented standard tradition, whereas the groupers endorsed a hierarchy derived from their development of an inordinate level of skill in manipulating paper costumes with the customary fringe. In keeping with the historical moment, the 1960s and 1970s experienced greater inclusivity, with members of social classes that previously stigmatized Junkanoo now joining Over-the-Hill organizations, and even the prime minister and other government ministers rushed (Wisdom 49). Junkanoo emerged as a suitable Bahamian cultural marker, contributing to a sense of national pride (Rommen, *Funky* 27–28), and extolled as the "National Festival of the Bahamas."

Along with the steel barricades for crowd control, this period produced structural order as well as many additional transformations. Structurally, costuming evolved in size and complexity, translating into a need for greater aesthetic space. In 1973, the Junkanoo parade achieved higher status when it was deemed by officials to be a "national artistic treasure" (Wisdom 51). In that year, according to junkanooer Arlene Ferguson, "The management of the parades was turned over to the Bahamas Government, and the National Junkanoo Committee was formed as a statutory body with the responsibility of overseeing the parades."[19] With the rule governed nature of this cultural production as well as the high quality of artistry, the judging of organizations fueled competition. Judging, nearly unchanged over the years, took place in eight categories: best (overall) adult group; best juvenile group; best adult individual and juvenile individual; old-time Junkanoo; best costume (adult and juvenile); and best music (adult category only) (Wisdom 54). Within a decade, the prize money had escalated from $1000 to $30,000 in the best adult group category. The five major membership groups were The Saxons, Valley Boys, Music Makers, Vikings, and The PIGS (Progress-Through-Integrity-Guts-and-Strength), with The Saxons and Valley Boys constituting the perennial favorites.[20] Yet, an assortment of innovations emerged, with the formation of the new trendsetting group, the Music Makers, credited with being the first to pioneer very fine fringe pasting and a brass section (1976), off-the-shoulder dancers (1977), and a show-dancing girls section (1984).

To introduce modern Junkanoo, the following comprehensive, thick description by Winston Saunders reminisces about the now-defunct traditional steps of the Junkanoo dance,

> . . . which in essence is a shuffle—two shuffles back and two forward, which in the Bahamas is called "rushin'." Today, on Boxing Day and New Year's Day, Bay Street is filled with the sounds of Junkanoo—the goat-skin drum, stomach throbbing in its rhythm, the horn, the trumpet, and the distinctive cowbell. The Junkanooers are magnificent in their stature, their tall headdresses reminiscent of the African heritage and their color depicting scenes from life present and past, making comment on the society as it stands today. The painted faces and the masks worn also relate this festivity to our African heritage. (245)

Traditionally, the "Junkanoo dance" relied on robust, repeatable, and rhythmic body movements: two steps forward, one step back.[21] With great cultural specificity and replicating the melody for the "Twelve Days of Christmas," a children's coloring book—*Junkanoo: The Most Colorful Celebration in the World*—revises the song as "Boxing Day was coming so this is what I got":

1 large cardboard box and a bag of tool
2 boxes of glue and glitter
3 cartons of crepe paper
4 types of tricks [trinkets] and decorations

The material culture and decorative arts are of special interest due to their salient and dynamic transformations from "sponge costumes, flour on their faces, [thrown] firecrackers to costumes costing $50,000 or more" (W. Saunders 246). Regarding item 4, Junkanoo "tricks" can be judged overdone with lay aficionados of Junkanoo deriding the overuse of beads, fake jewels, and silk, critiquing the internalization of outside globalizing influences such as Mardi Gras, the emphasis on competing, and reconfiguring the singularity of simply rushing (K. Thompson, "Destroying" fn. 101).

One innovation, which possibly also led to the emergence of modern Junkanoo, testifies to the rules mandated by the masquerade committee: "those not fully costumed were prohibited from rushin." The increased spectatorship eventually resulted in the installation of bleacher seating and box office ticketing. Along with instituting prize money, Winston Saunders bemoans how these practices "had the effect of diluting somewhat the old spontaneity associated with everyone having a good street dance" (246). Although in the scoring rules, 50 percent of the points are allocated to an organization's costumes, "everyone knows that the music is the soul of Junkanoo" (Ferguson 32). Nassauvian Boxing Day Junkanoo has developed into a fully blown spectacle, a competitive parade with massively costumed, bespangled bands, comprising up to a thousand members. Bands take to Bay Street in the wee hours, 'rushing' before the judges' stand throughout the night, taking two and sometime three laps around the stand until the breaking of day, and displaying a stamina that is beyond compare. Director of the Bahamas Archives Gail Saunders emphatically proclaimed, "It is the soul of the Bahamian!" (*Family* 11).[22] Centralizing the fete into a more spectator-driven festival with an augmentation of group participation enlarged the Junkanoo experience. Although the event is televised live, one person said the transmission's value was "showing the public that it is safe to come out of their homes and coming to bay street to watch how our culture have grown and by doing this they will see that watching it on television is not a great experience unless you are there" (N. Bethel, "Violence").

Of all the Boxing Day celebrations, the present-day Bahamian Junkanoo follows the most African-centered aesthetic model (W. Saunders 88). In discussing the earlier Consolation Act, Whittington Johnson explains how the law aggrandized the Creoles, differentiating them from the Africa-born. This resulted, then, in "a much stronger African cultural presence pervad[ing] the Bahamas than the American South" (188). This cultural continuity is now commonly understood as meaning that, while actual African retentions do not infuse many everyday customs and naming in The Bahamas, Junkanoo's picturesque masquerade iconography, dancing, and goombay drums are the exception (Craton, *History* 188). As a matter of fact, left to their own understanding, E. Clement Bethel reports that, based on the ephemeral materials in use, Junkanooers believe that the festal name derived from the word "junk" because the "early junkanoo participants were skilled at taking such 'junk' materials and forging them anew, turning them into works of beauty" (10). They made their goombay drums more decorative with the addition of radiant pieces of glass, bottle caps, and other shiny objects.

An island legend, John "Chippie" Chipman, also known as "the king of the goatskin drum," epitomizes Junkanoo and is one of the few to achieve international acclaim in promoting The Bahamas as a tourist destination.[23] His acclaim derives from his construction of goatskin (gombay) drums and his championing of these percussive instruments. Although he is a consummate Junkanoo dancer, he credits his wife, Becky, deceased for over a dozen years, as the island's best performer. His Junkanoo group, Chippie and the Boys, is recognized for revolutionizing costumes with the use of crepe paper as well as being the first to rush out with three women Junkanoo dancers, including Chippie's wife. Winston Saunders captures the essence of the tradition's standard:

> Junkanoo includes a colourful parade, with impassioned dancing, live music, elaborate costumes and main sculptures called lead pieces. Goombay drums, used to create the beat, consist of wooden barrel covered at the top with stretched goat or sheepskin. The drummer plays his instrument with his bare hands after heating the drum to obtain maximum sound. Other musicians use various combinations of guitars, cowbells, whistles and additional drums. (89)[24]

Like poetry in motion, several hundred musicians with bugles, whistles, horns, and cowbells lead the floats, while dancers in bright fringed costumes wind between them, moving with intricate steps to the Gombay beat. Among the Saxons' 2500 members strutted eighty-five goatskin drummers, forty-five in the brass section, and forty bellers (Poitier). Rommen says it is the second line of bellers that authenticates the "most common bell pattern" ("Funky" 28). Cowbells are a seminal Junkanoo instrument that continues to evolve.

Deriving its name from the onomatopoeic sound that the cowbell makes in Junkanoo music, Kalik, produced by the Commonwealth Brewery, is thought to be another national treasure. Vivian Wood presents a hermeneutical interpretation of the extratextual meaning underlying the chanting:

We don't want no Beck's
Beer, We don't want no
Heineken, Kalik! Kalik! (92)

Beyond utter amusement, the lyrics make a cultural critique, deriding foreign impact on the culture and Junkanoo (Wood 93). The chant also critiques
Heineken International's gaining ownership of the company in 1988 and the
out-marketing of another conglomerate—Beck. Addressing the propensity for
innovations, the One Family Junkanoo group introduced a new instrument,
the "Konklu," which creates the sound "Kong ku lu." Some organizations have
embraced it, while the Saxons refused: "They're sticking to the old Junkanoo.
But Junkanoo evolves because, at one point, there was no brass section."[25] This
multimodality evinces the "free nature" of Junkanoo's music and performance
style (Hedrick and Stephens 6).

    In the realms of artistry, construction, musicianship, and dance, Winston
Saunders draws attention to the competitiveness of Junkanoo—"called the
single most Bahamian feast" (245–46). Wood also authenticates contemporary
Junkanoo practices, delineating the Bahamian indigenized formalities that constitute such a gargantuan spectacle:

> Junkanoo groups range in size from ten to one thousand members. The larger
> groups have established fierce rivalries that have existed for three decades in
> some cases. Each group has a leader or groups of leaders who are wellknown in
> the community and who, along with their costume designers, determine what
> the group's costumes will depict for each parade. All groups have their own musi-
> cians [and] traditional Junkanoo instruments (cowbells, goatskin drums, horns
> and whistles) as well as western instruments such as trumpets, trombones, saxo-
> phones and sousaphones. (5)

As part of the cultural surrogation process, even Western brass instrumentation
can be said to have become Bahamianized.[26]

    Still, it is important to note a Junkanoo legend, Tyrone "Dr. Offfff" Fitzgerald,
who embodied Junkanoo as a popular music style. Having begun his participation by the age of five, he referred to Junkanoo music as the "sound of life."
Born into a musical family, his father was a Junkanoo drummer, and his older
brother was a founding member of one of the premier Junkanoo groups, the
Valley Boys. Invoking Junkanoo music as an expressive art form, Fitzgerald said:
"[It] vibrates the organs of the body. The drums are the heartbeat; the cowbells
the rushing blood; the whistle the nerves; the horn the flesh" (qtd. in Wood 357).
Winning a Grammy Award for the release of the hit pop song "Funky Nassau"
permanently endears him as a musical genius to Bahamians. Known as a man

with a thousand ideas and an innovator as well as an attorney, he established his own Junkanoo group, P.I.G.S. (Power, Integrity, Guts, Strength), which introduced its own distinct choreography. After his death in 2002, he was officially commemorated with the Tyrone "Dr. Offfff" Boxing Day Junkanoo Parade.

Of most relevance, each spectacularly costumed group vies for prizes by "bringing" a theme. The Tyrone "Dr. Offfff" parade premiered the overarching and innocuous theme "The Twelve Days of Christmas" compared to One Family, which brought the winning theme— "Liberty and Justice for All"—featuring the World Trade Center's tragedy. Notably, this globalizing theme was writ large, resisting the impulse to delimit such fetes strictly to a sense of what enslavement wrought within the Black Atlantic World (Gilroy). The following assertion by Roger Abrahams contextualizes this idea: "At Carnival in Trinidad and Tobago; Mardi Gras in New Orleans and Memphis; Christmas Sports on Nevis, St. Kitts, and Jamaica; and the Bahamian Jonkonnu, enslavement and liberation are replayed" ("Questions" 77). "Sublime" is perhaps the word that should apply to the 9/11 disaster, which affected us all powerfully, both emotionally and physically. In practice, more currency is given to globalizing themes, including the intertextual revisioning of past winning Junkanoo themes. Glocalism appears in the Bahamian appropriation of themes from mass media with multinational awareness, as framed by Sarah Fernandez, by a merging of global forces with local cultural tradition ("Theory" 27).

The One Family group leader, Gino Rolle, explains the gist of the 9/11 theme: "Our presentation will take the parade through all the states. We will start with Florida with the Florida Everglades. Then a Fourth of July celebration, Thanksgiving, and the tragedy that happened in New York City" (qtd. in Poitier). This theme speaks to the interconnectedness of global mass cultures but not their potential unification due to globalization alone. The Bahamas hovers off the US eastern coast, betwixt and between two worlds. Regionally, there is much criticism of any dissolution of local cultural environments. The indigenization of American culture, the collapse of national borders, and local US history (both past and present-day) undergo a negative shift in implications by those on the margins. The island's local residents blame rampant American balkanization and US corporate sponsorship for the increase in ticket prices for prime bleacher seating along the parade route. As one distraught letter to the editor expressed: "The Government should be encouraging us to support our culture, which is being watered down by influences by our neighbors to the North the U.S.A., and not taking it away from us."[27] Yet, paradoxically, transformations are endemic to these traditionalized, dynamic cultural productions with decades of malleable antecedents.

Local history credits the Valley Boys Junkanoo Group with the introduction of themes, such as Scottish Highlanders in 1960 (Ferguson; Wisdom; Wood).

Annually now, each group's "design think tank" devises themes for both the Boxing Day and New Year Junkanoo. Each theme must withstand two considerations: "be fertile enough to support a multitude of different designs" and "not closely resemble any recent" motif (Ferguson 24). Yet, frequently, groups masquerade as pirates or iconic characters from Greek and Roman mythology. These choices often lead to a strictly binary association with European masking traditions. However, such comparisons are ignorant of the Bahamian sense of place and use of metaphor. When it comes to Caribbean piracy and privateering, they are a thoroughly documented part of The Bahamas' ignominious history and thus inform masking. In particular, the reference to Greek and Roman mythology is consistent with their past as well. E. Clement Bethel traces the first appearance of Neptune and Amphitrite to an 1854 press report. He emphatically states: "It perhaps seems strange that these two characters from Greek and Roman mythology should find themselves in the midst of what was essentially a West African festival in The Bahamas" (27). He then provides an in-depth interrogation of the traditionality of these ancient mythological figures by affixing them to a sea-faring initiation rite that appropriated some aspects of masking. Upon crossing the Equator, "someone disguised as Neptune [who] . . . sometimes was accompanied by his wife, Amphitrite" (28). Therefore, rather than just hybridity, Bahamians lay claim to a root metaphor pertaining to locality and identity.

Arlene Nash Ferguson, a Junkanooer since the age of four, is a living legend, too, due to being the first woman to break rank as a dancer and to carry a lead costume. When it comes to costumes, she is a preeminent authority and differentiates between "Old-Time Junkanoo" and what is now known as modern Junkanoo, based on the plastic arts or three-dimensional designs. She describes the Old-Time costumes as "fringed in tissue or crepe paper, and the colours placed in simple horizontal stripes. The pointed hat and wire mask were also standard features" (14). As a part of her family history, with allegiances to the Valley Boys, an uncle formed his own group—the Vikings—transforming Junkanoo forever: "Now when I rushed with the Vikings in the 1960s that was rushing! Do you know how three-dimensional costumes started? It was us!" (14). That year they rushed as "The Hibiscus: Tribute to Bahamian Beauty," adorned with cardboard petals and breaking the color code as well from red, white, blue, yellow, and black to those consistent with the flower—red, white, pink, and orange. They caused a paradigm shift in costuming: "After that, everyone had 3-D costumes" (15). Ferguson estimates that these fabrications fueled three decades' innovations, "resulting in shorter fringe, flour paste gave way to white glue, and cardboard and aluminum rods eventually replaced wire costume frames covered with fabric" (16). Structurally, these transformations allowed for larger costumes, with shoulder pieces and skirts, and huge lead pieces with certain height restrictions, commonly referred to as "3-D sculptures in motion."[28]

There are two categories of dancers: off-the-shoulder and showtime dancers. The intricate costumes of the former are bulky, making them too heavy for
choreographed movements, whereas the latter are well choreographed. During
construction, their off-the-shoulder costumes are tested for weight, visibility,
and balance (Ferguson 29). Accordingly, Ferguson writes: "The Junkanoo costume is a marvelous feat of engineering in which a single performer wears an
ensemble that weighs between twenty to fifty pounds, and rises anywhere from
six to ten feet in the air." In this context, banning motorization in such a large-
scale contemporary US parade would be unimaginable. Another Junkanooer,
Valeria Moss, reports that the comparative size of the costumes restricted
movements, making the wearer more sedate compared to the past "wild melee
of dancing bodies in the centre of Bay Street" (163).

One of the main texts written from an emic (insider's) perspective to describe
Nassauvian traditions is *Bain Town* by Cleveland Eneas, a memoir constituting a "Caribbean narrative of belonging" self-published in 1976.[29] This narra-
tive presents descriptive and expository portrayals of mid-twentieth-century
Junkanoo parades and costuming, projecting a "cultural intimacy" (Rommen,
"Home" 72). For instance, Eneas writes, "The emphasis was placed on the masquerades. Some of the junkanoos tried to add some beauty to their costumes
by using crepe paper, and that is the part that we have happily retained" (50).
However, Eneas marked the period of World War II as the moment in which
"Nassau began to clean up the Junkanoo act" (50). Letters to the editor such
as one by local diehard Bob Nevil on October 21, 2013, in the *Nassau Guardian* still lament any bowdlerizing transmutations: "If Bahamians love Junkanoo
so much, we should take it Over-the-Hill where it belongs."[30] This viewpoint
contests the current commodification of Junkanoo as a central symbol of the
nation, in which the all-night parades along the main thoroughfare are shown
on jumbotrons to entice tourists off cruise ships since otherwise their perception is "they are horning in on a private local function." Along with his discourse
about "kinesthetic imagination," theorist Joseph Roach introduces the principle
of "vortices of behavior" as informing ludic spaces for intercultural encounters:
"the gravitational pull of social necessity" that legitimates the synergy between
audiences and performers (28).

Jankunú in Dangriga sustains another behavioral vortex, while constituting
a historical as well as cultural anomaly in the ACW. The anomalies reflect how
the British came to be the only English-speaking state in an otherwise Spanish-
speaking linguistic subregion along with the cultural history of its Garifuna citizens. For centuries, the British built outposts there under Spanish sovereignty;
during the seventeenth and early eighteenth centuries, the first British newcomers were ex-buccaneers and adventurers called Baymen, who arrived to extract
timber (Bolland, *Colonialism* 22). Formerly known as British Honduras, one of

the lesser known countries of Central America, Belize continues to sustain a long history of territorial disputes; from the time the nation-state was a British Crown Colony, even Guatemala maintains that it inherited a claim to parts of Belize.[31] Adding to the complexity, "For reasons of empire, shipping had always been via Jamaica, the former seat of government of British Honduras" (Judd, "Name" 139). Upon becoming a colony in 1862, British Honduras was governed from Jamaica, until a separate colony was established in 1871. A further incongruity is that, rather than British common law, with the rest of the southern Western Hemisphere, initially "the legal tradition [was] Roman," based on common law (Thomson 1). Under Spanish sovereignty, British loggers divested the land of its mahogany; and with the dominance of timber exportation, the country's development of agriculture and its infrastructure suffered. Another enduring legacy prevented newly freed Africans from purchasing land to survive, relegating them to work only as mahogany cutters. As a result, Judd noted, "The colony passed from the nineteenth to the twentieth century with no roads and railroads nor electric lights, and almost without a local modernizing capitalist class or a free wage-earning class" ("Name" 135). It is within these historical and political contexts that Jankunú emerged in this sector of Central America.

Regionally, it is not considered an overstatement when Belizeans claim their population is the most diverse—culturally, ethnically, and linguistically—on the planet. The country's largest ethnic group consists of mixed descendants of Mayan and Spaniards, recognized as Mestizos. However, the latest census results reposition this demographic fact as being in flux. Creoles constitute the majority population in Belize City, once the capital, and are the most populous nationwide. The term "Creoles" referred, historically, to the descendants of enslaved Africans from Jamaica who intermixed with the English and Scottish Baymen.[32] Europeans and North American expatriates may also be included. Garifuna (whose name signifies their culture and language like the Gullah in the US Sea Islands) are a small percentage, living in the Stann Creek District, particularly Dangriga (which means sweet water). The language is Arawakan and is also spoken in Honduras, Guatemala, and Nicaragua. Their language is primarily derived from Arawak and Carib, with English, French, and Spanish to a lesser degree. The Central American nation also includes East Indians, Syrians, Lebanese, Chinese, Taiwanese, and Mennonites. Linguistically speaking, besides English and Kriol (Belizean Creole), the Mennonites retain their distinctive German Dutch, while many Mestizos only speak Spanish along with Spanglish (creolized Spanish). Acknowledging their transculturalism, most Garifunas have surnames that are French (Rochez) as well as English (Thomas, Perry, and Lambert), Spanish (Alvarez, Martinez, and Aranda), and Portuguese (Moreira, Cabarello). Paradoxically, while whites dominate economically, "a creole (now predominantly black) elite has historically dominated political life" (Johnson and Watson xiii). Creoles strived for political dominance, being among the first to populate the nation (after the indigenous peoples) and feeling ordained to do so since the country was decolonized in 1981 and they gained power (Mwakikagile 149).

Moreover, the other historical anomaly engages the Garifuna's cultural preservation within their own settlements. November 19, 1823, marks their arrival into Central America from St. Vincent (Yurumein in the Garifuna language). The origins of Garifuna people were some recalcitrant runaways and shipwrecked Africans from the slave ship *Palmira* bound from the Bight of Benin in 1675 who then landed on St. Vincent. There, they intermingled with the indigenous Carib population; therefore, they are African Amerindian people.[33] Joseph Chatoyer became a national hero in St. Vincent and the Grenadine Islands because, in 1772, he led a rebellion resulting in the First Carib War and the British being forced to sign a treaty. This was the first time Britain had been forced to sign an accord with any indigenous population in the Americas. His military prowess, which included welcoming defeated French soldiers among his ranks, enabled him to survive two Carib wars against the British. On March 14, 1795, true to his bellicose nature, he challenged a British major and died in a duel. In 1979, following independence in St. Vincent and the Grenadines, Chatoyer was embraced as a symbol by the new nation and proclaimed, "Right Excellent Joseph Chatoyer, the First National Hero." Due to the ferocity of the Black Caribs in their independence war, twenty-five years after commencing their rebellion, the British finally forcibly transplanted this indigenous population to Central America. Presently, April 12 is the date when the Garifuna people commemorate their arrival on the large Honduran island Roatan, in 1797. Even today, anthropologist Joseph Palacio reckons the Garifuna people are one of the greatest transmigrant people in the Caribbean (175).

In Belize, Settlement Day became a national holiday to commemorate the Garifuna's arrival in Dangriga from Honduras on November 19, 1832, led by Alejo Beni. Later, the Garifuna were denigrated because they are phenotypically more African and called Black Caribs, so other Blacks with Creole status regarded the Garifuna as "a most dangerous people" (Thomson 46).[34] Discriminated against by all, when a British law granted property rights to other subaltern subjects, they received prejudicial treatment, making them squatters on Crown lands and being settled on reservations. Over time, though, they gained recognition for their quiet industriousness as an additional labor resource by the British. Nonetheless, contemporary Belizeans disavow racial prejudice with a general disdain of the so-called race card, which accords with Judd's assessment: "In the Caribbean, even where a strong white local elite is present, race is defined socially" (qtd. in Johnson and Watson xv). Explicating this sentiment, in his mother tongue, Belizean artist Phillip Lewis eloquently stated:

A tink a si wan new Belize weh di creole man, di mesizo, di Garifuna, an di Maya, no separate as a lis dem but instead all da Belizeans.

I think I see a new Belize where the creole, the mestizo, the Garifuna and the Maya are not separated as I have listed them, but united as Belizeans. (qtd. in Perrottet 67)

A commonly used Creole expression is "All a we mek Belize"—we all make up Belize. In a recent letter to the editor in the *Amandala* newspaper, a reader presents the allegiances achieved by the Garifuna within this multicultural nation.[35] While racial tensions exist, race conflict is rare.

At one time in Belize, the logcutting enterprise demanded that its laborers work away from their families in six-month stints. The contract laborers typically left their families in town while they worked in the forest, broken only by the Christmas holiday (Judd 138). Along with the other British colonies, the Christmas season granted laborers a well-deserved break. Thomson reports that, in the early nineteenth century, "Christmas hilarity was opened with a 'discharge of small arms in every direction' and marked with singing and dancing, dory and pitpan racing, and drinking. Other pursuits were fishing from the cays and shooting in the bush" (46).[36] One of the foremost authorities on Garifuna culture, Oliver Greene, situates the Garifuna Jankunú in Belizean English Creole as derivative of the men being coworkers with Creoles in mahogany camps in the nineteenth and twentieth centuries, providing the following transcription.[37]

Belizean Creole	Translation and Transliteration
Call	
Play, Jankunu Play	Dance, masked dancer, dance
Give them a kissey	Give them a kiss (money)
For New Year pleasure	As a New Year's treat
Response	
Ah Willi-yamo,	Ah! William
Blessy massa	Blessed master
Who live to see aye	Whosoever lives to see them
For next yearay	For next year.

As of 2001, in ten communities on the coasts of Honduras, Guatemala, Nicaragua, and Belize, an estimated 11,500 Garifuna speak the language as their mother tongue.[38] Along with Jankunú, their language retention supports validating Dangriga as "The Culture Capital of Belize."

To open and close the *Wanáragua* season, traditionally, on December 24 and January 6, *Warini* was performed until the mid-1990s (Greene 210). It is now defunct, due to safety issues, but it serves to demarcate the period customarily allotted for Christmas carnivals. According to John and Miles Hadfield, "Christmas Eve has never been part of the Feast of the Twelve Days" (53). Then, there must have been some alternative explanation for this ritualistic beginning and the termination of the ceremony. Dancers wore costumes of dried plantain leaves, carrying work-related objects and gesticulating with them (Greene 210). Along with the perfunctory drumming, they performed *Warini* songs unique to this occasion. One mythical explanation resurrects cultural memories dating back to their homeland, Yurumein, and the group's partnership with the Guarini, whom they visited and celebrated with over Christmas. After their exile, "when Christmas comes they start thinking about their neighbors and friends, Guarini, and the way how they used to dress, so they disguised themselves like that and composed a song" (Greene 211). Greene decisively situates the ritual as predating John Canoe and to be of direct African derivation, meaning it also possibly predated the participants' conversion to Christianity.[39]

Commencing on Christmas Day, now *Wanaragua* functions as the official Jankunú performance cycle opener with spontaneity and without fanfare (Greene 214). There are designated male group leaders, abuti(s) or banquata(s), who act as the bossmen or master of ceremonies much like the Gombey dancers' captain. Rather than the tall peacock headdress of the Gombeys, however, their *wababan* (headpiece) is constructed of cardboard and bears more generic feathers, colorful papier-mâché balls, and reflecting mirrors appearing to be more turban-like. As ethnographers Kerns and Dirks write, the end results "resemble fanciful crowns" or "spectacular hats" (6). With necks completely concealed, a screen mask (common to masking in Bermuda and St. Kitts) features painted-on "staring eyes, black eyebrows, and red lips" (7). The most significant aspect of the costume is the crisscrossed pink and green ribbons because there is a militaristic component with the *Wanaragua* ritual dance, satirizing and reenacting colonial domination by wearing their beribboned ensemble to mock the doubled bandolier uniforms of their oppressors.[40] The stylistic dancing engages mimicry, mockery, and mime as critical carnivalesque characteristics. A wooden sword commonly complements the disguise along with sneakers, black stockings, and white gloves. To establish the credibility of *Wanaragua* as a cognate rite of European derivation, Dirks emphasizes the sword dance: "Frequently, dancers hold swords and in some versions wield them in ways suggesting ritual execution," replete with dramatic spoken words ("Evolution" 94). Yet, by 2013, this prop had disappeared and evidently, in this iteration of mumming, dancers always remained mum (pun intended). However, costuming, dancing, and musical components persevere in which "little, if any, of the body is left exposed," a cognate of mumming (Kerns and Dirks 6). Audience members must rely on the dance styles of individuals for identification purposes. Leg-bands (*yawai*) are another enduring idiophonic instrument: "Fashioned from hundreds of tiny shells which are sewn on narrow strips of cloth, these bands are not simply decorative" (8). Essential to the merrymaking, being both audible and visual, the more vivacious dancers use the jangle of the seashells to make sounds congruent with the drumming. The primary kinetic movements ensue below the waist, with "the legs and feet in perpetual motion" (9).

The Garifuna, with some variations in construction, retain an African-based membranophone tradition of skin drums also affiliated with Nassauvian Junkanoo.[41] Specifically, according to ethnomusicologist Oliver Greene's official website, "they employ only two types of drums (garawoun, in Garifuna). Both garawoun are identical in construction but differ in size and musical function. The segunda, a single-headed bass drum, is approximately 90 centimeters high and ranges from 60 to 90 centimeters in diameter" (236). The cylindrical body of the drum is typically made of the mayflower or another hard wood. The head is made of dried deer, peccary, or goat skin and is attached to the wooden base by beach vine and small nails.[42] In conformity with African percussive musical systems, the primero drum is a high-pitched tenor and plays lead. Handcrafted from the same log and gendered female, the larger identical segunda drum is said to have birthed the primero, womb-like carved from its inside. By necessity, the segunda is lower in pitch and like the bass provides the basic, repetitive rhythm, which is the foundation for enhancing improvisatory passages played on the primero. The primero's principal function is to interpret the movements of the solo dancers, especially during the Wanaragua masquerade.

In the instance of the Garifuna's Wanaragua dancers, Belizean scholars insist on their bond with African egungun masking, symbolizing the spirit of the dead. This position centers the scholarship that recognizes the African-based masquerade, dancing, and drumming ritual arts traditions as retentions. More specifically, this stance concedes that the apparel of egungun masqueraders still informs the local aesthetic ideal (Greene 205). Just as St. Kittitians are recognized for revitalizing Bermuda's Gombeys, there is a theory that Jamaican Jonkonnu informs Belizean Jankunú.[43] The proposition derives from Judith Bettelheim's work and has been validated by other scholars.[44] The first cultural transmission route, allegedly, occurred from the late nineteenth to early twentieth centuries and depended on Jamaican workers' migrating to Belize to improved labor opportunities. Bettelheim specifies the transference of some elements such as wire screen masks and the quasi-military uniform, with Kerns and Dirks advocating for the implementation of ox horns and wooden swords (Greene 200). In 1976, the Caribbean festival arts exhibition in Jamaica included Belizean participation. This international recognition granted the Garifuna the cultural collateral and esteem needed to attract their government's approval. In 1981, belatedly, Belize obtained its independence, and establishing a more derivative national identity became the mission of the winning political party.

The same year, the National Garifuna Council was also formed and directed its efforts to reconsidering elements of their Jankunú revitalized from Jamaica. However, one must note that in "no two places are the festivals exactly the same" (Bettelheim, "Jonkonnu" 39). It merits pointing out that their *Wanaragua* headpieces, legwear, and African gombey drums continue to be uniquely their own and not part of a Jamaican continuum. These interpretations apply to the material culture as a text, but the extratextual meaning of their performativity is rooted in Garifuna history. In Dangriga (affectionately known as Griga), performers showcase an allegiance to masked festive traditions, freely adding their own twists. Comparable to past mummery in the UK and the contemporary Gombeys, the social element is the decisive factor with the aim of moving from location to location, celebrating, and entertaining a growing entourage of spectators along the way as an exciting stimulus.

On Boxing Day, Garifuna families celebrate *Charikanari* (also known as the Pia Manadi dance), which differs from the masquerade tradition exhibited on Christmas Day known as *Wanaragua* (which means "mask"). *Charikanari* foregrounds dancers, drummers, and the payment of restitution to visit neighboring households that have requisitioned dancers to stop by and perform on their premises. Specific to the Christmas holiday season, the *Charikanari* processional from house to house and dance performances spotlight *hianros* (traditionally men and boys dressed as women).[45] While crossdressing is shared with other masking traditions, when describing this performance art, Garifuna descendants center this gender role reversal as a ritualized reenactment of Garifuna men intentionally dressing as women during the Second Garifuna War in 1795–1796 to avoid capture and execution by the British.[46] A sexualized satiric dance is part of the antics of the *hianros* and includes, on occasion, teasingly grabbing a male spectator in a bear hug to frolic with him. While gendered, the disguises are far from sensuous and evolved from those described by Kerns and Dirks as being "extravagantly festooned with ribbons, sashes, and streamers, so that they are hardly recognizable to their owner" (8). Nowadays, *hianros* are well accessorized, wearing feminine wigs, pocketbooks, and white mesh masks festooned with female features that conceal masculine traits like facial hair. In keeping with the carnivalesque masquerade transgressive aspect, they engage in displays of ludic transvestism. One resident volunteered a tragic narrative alleging that one time a young boy, unable to process this kind of ludic behavior, drowned in attempting to escape the gender-bending role playing.

Other cultural dynamics inform *Charikanari* and other Garifuna ludic celebrations with the appearance of two stock figures—the two-foot cow and devil characters. Indicative of the stock figures, animal head masks are deemed to be African-derived and the satanic masks Western-derived (Bettelheim, "Jonkonnu"; Harris). As noted earlier in Hurd's remembrances, children particularly delighted in the appearance of these characters (Greene 215). On the one hand, the major function of the stock two-foot cow and devil characters, paradoxically, is to elicit fearful responses from the youngsters who nevertheless participate gleefully (Greene; Bilby; Dirks, "Evolution" 97).[47] These traditional figures may spontaneously participate in the dancing; but the real focus is harassing the children by administering blows with the weaponized implements they carry, remaining in character throughout the cultural performance. The *Charikanari* two-foot cow affords great amusement, "motion[ing] for the children to move out of the way to clear a path for him to run through the crowd. Surprisingly most observers knowing what would happen next did not move. Two-Foot-Cow suddenly lunged forward, striking an older boy in the chest.... The Boy laughed and seemed unharmed" (Greene 216).

The devil character, in particular, rages universally throughout the Black Atlantic World, even making an appearance of sorts in north Florida. Just as the fife was once a prominent musical instrument, there was also a peculiarly attired Santa Claus. On the 26th, I personally saw on one occasion a Santa in full St. Nick regalia, toting not a sack of treats, but a baseball bat in order to gleefully harass children. Unlike the white-bearded North Pole figure, this entity traditionally conformed more to the devil, a well-known Jamaican Jonkonnu character. George Henry described him to me by name: "Candace Hayes would portray the Santa Claus. He was an elder man who had lost some teeth in front, kind of heavy set, a brown skinned guy with fair hair and fair skin. He would put smut or something all over his face and make him look like a Santa Claus, and he'd dress up with all kinds of clothes on." The figure alluded to as Santa also was depicted as not only appearing in something "akin to black-face minstrelsy" (Reid 356), but with red paint around his eyes. He arrived in a mule-drawn wagon and threw candy to the children, but he was also said, foremost, to frighten them.[48] This description closely align with Jamaican Glen Hurd's description of the Jonkonnu figure, whose explicit role was a fear-provoking one: "They were all pretty scary, the costumes, from the perspective of a child. So if you saw them coming, you're at the gate. You saw them coming; you'd run back inside and peep out for them. They know children were scared. So if they see you there, they'll frighten you somewhat."[49] Piersen reinforces this idea when he wrote that "interaction between performer and audience is an essential part of African American festive style" ("Festive Style and Creation" 260). Offering hours of entertainment, this form of hijinks titillates and excites the younger spectators, who relentlessly taunt the characters and showcasing a coarse tradition with transgenerational appeal. Judith Bettelheim, in a Jamaican rural context, observed: "They scare, but they also amuse. They invoke both fear and courage" ("Jonkonnu" 53). The all-day performance never invokes a mumbling word from the masked characters, which can include the "hunter man" in surrogation for the devil actor.

The sexualized dancing, however, comprises the most dynamic public display in the *Charikanari* cultural production. In *The Black Saturnalia*, Dirks termed the dancers a "paternal fraternity of men"; yet, at each stop, the dancing is delimited hierarchically by age sets (8).⁵⁰ An apparent hierarchy exists based on a rank-ordered seniority as each dancer enters the ring, beginning with the youngest boy, to exhibit an increasingly provocative vocabulary of scintillating movements (9). Customarily, the performance entails the same door-to-door model of today's Bermuda Gombey dancers, which also privilege age sets in performance, except the Garifuna visitations are mostly prearranged as they unrelentingly traverse the city into the night. Their troupe includes a flagman, who travels in advance to request permission from the occupants to plant the flag, fulfill already established requests, and signal the next dance venue. A circle of spectators gathers with women choral singers standing behind the seated drummers. Traditionally, the principal dancers are a King and Antics Man, but all of the dancers in turn briefly show off their faux heteroerotic dance vocabulary. Duplicating the Gombeys, monetary gifts are collected in a purse or bag as also will be discussed among masqueraders in St. Kitts, where the proceeds are equally divided. Collective economics motivates and is the sustaining force behind these carnivalesque gatherings as a retention of a communitarian outlook (Bashi).⁵¹

In response to past exogenous propensities among scholars, derived from their own subjectivity under the veil of impartiality, today's ethnographers tend to privilege the endogenous perspectives of the cultural producers. Sociologist Orlando Patterson advanced "cultural configuration," a concept devised by anthropologist Ruth Benedict, and defined the "knowledge activation theory," recognizing the heterogeneity represented by the microdynamics of cultural practices. These aestheticized constructs speak to the accessibility of particular ways of knowing and the use of shared cultural knowledge. Whether referencing Boxing Day Junkanoo or Jankunú, these idioms derive from the same morphological linguistic system, yet each comprises distinctive historical configurations that led to unique innovations within ever-evolving masking traditions. Although Patterson's cultural study interrogates young African American masculinity, his assessment's articulation of cultural configuration works in an interdisciplinary way: "Differences exist, to be sure, but only in degrees of emphasis on certain practices; however, the knowledge structures, norms, and values of the configurations are strikingly similar" (58). Bahamian Junkanoos communicate a fraternal association whose cultural configuration is multitudinous and well choreographed to promote glamour and splendor in competition but in the spirit of customary celebrations, increasingly defined by glocality. The unpaved roads and lanes in Dangriga are most conducive to a cultural configuration consistent with the past, for example, featuring a small relatively ragtag contingency of drummers, Charikanari dancers, and other familial members delivering collective joy door-to-door for the entirety of the day, with hints of competition. This argument intends to offer a dialectical analysis to evaluate the wide diffusion of behavioral patterns propagated by differing socioeconomic conditions but keyed to the same emphasis on certain practices.

In the next chapter, I will focus on two of the Leeward islands, St. Croix and St. Kitts, because Boxing Day's Christmas Sports' cultural configurations deviate most at these two sites, attuned to the transnational cultural flow within the Black Atlantic. I will address how the infusion of Trinidad's Carnival complicates these islands' cultural production of playing mas "foreday morning," meaning in the wee hours. Paraders engage in what is called the "jump up" as members of different Mas camps surround trucks bearing refreshing adult beverages and sound systems blaring out competing road march tunes. However, masquerade characters still spontaneously make cameo appearances befuddling or overlooked by those who lack a high context for how Boxing Day used to highlight traditional figures like Pitchy Patchy, Mudman, and the Cane Cutter with his Burro engaging festivalgoers without causing any sensation, except for my own glee on seeing these characters for the very first time. In essence, as a survival imperative, choosing to play in the dark (especially to play mas) comprises a form of cultural logic or mutual assumption divorced from European reason. Defining mas in vernacular terms, a self-proclaimed masman said, "Mas is living art." Anthropologist Alleyne-Dettmers describes mas with equal succinctness: "unscripted dramatic costuming" ("Ancestral" 201). The next chapter reveals the virtual lack of masquerading "Foreday Morning."

CHAPTER FOUR

J'ouvert

On St. Croix and St. Kitts, celebrants play mas, known as J'ouvert (Carnival), at "foreday morning": "J'ouvert" combines the French words "jour" (day) and "ouvert" (open). As a French Creole expression, the term generally, though without consensus, translates to mean "daybreak." Wherever it is enjoyed, usually J'ouvert (pronounced joo-vay) extemporaneously erupts in the streets at least a couple of hours before dawn.[1] Most observers associate J'ouvert exclusively with Carnival in Trinidad and Tobago, where it inaugurates the pre-Lenten season's Carnival as a rite of spring. Boxing Day Carnivals possessed their own long-standing masquerade traditions; yet Trinidad and Tobago are the two islands that most obviously personify what is meant by transnational cultural flow. More recently, they have been heavily carnivalized by appropriating the festival art common to Trinidadian bacchanalia. The Anglophone Trinidad was never colonized by the French, but the tradition is affiliated with the influx of French Catholic planters migrating there.[2] Folklorist Stephen Stuempfle further historicizes the celebration, writing, "J'ouvert was a reinterpretation of the old Canboulay tradition and featured percussion, aggressive action, eerie figures, and satirical commentary" (25). St. Croix and St. Kitts represent examples of "successful hybrids," heavily carnivalized by transcultural flow from Trinidad, called the mother of all West Indian Carnivals (Mason 166). In the process of cultural globalization, the flow of ideas across borders "is instigated by cultural glocalisation, where cultures continuously interact" (Robertson 25).[3] The transmigration experience supports multidirectional networks that facilitate the circulation of indigenized practices and creative ideas.

Located in the eastern Caribbean, these Leeward Islands demonstrate fascinating and paradoxical cultural and historical intersectionality; for instance, St. Croix is the largest of the US Virgin Islands. "Croix" means Holy Cross, and the island was given distinct names as it was colonized by different countries—Spanish: Santa Cruz; Dutch: Sint-Kruis; French: Sainte-Croix; and Danish:

Sankt Croix. Commencing with Columbus, St. Croix has been called the "land of seven flags"—Spain, Holland, Knights of Malta, France, England, the Danish West Indies Company, and the United States. On his second voyage in 1493, Columbus named all the isles throughout this archipelago, labeling them "Saints and Virgins" (Verrill 31). All of the Saints came to be Danish colonies, while England claimed the Virgins. Destined to become a US territory, St. Croix was lastingly colonized by Denmark (from 1733 to 1917), and it retains many Danish sociocultural influences as well as architecture and windmills.

Outside academic circles, Danish and Dutch colonialism in the Caribbean is generally unacknowledged, receiving little attention on a concrete level. Anglophone researchers are often unable to read Danish to access most of the source material, whereas Danish researchers have facility with English but do not generally publish in English. Even US history often ignores that, in 1619, the Dutch were the first to transport to Jamestown, Virginia, the indentured African servants whose descendants became chattel slaves in perpetuity. Nicknamed the isle of rum and sugar, St. Croix had fertile soil, which resulted in its rise in value, being larger and better suited for sugar cane production than the other possessions—St. Thomas and St. John—in the Danish West Indies (Ober 324; Bayley 127).[4] At the time of Danish colonization, about 150 British inhabitants on St. Croix (with about 400 to 500 enslaved Africans) ultimately swore an oath of allegiance to the king of Denmark (Dookhan 45).

St. Croix's history of colonization includes a brief period in the mid-seventeenth century of simultaneous Dutch and English rule, with the Dutch occupying the west coast (Frederiksted) and the English the east (Christiansted). In *The Dutch Slave Trade: 1500–1850*, historian P. C. Emmer interrogates the "dark side of the Dutch Golden Age." He outlines the early, active colonizing mission of the Dutch throughout West Africa, Brazil, New Netherlands (the present state of New York), and the Caribbean. Compared to other "Caribbee Islands," St. Croix was small and deemed unattractive, while nearby St. Thomas was "aptly described as 'the place which is on the way to every other place'" (Dookhan 1). The Dutch perceived these formidable characteristics as assets, conceding the islands to the south to be colonized by other nations. The era also condoned piracy: "following the end of the Spanish/Dutch truce in 1621 Dutch 'zeerovers' utilised the Virgin Islands as a base from which to harass and pillage the Spanish settlements to the west" (Harrigan and Varlack 3). In the 1780s, with a diminished slave trade in the Leeward Islands, the enslaved population was primarily native-born, resulting in an Africa-based creole culture informing dress, dance, music, and obeah. Historians interpret these retentions to be due to the fact that "the white overlords, while they never slackened in the political control of slaves, saw it as no part of their function to 'civilise' them" (Harrigan and Varlack 32). A table in Tyson and Highfield's *The Kamina Folk: Slavery and Slave Life in the Danish West Indies* shows that the enslaved population on St. Croix always far exceeded those on St. Thomas and St. John by up to 80 percent (xi).[5]

The Leeward Islands share a long history of coexisting and open reciprocity. The proximity of Puerto Rico, a Spanish colony, further complicated matters for slaveholders in the Virgin Islands:

> It can also happen that a man can be ruined in one night if his slaves plot and run away to Porto Rico. The latter is an island belonging to the King of Spain, located some eight or nine miles to the west of St. Croix (Danish Miles). This island has brought many people to tears for they and their entire families were ruined when in a single night 20 to 25, indeed sometimes more, deserted to that place. (Tyson and Highfield 32)

With a mere seventy miles separating the two colonies, a Crucian slaveowner's entire enslaved population could disappear to Puerto Rico overnight. A unique sociocultural bond continues between inhabitants of the two islands, most indicative by the merger of Christmas traditions.

In the US Virgin Islands, St. Croix experienced several notable insurrections; and playing mas, meaning revelers marching with a band, often disguised an open rebellion.[6] Planter Thurlow Weed documents the St. John Slave Rebellion of 1733 as well as the slave conspiracies of 1746 and 1759, both uprisings set for the Christmas holidays (166–71). Then, in July 1848, freedom fighters burned down plantations and sieged Frederiksted on St. Croix's west coast. Insurgents signaled the start of the rebellion "by the ringing of bells and the blowing of conch shells" (Weed et al. 176).[7] In the aftermath, the most outstanding and unpredictable outcome of this notorious uprising was the emancipation of the enslaved people (Heuman 86). Unlike other Anglicized Caribbean locales, American regional politics did not unduly influence race relations in the future US Virgin Islands. When the Emancipation Act came, the elite landowners anticipated a marked societal and economic transformation with the once-enslaved persons dominating the population by twenty-five to one. According to the planters, the enslaved population already lived "in a condition of considerable ease and comfort" (Harrigan and Varlack 92). It must also be stressed that despite not having an organized abolitionist movement, Denmark, in contrast to England and France, was the first to eliminate the slave trade (Green-Pedersen 215). An edict in 1792 sought to eliminate the Atlantic triangular slave trade, not because of altruism but in recognition that it did not pay in economic terms. Frederiksted gained fearsome notoriety thereafter and proudly called itself "Freedom City."

After an investigation by the king of Denmark revealed mortality rates to be high and fertility low, the Crucian president by 1858 boasted that nowhere within the West Indies was there greater evidence of improvements.[8] Harrigan and

Varlack write, "If we turn to the more prosperous lower class, we find them for the most part engaged in not unprofitable pursuits; many in possession of comfortable houses and well-fed flocks and herds, well-clothed, with an air of independence not unaccompanied by respectful demeanour which certainly ought to delight friends of emancipation" (93). The more humane treatment reflected a commensurate change in living conditions. The overall transformation also created a difference in perceptions about race-based social stratification from that of other Caribbean islands (Harrigan and Varlack 104). Essentially, the most successful and progressive of the emancipated were deemed honorary whites and gained social and political equality (Dookhan 147).

Yet the Fireburn Unrest of 1878 has everlasting historical significance since three legendary women led the revolt that erupted in Frederiksted, half of which was burned down (Willocks 212). In an oral history interview with Richard Schrader, George Alexander Cornelius (speaking creole English) conveys the leaders' inspirational role: "Three women, deh call dem de three queens: Queen Mary, Queen Matilda and Queen Agnes, were de pushers and leaders behind the uprising. Man, deh burn canepiece foh spite. And deh kill couple of buckra [white people] toh. This happen after a Danish soldier shot and kill ah woman big with child. De women were tried and sent to jail in Denmark. When deh time was up, deh send dem back home" (21–22). While the captured and prosecuted males hailed from other islands, the "three queens" were all homegrown and were tried in Denmark (Terborg-Penn 53–56). The most renowned of them, Queen Mary, relentlessly galvanized the rebels in the burning of houses, sugar cane fields, and about fifty plantations. Representations of these rebel queens appear in the island's present-day preoccupation with beauty queen pageantry, integrating a rhetoric of empowerment not imperialism (Oliver, *Queen* 30–33). The Fireburn (as it is known) still rages symbolically as a historical reference point throughout Frederiksted in beauty pageants, graffiti art, and other cultural productions.

During World War I, for strategic purposes, the US purchased the three islands (St. Croix, St. Thomas, and St. John) for $25 million (Willocks 240–48). Sarcastically, beforehand, Ober described St. Croix as being "more American than Danish, as also is St. Thomas, and the sum and substance of European domination is expressed by about three dozen stolid soldiers, a flag, and a few obsolete forts" (325). However, Harry Franck's condescending remarks probably encapsulate the mindset of many Americans at the time: "I have yet to find any one who knows just why we bought the Virgin Islands, still less why we paid twenty-five million for them" (315). Begrudgingly, he reports the comment of a navy man: "it would have been worth a hundred million to keep Germany from getting them." Franck also laments the continued Danish ownership of the land and the retention of their laws (318). Indeed, islanders still drive on the left-hand side of the road; the legal drinking age is eighteen; and of greater pertinence to my study, Christmas may extend for twelve days.

This pattern embodies the greatest anomaly in that residents of the "American" Virgin Islands have the longest Christmas holiday season of any in the ACW. In 1733, when the Danish purchased St. Croix, the Europeans retained their own mask, mumming, and disguise traditions. Christmas Eve initiated the holiday season rather than Christmas morning, establishing two holidays—First Christmas Day and Second Christmas Day, which remains an official observance in the Netherlands. Ironically, these American possessions prolong their holiday celebrations longer than any of the other Anglicized islands.[9] Only recently have fetes been curtailed, contingent on the calendar—always culminating on the Saturday after New Year's Day. However, in 2017, January 1 occurred on a Saturday, which led to a plethora of prolonged nightly entertainment as in the past. Notably, Boxing Day is one of twenty-one holidays for government employees in the Virgin Island Code, while the US observes a paltry ten.

Pertaining to St. Croix, Isaac Dookhan provides one of the few descriptive, eyewitness accounts of Christmas and Boxing Day celebrations, noting that, by law, enslaved Africans obtained the right to observe not only Christmas but the following day, called Second Christmas. Perhaps, with a degree of malice, one eyewitness added that the enslaved persons contrived "to do very little work between Christmas and New Year" (152). The following account supplies thick ethnographic description, narrating layers of details about the enactment of a folk drama and introducing a full cast of its royalty, musicians, and lead singers:

The Dance opened by the King and Queen. The Prima Donna sings ballads, while the whole gang unite in the chorus to which the Drums furnish a very bass, but truly appropriate accompaniment. When the Royal pair are exhausted, they introduce the Prince and Princess, who in turn call up those of inferior rank. The Dance opens with such gravity, but in its progress Dancers and Singers warm into enthusiasm. The voice of the Prima Donna rises; the chorus swells; the drummer turns up the white of his eyes and displays his ivory; the Queen swoons; is supported by maids of honor who sprinkle "Bay Rum" and ply their fans until she recovers and joins in the Dance with renewed energy. And thus the revelers consume the day and night. (153)

It was customary for the white Crucian elites to regale the performers with refreshments and gifts. As described in 1840, "Christmas day and the day thereafter . . . our boarding-house was visited by several hundreds, who danced for our amusement," descriptively conforming to most written reports in the region (Nicholls, *Jumbies* 79). Afterwards, "[they] went the rounds among them, and were generally received by some complimentary line thrown impromptu, into their songs" (Dookhan 29). Olwig suggests that such Christmas sports emerged from a culture of resistance: "By boldly displaying this important aspect of their culture within the framework of English folk traditions right in the homes of the planters, the slaves thus challenged the planters on a cultural terrain which implicated the planters themselves" (*Global Culture* 56). If not for the enslaved population, Christmas was of little importance to the elite planter class (Irene Armstrong 152–53).

Perhaps, due to its multiplicitous history, the US Virgin Islands also maintained an array of customs distinct from the rest of the ACW. For example, the "Introduction" to Carroll Fleming's *Virgin Islands Cooking* underscores a magnitude of standard folk traditions: "On Christmas Eve, there were midnight church services and the stores stayed open until one in the morning. There were tramps and plant moving, as well as other mischief. If you had potted plants outside you had to bring them indoors on Christmas Eve or know that in the morning they'd be gone—moved upstreet or downstreet or sometimes you never would find them." As Kate Melone notes, "There was no carnival as we know it now. But on the day after Christmas, called Christmas Second Day, there was the masquerade and 'Moko Jumbie,' horse racing, and troupes dancing in the streets. Troupes began the day dancing in the country-side, and reached the towns by midday where the festivities continued until late evening."[10] What is of note here is the allusion to the kinds of pranks analogous to those in the Halloween trick or treat tradition in the US, except here occurring on Christmas Eve and coinciding with the Christmas gift-giving. The holiday season offered a way for enslaved persons to counteract their marginalization as "socially dead property" within the plantation systems (Olwig, *Global Culture* 58).

Nonetheless, after emancipation, while government authorities permitted masquerading, it ruled "Gombay dances—dancing to African drumming—would not" be allowable.[11] Afterwards, this prohibition resulted in open retaliation, causing the death of three revelers and the wounding of eight policemen. According to Wayne James, "Though masquerading was tolerated—perhaps because of its outward similarities to European-style masking or 'mumming' traditions, many white people always felt threatened by the infamous Gombay and street dances, both of which necessitated African drums" (Part II, 1). Still later, islanders reminisced about the masqueraders, without mention of any barbarous dancing and Gombay drumming. Instead:

> On Christmas Second Day there was the masquerade or mocko jumbie. We had beautiful picket fence of a kind I have never seen since. I remember standing by the fence looking out when one of the "devil men" came to the fence. I tried to run away but my foot caught on a picket and he lashed at me with his whip. . . .

At those old masquerades every masquerader had a whip, which was just a thin piece of stick ornately decorated. There would be such a lot of masqueraders, going from street to street and stopping to perform their acts at the houses where people were gathered. The audience would throw them pennies or give them food. I am sure the masqueraders enjoyed themselves as much as the people they entertained and, thinking back on it now, I think the money they collected helped to pay for their costumes, some of which were quite elaborate. One member of the masquerade troop was responsible for collecting the money, it was always given to this designated person. Later the money would be divided up among the musicians and members of the troop. (Rivera 16–17)[12]

This description aligns with the dance complex and the festival arc of old-time Gombeys and Junkanoo/Jankunú customs throughout the ACW.

Ironically, a century after the previously mentioned revolt, Christmas festivities became more organized with government officials' decision to open a festival ground to contain events. As Robert Bayley reports: "One of the charms of St. Croix is holidays. Cruzans have all the national holidays, plus Virgin Island holidays, plus some of their own. There's a big Christmas Week Carnival with costume parades, bands, a Carnival queen, floats, horse racing, fairs and calypso tents—a real jump up" (134). Considering the historical dynamism of jump-ups, the Crucian Christmas Festival idea exhibited its own cultural flows and negotiations. Similar to Junkanoo's transitional periods, originally the fete was called the "old Fashioned Christmas Festival" and then given the more generic title, "big Christmas Festival" (when it featured the grand parade on Christmas Second Day); the latest incarnation shifted again so that the parade would coincide with Three Kings Day (Heyliger, "Origins"). Thus, it differs from events in The Bahamas and Bermuda by traditionally unleashing twelve nights of bacchanalian excitement, energy, and enjoyment.[13]

What came to be known as the Crucian Christmas Festival (CCF) began in 1952. Celebrating its fiftieth anniversary in 2002, one newspaper report proclaimed: "This wasn't a stretch for Crucians, who for more than 200 years on holidays had dedicated themselves to hip-gyrating, drumbeating, costume-wearing parties in which masqueraders moved from house to house."[14] In 1956, Christiansted's festival program highlighted a "Costume Tramp" (parade) ending at 7:30 p.m. Thereafter, the festival combined daily events from merely "Merrymaking" and boat races to no fewer than six parades, including two "Lantern Parades" in Frederiksted and a Kiddie Parade in Christiansted. Ongoing until the customary January 6, which happened to be on a Sunday, it boasted a Puerto Rican Parade and a Three Kings Parade. By 1958, the two towns began to alternate, with the Festival Village being a well-established aspect of the seasonal celebration. That year, the Festival Village opened on Christmas Eve and, on Boxing Day or Second Christmas, a children's parade launched the holiday's events, which included horse races; but the official program has no mention of any other road tramps. Instead, there was a musical emphasis: a Steel Band Competition on December 27 and Calypso Night on January 3.[15]

"Floupe" is a portmanteau term assigned to a float in combination with a Carnival troupe, comprising two distinct competitive categories based on the group's size. Crucian designer Wayne James dates the first floupe to January 2, 1893, with *The Avis* reporting, "We had the streets thronged all the afternoon, the attractions being masqueraders, pole platters, and a guitar band, but above all, a model ship of considerable size drawn through the streets (by four small ponies). There was a numerous crew, who walked behind. . . . the sailors were all in uniform" (2). James also attributes this inspiration to the 1970s, being influenced by Trinidadian immigrants working at Hess Oil: "troupes became less character-based and more theme-oriented, and less theatrical and more free-dance" (Part III, 3). Keith Nurse credits the globalization of Trinidadian Carnival as being due to its population being a cheap labor source and the expansion of the Caribbean diaspora (80–81).

Aligned with its Puerto Rican citizenry, who primarily immigrated to cut sugar cane in the early 1900s, Three Kings Day promotes island diversity, which extends to a large Dominican population as well. Along with St. Croix, Puerto Rico is an American territory, and according to James Barnett, instead of Christmas Puerto Ricans celebrated Three King's Day on January 6 (143). One descendant salutes this cultural holiday's preservation: "[my grandparents] missed the closeness of the family life as they knew it back home. So they decided to have at least one big get-together once a year, and the most logical time was Three Kings Day" (Pelzer 4).[16] It is generally accepted that the first celebration of the Nativity occurred in Rome, coinciding with the rise of Christianity (Hadfield and Hadfield; Dyer). In honor of the three wise men, Christmas and Epiphany were, for a long time, concurrent observances to conform to a belief that the star rising in the East and Christ's birth coexisted (Dyer 452). Traditionally, as part of its Crucian festival, the final parade of the season coincided with the Feast of the Three Kings, also known as the Epiphany.[17]

In 1960, the Puerto Rican community approached the legislature with a resolution making Three Kings Day an official holiday; that recognition persisted until 2012. Frederiksted's Crucian Christmas Village reserves a Latin Village night to celebrate the island's diversification. Other innovations may occur annually as well. For instance, since January 6, 2012, was on a Sunday, fireworks provided the climax on the Eleventh Night, with the Village opening ceremony on December 27.[18] Another British transition separated the two into "new Christmas" and "Old Christmas," until as R. Campbell remarks, "common sense prevailed" (21). While the Crucian Christmas Festival (CCF) in Frederiksted devotes one of its twelve nights to Puerto Rican immigrants, in Christiansted, the St. Croix Landmark Society nowadays hosts a Crucian-Rican and an All Ah We Three Kings Day Tramp.

The Carnival adult parade became a discernible, favorite part of the CCF holiday season.[19] Currently, as in Trinidad, costuming is "outsourced": instead of reflecting the artistry by individual participants, costumes are created by local troupe leaders at a Mas camp.[20] Mas camps are a site where masquerade costume designers, costume assemblers, and costume order takers get together a month or two before a major Carnival event. Carnival participants can visit the Mas camp for complete information on Carnival masquerade bands, view costumes in each section of a masquerade band, be fitted for a costume before purchase, and preview other related activities that occur during Crucian Christmas. Mas camps, like Simply Sophisticated, operate Facebook pages with year-round updates to their fan base such as the following:

> Happy Thursday party people! With only 44 more days to go until *Crucian Christmas Carnival* 2014 [effective 2013–14], we would like to keep you informed about a few things:
> 1. We have a few members who haven't paid their 2nd payment as yet. We ask that you please try your very best to do so ASAP!
> 2. To all members who haven't submitted shoes as yet, we continue to stress that you make every attempt to drop it off to the Mas Camp at your earliest convenience.
> 3. Dance routine practices will start on Thursday, December 26th. Time & location to be announced very soon.
> It's almost that time!! Are you ready?![21]

Boxing Day, or Second Christmas Day, now functions as time for camps to rehearse choreography in preparation for the adult parade. Many troupe members travel from neighboring islands and from abroad to participate and sometimes later go on to Trinidad for Fat Tuesday, meaning there is also the extension of reciprocity among masqueraders. The main objective is always to fondly compete and reap the first-place prize, and the mass-produced costumes they stitch enable the later playing of pretty mas on New Year's with feathers and beads.

At the Crucian Christmas Village site, the CCF committee also awards Booth Prizes to the vendors who occupy the space nightly.[22] The term "booth" is the current euphemism used in St. Croix for what are called shacks ubiquitous throughout the circum-Caribbean. On St. Croix, that includes vernacular architecture. These are not stereotypical living accommodations but sites for engineering a livelihood, year-round or during festive occasions. Even in north

Florida, wooden planked food stalls manifest, subliminally, as a linear barricade to better serve the assemblage who position themselves nearby in a circular formation around the raging bonfire. Various Henry family members operate these food shacks selling a variety of fish dinners native to the region—spot, whiting, or mullet—in a veritable fish fry. These sales are conducted in the spirit of family ancestor Florida Knight who, according to George Henry, "want[ed] in on the action. So she would get a big pot of greens. I was a little boy. So I had to get the wood and make sure they had plenty of wood because they had iron stoves at that time. And she would cook up these pots, big pots, of greens and sell them to make money." On the periphery behind these shacks, men clandestinely sell their homemade wine, cane buck (moonshine), and beer to further invigorate the crowd and support another level of enterprise.

The Bahamas offers a specialized case, too, besides the fish fry on Arawak Cay where food and culture meet. "Shack" is the name given to what amounts to their "Mas" camps. Arlene Nash Ferguson states, "Because of their size, Junkanoo costumes cannot be accommodated in even the most spacious of homes. The buildings used for the preparation of Junkanoo costumes are called 'shacks'; and many Bahamians have yet to see the inside of one" (20).[23] Some of them are built specially for this purpose, while others are restored warehouses or other large buildings, but nothing like the usual connotation of shack as a dilapidated house. Wood's dissertation adds, "The actual creation of costumes takes place in shacks, which are structures that range in size from a one-room building to a large warehouse, and entry into which is usually restricted to group members" (178). A thick description by Arlene Nash Ferguson delivers an additional emphatic commentary engaging local color:

> It was always strange to go into the shack for the first time for the season. This room, illuminated under the unforgiving glare from the crude ceiling light fixtures, this home for so much rich creativity, now stood naked, still, empty. The walls were bare, crude, stark. All the debris and casualties from the past parades had been cleared out, and only traces of glitter on the floor remained. A single, lonely stack of cardboard rested in the corner beside aluminum rods of various lengths and thickness. The room screamed for costumes. (24; her italics)

Nowadays, large Junkanoo bands have numerous shacks where they secretly construct another set of masterpieces from a repertoire of spectacular visual art images collected from pictorial resources.

In St. Kitts, prototypical shacks are used in Basseterre to promote everyday commerce. In the travel literature, they are described as colorful shacks selling food and drink. Without the governmental sanction as in Nassau, they approximate the utilitarian stall-like venues in north Florida. Entrepreneurs foster community, operating along the town's trade routes—by the taxi stand and the frigates. Sundays are the only day of the week when there is no hustle, bustle, or sound from loudspeakers pumping out island music. Otherwise, even on Christmas Day if it falls on a weekday, these stalls emit lively sonic reverberations to suit their customers. On Sunday, apparently the vendors rest at home with family and friends, with ringing church bells replacing the clamor of the everyday soundscape and leaving fewer options for purchasing meals and drink. The truth of the matter is that the best chefs are often headquartered at the least likely looking shacks. They appear throughout the Caribbean isles as well as globally, but as a part of St. Croix's CCF revelry as competitors. The CCF shacks are stylized, individually named, and decorated with iconic, scrumptious visual representations and are currently being sponsored by one supplier—Home Depot.

Kenneth Bilby's findings propose a set of commonalities regarding the Black Atlantic Carnival arts: "almost always, there is some combination of masking (or at least costuming), parading, drum-based music, and dance" ("Masking" 1). Due to recent innovations in the tradition, J'ouvert in St. Croix and St. Kitts challenge without abrogating his first valuation. For instance, the throng of celebrants seldom masquerade in keeping with the customary carnivalesque archetypal masquerade figures. As in Trinidad, contemporary costuming now includes casual wear: T-shirts, short shorts, and miniskirts along with topless men in baggy jean shorts. Other revelers may wear colored wigs, feathered headpieces, oversize sunglasses, school uniforms, ballerina tutus, masks, and hats.[24] Historically, clashes described stick fighting throughout many parts of the Caribbean. In Trinidad and Tobago, Mason defines stickfighting as when "two opponents attempt to block each [blow] by holding his stick between two hands, one at each end" (148). Known as Calinda, it is now the martial art of Trinidad and Tobago and no longer observed during Carnival. Instead, on Carnival Tuesday, it is when rival bands' deejays clash. More metaphorically, to clash nowadays represents fashion faux pas—things that shouldn't ordinarily be worn together, a quasi-costuming. Evidently, the impulse is no longer for celebrants to lose themselves totally in anonymity but in pursuit of a riotous spirit in a do-it-yourself fashion.

Over the course of the holiday season, both St. Croix and St. Kitts support a multitude of luxurious Carnival parades; but it is J'ouvert morning that introduces the world to some quintessential processions par excellence. In comparison to the Gombeys and Junkanoo/Jankunú, J'ouvert conforms the most to the carnivalesque as an "excuse for disorder" (P. Burke 199). Peter Burke's assessment of Carnival in early modern Europe appears applicable here: "Carnival did not have the same importance all over Europe. It was strong in the Mediterranean area, in Italy, Spain and France; fairly strong in Central Europe; and at its weakest in the north, in Britain and Scandinavia, probably because the weather discouraged an elaborate street festival at this time of year" (191). The ACW does not disappoint. On Boxing Day, as Bakhtin wrote, "Carnival is not a spectacle seen by the people; they live in it, and everyone participates because its very idea embraces all the people" (7). In these Leeward Islands, J'ouvert explodes before the morning sun with a gyrating mass crowd engulfing all in its wake—even I was jerked into the fray by a whirlwind of strangers who refused to let me be a mere spectator.

Steve Stuempfle, in *The Steelband Movement*, asserts that "the restrictions on drumming did encourage the development of new forms of percussion for Carnival" (23).[25] However, innovations in the northern Caribbean require musicians to hold on to their drums, particularly in The Bahamas where parade rules specify that no motorized vehicles be deployed. However, in the two Leeward Islands, percussion sound trucks function like pied pipers, inciting swarms of people to cavort exuberantly at a mobile street party. Accordingly, during Trinidadian Carnival, "the bands inch slowly through the dark and crowded streets" (Stuempfle 203). Typically, massive flatbed rigs (also pulled by tractors) transport a wall of speakers powered by a large generator, so musicians with their electronic equipment and instruments can perform unencumbered along the parade route. Bands still clash in competition at crossroads where they intersect, vying for the title of Road March Champion. In Trinidad, at first it was the elites who "maintained a distance by masquerading on the back of lorries (trucks) rather than parading and dancing on the street with everyone else" (Stuempfle 29). With the demise of masking and the advent of more J'ouvert DIY casualwear on the road, social class distinctions are diminished.[26]

During J'ouvert, "wining" fulfills the dance component and is the most carnivalesque feature of the morning, privileging lower bodily extremities. The downward thrust of hips with bended knees and widespread legs, contorting the body to touch the ground, fits within the spirit of Carnival.[27] Wining is now popular worldwide; usually two or more dancers sensuously gyrate their hips at a slow or fast pace with their pelvic areas touching. Wining in the street, dancers spontaneously erupt in constant motion, extricating themselves and moving on to other partners at will. Urbandictionary.com humorously defines "wine" as "a west indian dance involving the hips, it is similar to traditional east indian dancing. It has nothing to do with Kevin Lyttle or Sean Paul, they have simply made wine popular in north America. It is also known as 'wuk up.'" Beyond just a wuk up, there's also a "freeing up" (Balliger 125). The dancing styles authorize optimal freedom of expression; and illustrating Joseph Roach's concepts of surrogation, bodies unleash a kinesthetic imagination via continuity and innovations in the celebratory tradition. In rough formation, friends and strangers grind their posteriors in an endless procession of wining, while couples and threesomes "dutty" wine without inhibition.

On Boxing Day, originally the carnivalesque CCF J'ouvert was advertised to begin at 5 a.m.; then, the isle supported an array of processions from road tramps to an ornate children's parade, concluding with a pretty mas, the adult parade. Correlating with the CCF's official opening of the fairgrounds, the first road tramp usually would follow. Variously, over the years, called the Festival Kick Off Tramp or Opening Night Tramp, it culminated at the festival village. As defined by *St. Croix Source*, a tramp's "essential ingredients are a lively band and a horde of dancers."[28] On November 28, 2004, another *Source* article—"Me Son! Crucian Christmas Festival Has Begun!"—featured the following announcement as a prelude to the main public event:

> It's beginning to look, and sound, a lot like Christmas—Crucian Christmas Festival, that is. Hundreds of revelers packed the streets of Frederiksted Saturday evening to officially kick off the St. Croix festival season with a traditional tramp. The participants were largely energetic teenagers and young adults, and the music was provided by the Heartbreaker band. The tramp, whose essential ingredients are a lively band and a horde of dancers, began at the Frederiksted Post Office corner and wound its way through the historic town, culminating with a street party in front of Buddhoe Park. Tradition demands that the event begin at least one hour late, and Saturday night was no exception. The revelers passed the time by lounging on the sidewalks and in and on top of cars, waiting for the band to begin. As soon as the first chords were struck, the dancers claimed the street, dancing and gyrating in unison. The band, perched on a flatbed truck, progressed slowly down King Street, enticing onlookers with an incessant beat to join the loose-limbed multitude.[29]

Such joviality is a hallmark of the festive life that annually generates immeasurable enthusiasm; the merrymaking is contagious, and the crowd veritably erupts, bursting with glee minus excessive, extraneous masquerading. As elsewhere, J'ouvert tramps no longer engage in traditional masking but don island casual wear. Therefore, the Boxing Day road tramp can exemplify an informal fashion outing, as I observed in 2008 when youthful revelers promenaded for hours along Frederiksted streets to model their new Christmas gear.

In 2012, the island celebrated the sixtieth anniversary of the CCF with the following slogan: "One time of year when happy and together." Therefore, to mark the anniversary, organized activities were more far-ranging. In honor of this anniversary year, the committee created minivillages to spread the wealth, so to speak. As a result, on December 26, the Mon Bijou J'ouvert kicked off days of festivities in a working-class neighborhood and was televised without media commentary. Without the formality of a mediated narrative, the attendees participated with carefree abandon, mostly unhampered by a heavy police presence. The next day, in Frederiksted, a more rudimentary road tramp to the village site occurred, only stretching out for under an hour possibly because of temporal changes, the shift back to the already well-traipsed urban locale, and even fatigue.

The CCF committee also designates one night in honor of the home-grown quelbe (kwail-bay) tradition of scratch bands.[30] In 2012, quelbe constituted one of the nightly concerts at the Crucian Village after inspiring its own tramp. The community at large demonstrated great respect for quelbe as a symbol of their musical heritage. These days, quelbe is synonymous with the Ten Sleepless Knights, esteemed as the music's true ambassadors. It was a hybrid musical form, at first, with instrumentation like that of the Gombeys and north Floridians— Old European military fife and drums—but guitars, banjos, the piano, and other percussive instruments including the indigenous asspipe (the exhaust pipe from a car) were added. Also, amplification along with Congo drums and the squash appeared. Scratch, therefore, is string band instrumentation that can also feature not only the guitar and banjo, but also steel (triangle), cuatro, bar-horn, and the baha (long boom pipe). These instruments and more were traditional from the days when playing mas included serenading from house to house.

Attracting a packed and responsive crowd, at least one night is devoted to the Calypso Monarch Competition, sponsored by the CCF but performed off-site. Also of Trinidadian derivation, calypso is another staple cultural production throughout the Leeward Islands. This musical tradition inspires songsters to compose the best new calypso songs of the year to earn the title of Calypso Monarch King and Queen. Gordon Rohlehr highlights the functional attributes of this art form: "celebration, censure, praise, blame, social control, worship, moralizing, affirmation, confrontation, exhortation, warning, scandal-mongering, ridicule, the generation of laughter, verbal warfare, satire" (1).[31] The words and tunes are all original. The most important function is to provide humor and always to entertain. For instance, Temisha "Blakness" Libert was a first-time winner of the crown with two powerful songs titled "What For" and "Nowhere Else like the Caribbean." The format includes a final competition with the six best singers selected for a final competition at the gala. Actually, more ludic activities and Caribbean musical genres occur there than anywhere in the ACW, continuing seemingly without a curfew and before audiences that never grow weary of the late-night cultural productions. Local radio and television stations blare out these sublime, imaginative sounds to home audiences along with the announcers' often humorous, esoteric (for outsiders) banter lasting for hours exclusively to entertain.[32] Another Trinidadian import, this music's inscrutable style grounds the community-builders in what is near, rather than far.[33] Calypso helps islanders fashion a sense of collective identity tied to the spatiality of their geopolitical location. Fashioned for social commentary from the oral tradition, these often-racialized songs originated to bewail colonialism and its lingering effect.

In the vernacular, "liming" is another transnational import, meaning relaxing, hanging out, or simply going out. Most significantly, Scher differentiates the ordinary from the extraordinary: "Carnival is the supreme liming time" ("Carnival" 94). Moreover, Thomas Hylland Eriksen deconstructs the "institution of liming," differentiating it from Westernized notions of mere idling, but rather being a performing art: "it is a kind of activity one wouldn't hesitate to indulge in proudly" (25). He contextualizes its everyday practices, rules, group affiliation of limers, and the aesthetics of good/bad limes and other pertinent contradictions. He concludes with a corrective, stating that liming should "serve as a reminder that facile assumptions about 'cultural hegemony' and the presumed dominance of bourgeois values in capitalist society deserve closer scrutiny" (40). Mason provides the most ethnographic investigation of liming as "hanging around doing nothing, cracking jokes and watching the world go by" (37).

St. Kitts's Boxing Day morning J'ouvert is the counterpart to St. Croix's, and both privilege the most carnivalesque and ludic Carnival at Christmastime. Roger Abrahams's "Christmas Mummings" positions St. Kitts and Nevis among "The Mother Colonies of the West Indies," along with Antigua and Barbados (120). Perhaps because of St. Kitts's longer history under British rule, the English manner of celebrating the Yule season was even more profound and long-lasting on St. Kitts and Nevis than elsewhere in the ACW (121). To assert the historicity of St. Kitts, Franck situates it as "the first island of the West Indies to be settled by the English, antedating even ultra-British Barbados in that regard by nearly two years, [and] its capital bears the French name of Basse Terre" (340).[34] Based on this claim, St. Kittitians have recreated their own ethnohistory. Relative to their history as a colonial settler state, locals identify their isle as Ground Zero. Due to its immense visibility and geographical location, early on the island emerged as a major stopping point for transatlantic migration. Robert Bayley describes the island thus: "St. Kitts is a pretty island. It has the shape of an oval with a tail like a kite, and the land rises gently from the sea, never too steep to cultivate, until it meets abrupt rise of the high central mountains. The highest peak is Mount Misery" (139). Named St. Christopher by Christopher Columbus in honor of the patron saint of travelers, St. Kitts figured heavily in the establishment of the Black Atlantic.[35] As the first English colony in the Caribbean, St. Kitts served as a base for further colonization in the West Indies. To denote their possession, the British shortened the name to St. Kitts.

The last principal island of relevance to the contemporary Boxing Day Carnival arc, St. Kitts lacks the centuries of scholarly attention received by other ACW islands. Instead, the informality of writers such as Robert Bayley reveals a great deal about perceptions of its place. For instance, he wrote, "The settlers of St. Kitts broke the Spanish monopoly of the New World. A mixed party of English and French colonized it in 1623. It is difficult now to see why they both-ered" (139). In the wake of the 9/11 attacks in the US, "Ground Zero" became a term with one absolute association—the World Trade Center in New York City. Before that, the term referred to nuclear explosions or the point below the denotation of atomic bombs in Hiroshima and Nagasaki, Japan. Kittitians began using the term to refer to the catastrophe associated with the genocidal slave trade in the Atlantic World. Thomas Jefferson's ancestors are credited with establishing the first plantation there, which centers St. Kitts as ground zero for the spread of Western imperialism.[36] Nevis, too, achieved notoriety for head-quartering The Royal African Company, which sold six thousand souls from its port from 1674 to 1688. Also, to gain a permanent foothold on the island, the British along with French militias massacred the remaining Caribs at Bloody Point, named for the carnage there. St. Kittitians' current expropriation of the ground zero metaphor honors having survived a holocaust with their psyche and spirit (as dispossessed sentient beings) intact.

A telling representation of the colonizers' mindset blames "the West Indian parasite" that is the "ubiquitous negro" for St. Kitts's impoverished agricultural state—then based on a sugar economy (Ober 336). Similarly, Bayley communicates this preposterous assessment: "Unhappy is the word for St. Kitts. There are more beggars there than I've seen on any West Indian island. The chief town of Bassaterre has a poverty-stricken look to it. The buildings are mean, and people hang idly around the street. Except when there is work in the sugar-cane fields, there is little employment" (139). Rather than blaming those victimized, Bayley adds, "The trouble is that the land is still owned by large estates. Hardly any of the common people own even a small piece of ground to raise vegetable on. Most of them live in estate-owned shacks and work on the plantation all their lives without a chance for anything else." The tendency is to excoriate the state-sponsored institution of slavery and colonialism but seldom repudiate the failure of the stakeholders to diversify crops. From the start of sugar cane production in 1643, this crop contributed to St. Kitts and Nevis becoming the wealthiest in the British Empire, similar to today's oil industry. Needless to say, life for laborers on these "Sugar Islands" was harsh, and the mortality rate extremely high.[37]

St. Kitts was the last sugar monoculture in the eastern Caribbean, and its J'ouvert is called "Sugar Mas" with the capital, Basseterre, being nicknamed "Sugar City." Ironically, in 2005, St. Kitts became the first in the Caribbean to forsake sugar production for sustainable tourism as part of its economic strategy, perhaps to follow the Bahamian model by embarking on a sugar industry diversification program.[38] Like Belize, St. Kitts belatedly gained independence from the British less than forty years ago, on September 19, 1983. In 2013, their momentous celebratory theme was "Stability, Creativity and Prosperity, Independence Thirty."

American folklorist Roger Abrahams, a premier theorist and prolific researcher with a concentration in performance studies, researched the centrality of festive play and public display events in the Caribbean. In *Man of Words*, he interrogated a proliferation of Christmas mumming plays that then persisted in Nevis but are now defunct (10–20). Educator Donald Matheson's *Folklore of St. Christopher's Island*, however, enumerates the various raucous groups making appearances in St. Kitts such as the "Christmas Morning bands, Big Drum bands, the Cakewalk band, various Singing bands, Maypole, Moko Jumbie Stilt Dancer and Nagur Business bands." The Christmas Morning band (also known as Shambololo bands) was the first to assemble on the road, suggesting an Africanized presence in counterpoint to the Christian holiday spirit. Walser's article imparts ethnographic insights from his observations in 1969. From his account, on the cusp of St. Kitts's ascendancy as the proprietary site for Christmastime revelry, one might project past merrymaking. Walser describes Christmas as "quiet"; "Then on the following morning—boxing Day, of course—guests at Nisbett's heard quite a racket from the circular driveway in front of the old plantation house" (160). Notably, Walser declares that the affiliate term—John Kuner—was extinct if ever of popular usage; this point is foundational to his effort to restore the possibility of a connection (161).

Although Boxing Day is commonly observed on St. Kitts and Nevis, the National Sugar Mas Carnival's J'ouvert occurs solely along the streets of Basseterre. The contemporary J'ouvert Boxing Day fete not only meets the predawn expectancy but elaborates upon it. Ethnographically speaking, its J'ouvert morning befits the ground zero trope, being that it best engendered the carnivalesque because of its appropriation and revitalization of a massive amalgamation of festival characteristics, both individual and collective. Without the publicity and fanfare of Carnival elsewhere, J'ouvert not only explodes freely in this small capital city by the sea, but mysteriously, without fanfare, the masses seemingly march out of the coastal waters while it is still night. Once the competing double-decked sound trucks begin to amble through the tight streets, revelers appear as dancing and prancing shadows. Within hours, in the tropics within a flash, the sun rises spectacularly. With corporate sponsorship, all-inclusive Mas camps have distributed hundreds of logo-bearing T-shirts, instilling a sense of rivalry while dispersing adult beverages to those wearing the prerequisite colors. Bodies flow seamlessly with swaying derrieres spawning wanton festive laughter.

Interlaced throughout instead of in an organized procession, traditional characters make cameo appearances—the Red Bull, a few Pitchy-Patchy, a Cane Cutter with his burro, and so on—with the most prominent appearance being any revelers caked in mud in a throwback to slaves' *canboulay* festival in Trinidad (Manuel et al. 203).[39] Earsplitting waves of soca music issue from the gigantic speakers, signaling the beginning of the Boxing Day festivities. Soca music is one of the more lambasted turns in West Indian popular music. Tania Isaac provides one of the most basic definitions: "Soca is party music, born out of a high speed, percussive style of delivery. It is associated with the road march, the wine, what [St.] Lucians call lydeye (commotion), the street fete" (260). Via Trinidad, the advent of soca shifted the focus to pleasure, dancing, and sexualized bodies.[40] Accordingly, Roger Abrahams in "Christmas Mumming" wrote that, with "the growing cultural pull of Trinidad with its emphasis on Carnival, Christmas remains the most important celebration of the year" (120–21). Significantly, Simon Lee contextualizes Christmas sports today: "The sports even in their postmodern form, represent what must be some of the oldest examples of creolization—the meeting and transformation of diverse cultural influences to create new forms—in the region." As part of acculturation, Lee addresses the reinterpretation of ideations or the surrogation process that reproduces or recreates culture.

To commemorate the fortieth anniversary of J'ouvert in St. Kitts, Mosimba self-published a history of the Kittitian Carnival in which he credits Basil Henderson who, upon returning from Trinidad and Tobago, introduced the festival art.[41] First occurring in 1957, Carnival here coincided closely with St. Croix's impetus to convene its Crucian Christmas Festival in 1952. Mosimba writes that Henderson undertook the revitalization initiative first by locating persons associated with the "Ole Time Christmas Sports" and encouraging them to "return on the road" (10). Although expressing reservations about Carnival fetes occurring during the holiest time of the year, government leaders did not suppress the idea, which "went off not with a bang but with several bangs," including an amalgam of standardized cultural performances and competitions such as calypso, Carnival queens, dance troupes, and bands competing in the road march along the parade route. Philip Scher defines "road march" in his glossary with the following thick description of Carnival in Trinidad:

> It is also a competition, the winner being the song played most frequently by bands as they march during the Parade of Bands. Each masquerade band is accompanied by a sound system and often by a live band as well. As the masqueraders move through the streets various popular soca hits are played. The one played by the most bands the most often is judged the winning road march. (*Carnival* 186)[42]

As appropriated in St. Kitts, following Boxing Day the repetitive soca music performed by the bands cascades from the outdoor speakers of local businesses, both deafening and vibrant. Again traditionalized in Trinidad, it conforms to what is called "The Soca Switch," the period after Boxing Day when the media and other outlets play the new soca tunes. Leu locates the significance of this switch in the music's becoming a trend at Carnival fetes in Trinidad, where the popularizing of songs depends on successful manipulation of the crowd to perform lyrical cues "executing the actions led by the singer, or echoing their chants" (49).

In 1964, St. Kittitians first instated an official oversight body, the Christmas Festivities Committee. A minority caucus from its Democratic Party fought to salvage "Ole Mas," and any remnants of traditional Christmas. Possibly because there was no Carnival in 1963, with only old-time Christmas Sports parading on the streets, the impetus was to restore the primacy of the masqueraders, too. This tension still exists, and Winston "Zack" Nisbett, known as "De Doctor of Culture," advocates for the preservation of the islands' folk culture and the history of St. Kitts and Nevis. Nisbett specializes in the preservation of folkloristic Christmas Sports such as clowns, masquerades, John Bull, and Plait the Ribbon.[43] In an interview with Mosimba, Nisbett elaborates about the clowns, the tradition with which he is most associated: "Our clowns that you see on the road were only used to flank the sides of the streets, to keep off the crowds but really and truly the clowns are court jesters" (Mosimba 60). On J'ouvert morning in both St. Kitts and St. Croix, clowns still provide an idiosyncratic presence on an individualized basis, whereas in the New Year's Day adult parade, the clowns' routine folk cultural presence implies a degree of degradation, as though an afterthought or mere concession.

Since the CFC's inception, Nisbett has crusaded to protect folk cultural traditions that are facing marginalization and condescension although he is an honored cultural advocate who curates his own International House Museum and Edgar Challenger Library. Lodged in his home, the museum is massive and contains a sanctuary for indigenous birds and animals, along with a range of artifacts and historical documents dating back centuries. Year round, he instructs local children in traditional string band musicmaking. In 2005, hailed as an unsung hero, Nisbett received a $5,000 honorarium from the First Caribbean Bank. Nevertheless, in 2009, the National Carnival Committee (NCC) withheld funds for his folk group's participation. On his behalf, he responded: "I would like them [committee] to come sit down with me and ask me to advise them because it's the same ol' thing we'll see. If they give me a chance to do what I have to do you will see a complete difference, and I think I'm the fittest person for this."[44] Although not pertaining to J'ouvert proper, the feud addresses funding practices by the government-controlled NCC, which oversees two separate categories for parading troupe registration: folklore and modern.

By the 1970s, island party politics negatively affected the holiday season in some ways parallel to the rivalry in St. Croix. Mosimba writes, "The situation reached its lowest point in 1970 when there were two separate sets of Christmas celebrations organised by two different committees: two separate Calypso Shows, two separate Queen Shows, two separate Troupes and Parade and so on" (19).[45] To promote sentiments consistent with Christmas—understanding, unity, peace, and love—the Labor government passed a resolution subjecting all entertainment at Christmas to the provisions of the St. Kitts-Nevis National Carnival Act 1971. Establishing the beginning of the Sugar Mas name, the act proclaimed: "It shall not be lawful for any person, society, club or other organisation during any Carnival period to designate, represent or advertise any function except with the approval of the National Carnival Committee, such function included queen shows, beauty contests, calypso shows, musical presentations and festivals, but not including the provision of music for dancing by the general public" (qtd. in Mosimba 20). Shifting canons of taste apparently resulted in hostilities that unfortunately still persist, with participation payment being lower for folklore groups.[46]

St. Kitts's J'ouvert offers an elevated possibility for witnessing a cornucopia of the traditional masking styles; the public displays extemporaneously come alive throughout the Boxing Day morning fete. As relates to the masquerade style in particular, Zack Nisbett assesses the status quo: "You might see a few masquerades but you don't see them dancing properly" (qtd. in Mosimba 25). His desire for the return of the old times mummers will not likely be satisfied. He requests the return of "the Children of Israel, David and Goliath, Cowboys and Indians and others" (qtd. in Mosimba 25).[47] Nonetheless, historically, St. Kitts is ground zero for its indispensable, inclusive approach to tradition in the face of an interregional globalization process.

Simon Lee positions St. Kitts as "the oldest example of creolization—the meeting and transformation of diverse cultural influences to create new forms—in the region."[48] For example, one popular character is Pitchy Patchy, "alias Shaggy, the bizarre, popular Jonkonnu character, [who] plays masquerade from Morant Point to Negril. Male dancer extraordinary, face masked in mesh, body and limbs swathed in restless layers of multi-coloured scraps of cloth—he is at once common yet inconstant. Common in that he is ubiquitous and predictable in the matter of his rags but like the chameleon, inconstant in manner and mask" (S. Barnett 19). At first, the blackface minstrel-like appearances by fully costumed masqueraders with darkened skin are disconcerting to witness. They capture the traditional characters darkened by canboulay (burning the cane), the rampant fires that devastated crops by accident or insurrection. Chained and forced to fight the flames, the enslaved people's faces and extremities would be covered with soot, making this figure a legendary aspect of the slave sublime (Tsuji 86).[49]

The Facebook page of LIME Xtreme Generation, a successful Sugar Mas troupe, annually includes posts to communicate phenomena applicable to J'ouvert, beginning in mid-September when the NCC first meets to consolidate plans. A winning J'ouvert troupe, LIME celebrates its annual launch in late November, when the band's Sugar Mas tunes also are revealed. Crowds of Xtreme J'ouvert revelers arrived very early to take full advantage of the discounted price of sixty dollars for the early birds who registered on Launch Day for the troupe. The package cost escalates incrementally thereafter. Ronnie Rascal is the mastermind behind Xtreme J'ouvert Troupe, which has been in existence for twelve years. Excitement builds with regular updates leading up to Sugar Mas on Boxing Day morning such as "XTREME MASSIVE YOU READY FOR THE ROAD?" in conjunction with announcing ten days in advance J'ouvert Jam, a pre-party from midnight, street jamming for hours on end to a powerfully upgraded sound system that cannot be beaten. Christmas Day will be devoted to "getting ready for the road," decorating the sound truck, positioning the massive speakers on it, and packing a massive bar. As in previous years, the J'ouvert morning experience will culminate with the much talked about WET DOWN, a major highlight of Sugar Mas J'ouvert.[50]

Ironically, St. Kittitians not only revived Bermuda's Gombey tradition but, along with Trinidadians, elevated St. Croix's J'ouvert too; for Bayley suggests an economics-driven exodus, writing, "No wonder so many young Kittitians leave their island to go to St. Thomas or St. Croix" (139). In formulating their J'ouvert jump up, St. Kittitians isolated experience-centered local-to-local connections stimulated by Trinidadian Carnival and imported its framing devices. This happenstance engages the key concept of translocality that emerged to theorize mobility and place (Olwig, "Cultural Sites").[51] Translocality and glocalization, not mutually exclusive in the context of the mobile and interconnected ACW, provide the incentive to move from the periphery and recenter lives by any means necessary. As exponential parts of transnational cultural flows, migratory patterns induce an influx of cultural elements in the regions of origin, but also in the regions of arrival (Schuerkens 202). The two or more sites are coeval in their historical desire to resist Western hegemony through the maintenance of their own "traditional life-worlds, [by] attempting at keeping up the authenticity of their cultures" (196).

Based on my empirical experience engaging multisited ethnography as well as onomastic research, a move towards Africanity in sociocultural production characterizes artistic expressions, whether regarding gospel music in Wiregrass Country or African American naming patterns. Certainly fetes in the ACW also have sustained and revitalized African-derived characteristics, both spatially and temporally. Occurring during the so-called postcolonial period, a politically conscious inversion of the acculturation process occurs. Boxing Day conserves the festive productions of the ACW rooted in a mas culture entrenched by creative collaborations, collective economics, and direct reciprocity—mainstays of traditional West African societies and traditional mumming (Santino, "Ritualesque" 16). The subsequent chapters have as their focus a tropological approach that breaks down the subtleties of noise, darkness, and spatiotemporality as part of a survival imperative in open defiance of the colonialism that still sustains hegemonic aesthetic and cultural representation.

In 2010, with Boxing Day on a Sunday and a nor'easter storm on Monday, troupes cancelled the road marches due to the height of the Gombey dancers' headdresses, but it did not deter the drummers.

In north Florida, the drums remain idle until the music begins spontaneously an hour before sundown.

Junkanoo in Nassau necessitates the retention of rustic, goatskin gombay drums.

The Garifuna community in Dangriga, Belize, celebrates its *Wanaragua* Jankunú on Christmas Day, beating Primero (lead) and Segundo drums to accompany the masquerade dancers.

In the two Leeward Islands, on J'ouvert morning sound trucks function as percussive musical instruments weighted down with gigantic speakers pumping out island music.

While for J'ouvert, on Boxing Day morning, sound trucks rule the streets in Basseterre, St. Kittitian troupes have not forsaken their traditional drums, which make seemingly daily appearances until Las Lap, January 2.

The 26th Shooting Match in north Florida is a possible "cousin" to the ACW's gumbe-complex.

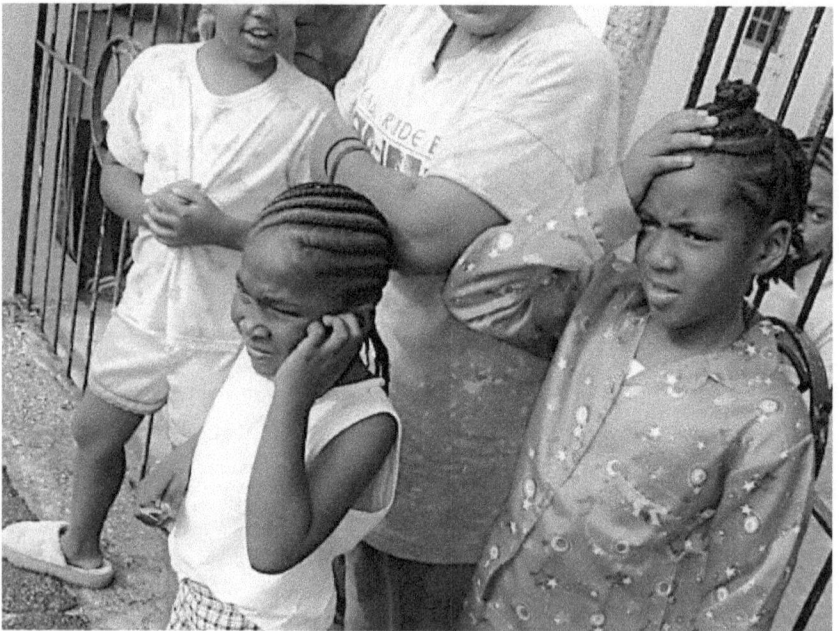

A Bermudian tradition is for residents to gather outside their gateway, still wearing pajamas no matter the time of day.

Junkanoos' embracing of brass instruments is uniquely Bahamian.

Along the main downtown street in Dangriga, at nightfall the Two-Foot Cow and the children apparently broach a truce.

J'ouvert (from the French term meaning "day opens") is not about beautiful costumes.

The J'ouvert road tramps to the Crucian Christmas Festival Village are inspired by transcultural flow from Trinidad and Tobago.

The Crucian Road March, besides the big trucks, feature a conspicuous soundscape that deploys all sorts of street music exemplary of "one grand noise."

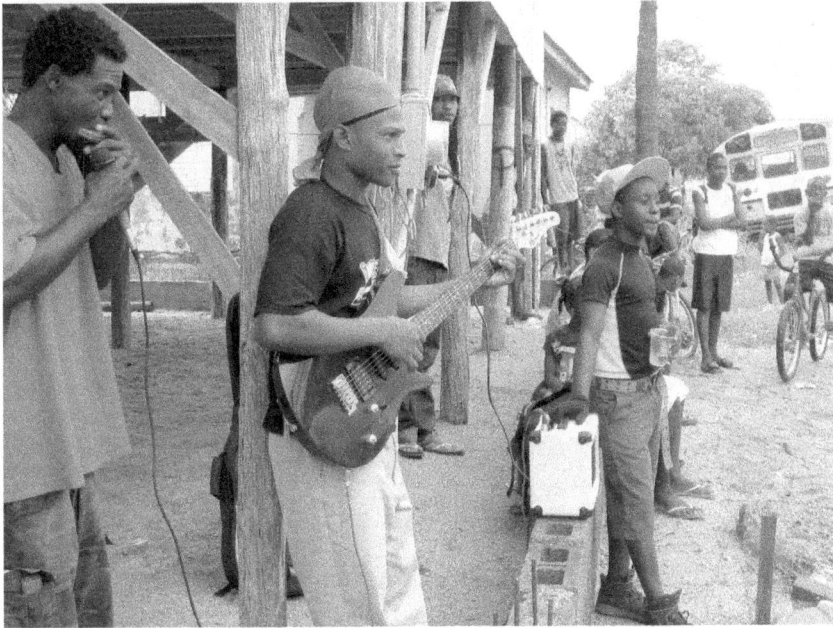

Roaming from house to house during *Charikanari,* the dancers encounter other musicians along their route and commingle the sounds.

Tallahassee elders assemble around the bonfire where, for generations, The 26th has represented a Black space of conviviality.

Under the cloak of darkness, J'ouvert offers a counterspace for young girls and women to exercise somatic freedom without inhibition.

Located back o' town in Basseterre, the International House Museum and Edgar Challenger Library are managed single-handedly by "Zack" Nisbett, "De Doctor of Culture."

After Boxing Day, King of Junkanoo Percy "Vola" Francis transitions to creating costumes for the New Year fete in one of the Saxon's shacks back o' town.

Designed to ritualize the future as in St. Croix, children's parades and a bevy of youth competitions fill out end-of-the-year calendars.

Perhaps the grandest of processions for children occurs in St. Kitts with Lime, a cable and wireless communication company, as a sponsor.

The Honorable Louise Jackson (now deceased), a member of Bermuda's Parliament, self-published an important history text, *The Bermuda Gombey: Bermuda's Unique Dance Heritage.*

Junkanoo King Vola, also Bahama's minister of youth, sports, and culture.

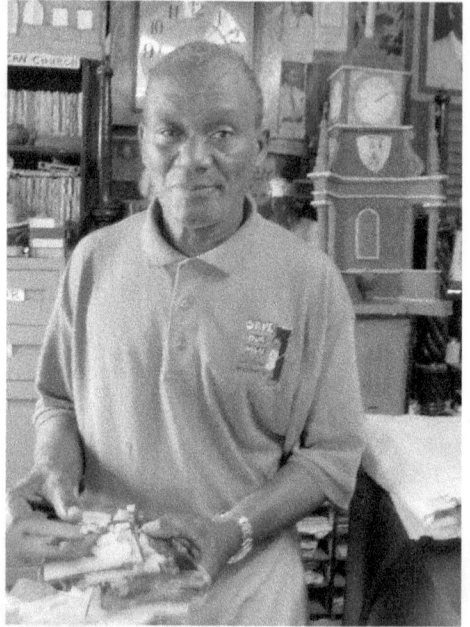

Cultural preservationist Nisbett displays his large collection of everything St. Kittitian, including a replica of the four-faced clock located at the Circus in Basseterre.

Ena McKell is a perennial returnee to play mas during St. Croix's Sugar Mas adult parade as well as Trinidad's annual Carnival.

CHAPTER FIVE

"One Grand Noise"

The Black Atlantic World abounds with soundscapes as a resolute part of the diversity within its gumbe complex. The sound politics of aurality, being noisy and undesirable, conflicted with European musical aesthetics and overdetermined their colonial move to subjugate, enslave, and racialize the human populations. At its ludic core, evoking variant interconnected sonic acts, traditional West African–influenced percussive music produced panoramic soundscapes, whether generated by traditional goatskin membranophones, military-style drums, or modern everyday technologies and amplified systems. Historically, according to Western aesthetic judgment, the region's festal rites produced an aural vibrancy that was judged both odd and odious. Folklorist Roger Abrahams notes, "The early reports of the New World settlements comment repeatedly on the profusion of noise: worrisome sounds that resisted sense, that seemed to communicate and be interpretable but never be quite understood" ("Questions" 79). Underscoring centuries of dismissal, Europeans considered the indefatigable soundscapes associated with enslaved Africans to be exceptionally noisome, linking them with disorder and wantonness. Due to the acoustical characterization of music, Andy Hamilton defines Western notions of noise as "irregular, unstable, non-periodic vibrations" (52). The "noise" of people considered to be "others" not only discombobulated Western ears; it provoked repudiation. In artistic terms, the music was described as noise—chaotic, disorganized, and disturbing—and the dances lascivious and offensive.

This chapter engages conflicting canons of taste by interrogating Africa-derived soundscapes as expressive and communicative resources that register as contributing to both an ignoble soundscape by Western detractors and a shared identity as upheld by those who were enslaved or colonized. Media expert David Hendy theorizes that noise possesses a "democratic quality," a symbol of an aural culture sustaining a power of its own (210). In the maintenance of their own aesthetic judgment, this possible understanding emboldened and conferred on enslaved persons another means of culturally resisting hegemonic forces. Regarding the few freedoms enjoyed by those who were enslaved, Hendy specifies, "But one they did have was the freedom to adapt the sounds their owners suppressed into new forms that took on a life of their own" (200). A propensity to construct strategies of resistance occasioned a "growing and distinctive audibility" (200). Therefore, a tropological approach to Boxing Day that theorizes noise in the frame of cultural imperialism uncovers greater agency and subversion of the coloniality.

The politics of noise also divulge a bipolar tension, delineating a large aestheticized divide in which silence signals "the sound of authority" and, despite enslavement and colonization, cultural opposition by a debased subaltern group for whom "noise" is diurnal and nocturnal. Unwanted sound, considered to be mere noise, is subjective as well as an instrument of colonial power, bounded by the intersectionality of culture, race, and class. Schafer asserts that before the musical sounds in our cities—church bells, the postman's horn—were replaced by mechanical noises and music moved into the concert hall, music and noise were not distinct categories (*Tuning* 103). He further situates the emergence of some music as unwanted sound back to about 1225 CE, signaling the trajectory for vilifying sound signals (exclusive to Africa and its diaspora) as a means for colonizers to arrogantly project their superiority (273). In the ACW, present-day sound events (endemic to Boxing Day celebrations) serve complex purposes: "because it is necessarily local, being available only in a specific place to a limited audience, it is particularly effective at serving a sense of community identity," a basis for collective joy (S. Smith 236). Celebratory fetes unleash a collective joy in commemoration of a historical past and the erasure of present liminality with the portent of future betterment.

Dancing in the Streets: A History of Collective Joy by journalist Barbara Ehrenreich describes this interrogation of the sonic trope under authoritative rule. She writes, "The European idea of the 'savage' came to focus on the image of painted and bizarrely costumed bodies, drumming and dancing with wild abandon by the light of a fire" (1). Such mythologizing is infused with Western metaphysical dualistic thinking. Africa-based acoustic territories in binary opposition to European norms reinforced dualistic suppositions of high/low cultures, civilized/primitive peoples, and superior/inferior races. The Enlightenment era reified Western dualistic thinking, creating philosophical polarities that persist and are often taken for granted as though universal.[1] In short, the traditions associated with people who were enslaved/colonized were viewed as needing eradication or, at the very least, control. This inclination was all the more reason for colonial administrations to discipline their captives: on the one hand, to avoid blurring the line between masters and slaves; on the other hand, to avoid sanctioning seemingly cantankerous assemblages due to their own fear of insurrection. Thus, the determination grew to suppress all undesirable sounds perceived as jarring because the morass of aural sounds were symptomatic of European dis-ease.[2] To this mindset, sonic events that centered African drumming and dancing were disruptive agents ruining the sanctity of Christmas.

Since in the Anglicized Protestant Caribbean celebration of Carnival transpires over the Christmas holiday season (rather than the pre-Lenten), Boxing Day fetes establish a grand temporal moment for subverting the holiest of seasons. The substance of historian Peter Bailey's argument is supportive, defining noise as "sound out of place" (23). On the one hand, Bahamian Nina Wood's dissertation affirms, "Some people have felt that Junkanoo and by extension its music desecrates the meaning of Christmas" (332); on the other hand, another result was the strategic social construction of a binary of one's own. According to interviewee Glen Hurd, "Like Sunday, Christmas Day was hallowed, a day of reverence, when everything was quiet. Christmas day there is a feasting of family dinner, but it was a quiet day spent at home. And everyone looked forward, especially the children, to Boxing Day because that was the day when you could run, scream, and get excited"—inverting the otherwise pejorative synonym for sound with the epitome of a more self-affirming expression. The requisite screams add another carnivalesque dimension. In it, the battery of ludic soundings demarcates merriment, just as Bakhtin highlights how noise unleashes levels of communication outside of everyday practice (10).

In "Noisy Spaces," Balliger proposes a counter-appropriation emphasizing the necessity in the Black Atlantic for "creating a hellish din that announced their [enslaved persons'] presence—and in a strange way—their humanity" (124). Therefore, African-influenced music was configured as noise, unwanted sound, to the elite authorities and as a strategic act of perseverance, memory, and subversive remedy for those dispossessed (Gikandi 255). The move to establish the bank holiday led to more subversive acts as, essentially, Christmas Day became Boxing Day Eve—the calm before triggering a barrage of playful and often-maligned fractious sounds, vernacularly codified as "one grand noise." Fundamentally, this expression captures the endogenous (insiders') perspective presaging an extratextual functional meaning that augurs an extension of the enculturation process in the sonorous ACW. As island communities fragment, some due to a push toward assimilation and others to the pull of emigration, practitioners may no longer seek just the carnivalesque psychic release but the heuristic value of symbolic action, directed toward the socialization of their young.

Heralding the auditory arts, an aesthetic of noise also embraces raucous laughter as a compound signifier for excessive and intensified vulgarity. Black laughter infuses a phonocentric world with its own forms of quotidian oral-aural communication. According to Neville Hall, authorities viewed the shocking

noises and derisive laughter outwardly exhibited by those enslaved as disre-
spectful (102). For Bakhtin, according to Bailey, laughter was a regenerative and
liberating noise that challenged the repressive seriousness of official authority
(24). Enslaved Africans deployed laughter as a free weapon, another form of
coded expression. Such laughter eased and even made tolerable a harsh, cruel
reality, functioning as a catharsis. Black laughter often still elicits derision from
the bourgeois-minded as being loud, aggressive, and counterproductive—pro-
voking stereotypes. Yet festive laughter gainsays those politically empowered
with disdainful mockery as well (Bakhtin 11–12).

An English visitor to Trinidad in 1845 summed up the typical Eurocentric
reaction to these seasonal exhibitions of collective joy:

> On Christmas Eve, it seemed as if, under the guise of religion, all Pandemonium
> had been let loose. . . . Drunkenness bursting forth in yells and bacchanalian orgies,
> was universal amongst the blacks. . . . Sleep was out of the question, in the midst
> of such a disgusting and fiendish saturnalia. . . . The musicians were attended by a
> multitude of drunken people of both sexes, the women being of the lowest class;
> and all dancing, screaming and clapping their hands, like many demons. All this was
> the effect of the "midnight mass," ending, as all such masses do, in every species of
> depravity. (qtd. in Cowley, "Carnival" 41)

This inventory of repugnance conforms to an additional volley of descriptive
adjectives: "noisy, crude, impious, and simply, dissolute" (qtd. in Ehrenreich
3). Symptomized as dis-ease (with the hyphen implying a psychological state)
among the white elites, they are insensitive to other aesthetic representational
practices and "hear only *noise*" (Abrahams, "About Face" 286; his emphasis).

Most importantly, such pejorative, elitist judgments degraded and traduced
the rhythms of drum music as the primary feature of an indigenist aesthetics.
Rommen quotes Tinkle Hanna saying, "Junkanoo is above all else, a rhythm"
(*Funky Nassau* 28). In this context, Wood produces quite a treatise regarding the role of drums in Junkanoo music, noting two type of drums—goatskin and tom-toms (249). To attend to Bahamian musicality, Wood identifies
three principal beats: the Slow Beat, the Hill or Up-the-Hill Beat, and the Fast
Beat. Each is complete with its own function such as the Slow Beat when tired.
Contrary to some popular belief, the objective is not how loud or fast you
play; instead, the goal is to synchronize and blend together (324). Driven by
the polyrhythmic beats produced by drums and percussion instruments, this
rhythm unveils the auditory arts of African peoples.[3] Martin Munro centers
rhythm as a sonic concept and a major shifting signifier. Accordingly, Munro
asserts, "Rhythm can to some extent be considered a sense in its own right; the
common term a 'sense of rhythm' suggests a general awareness that the sen-

sory experience of rhythm is not quite hearing, not quite touching or feeling, but an amalgam" (5). In this context, rhythm operates as a dynamic marker of resistance and "impenetrable black subjectivity" (15). Such immersion indicates cultural noise to be a form of pleasurable resistance, running counter to European aesthetics.

Along with gombay drums, reports as early as 1823 from Jamaica mention other musical instruments with sonic markers that added to the rebuke: "The girls also danced without changing their position, moving their elbows and knees and keeping time with the calabashes filled with small stones" (qtd. in Beckwith, *Christmas* 4). Based on a nineteenth-century anthropological resource, Beckwith confers on this instrumentation an African provenance: "Drums and rattles of the kind he describes are also found on the West Coast." Cowbells, at one time, infused the music even more than the drumming. Winston Saunders positions them as a "ubiquitous noisemaker," further noting that "the cowbell sound has now become familiar with any Bahamian celebration, from welcoming heroes home to parading beauty queens through the streets of Nassau to creating the finale of a folklore show" (246).⁴ Overtime, bellers' inventiveness advanced other transformations among the musicians who customarily struck their bells together; starting in 1983, a Saxons' beller credits himself with the self-explanatory "no-knock ring" (Wood 392).

In Nassau, brass instruments, too, move to the forefront, but do not commence with sound until the entire rhythm section congeals, establishing a steady tempo. With the advent of brass instruments, Wood also says there was an increase in religious songs (332).⁵ Nonetheless, the brass section served legitimate functions, providing "the melody for the Showtime dancers in front of them, and for the enjoyment of the fans" (370). In the 1970s, Jamaican scholar Rex Nettleford published an essay, "Melody of Europe, Rhythm of Africa," which while rejecting Eurocentric ideologies of superiority, espoused a syncretic mutuality dependent on the harmonizing of the two: "a cultural fusion rich and cohesive in its diversity" (210). Junkanoo music seemingly mirrors this standpoint and supports Jacques Attali's contention of the musical process structuring noise, with music being a mirror of society "structured like it, and chang[ing] when it does" (9–10), as an extension of the political economy.

In West African cultures, dancing and music intersect, a carryover that also caused colonizers much dismay. Leonard Barrett affiliates the two, writing, "[Dance], like the drum, was the instrument of non-verbal communication. In Africa, the dance occupied and expressed every significant emotion. There was a dance for every occasion—even death. Dance was not a separate art, but a part of the Whole complex of religious and secular life" (73). Reverend James Phillippo was a British Baptist missionary and renowned abolitionist who spent fifty years in Jamaica. He is credited with this thick description of Jamaican dance:

The dance was performed to a monotonous music which was manufactured in Africa. . . . The people were arranged in a circle, with a leader in the center. Male and female danced to the music of the drums. A female led a chant followed by choral response from the rest. This was accompanied with the stamping of the feet, with strange contortions of the body; the head of the dancers sometimes erect; sometimes inclined forward; the hands united in the front; the elbows fixed pointing sideward, the lower extremities being kept firm; the whole body was made to move from the ground without moving the feet off the ground. (qtd. in Barrett 73)

In addition, Barrett cites a Ghanaian scholar, Mawere-Opoku, who explicates the centrality of dancers in African life: "in his subtle flexions of hands and fingers, our prayers; in his thrusting arms—our thanksgiving; in his stamp and pause—our indignation; in his leap and turns, our frivolity—our foolishness; in his tensed frame—our defiance; in his bow—our allegiance; his halting steps—our reverence" (qtd. on 74). More specifically to Belize, the implication is that without drumming (rhythmic accompaniment), dancing cannot be enacted, and vice versa (Whipple 99).

Before modernity, the drum-based bamboula, an African-derived dance, was excoriated as a "sex dance, pure and simple."[6] Since the Lateran Council of 1215, Christians had waged a war on lascivious dance, branding it a confessable sin (Ehrenreich 81). However, bamboula reportedly "functioned as the eyes and ears of society," as "the local tabloid and scandal sheet all rolled into one" (Emanuel n.p.). The themes of the songs accompanying this dance privileged local gossip. Roger Abrahams asserts that gossip is basically a predictable performance of everyday life ("Performance-Centered" 293.) In the final analysis, Emanuel reckoned it to be a proficient weapon, "heap[ing] personal abuse, vituperation, scandal, and blackmail upon all and sundry." Such noisy dancing might be an even safer tool for self-assertion, ridicule, and criticism than song: "If the songs of the slaves in which they voiced their disapproval of slavery were not understood by whites, the dance was even less understood and therefore a much safer form of self-assertion" (Hazzard-Donald 121). The songs could serve as scornful editorial commentary because they were usually grossly misunderstood and considered mindless repetitive practice that simply exercised the lungs (Cowley, *Carnival* 97).

In the past, slaveholders often kept meticulously documented diaries such as the one by Thomas Thistlewood of Jamaica from 1750 to 1784 (Burnard; D. Hall). Thistlewood's diary is unusual in containing decades of copious details specific to the Christmas holiday. Christmas was widely accepted as the occasion when planters would "box" up their leftovers for distribution to enslaved persons, as a carryover from the English custom. Thistlewood's diary catalogues his annual distribution of foodstuff. For example, in 1778, Douglas Hall reports:

On Christmas Eve Thistlewood had shot one of his cows, "a trouble-maker." . . .
On Christmas Eve night he had given them the head, liver, lights and guts for their
supper. With the meat there was the accustomed distribution of rum, and a special
12 bitts to Abba, "to assist her." Phibbah got seven bottles of rum, John got "a pair of
new shoes, the only remaining ones of the light sort," and friends around received
gifts of fish, fruit, or flowers. (261)[7]

For enslaved Africans, this custom ushered in a season of jubilation of their
own making, often as a hard-won concession (depending on the planter family).
Burnard's text acknowledges, "At Christmas, he allowed his slaves to celebrate
and watched 'Creolian, Congo and Coromantee, etc. Musick and dancing'" (4).
This description endorses identifiable components recognizable throughout the
African diaspora.

Therefore, it should be no surprise that most journalists, from colonial settler history to the present, adhered to Western binary opposition. Craton and
Saunders, for example, report on an editorial in the *Bahama Argus* that equated
ordaining Black Baptist preachers with a "'John Canoe' exhibition in which
there will be an abundance of followers we admit; but their worshipping would
be more in conformity with the noisy rites of Bacchus, than with the sober doctrines of the Christian faith" (334). This dismissal of Black ministers is based on
a binary opposition of the sacred and profane. Michael Anthony contrasts celebrations of Carnival in Trinidad in the nineteenth century by a genteel French
plantocracy with those of the then newly emancipated: "the attitude changed
swiftly when slavery was abolished and the masses came out onto the streets"
(6). Journalists catering to the predilections of the ruling class, dehumanized
the formerly enslaved persons as "semi-primitive hordes yelling at the tops of
their voices" and endorsed banning such events (7).[8] In describing their historic
Canboulay rituals, Anthony also captures the opposing perspective of those
who were enslaved: "These must have been the only enjoyable moments, the
only moments of freedom and fun and laughter, when slaves from different
estates met and chatted, some for the first time" (9). Increasingly, newspaper editorials besmirched their social noise, sexualized dancing, and satirical mimicry
as possessing no redeeming potential (W. James, Part I, 1). In 1893, *The Gazette*,
a Trinidadian newspaper, lambasted Carnival as "one of those relics of medieval
barbarism which should not have been permitted to exist in the enlightenment
of the 19th century" (Ottley 71).[9]

Hailed as the Age of Reason, the eighteenth century experienced new knowledge, exploration, and the Industrial Revolution with many advances including
printing. The overblown title of Charles Leslie's publication is indicative of the
period: *A new and exact account of Jamaica, wherein the ancient and present
state of that colony, its importance to Great Britain, laws, trade, manners and reli-*

gion, together with the most remarkable and curious animals, plants, trees, &c. are
described: with a particular accoun (sic) *of the sacrifices, libations, &c. at this day*
in use among the negroes. Leslie's "exact account" subliminally pairs "the most
remarkable and curious animals, plants and trees" with the objectification of
"negroes." And, of course, there is the omnipresent noise factor: "Sunday Afternoon the Generality of them dance or wrestle, Men and Women promiscuously
together. They have two musical Instruments, like Kettle-Drums, for each Company of Dancers, with which they make a very barbarous Melody" (Leslie 282).
Richly revealing, such Enlightenment era reactions toward enslaved Africans
were like decanters dispensing an outpouring of rabid Eurocentric discourse.

Travel writing evolved as one of the primary means of recouping extraneous Western perceptions that unwittingly acknowledged the asymmetries of
power.[10] Mary Louise Pratt, for example, considered "how European travel writing interacted with enlightenment natural history to produce a Eurocentered
form of global or 'planetary' consciousness" (4). In one of the first accounts of
the Junkanoo tradition by an American, Dr. Townsend in 1824 wrote a diary
about Nassau's social elite, but his portrayal of Christmas imparted clues about
social life beyond that of elite whites (Craton and Saunders 248). In keeping
with the distorted nature of this genre, noise appeared as a burgeoning trope.
Dr. Townsend, for example, wrote that "We should not have noticed ten times
as much sound in New York but in this still town it seemed quite grating. We
were also regaled last night at Christmas eve until 3 or 4 in the morning with
some bad music on hoarse cracked drums & fifes by groups of negroes parading the streets" (qtd. in Craton and Saunders 248). Fully aware of the Bacchanal
nature of their Christmas season rites, Junkanooers viewed the disruption of
religiously imposed solemnity positively with an unabashed "grand noise."

Dualist thinking may also cause some to have trouble accepting the fact that,
throughout the Anglicized New World, British Boxing Day reigns supreme as
a much-loved holiday tradition. While the term "Gombey" means rhythm, for
the most part, percussive sound emanates from bass and snare drums, whistles,
cowbells, and an assortment of other idiophones.[11] Western musical instruments and technology take on new meanings and rhythms. Few speak to how
the heterogeneity built into the present-day African diaspora leaves room for
the reinterpretation of homogeneous Anglicized practices, with the possible
exception of Joseph Roach's surrogation performance theory.[12] These Boxing
Day public display events are rich in symbol, metaphor, and life. Simon Frith
noted, "Music constructs our sense of identity through the direct experiences
it offers of the body, time, and sociability, experiences which enable us to place
ourselves in imaginative cultural narratives" (qtd. in Rommen 72). For the
descendants of the Henry family whom I interviewed, Roach's "displaced transmission" empowers a collective identity depending on the perpetuation of their

intangible culture, via the cultural production of "one grand noise" passed on and refunctioned in a north Florida context.

Mary Louise Pratt introduces the concept of "contact zones" to define social spaces "where disparate cultures meet, clash, and grapple with each other" (7). For most colonizers, the novelty of experiencing different, first-hand musical arrangements created a negative affective response. For example, Peter Marsden's description acknowledges rancor towards the playing of an African chordophone: "They used formerly to have no other instrument than a bow with two or three wires, which they struck with a stick, making a noise strangely dissonant and uncouth" (34). In the words of Paul Miller, "These negatively articulated notions of 'syncopation' and 'dissonance' as disruptions of normalcy reveal just how strictly codified and contained 'Western' music had become by the end of the nineteenth century" (64). These examples expose an insistent affective tone that coalesced into greater vituperation, prejudice, and even hate.

As a by-product of the burgeoning tourism in the Caribbean, an American visitor to Nassau, Charles Ives, fancied himself to be a literary genius, looking to capitalize on his exposure to those who were othered. He declares hearing "a voice saying unto him 'Write!' and without pausing to think or inquire whether the injunction came from heaven or elsewhere, he obeyed with alacrity" (7). In his self-published book, the preface records his primary incentive: "To gratify and amuse his friends at home, many of his impressions and pictures were forwarded for publication in the New Haven Journal and Courier." In chapter III, he describes "The Poor but Happy Negroes" in Grant's Town (55). By chapter IV, he has tried to assume the role of ethnographer to record the "Sacred Songs of the Negroes," which "probably have never been printed or reduced to writing" (74). Around Nassau, he expressed amusement by "the colored boys [who] came to scramble in the most laughable manner, for pennies, thrown to them for that purpose upon the hard pavements of lime-stone and brick" (73). It is even more disconcerting and disheartening that after Ives transcribed sacred music performed in his hotel's courtyard, he writes, "At last the penny scramblers and the sweet singers of Nassau caused so much noise, and such a disturbance of the quiet which usually pervades these dreamy shores, that a man with a long unsentimental whip was sent, whenever they assembled, to drive them away" (78).[13] Tourists, according to Wheelock, seldom acknowledged the corporal punishments resulting from their own barbaric culture of savagery amid civility.

Nonetheless, straight from travels to Miami and Havana and arriving in Nassau to be an eyewitness to Junkanoo when rushin' occurred on Christmas Eve in 1924, Alan Parsons seemed more receptive, stating, "The noise is terrific" (101). Although including some racialized signifiers, Parsons's thick description is more ethnographic than demeaning as he describes "the Christmas orgies of the natives" and their "strange and primitive business." He documents the extent to which Junkanoo was apparently now being regulated. For instance, he records that there were two timeslots: from 8:00 a.m. to noon and 4:00 a.m. to 8:30 a.m. Not going into much detail about costumes, he described them as "most fantastic fancy dresses." Regarding the Junkanoo music, he only identifies two instruments, calling them tom-toms and trumpets in "queer survival of their African origins." If the trumpet was indeed played, this description may be the first recognition of the use of a brass instrument. He concludes by comparing the participants to the British elite: "They are apparently moderately sober, and don't fight much; quite respectful to the spectators, and only intent, as one used so often to be at Oxford, on getting as much noise as possible from one's own private musical instrument." Parsons's ability to identify with the cultural sounds of Bahamians shows an uncommon humanizing capacity. According to Guilbault, the elite members of British Victorian society positioned themselves as the height of civilization, and "everything else as unworthy of respect" (41). Placed within this context, colonizers unrelentingly viewed this cultural production as barbarous, demonic, dangerous, or, at best, silly, irresponsible, uncontrolled, and unimaginative. Still, Junkanoo aroused curiosity and interest among members of the white European elite and the Creole middle and upper classes. In such contexts, the establishment deemed noisy music and noisy dancing offensive curiosities and murderous.[14]

What Western critics have often demeaned as noise from slavery to the twenty-first century may reflect a privileging of (white) intellect over (Black) soul. Popularized by African Americans in the 1960s, the concept of soul was parlayed into vernacular expressions such as soul music and soul food, with the word "soul" incarnating an internal, emotional chord. What the religion scholar Leonard E. Barrett says is apposite here: "Soul is visceral rather than intellectual, irrational rather than rational; it is art rather than logic" (2). On the surface, his statement appears to express only stark dichotomies, but with it, a dialectic is given voice. Soul is indicative of an Afrocentric slant to the carnivalesque, with noise at its core. Barrett goes on to create a compound phraseology: soul-force. Defining "force," he writes that it "connotes strength, power, intense effort and a will to live" (1). As Junkanooer Arlene Nash Ferguson says, "*There was in those of us called to carry on the tradition, the subconscious realisation that Junkanoo was the place to keep our souls*" (30; her emphasis).[15] Noise, then, from an endogenous perspective, embraces a survival imperative that invigorates the soul to stave off destructive oppression models intended to traumatize. At the quantum level, drumming and dancing protect their very souls from disasters, atrocities, abuse, and even diseases that ravage Black bodies.[16]

Especially among missionaries in Africa, the drum contributed to a strong sense of revulsion because of a sense of its empowerment. As Ehrenreich asserts in *Dancing in the Street*, "Henri Junod, a nineteenth-century Swiss mission-ary among the Ba-Ronga people of southern Mozambique, complained of the drums' 'frightful din' and 'infernal racket'" (4). African drumbeats projected a world outside of the missionaries' cognizance. Voicing reductive notions, they asserted that "the essence of the Western mind, and particularly the Western male, upper-class mind, was its ability to resist the contagious rhythm of the drums, to wall itself up in a fortress of ego and rationality against the seduc-tive wildness of the world" (9). Kenneth Bilby best articulates the demand on European sensibilities: "The loud drumming and singing, 'wild' dancing, and 'extravagant' costumes topped with horned animal masks and towering head-dresses overloaded the sense of these white onlookers, and suggested to them something inscrutably and dangerously African, even when certain European elements could be recognized within the unfamiliar mix" ("Surviving" 179). Clearly, these Europeans were prone to essentializing both their own and Afri-can cultures.

A more contemporary travelogue by Mark Hudson, *Our Grandmothers' Drums*, yields a pastiche of ethnographic observations. At one point, Hudson observes, "A drum, particularly in Africa, is never a wholly silent object. Even if it is only sitting in the corner of a room, its capacity to create noise and excite-ment and emotional disturbance gives it a power which goes beyond its poten-tial as a decorative object" (131). Then, however, he offers this comparison:

> Unlike in the West, where the beating of drums is used largely as an accompani-ment to melody, in Africa it is not seen as music as we understand the word. The rhythms are inextricably bound up in the rituals and processes of the people's lives. And like these processes their forms are precise, and prescribed. To rhythms which, to a European, may sound equally precise, meaningful and satisfying, may be, to an African, as different as a well-honed sentence and a stream of gibberish. If it is not one of the traditional rhythms of their culture, it is nothing. They don't even hear it is a rhythm. (137)

The significance of this observation cannot be overstated. Sounds can vibrate within the human body, speaking to esoteric/exoteric factors, including Hud-son's own.

Discourse related to the drum is foundational in revealing the dynamics of intergroup perceptions of creating social bonds. Nina Wood's ethnographic dissertation, based on participant observation, stresses the Junkanoos' sense of group identity in relationship to the larger world. She quotes Robert Ferguson in an interview in 1994 saying, "you know our Junkanoo music sound is, it's no sound like this nowhere in the world, because once it hits you and gets into your soul, and once you a Black person . . . once you from African descent . . .

and once that rhythm, that rhythm gets into you, one you hear them drums, the **drums** is what makes you move—it's not the bells, you know, it's the drum" (357; his boldface).[17] Another interviewee confirmed to Woods, "Without the drums, ain't nothing happenin." Part of the mastery of drumming techniques is moving others, causing the adrenaline to flow. Blues aficionado Robert Palmer's description applies here as it relates to the appeal of drumming on The 26th in north Florida: "The snare and bass drummers played syncopated cross-rhythms that rarely fell directly on the downbeats and were designed to stimulate uninhibited, improvisational group and solo dancing" (39). No matter the drum design, rhythmic technique, and patterns, the musical arrangements always include two or more drums.

The hand drum is so privileged in African musicology that the prevalence of drumsticks in musicmaking is often obscured. Emerging from a breakthrough conversation with Dogon's Ogotemmeli, French anthropologist Marchel Griaule uncovered some cosmological mythic narratives related to the hierarchy of the African drum. Of particular interest are remarks on the ninth day of Griaule's interviews pertaining to the drums of Ogotemmeli's society. While their family of drums does not approximate the festal heritage found in the Anglicized Caribbean, he divulged the cosmology informing drum beats, especially the allure of the drumstick against the one designated as the armpit drum: "The blows of the drumstick make the sound leap from one skin to the other inside the cylinder" (65).[18]

Ultimately, the one commonality across the spectrum in the Boxing Day arc of cultural productions is the bass rhythm (Wood 382), which even informs the sonic force of soca playing via mobile sound systems. Hip hop music builds on deep bass tones; similarly, soca music's bass line is overamplified, recorded in the red when mastered, and then loudspeakers transmit in the red, keeping the drums up front and boosting the bass (Rose 75).[19] Perhaps, with the banning of drums until the late 1930s, Trinidadians' lack of dependence on African or military-style drums resulted in musical innovations such as steelpan and now soca that seemingly lack the same trajectory as well as this distinctive transnational identity (Guilbault 5).[20] Then, too, even steelpans vanished, unable to compete with "the modern impact of the big trucks and their huge, earth-shaking sound systems" (Mason 74). Julian Henriques speculated that sound systems led to terminologies—sonic dominance, sonic body, and the triangulation of sonic logos—to articulate the move from visual representation to a bass culture "in which hearing overrides the other senses" (qtd. in Goodman 27).

As it relates to Jamaican dancehall music, Henriques's interrogation led to a much-needed paradigmatic turn in sound studies. Regarding sonic dominance, Henriques uses this thick description as an example of experiencing the sonic force of sound systems: "It hits you, but you feel no pain, instead, pleasure.

This is the visceral experience of audition, to be immersed in an auditory volume, swimming in a sea of sound, between cliffs of speakers towering almost to the sky, sound stacked up upon sound—tweeters on top of horns, on top of mid, on top of bass, on top of walk-in sub bass bins" (1). He further contextualizes this sonic dominance as de rigueur for the energizing of "sonic bodies" and defining it to be in tune with the sound system's bass line as its corporeal embodiment. Principally, Henriques theorizes the sonic body inside the sound system: "This makes the dancehall session a unique living laboratory—an auditory Galapagos—outside the usual dominance of vision." After establishing his preamble, "thinking through sound" *ad infintium*, his text concludes with the triangulating of sonic logos, which is a way of thinking "not bound up with language, notation and representation" (2). His triangulation schema ultimately is non-binary negating dualities: "mind and body, viewer and viewed, subject and object, internal and external worlds" (16).[21]

My intent is not to dismiss European influences or to reify Africanity; rather, I am proposing that, at their core, these festive practices possess a deep structural unity with an African aesthetic autonomy. To articulate evidence of Africanisms is not to essentialize, making assessments attesting to purity, homogeneity, superiority, or sentimentality.[22] Essentially, as Ehrenreich asserts, "Carnival provided one vehicle for the preservation of African traditions" (169). In *Singing the Master*, Roger Abrahams discusses the propensity to fabricate hybrids about African-descended peoples' maintenance of "an African-style system" (125). Relishing the genius of their festive displays, Abrahams admires the mutability of the "representative performers" to artistically excoriate the stakeholders who ultimately commodify their kinesthetic imagination (158–60).[23] Cheryl Ryman hypothesizes a neo-African hybridizing process, which she defines as the "end-product": "those forms developed in the new world by African peoples, who draw largely on a body of cultural knowledge (African) to interpret both the new environment and cultural modes" ("Jamaica" 13). Gikandi best describes the process: "Out of the ruins of Africanism, slaves could have a vision of their location and dislocation in both the new and old worlds" (236). Subsequently, like their ancestors, participants embrace new identities to dismantle their sense of marginalization (Gikandi 236).

At the close of the nineteenth century, it was common for writers to mention the prevalence of African-specific interpretations of these cultural performances. In 1895, writing under the pseudonym Tom Cringle, Michael Scott fictionalizes the following account: "This day was the first of the Negro Carnival or Christmas Holidays, and at the distance of two miles from Kingston the sound of the negro drums and horns, the barbarous music and yelling of the different African tribes" (261). Even in 1908, Ober issued this ethnocentric observation: "African huts are half concealed amid tropical foliage of cocoa-palms, etc.; but they seem to be occupied rarely, as all the people cook, eat, and probably sleep out of doors" (49). Clearly, these remarks reflect failure to negotiate cultural differences without prejudice. Given the colonial mindset, of course, "African" was equated with barbarousness and savagery, as well as being "out of doors" regardless of celebration, climate, and cultural proclivities. Hendy corroborates this distancing by Europeans: "lumping together all the complex languages and varied musical traditions of the indigenous peoples they met into some amorphous category of 'savage' and meaningless sounds, it was a convenient prelude to denying the people themselves any claim to equal rights, even over their own land" (331). Even moreso, local white writers in the present day deny Boxing Day cultural productions any European derivation, by privileging the generic African (Moss; Cassidy, *Jamaica*; Craton, *History*).

From an endogenous perspective, likewise, there is more of a turn toward unapologetic acknowledgement of the centrality of West African festival performance genres, without referencing hybridity.[24] For instance, with a sense of national pride and in defense of Junkanoo, E. Clement Bethel declares: "For years, too, Junkanoo has provided links with the Bahamian's unique African heritage; its very survival has indicated that the Bahamian celebration cannot be viewed as being simply an offshoot of the more well-researched Jamaican John Canoe. In this regard, then Junkanoo may be viewed as public symbol of the Bahamian's Africanness, and may provide clues to the meaning of other Caribbean festivals, rather than vice versa" (ix). Another Junkanooer, perhaps with more ignominy, noted, "the only thing Africa ever gave us was the drum!" (Wood 341). Speaking to functionality, Martin Munro wrote, "The drum is, moreover, a means of racial remembrance, containing the bitter memory of past servitude and, more positively, the memory of revolt," making sound a depository of memory (66). Hendy writes that, during slave rebellions, it was the drum beating that unnerved plantation owners the most (193).[25] The current re-Africanizing process is recuperative; unlike the essentialism by 1960-era Black Nationalists, grassroots actors do not disregard their own indigenous practices in order to romanticize an African past. They subliminally (or otherwise) parade culturally transmitted traditions, allowing for innovation and the improvisational as permissible adaptations within the given concomitant structure.

The intensity factor is another key to Junkanoo and other Africa-based performance traditions from among a range of retentions: density, polyrhythms, staggered entries, and call-response (Wood 343). Of these, intensity is the one most in sync with the African diasporic auditory arts as an essential source of communicative power.[26] Wood's interrogation exhaustively explores Bahamian Junkanoo in regards to drumming and noisy dancing through which the intensity possesses wider implications. First, she enlarges on intensity by illuminating volume and analyzing drumming from an emic (insider's) perspective as "a very dense ball of sound" (345). Also, Wood forthrightly addresses the sound factor in which musicians produce "more noise than definite pitches" to attain a level of intensity that is "aesthetically desirable" (345). Percy "Vola" Francis told her that "music is not noise, but Junkanoo. The more noise you make the more feeling you get from the sound" (qtd. on 346). Next, Wood says that, as part of the desirable aesthetics, the layering of instruments (cowbells, foghorns, etc.) adds contrasting textures, rhythms, and attitude. Finally, Wood specifies how the horn blowers hype themselves as the "icing on the cake" (369). Therefore, the intensity factor addresses the depth of enjoyment attained through Junkanoo music's auditory excesses.

What Wood regards as "in the groove" (for Junkanooers) pertains across boundaries and levels of participation: "When a Junkanooer is in the groove, he/she reaches another plateau in the performance and may begin to improvise by playing more complex rhythms" (411). Introducing the "running hot stage," Wood pinpoints the epicenter of Carnival, when one loses consciousness of those around by directly engaging in an intensive, radiant experience (413). Muir explores Bakhtin's interrogation of Carnival as more than a "safety valve"; instead, he says it "liberated human consciousness and permitted a new outlook by allowing common people to organize themselves 'in their own way' as a Carnival crowd" (91). To center his expression "running hot" within a West African musical aesthetics, John Collins gives persuasive examples about the "balance of sound and silence" (5). His fascinating thesis discerns a clandestine rhythm secreted within a turmoil of sounds, "like the quiet in the eye of a storm" (7). He advances how a master musician is "poised between cool silence and hot sounds, the hidden rhythm and the overt beat" (7). In this manner, the desired aesthetic encapsulates a dialectical interdependency, with rhythm defined as silences between tones (Hamilton 53).

Along with the polyrhythms, consistent with my research, come other pronounced African retentions: processionals, competition, hospitality, reciprocity, and collective economics. To avoid a utopian fantasy of sameness by the refusal to universalize them, these characteristics are enduring and are rife throughout sub-Saharan Africa and the Black Atlantic World.[27] The objective is not to argue that such public display elements are solely the cultural domain of African peoples but to account for distinct moral and aesthetic purposes (Abrahams, *Singing* 160). Traveler Mark Hudson observed, "It was only in Africa that I had seen such complete unreservedness, such total abandonment to rhythm. And unlike in Europe, where such abandonment seemed to lead inevitably to violence or self-destruction, there was no element of aggression" (131). Hazzard-Donald identifies two factors conducive to the survival of African-based traditions: "one, that the surviving culture prove functional for the practitioners; two, that it be somehow functional and perceived as relatively non-threatening for the slaveocracy" (102).[28] Moreover, rather than being monolithic, the intense soundscape of each Boxing Day fete has similarities as well as differences. Bilby, for example, has noted that these indigenized traditions, "though they ultimately stem from a common source, show great variety" ("Masking" 4). It is the inexorable predominance of rhythm that marks these celebratory moments as simultaneously Afrocentric and diasporic.

From two academic disciplines, both anthropologist Margaret Drewal and historian Sterling Stuckey have recognized the salience of processions in West Africa and its diaspora.[29] In her study of the ritual process in Nigeria, Drewal shows a printed program announcing an upcoming anniversary of a secret society with the heading "PROCESSION & PARADE OF ALL EGUNGUN" (2). The all-capitalized words accentuate the centrality of such cultural performances in engaging auditory saturation, which Drewal equates with an ontological journey.[30] In his introductory chapter, Stuckey engages the cultural symbolism of the circle, but not at the expense of the line. In capturing the essence of John Canoe and northern Pinkster traditions, he writes, "The evidence suggests that the parades of kings and governors were parts of a larger cultural configuration, and this reinforces our claim that a Pan-African culture existed in the Americas" (80).[31] Thus, "Structurally the line and the circle were both surviving commonalities which many of the West African ethnic groups shared" (Hazzard-Donald 106).[32] The key component for processioneers is a "type of danced walk" (Bettelheim, "Caribbean Festival" 64). While prominent, the use of parades and processions are customarily limited to specific festive occasions, or "in most cases they perform in one specific location" (Nicholls, *Jumbies* 215).

The principle of competition in economic, social, and aesthetic spaces is the living heartbeat of Africa-rooted culture in the Americas.[33] Defining the essence of Carnival in general and Boxing Day in particular, Maude Dikobe says, "Sometimes it seems as if Carnival is nothing but a series of musical competitions" (14). In Bermuda and Belize, Gombey and *Wanaragua* dancers compete to establish the superiority of group and individual performers. Monetary rewards and bragging rights fuel a high degree of virtuoso contests in The Bahamas, St. Croix, and St. Kitts. In St. Croix and St. Kitts, the growth of a sort of cottage industry (Mas camps) drives the competition year-round. In 2018, for the New Year's Day Grand Carnival Parade in St. Kitts, there were six Mas camps with the following names: Kitti-Vincee Artisans, Solid SKB Mas camp, Phunn Vybz, DFX, Fun Teenz, and Ultra Carnival. The mobile unit of each is decorated, showcasing its corporate sponsors, and dispensing beverages to hydrate or further intoxicate their particular band of merrymakers, who compete for greatest number of dancers as well as best music.[34]

Regarding competition, the December 26th Shooting Match in north Florida also features African-stylized sonic contests. Participants fire shotguns aiming for the pellet holes to produce an indentation closest to the x on a cardboard square nailed to a distant stake in the ground. No doubt, with their side bets, the men involved in the turkey shoot are gunning for more than the grand prize and bragging rights. Roger Abrahams describes the everyday use of competitive and allusive play as "wherever the men hang out, rhyming or joking with each other, playing the dozens, ragging, playing at the game of 'busin' (abusing), or jiving" (*Singing* 110). Documenting Junkanoo, Wood rightly positions "Boxing Day as Battleground." She pinpoints the historical moments leading to this cultural transformation: "Prior to 1948 Junkanooers participated primarily to have fun and to release anxieties of the previous year. After 1948 competition for prizes gradually became the motivation for participation, first on an individual basis and, from 1954 on, at the group level" (110–11). On the level of spectatorship, crowds gain vicarious bragging rights vis-à-vis their individualized selection of the champions.

Hospitality, collective economics, and reciprocity all reflect a communitarian outlook. In my research of urban to rural sectors in the US and now including the West Indies, I have found these three principles go hand in hand. This is not to suggest that all exist together without conflict, but greetings along with liming are indicators of hospitality. In Bermuda, even the tourist literature informs visitors that the failure to offer a greeting is considered an abomination. For instance, Fodor's recommends: "Always greet bus drivers with a friendly 'good morning' or 'good afternoon' when you board public buses. This is an island custom, and it's nice to see each passenger offer a smile and sincere greeting when boarding and exiting the bus" (Fodor 37). This etiquette pertains throughout the Black Atlantic, although depending on social class and age, all may no longer adhere to it. Of equal importance, collective economics and reciprocity can be said to be sacrosanct, constituting the *raison d'être* of organized groups and Carnival en toto.[35] Regarding the Shooting Match, lay historian and master drummer Otis Hill told me that, for African Americans in the region, "There were three main Shooting Matches throughout the vicinity each year. On Christmas Day, Johnny James had his big thing; the day after Christmas, on the 26th, that's when the Henrys had their big thing; then on New Year's Day, that when Sam Adderley had his. And these three Shooting Matches went on for years, as far as I can remember." Collectively, these occasions bring the noise, as a rallying cry stressing the centrality of social interaction as an affirmative cultural mandate.

Also, on December 26 in the Florida panhandle, there is no need to suppress noise making, and blasts of music freely echo across the Henry family's compound into the night. Whether dancing the electric slide or stepping jauntily to snare and bass drums, partygoers are free to talk boisterously over the noisy din of their own sounds. By so doing, they stand their ground, the foundations of which were issued generations ago, and pay true homage to their ancestors.

In this context, annually, the firing of guns on one's own property provides a touch of retribution, providing a redefinition of self. In terms of racial tension, socially a great deal has changed. The Henry property is today the site of what is now known as the Bradfordville Blues Club (honored with a Mississippi Blues Trail historical marker attesting to its authenticity as one of the few jook joints outside the state where the blues began), although it is now frequented mainly by local white enthusiasts each weekend. However, every December 26 several hundred African Americans, many of whom have migrated northward, return for the holiday season and reclaim this space. With urban sprawl, it is their white neighbors in nearby subdivisions who complain about disturbing the peace. For the Henrys, the annual Shooting Match operates on ceremonial ground, as these tradition bearers maintain not only land possession, but control over its sonic waves, affirming their property as an authentic site for gleeful black noise of their own creation.

Calling for greater comprehension is the embeddedness of sound, its connection to the social. Soundscapes resound throughout Africa and its diaspora as quotidian parts of the environment, spaces with few prohibitions or inhibitions regarding the audible.[36] A soundscape is defined as the overall sonic environment of an area.[37] Against a political hegemony intent on eradicating all that it judges to be obnoxious and different, Africa-derived soundscapes achieved a decibel level above what the colonizers viewed to be sociable. On the one hand, noise is an aural vibrancy that may be abhorrent and loathsome to the Western cultural imaginary. On the other hand, even though many traditional African societies did not conceptualize music in accordance with Europeans, their capacity to adapt to Western cultures' conception of the term "music" indicates the concept subsisted, "integrally, even where no term is available" (Hamilton 51).[38]

Theatre scholar Errol Hill published the first major study of Trinidadian Carnival, and later he introduced Nigerian scholar Laz Ekwueme's contention that African and diasporic cultural expressions consist of two parts: one appealing to the visual senses and an acoustic part appealing to the aural senses. He wrote:

> No one, whether in Africa or in the New World goes merely to hear black music; people go to see it. . . . The point here is that black people do not make music, or for that matter any creative art, only for one of the senses. A drummer is not just beating out rhythms; you have to see him do it in order to appreciate in any sense what he is doing. His costume, his facial contortions, his gestures, are all part and parcel of his art of drumming. This extra-acoustic (visible) motion is as essential a part of drumming as the sound produced. (*Trinidadian* 221)

The idea of noise as irritation typifies the repressive defenses inherent in colonialism and bourgeois culture. However, for the festive music makers, the objective is to produce a sweet sound that electrifies spectators as well as stimulates fellow performers (Wood 325).

Of course, there is an ideology of sound as well, based on some core assumptions. Ideological assumptions about music tend to privilege Western notation, written scores, and pitch/duration over timbre. Said's *Musical Elaborations* notes that there is also a transgressive element in music. Although theorizing European classical music, he writes, "Secular transgression chiefly involves moving from one domain to another, the testing and challenging of limits, the mixing and intermingling of heterogeneities, cutting across expectations, providing unforeseen pleasures, discoveries, experiences" (55). By espousing a philosophy of music as transgressive, he explores an imaginary with certain irreconcilabilities, wherein there is never a possibility of harmony of polar oppositions. While his theoretical discussion privileges classical music, the discourse is at home in the hybridities of postcolonialism, in which creating a vital atmosphere depends on anti-assimilationist musical sounds.[39] Having endured British colonialism too, for example, the Irish have a sense of cultural identity via mumming that, according to Glassie, "was among their geographical signs: it helped them locate themselves, eliminating anomie and giving precision to the idea of 'our district'" (75). In this manner, the transgressive theme repeats each in its own way with homogeneity and heterogeneity. No matter which observance, people experience music in distinctive localized ways in which sounds form part of the cultural landscape. David Morley notes that "local" is not to be considered an indigenous source of cultural identity, which remains authentic only insofar as it is unsullied by contact with the global. Rather the "local," he says, is itself often produced by means of the "indigenization" of global resources and inputs (9–10).

Moreover, the British and French employed distinct styles of colonialism, with the British ruling with greater chauvinism and the French with greater diplomacy. Therefore, the British colonial approach was to suppress local culture. Martin Munro recognizes an equivalence in Trinidad where there was a dual presence: "Just as in Britain, where there was a continuing struggle between 'refinement and vulgarity' that was often figured around questions of noise, music, and the bourgeois desire for silence, in the colonies, too, the transplanted colonials sought to repress the carnivalesque 'rough music' of the masses" (84). Principally, the two colonial systems shared historical parallels at home regarding the prohibition of street sounds by the poor as a form of sonic pathology.[40] In designing models of oppression, "The continued concerns over the incompatibility of rhythmic, Africanized music and dance and 'civilized' morality combined with the ever-present possibility of public disorder during Carnival, led to new, stringent ordinances in the early 1880's" (105). For example, a Musical Ordinance banned or restricted the "unlicensed playing" of percussion as well as "European" instruments. Similarly, in St. Croix, the colonizers' "civilizing" mission demanded more bifurcation: "editorials made it perfectly clear: masquerades and street processions could be tolerated and even encouraged; African drumming and dancing, however, could not" (W. James, Part I, 1).[41] Ostensibly, noise conquered all; for a loud soundscape yet saturates the ACW, especially with the advent of new technologies that amplify the acoustics.

Today, it is dancehall soca that contributes the most to the soundscape with its grandiose amplified sonic wave. Transcending geographical boundaries, soca is a hybrid form that combines calypso with African American funk bands of the 1960s and privileges the bass and electric guitar. The music's name combines soul and calypso. Mason explains, "Essentially soca was a more up-tempo, freer-flowing and louder version of calypso with a more laid-back bass line and a touch of Indian drumming, although still with the essential horn section" (29). To further differentiate the two, calypso is lyrically based, with soca being rhythmically based dance music (Balliger; Guilbault). Mason contextualizes soca as a dynamic music that governs contemporary Carnival fetes, eclipsing the once popular calypso tents, due to its promotion of gimmicky dances and audience participation (30). The intention is to compose "dynamic and powerful soundings" (Guilbault 219). It was this form's transition from the dancehall to the road that furthered carnivalesque dictates. Since soca music is synonymous with "party" or "festival music" with its sonic power, it has been called superficial and "without content" (Balliger 145).

This chapter has historicized and theorized noise as a living trope in the ACW. Into the twenty-first century, earwitnesses and journalistic accounts are helping to develop the trope of noise over time and acoustical space.[42] With culture contact, Europeans encountered a distinct Africa-derived aesthetic, which they interpreted as noise. While moves to suppress noisemaking were an intrinsic, universalizing response by colonial authorities, this propensity is complicated when racialized. Noise can function as a metaphor, threatening bourgeois ideologies.[43] European newcomers to the Atlantic World expected to tame the wildness and the wilderness. Fundamentally, noise is gradient (conceptually different) and highly phenomenological (Nechvatal). Today's soundscapes also are rife with postmodern noise: "Noise was not only an important component of the modern everyday but also of popular culture—whether rural folklore, children's street games, the practices of urban subcultures, or electronically relayed images and sound" (Suárez 11). One cultural group's noise is another's artistic communication. As Peter Bailey writes, "[Noise] is an expressive and communicative resource that registers collective and individual identities, including those of nation, race and ethnicity. . . . it is a ready form of social energy with the power to appropriate, reconfigure or transgress boundaries; it converts space into territory, often against the social odds" (34). The end result was an "immersion into—cultural noise" comprehending fluctuations.[44]

Consigned to a hermetic world music niche, the auditory art of the Caribbean faces not only annihilation but commoditization. What was once derogatory noise gains ascendency by becoming elevated and consumed within a global system of neoliberal capitalism. In Michael Stone's meditation to contest the fetishizing of Garifuna music, he declares: "Many observers celebrate the transculturation of local traditional musics as a mutually edifying synthesis of dissimilar cultural influences conducive to a more generalized democratizing of the planetary sonicsphere, and as a welcome interaction of world musics seen as indexing a more egalitarian 'multicultural' future" (59). In addition, Guilbault was among the ethnomusicologists to research and extol this turn toward Western consumption (zouk). Stone perceives a bipolar tension unfolding with this exoticization of "world-music-as-commodity" that ironizes the construction of "sonic otherness." Yet via new media, digitization, and the democratizing of the internet, the subaltern also speaks back on Facebook, YouTube, and Soundcloud, uploading vistas of sound within hours of Boxing Day fetes. Thereby, they not only indigenize the trope that is "one grand noise" (whether from Shooting Matches, the beating of drums, or mobile sound systems) but make it their prerogative to be in full possession of their own intellectual property, keynote sounds that resonate relentlessly into the night. The next chapter, "Foreday Morning," explores "endarkenment" as a construct not in opposition to the Enlightenment, but as the actualization of another phenomenological aesthetic judgment.

CHAPTER SIX

Foreday Morning

As a common vernacular expression, "Foreday Morning" denotes the early morning hours before sunrise. Boxing Day's foreday morning orientation elevates most of those celebrations to being tantamount to a way of life.[1] Those celebrations show a definite preference for festal public display events that occur during the transition from night to day. The wee hours are, functionally, a temporal response to transgenerational performance practices consistent with collective folk cultural belief. While fear of the dark is widespread, the traditionalizing of collective nocturnal experiences—under oppression—is an act of notable defiance, as described in the following:

> Village life, by contrast, took place during the evening and night. Under the cover of darkness, the kamina folk profited from a small measure of freedom to pursue their own way of life, to establish and develop interpersonal relationships, to communicate their innermost thoughts and feelings, to move from village to village and to define and practice their cultural traditions. In the fields, their time and their labor belonged to their masters. In the villages, they reclaimed themselves to a degree through community and culture. (Tyson and Highfield xiii)

Challenging the usual dichotomies, those villagers sought an equilibrium, a harmony between their nighttime and daytime experiences.

In 2003, while vacationing in Jamaica for a week, I befriended several taxi drivers, and one Sunday they took a friend and me—gratis—to a beach site called Boonoonoonoos, roughly translated into a range of words from "pleasure" to "super." To my surprise, in total darkness, a sizeable dancehall-like outdoor fete was taking place. Definitely off the tourist map, rows of parked cars surrounded the wooded area. When our headlights were extinguished, the darkness was only briefly broken by the headlights on lines of cars that continued to arrive at the scene. Further within the site's main open-air domain, not even shadows appeared. One could only see a shadowy person directly in front of oneself. Two towering speakers pumped out eardrum-splitting dance-hall music. As my eyes adjusted to the dark, I could make out a swarm of bodies "wining" (moving erotically) to the music, providing another context for one grand noise.[2] I found myself intrigued, but my friend had to ask, "Why does it have to be so dark?" Seemingly perplexed by the question, Jonathan, one of the drivers, replied, "If it were not dark, then we would ask to turn off the light." This collective embrace of the dark first broadened my perspective on darkness, which now appears in this study.

Collective endeavors out of doors at night support a binding indigenous belief system. Historian Robin Kelley, theorizing about "building community in the dark," wrote, "Many African American working people pierced the stillness of the night with the sounds of blues and jazz, laughter, and handclapping, moans and cries" (44). He acknowledges that nocturnality represents a "hidden transcript," sites where "thoughts, dreams, and actions that were otherwise choked back in public could find expression." In this manner, the dark of night granted affirmation of those individuals as sentient beings, beyond being mere workers (50). As Hanna noted about Boxing Day in The Bahamas, "This night no one sleeps, even the boys and girls are allowed to stay up to go to Junkanoo." Instead of a negative preoccupation with "things of darkness," the ACW socialized their young to positively embrace the dark as pitch-blackness.

Foreday Morning transforms the shadows of history and ideologies of darkness that could prove traumatic to Africa-descended peoples. Back in the Early Middle Ages, Europe was certainly isolated—as isolated as Africa had ever been (Bohannan 4). Kim Hall's *Things of Darkness* explores the Renaissance "aura of blackness" with regards to British engagement with dark-skinned Africans (2). In her seminal study, Hall argues, "In actuality, Africa, particularly the darker peoples of the central interior and southern portions of the continent, played a key role in the rapid change of England from 'an underdeveloped country' in its own right to the empire that would dominate the globe for the next two centuries" (16). By the nineteenth century, however, Europeans referred to Africa as the "Dark Continent," signaling their own xenophobia—an intense, irrational dislike of people from different cultural spheres and considered Other. This derogatory metaphor served to debase Africa and all that flowed out of it, negating the history of vast trade routes while Europe experienced its own "Dark Ages."

Stefan Wheelock calls the preeminent eighteenth-century historian Edward Long's *History of Jamaica* "a decidedly bold proslavery manifesto," for it inaugurated a specific form of vitriolic color-racism (37). Published in 1774, Long's text cast enslaved Africans as subhuman based on dark skin pigmentation and, therefore, a separate species. Deconstructing the evolution of Black villainy in American life, William Van Deburg writes, "Just as chimpanzees and baboons were said to approximate the behavior of 'Devils whom they resemble,' black Africans, too, came to be seen as being biologically wedded to the powers of darkness" (17). Therefore, from a colonizing perspective, the desire was "to enlighten"—that is, vanquish the darkness. To enlighten meant to buttress a sense of European superiority, which emerged during growing anxieties over a Western nationalistic identity and culture in a time of imperial expansion.

Thus, Europeans developed an ideological intolerance for darkness and blackness in contrast to valorized lightness, in a binary opposition resulting in a specious connection between evil and darkness/blackness. The Christian church was principally influential in defining and promoting "a spiritual battle between light and darkness" (Bildhauer and Mills 136). Deborah Young and Simon Harris's "Demonizing the Night in Medieval Europe" chronicles Western Europe's deep-seated fear of the "unknown dangers that night was believed to contain" and how it "became home to imagined horrors" (135). To deter fear, the ceremonial lighting of candles helped empower people against the terrors that came in the night. Western Europeans also called for greater security from hooligans, "criminalizing their movements" during the hours of dark, as black as sin (144). Most problematic was the conflation of blackness/darkness with evil, despite their differences: darkness equals an absence of light, whereas blackness exists as a known property without the possibility of light. The associative prohibitions expose hegemonic policies that later affected colonized Africa-descended peoples.

In contrast, this chapter argues that enslaved Africans culturally inverted this Western dichotomous ideation system, endarkening it as a means of stabilizing their own sense of Africanity. "Endarken," the key word, speaks to its lexical meaning as well as a more politicized connotation. Dictionaries today either define the word as an obsolete term for "darken" or say it is restricted to literary usage meaning to obscure, to obfuscate, or to confound. These words signify bewilderment, incomprehensibility, and ambiguity—areas of consciousness positivists dismiss. It is also possible that "endarken" leans toward racialized sentiments projected upon those considered Other—defining them as devalued, pathological, even subhuman. Nonetheless, the so-called Others spoke back, engaging the concept to theorize their own ways of knowing that were antithetical to Western hegemony. Cynthia Dillard posits an endarkened feminist epistemology in a move to decolonize scholarship pertaining to African American women by privileging more experience-centered methodologies. Dillard's theory supports the intentionality and design of this chapter. The term also equates with empowerment and recognizes intersectionality by nonbinary scholars. Indeed, the present historical moment is facing a backlash toward political correctness, defining endarkenment in a pejorative vein destructive of Enlightenment values.[3]

Realizing this nocturnal orientation led me to pursue those celebrations taking place in darkness. My pursuit of darkness gained momentum from my first
visit to The Bahamas on Christmas Day 2005, which was a Sunday. Once I was
aboard the shuttle at the airport, the driver informed me that local officials had
postponed the traditional Junkanoo Parade due to an early morning rain. Scheduled to start at 2 a.m. on Boxing Day, the parade, I was told, would instead commence Tuesday at 8:30 p.m.[4] This announcement caused me some confusion due
to my expectation of an all-night parade until daybreak on Monday. Much later,
I found out that the shuttle driver was a Seventh Day Adventist and relied on
his religion's sunset calendar for Sabbath keeping—meaning when we spoke, to
him it was already Monday, rather than Sunday. Junkanoo rushin' actually was
rescheduled to begin on Boxing Day Monday at 8:30 p.m.; so while not in the
"wee hours," the competition still happened after sunset until near dawn.

At the time, thinking I had about fifty-six hours to fill, I investigated a wave
of sounds that led me to the spot locally known as Fish Fry. It amazed me that,
on Christmas night, locals by the hundreds and of all ages converged there
in almost total darkness. Located on Arawak Cay, Fish Fry is no tourist trap
(although touted by cab drivers to travelers), but a place where chiefly working-
class Bahamians assemble for lunch and dinner. Fish Fry, with over a dozen distinctly designed structures, defies any Americanized expectations based on US
strip malls. Each is dedicated to serving local cuisine and more as one resident
stated on the "Junkanoo Spirit" website:

> Some of the best Junkanoo times I have had have been down at the Fish Fry
> (Arawak Cay), watching the Junkanoo practices and sometimes rushing with the
> groups, listening to the high-spirited Junkanoo talk, enjoying the cultural activities
> during Junkanoo Summer—the local food and crafts, concerts, and of course, the
> ancestral love of my soul—the Junkanoo rushouts held not one time but two fabu-
> lous times on those Saturday nights.[5]

However, not all of the restaurants were open for the long, long weekend—lasting through Tuesday, December 27, that year. With Christmas on a Sunday and
Boxing Day to follow, local businesses and government offices remained shuttered until Wednesday. When a holiday happens on a weekend, statutory holidays "carry days" until the next available working day.

Pointing out another aspect of darkness, Percy "Vola" Francis, considered the
King of Junkanoo in The Bahamas, said in an interview with me that "The nighttime offers its own mystique." Alluding to Dracula and vampires, he acknowledged a profound antipathy to the dark—night being the most dangerous time.[6]
Traditionally, throughout West Africa and the African diaspora, pitch-blackness
is especially foreboding. In *Mama Lola*, anthropologist Karen McCarthy Brown

offers a persuasive example: "In the remote mountain villages of Haiti, night is taken seriously. People treat it with respect. No one wants to take the chance that bad air or, worse, bad spirits (which, as everyone knows, wander freely at night) could find their way inside. So doors and windows are barred and, where possible, chinks and cracks are stuffed with rags" (23). The oral literature supports a belief system that employs themes of malice and horrific events taking place under the cloak of darkness.[7] Stories about the Caribbean duppy far outstrip Western ghost tales in terms of frequency and fluidity. According to Moore and Johnson, a duppy is "not simply the local equivalent of the English ghost" (36).[8] Generally, believed to be malevolent, duppies love the night and populate sociospiritual landscapes, but are distinct from the ancestral forces of deceased family members.

The funerary customs of Africa-descended peoples' wakes and funeral rites have been customarily relegated to the nighttime. Seventeenth-century traveler Bryan Edwards reported, "The strangest of all their [Bahamians'] customs is the service of song held on the night when some friend is supposed to be dying. . . . Long into the night they sing their most mournful hymns and 'anthems,' and only in the light of dawn do those who are left as the chief mourners silently disperse" (17). He proceeded to describe the "settin' up" as being comparable to other great occasions such as "Augus' eve'night" (emancipation celebrations) and "Chris'mus" (18). His thick description yields an abundance of songs that punctuated "the beautiful night." His ethnographic account concludes poetically with the following rhetorical questions: "But how can one describe this music, vibrating in the dead of night to the pulse-beat of human hearts? As well try to describe the song of the thrush or the voice of the palm?" Edwards's privileging of unilluminated space bespeaks intercultural differences. For example, Ninth Night funerary rites engaged a complex of traditional dance music to ensure absolution from any "unwanted spirit" (Ryman, "When Jamaica" 121).[9] Vincent Brown elaborates further: "Night after night, in slave villages or secluded clearings all over the island, diverse assemblies of mourning slaves showed contempt for the conditions of their enslavement by articulating their own ideas about the proper social arrangements in the temporal no less than in the spiritual world" (63). Therefore, enslaved persons possibly capitalized on the planter class's abhorrence of darkness by collectively retaining Africa-based beliefs and customs to benefit their own sense of deepening empowerment, autonomy, and self-determination.

As part of this nocturnal world, stilt-walkers constitute ancestral spirits and wear disguises that hail from West African traditions (Drewal; Nicholls, "Mocko Jumbie"). Called Mocko Jumbies, they are quintessential Carnival masquerade figures on stilts that augustly embellish Caribbean cultural productions. Creative writer Earl Lovelace's imaginative reconstruction evocative of the Mocko Jumbie described it "as a majestic ancestral spirit towering above the community, with the height to look back to where his people have come from; and the perspective to see out into the future to which they might pledge themselves" (qtd. in Falke and Anderson 13). In his book, Robert Nicholls more painstakingly attests to jumbies' affinity with West African Egungun masquerades (*Jumbies* 145–75).[10] Drewal reports their mandated cultural performativity: "Egungun perform during the play segments of funerals or biennial Egungun festivals held in communities throughout Yorubaland" (90). While ritual masks are known to represent spirits mostly of the dead (Pernet 45), in traditional West African societies, they are raised on stilts because their elevation symbolizes the power of God.

Customarily, Mocko Jumbies walked at night, with some regarding them as protection from evil spirits.[11] In West Africa, libations are poured in their honor and altars built. Quoting Schrader, Nicholles reports the precautions locals took to "prevent a jumbie from entering your home by turning your clothes inside out and hanging them on a line across the room. The jumbie will walk up and down outside, but it could never enter" ("Jumbies Playing" 13). A personal experience narrative by George Alexander Cornelius of St. Croix includes the following particulars:

> When I was a young boy there were a lot of devilishness. I used to go from Betsy's Jewel to Glynn every night to play ring with dem gel. Sometimes we played until 12 o' clock at night. And every night I used to cry when it was time to go home. I was always afraid to walk that dark road home, and I didn't want to butt up on noh jumbi. Yet I returned to Glynn to play and dance each night. The fear was great, but the fun was sweet. One night a deer almost kill me. As I walked, frighten, like a cat along the road, suddenly this thing ran across the road in front of me. Then there was a quick sound: WHEE, WHEE, and it dashed into the bush. It was a deer. I was so frighten I wanted to bawl out, but was afraid I would wake up a jumbi. (qtd. in Schrader 18)

Such experience-centered narratives are termed "memorates," symptomatic of the individuated foreboding associated with traveling unaccompanied at night.

On the other hand, exhibiting a relatively low context, ethnomusicologist Emory Whipple transcribed "Lyrics for the John Canoe" although, in his analysis, he characterizes such memorates as plain "spooky in nature" because they favored supernatural themes:

> Nighttime catches me.
> Nighttime catches me my dear.
> I saw a spirit open its wings:

In front of me, my dear, at midnight.

Joy, joy, they shouted.

I saw a spirit open its wings

In front of me, my dear, at midnight.

I keep on running, running,

I, running, running, my dear, at midnight. (48)[12]

Instead of being merely spooky and sinister, such nighttime sightings serve as a metaphor for not only the spirit in pursuit of the speaker, but the objective beliefs of a people. For comparison, Miss Bea (also known as "Doctor Johnson") narrates a memorate about a personal encounter one night and mentions a remedy: "Some people who lub foh walk 'bout late ah night use foh tek bush bar" (qtd. in Schrader, *Kallaloo* 87). Also, instead of constructing a binary, Louis Moore captures the traumatizing, fearsome effect of a gardening community: "So ingrained were the beliefs that at dusk, when the spirits were thought to be about to go abroad, people reputedly flocked home from their provision grounds" (37). In contrast to sheer apprehension, Belizean N. O. Bolland substantiates, dating back to 1806, the persistence of nighttime escapades involving gombey drums and dancing in Belize. He depicts, seemingly, a collective love of darkness as "the enslaved [are] accustomed 'to beat Gumbays or other Instruments sounding like drums, and to be strolling about the Streets at all hours of the Night'" ("Timber" 47).[13]

Gikandi contends that, nevertheless, the forms of play of persons who were enslaved alarmed planters, occurring in a "dark, secretive world" (263). Under the veil of darkness, the threat of slave rebellions created the greatest presentiment of dread among colonizers; moreover, in the West Indies, fire imposed another constant threat. Cowley notes the lyrics to a song, "Fire in Da Mountain," which operated as a signal "to burn down the canes" (*Carnival* 19). Canboulay, Canoule, Kambule, Cane-bouler, Cannes Boulees, or Brulees are the terms variously associated with Carnival on particular islands (Warner; Harris; Alleyne-Dettmers). While related to Crop Over, the sugarcane harvest, the intentional burning of crops dramatized political unrest. For example, in 1896, a St. Kittitian newspaper article entitled "One Vast Wall of Fire and Flame" reported: "Noisy bands of striking men were said to control the roads at night, parading with drums and armed with heavy sticks and lighted torches" (qtd. in Richardson, *Igniting* 171).[14] Contextualizing the use of torches, especially in Trinidadian Carnival, Warner-Lewis provides more detailed information:

It was called kambule, a word which both past and recent commentators have derived from French Creole *cannes brulees* "burnt canes," associating the procession with the task of the slaves to put out untimely fires on the sugar plantations. No reasonable connection has, however, been made between revelry—represented by masquerade—and work, unpleasant work at that. Why should people about to celebrate remind themselves of being awoken after twelve or more hours' work to put in further hours amidst the heat of burning canes? Furthermore, kambule involved the lighting of open-flame torches, whereas *cannes brulees* or cane fires involved the extinguishing of flames." (221)

Sugarcane fires fanned more than flames depending on the context, functionality, and meaning.

Ironically, fires during the British yuletide syncretized well with West African customs. In his social history, historian Mark Connelly wrote, "Englishmen were true Englishmen when they celebrated Christmas properly and that meant taking part in outdoor activities" (24). Besides enlivening the Christmas holiday period in Britain, bonfires pertain more specifically to Guy Fawkes Day. Also called Bonfire Night, the Fifth of November commemorates the action of the historical figure who led the 1605 Gunpowder Plot to blow up the Houses of Parliament and James I, who was the first of the Stuart kings of England. The plot by Catholic conspirators was thwarted, and many including Fawkes were tortured and hanged. Bonfire Night celebrations continue into the present era, traditionally with fireworks and the burning of Fawkes in effigy.[15] In the Bahamas, historically, "Every 5th of November his effigy is carried in procession with bands of music and torches, and solemnly hung on a gallows prepared for that purpose" (Powles 147). Matheson questions its significance in St. Kitts, where bonfires and fireworks marked the day at "Monkey Hill and other parts of the island." Still, Guy Fawkes Day heralds the start time for Boxing Day preparation by the faithful in the AWC (Bastian; R. Sands).

Based on a literary source, Maureen Warner-Lewis reports on the "iconography of fire," saying "dances often continued 'for a whole night long, or in dark nights as long as the great heap of dry grass that they have provided lasts—the illumination being obtained by burning wisps of this grass'" (221–21). Warner-Lewis further discusses fire as a "life-giving energy" with mystical power to sanctify the moment and to engage in a ritual act outside the normalized routine (221). Marcia Gaudet, in "Christmas Bonfires in South Louisiana: Tradition and Innovation," refers to lighting bonfires on the levee there on Christmas Eve as conforming to French custom (81). She also notes, "There is no definite time to light the fire other than 'when it gets dark'" (82). However, in north Florida, this stipulation does not apply for the Shooting Match since the weather can be chillingly brisk and a bonfire burns from the start. In 2001, by 10 p.m., temperatures dipped down to 29 degrees. In contrast, 2004 was one of the warmest years of the celebration, causing someone jocularly to exclaim, "You'd better save that wood for next week when it gets cold." While the Christmas Eve bonfires are more of a public display event for tourists in Louisiana, the mass crowd at the Shooting Match huddles closely together around the fire, greeting newcomers, watching the drummers, and spontaneously dancing (also known as "catching each other around the fire"). Bonfires often occur along with outdoor events featuring drumming. As the daylight wanes, the men who participated in the Shooting Match add to the conviviality around the fire. Everyone becomes shadowy figures unless standing in the direct glare of the billowing blaze. The bonfire also lends itself to a naturally circular seating arrangement, as "permeable circular formations" inspire a communal and interactive spirit (Piersen, "Festive Style and Creation" 267).

At first, the bonfire appears to be a response to the winter weather, except folklorist David Evans mentioned them, too, at picnics on Independence Day and Labor Day in Mississippi. According to Evans, they were "for the purpose of warming and tightening the drum heads in the damp night air" (99). In addition, Martha Beckwith, documenting Jamaican folk culture, avowed how at Christmas the maroons "all gather about a fire at night and drum and sing while individuals spring into the circle and perform dances" (*Black Roadways* 192). It also was customary in St. Croix to light a bonfire to commemorate Old Year's Day: "Get rid of all the old year bad things. Curse the bad things of the old year and throw them into the inferno" (Heyliger, "Crucian").[16] In his oral history memoir about coming of age in The Bahamas, Cleveland Eneas illustrates what is meant by the "iconography of fire" as well as troping darkness:

> In the middle of the yard, there was kindled a massive fire, which provided illumination as well as a spirit of warmth and jollity to the event. It also served to tune the goatskin drums, which they used to provide the rhythm for the dance. The adults formed a ring, and to the rhythm of drums, augmented by folk songs, akin to calypsos, they danced the night away. From the ring anyone moved by the rhythm and music could jump into the center of the ring and dance to his soul's delight. His movements were always lascivious and directed to a member of the opposite sex whom he favored to take over for him. He then moved to this person, and caused her movements to rhyme with his in perfect coordination, she took his place in the ring. The process went on repeatedly until the wee small hours of the morning, when everybody was surfeited and exhausted from fatigue and rum. A "jump-in" dance was fun out in the open, under a hunter's moon. (21)[17]

His description brings to mind the uniquely Bahamian fire dance, which James Stark in his early guide described thus: "A form of open air dancing has a great hold upon them; it is called a 'fire dance,' and is no doubt a relic of their previous savage life. The people form a circle and a fire is lighted in their midst. The music consists of two tom-toms, that will not work unless frequently warmed at the fire" (188).[18] Famously, Zora Neale Hurston recorded and documented this kinesthetic dance among Bahamian migrant workers in south Florida and subsequently traveled to conduct research in Nassau.[19] Adding to the discourse on darkness, she observed, "Every dry night the drums can be heard throbbing, no matter how hard the dancers have worked that day, or must work the next" (295).

These nocturnal events conjure up literary theorist, poet, and cultural worker Elizabeth Alexander's collection of essays entitled *Black Interior*, which she defines as "a pragmatic space in which [Black people are] not only visible, but also safe" (9). Frank Roberts's review of the film *The Butler* articulates the thrust of Alexander's "black interior" discourse, describing it as "those intimate, joy-filled (and often-raunchy) counterpublic spaces where black folks can congregate, care-for, and cater-to one another without being subjected to the surveillance of a white gaze."[20] Historically, even when unavoidable, enslaved operatives masterfully directed this white gaze to preselected focal points that exploited European exoteric views of them. According to Tyson and Highfield, "In effect, [planters] observed what they had come to observe or were capable of observing. And to a certain extent they saw mainly what those who were being watched allowed them to see, because survival tactics had long instilled in the enslaved population a sense of European expectations and the means with which to satisfy them" (xiv). By gathering en masse, this black interiority enjoined individuals to feel agency and even more protected, more secure, more empowered. Ultimately, Alexander describes the black interior as "Black life and creativity behind the public face of stereotype and limited imagination" (x). The prolongation of fetes late into the night, outside of the gaze and control of whites, was perceived by them as a challenge to their authority. It was a sign of irreverence on the part of the revelers, who allowed themselves more license than had been tacitly granted; this perceived transgression suggested to them the possibility of further disorder (Fabre 60).

Here, we can see how, as a collective response and with the hint of a taunt, iconoclastic revelers would claim the darkness as resistance art to exploit the lurid, prevailing mythologies of race. By so doing, in total darkness, adherents also transformed public places into "ludic spaces" as a vortex to engage in the magical lifting of their communal spirit. As Junkanooer Percy "Vola" Francis said when I interviewed him, "God has given us all something to celebrate." Among a collective, darkness transforms and becomes lighthearted, perpetuating a countenance of joy. In an early publication by the American Folklore Society, *Bahama Songs and Stories*, folklorist Charles Edwards included an appendix with the following description of traditional West African grand festivals: "The dance takes place at night about a great fire, and is especially enjoyable when there is moonlight" (104).[21] Fundamentally, Edwards surmises a nocturnal acclimatization to be consistent with a particularized festal heritage: "The well-known custom of sitting up and singing all night . . . has been described among the native tribes of Africa by every explorer" (110). Otherwise, as Bildhauer and Mills noted in their introduction to *The Monstrous Middle Ages*, early Western theologians created temporal boundaries to "the monstrosity of the night in order to underline the glory of the light" (10).[22] Such polarities of dark and light articulate lingering cultural and social disparities, whereas, in the vernacular culture, the dark hours, foreday morning, signify a collective's greeting to the imminent first hours of light or the welcoming of the dawn of a new day never seen before.

Historically, in the Caribbean, Sundays amounted to another day allotted to leisurely recreation. One early descriptive account of Jamaica from 1790 stated: "They generally meet before their houses, and sometimes in the pastures under the shade of trees, where, if allowed, they continue their favourite diversions from night to morning" (qtd. in Beckford 289). Apparently, some planters intervened and limited these leisure activities with an even more judgmental account, as one noted, "Sunday is a day of festivity among the slaves. They are passionately fond of dancing, and the Sabbath offering them an interval from toil, is, generally, devoted to their favorite amusement; and, instead of remaining in tranquil rest, they undergo more fatigue, or at least more personal exertion, during their gala hours of Saturday night and Sunday, than is demanded from them, in labor, during any four days of the week" (qtd. in Abrahams and Szwed 293). Enslavement prompted a subversive response to darkness as another site for day-to-day resistance as Edwards recognized: "The evening is the playtime of negroes" (17). As a "double-edged blade," according to Tucker, the night afforded concealment for enslaved persons to shroud routine acts of autonomous resistance (88).

Plantation owners often refused to approve marriages of those who were enslaved out of the plantation; however, since enslaved persons usually exemplified an exogamous people, they refused to participate in acts of carnal knowledge with blood (or fictive) kin. Therefore, it was common to risk punishment and the inky night, rather than abide by the slaveholders' boundaries. For scholars, Jamaican planter Bryan Edwards captured a defining moment during a period of social and cultural transition. This eighteenth-century scribe expressed how "No perils can abate, nor impending punishments restrain, the ardour of his passion. He leaves his master's habitation, and traversing the wilderness by night, disregarding its noxious inhabitants, seeks a refuge from his sorrows, in the bosom of his faithful and affectionate mistress" (qtd. in Abrahams and Szwed 74). With less sentimentality, Errol Hill reported that enslaved persons "were known to walk ten or twelve miles to attend a dance, or as they called it, a play; they would stay up all night enjoying themselves and yet return to the plantation in time for work the next morning" (*Jamaican Stage* 223). Nighttime mobility, then, served as compensation for the restrictions imposed against inter-plantation excursions (McDonald 34).

Peter Marsden confirms the commonality of such gatherings as well as derision toward the ludic privileging of play overnight by workers:

> Every Saturday night many divert themselves with dancing and singing, which they
> still play; and notwithstanding their week's labour, continue this violent exercise all
> night. But their own way of dancing is droll indeed; they put themselves into strange
> postures, and shake their hips and great breasts to such a degree, that it is impossible
> to refrain from laughing though they go through the whole performance with pro-
> found gravity, their feet beating time remarkably quick; two of them generally dance
> together, and sometimes do not move six inches from the same place. (33–34)

Although their "play" was certainly a way to relieve tension, viewers like Marsden could not escape their ethnocentrism. Because play meant doing something
for its own sake whereas work was a means towards play for white laborers, elit-
ists' hierarchical ideology led to a sense of their own superiority when viewing
performative scenes. For the dancers, the balancing of the play–work dichotomy imbued a sense of personhood under otherwise dehumanizing conditions.
As Du Bois pointed out in *The Gift of Black Folk*, "As a tropical product with a
sensuous receptivity to the beauty of the world, [the enslaved African] was not
as easily reduced to be the mechanical draft horse which the northern European
laborer became. . . . He brought to modern manual labor a renewed valuation
of life" (53).

In *Jamaican Stage*, surveying slave performances, Errol Hill argues for a significant juncture at which, on the emic level, improvisational music and dance
engaged "play." Hill writes, "Calling their dance 'a play,' which several writers
noted, would seem to imply that the blacks viewed the occasion as a form of
theatre during which certain pantomimed actions were performed by the dancers toward each other, no doubt in response to suggestions made by the drums
and the lyrics of the songs. Thus, a dynamic relationship would be established
between all the performers not unlike that of characters in a drama" (223). Supporting this contention, which related to Yoruba culture, Margaret Drewal sur-
mised that play is "more specifically, an engaging participatory, transformational
process that is often, but not always, competitive" (15). Play, then, would embody
the center of life. J. P. Toner's definition of play is central to this interrogation as
well: "*Play is a system of symbols which establishes a feeling of freedom and spontaneity, amusement and stimulation by formulating a sense of non-seriousness,
fantasy, and chance*" (20; his emphasis). In "Ancestral Voices," Alleyne-Dettmers
associates Carnival play with "meta-masking," a term she neologized to address
cultural signifiers that forge national and other identities.

Playing is one "protean realm of activities," what Roger Abrahams called "getting away and into play," implying to "get away from it all, even into a parallel

realm in which the motives of everyday life are replayed with no obligation to commit to anything but the flow of the play itself and the rush arising with the focused expenditure of energy" (*Everyday* 98). Abrahams's academic career was built on the documentation of play throughout the Anglophonic Black Atlantic. He complexifies public activities in which reputations can be built on one's commitment to play bodaciously ("Play" 34). Moreover, play is a collective venture at festival time such as Carnival or Christmas sports, which nourished negative stereotypes of laziness, indolence, and being childlike. To play/be playful was translated into criminality (loitering) to further articulate the superiority of whiteness. Black persons' seasonal fun proved antithetical to the Western hegemony's work ethic. These ideological distortions countermanded the necessity of advocating for a play world by those of African descent.

In contemporary island parlance, "liming" is a term in wide circulation, having migrated transnationally. Abrahams writes, "The vernacular has been immeasurably enriched by the language we use for play" (*Everyday* 99). Liming is a case in point. The term signifies any happening in which the objective is to achieve ludic license to play. Stern's *Say It in Crucian* has the subtitle *A Complete Guide to Today's Crucian for Speakers of Standard English*. Intended for the tourist market, this book defines "lime" as a "fun place to hang out, a party, i.e., 'Wha pa de lime deh?'" (84). The book defines "limin, liming" as "relaxing, hanging out, going out," as in "Leh we gane limin no?" Therefore, it embodies an economy of pleasure; in keeping with Carnival, it constitutes having a great time liming with the masses. More specifically to this chapter, Stephen Stuempfle writes that "this activity [liming] occurs at night" (184).[23] Liming disrupts the dichotomy of bourgeois ideologies as an all-consuming artful way of life. Annually, iconoclastic revelers use their bodily kinesthetic imagination to revitalize the cultural holiday under the cover of darkness, liming the night away.

In *The Future of Ritual*, Richard Schechter suggests that "dark play" differs from the usual inversion associated with the carnivalesque. Instead, it is steeped in "Playing out selves that cannot be displayed at work, or with family" (38). In this regard, Boxing Day cultural productions move from playing in the dark—to deceive and to manipulate authority—to the appropriation of dark play to perform alternative selves and (for continuity) to socialize their young. Martin Munro observed a Haitian tradition *bat Tenèb*, or beating back darkness, at which at some level the rhythmic beating of percussive objects coordinates a "discourse of resistance" (77). When asked in a survey about Junkanoo portending violence, a respondent said, "Junkanoo shouldn't be 'safe.' . . . The risk, the intensity, the vile railings and emotions is a part of the authentic experience. . . . Though I feel safe, it's simply because I choose not to be paranoid. The thrill is in the risk, if that changed I wouldn't attend" (N. Bethel, "Violence" n.p.) In an instance of Western metaphysical dualism, Friedrich Nietzsche associated the Dionysian spirit with lunar-nocturnal creative and imaginative power in contrast to critical and rational Apollonian qualities represented by the solar-diurnal (Thrall et al. 156). Even then, seemingly, the power of darkness possessed parallel value in Western early modern popular culture.

Notably, inspiring a form of deep play, total darkness especially emboldens diehard women enthusiasts. Deep play bespeaks the tension of engaging in ludic activities that carry a degree of risk in the claiming of radical sexual subjectivities, if only for one night. For women, the implied risk factor is in going against the grain of bourgeois respectability by deep playing in the dark into daylight and performing acts of alloeroticism by dancing sensuously with strangers (male and female) while being scantily dressed as part of a public display for which women have been derided historically. Such inversion and transgression still undergo scrutiny from one's family, church, and in the press—mostly via letters to the editor.[24] Recent analyses have addressed the prevalence of women liming outdoors in total darkness to bring in the first hours of light (see, for example, Balliger; Franco; Mason; Rohlehr, "State"). Balliger writes, "The most blatant policing that occurs during Carnival season centers, not on violence, but on the expression of female sexuality" (172). In Trinidad by 1988, "there was a concerted effort to revive and reposition traditional mas characters" (Franco 25). Franco views this as an effort to suppress the dominance of wining, sensuous women on Carnival Monday and Tuesday.

Elsewhere, some local customs disallow women's participation, others segregate them, and, in others, women now represent the majority. Today, women rarely take up the drums; given the nature of the sporting event, men predominate in attendance and most activities. While women are not barred from participating in the drumming, their interests lie elsewhere around the compound. Although normally passive onlookers or sedentary conversationalists, girls and women of all ages, enticed by the music, occasionally erupt with gyrating, wining hip movements. Once darkness sets in, flirtations in the light may shift to "hook ups" by nightfall.

Bermuda's Gombeys, however, being transgenerational, disallowed women because they were constituted by male affiliation to the troupe that their father founded or belonged to. Nonetheless, change did come, but only a few names have emerged, each with a personal experience narrative usually involving deceit. The documentary film *Behind the Mask: Bermuda Gombeys Past, Present and Future* features the voices of prominent young women who challenged the status quo. Algina Warner, the daughter of Alan Warner, one of the main Gombey patriarchs, reports that she rebelled to show that "girls can dance Gombey, too" by transgressing gender boundaries in the restorative act of utilizing masquerade to disguise her presence among the male dancers during one road march. Eventually, she founded and commanded her own Alisha Kani

Girl Gombeys troupe. In spite of these few examples, "growing up Gombey" still defines the tradition as principally masculine. Although males typically construct their own costumes, the artistry of women costume makers receives admiration for their masterful contribution to the decorative art festooning the dancers' creative array.

In Junkanoo, women perform more diversified roles; primarily, they are the choreographed dancers, but they may also wear lead pieces, function as contract workers, and play brass instruments. They also serve on the National Junkanoo Committee and as judges, although seldom in the leadership role of chairperson (Wood 214). Dating back over seventy years, performers such as Naomi "Queenie" Taylor Caesar and Maureen "Bahama Mama" Duvalier are legends. In an interview, Duvalier boasts about how, at age seventeen, she was among the first to take a group of women to Bay Street (R. Sands, "Conversation" 95). She was a professional entertainer in nightclubs along with the women in her group, which reduced the shock value. As two other renowned female Junkanooers, Rebecca "Becky" Chipman accompanied her male counterparts as "all-rounders"—dancers or musicians—and Vivien "Aunt Sue" Ingraham was a cowbell player.

In these situations, women have been the object of much derision and gender stereotyping, particularly displays of excessive male chauvinism. Wood presents one long oral narrative by a man attesting to how the "women who participated in Junkanoo [were] a jinx," resulting in his group banning women for twenty years (216). Yet, to his credit, he now appreciates their inclusion: "Twenty years it took us to bring girls back in! Y'know, we figure well, it's a no-no, but now you can't, you can't do without 'em" (217). Historically, women's participation was mainly relegated to scrap groups, bands that do not obsess about their theme, costumes, or music (Rommen, *Funky* 233). Scrap groups gave women a sort of apprenticeship from which they might ascend to a more competitive organization (219). Arlene Ferguson's long-standing participation, despite her social class attainment as a school principal, continues over twenty years after first being content with joining scrap groups and then serving as a prestigious member of the National Junkanoo Committee. Still, in the premier groups, women are rarely in the back lines, among the musicians.[25] According to Ferguson, the daughters of renowned cowbell-maker Denzel "Uncle Donnie" Huyler rushed as bellers for years, and Ferguson's daughter began rushing as a drummer at a tender age (218). Besides, most women junkanoos prefer participating as Showtime dancers in the front lines of an esteemed organization such as the Saxons or Valley Boys (220). Once more women from the middle class gained esteem as Showtime dancers, that situation removed any further stigma and allowed a formidable number of women to gain acceptance (221). Wood further breaks down the dialectic of being involved with the front or back line: "polish (fluid, choreographed dance movements) versus ruggedness (fierce, forceful beating of the drums and ringing of the cowbells" (221).

As perhaps would be expected, the response of the Christian community in The Bahamas speaks for many. In 1992, Wood interviewed several religious leaders, including Rev. H. Oral Brown. about Junkanoos' appropriation of sacred music. Brown stated:

> To further insult Christians, the music was soon joined with a horrible display of vulgarity exhibited in the shaking of the bodies of young Bahamian girls in what is called choreography, that is unseemly. . . . Now, for fear of being labeled a prophet of doom, I must add that I see worse things happening, if we continue to insult God by taking his sacred music out of the temple to what can be labeled our mid-night ball. Please stop while there is still time. Junkanoo to me is still a good Bahamian art form. But we are ruining it. (qtd. in Wood 335)

The derisive reference to Junkanoo as "our mid-night ball" adds a forbidden narrative, featuring women of the night cavorting hellishly. The narrative also articulates a revelation with a stark outcome. Among Bahamians, a conjecture is made about "Junkanoo babies," born nine months after "the rushin'." Now, a Christian group named Chosen Generation participates, rushing not only during Boxing Day Junkanoo but at other "mid-night balls."

In Belize, participants play mas on Boxing Day, called *Charikanari*, by engaging in gender-bending masquerades and dancing. Women are relegated to accompanying the troupe as the songsters, as well as to bag the monetary donations. In essence, *Charikanari* is a truly ludic public display event with several households requesting house visitations in advance, directing the procession's all-day promenade. By all appearances, the phenomenon invokes Western charivari as a cultural appropriation but instead signifies "transmission by surrogacy" by the retention of knowledge across time through reinvention (Roach 28).[26] In reality, these masquerades engender more than a universalizing fantasy or hybridity within the heightened context of colonialism and imperialism. Cultural evidence suggests otherwise since, traditionally, gender variance long existed with great fluidity and the festal rites' raison d'être is to engage performance practices that privilege deep play. Furthermore, it is the bull (cowhead) and devil characters that captivate young spectators into the night, when their antics no longer target only children. By nightfall, they indiscriminantly harass passersby, surreptitiously wielding their sticks and aiming them especially at skimpily clad young women.

While women and children are mostly relegated to spectatorship, as in West Africa, successful masquerading depends on their willingness to engage these illusions, accepting their marginalization (Franco 33). While cisgendered

women do not mask during Jankunu, customarily, they are the cultural producers of songs that accompany the drumming. It is during the Settlement Day
festival in November when "it is said that the women, when dancing, can do up
to 200 hip rolls a minute. Some call this provocative, some call it backbreaking.
It is supposed to be a re-enactment of the cock-and-hen mating dance, where
the one dancer tries to outdo the other" (Lougheed 324). It is also said that their
punta dancing is an expression of sexual politics while singing songs of social
commentary about the plight of women. Abrahams suggests that cultural displays consume all because even spectators gain from the exhilaration.

The domination by women in Trinidad has inspired scholars to theorize the
body politics of soca, an emergent musical structure that reinforces a mind-
body dichotomy. Gendered as female, soca surfaced as engaging "the 'unthink-
ing' body" (Ballinger 129). For example, Rohlehr situates soca as the music of
"winer women," objectified by masculine lyricism, which demands them "to
wine, grind, jump-up, jump-down, move, groove, do this or that with various parts of [their] anatomy" (129–30). Ballinger theorizes a more dialectical
response, based on ethnographic interviews with female soca fans regarding
their subjectivity. These women exercise agency and say they are not kowtowing
to masculinist texts but, along with the crowd, are involved in the collective formation of a social body, "with everybody moving together" (131). Carnivalesque
behavior occupies the realm of the body, nonetheless, usually in the guise of
the phallic male body or cross-dressing men, especially among mummers. The
female body becomes amplified and stigmatized due to the sexual energy mas
exudes, enhanced by the move to play mas in Rio-style string bikinis, another
sign of transnational cultural flow (Mason 106–111, 133–36).[27]

Commenting on the prevalence of solo female soca artists, Guilbault recognizes another instrumental factor in the demonizing of women's bodies (57). In
her opening remarks introducing Jamaican dancehall sensation, Lady Saw, who
helped to articulate the presence of new gendered subjects, Carolyn Cooper
notes, "The flamboyantly exhibitionist DJ Lady Saw epitomizes the sexual liberation of many African Jamaican working-class women from airy-fairy Judeo-
Christian definitions of appropriate female behavior" (99). Mason suggests the
following analogy: "Fetes are to Trinidad what the dancehall is to Jamaica" (11).
If only on Boxing Day, women receptive to the transnational practices generated by Jamaica's neighboring isles take the license to perform hypersexualized
dances, with minimal rancor. According to Pamela Franco, by 2005, "For the
first time in its recorded history, women are very visible in the historically male
enclaves of calypso and steelband, and are also the numerical majority in the
street parade on Carnival Monday and Tuesday" (25). Apparently, in accordance
with the globalizing of Trinidadian Carnival, this transformation is most prevalent in neighboring St. Croix and St. Kitts. In Trinidad, Mason documents the

effects of the large influx of women, such as adding revealing costume designs, augmenting the size of bands, increasing dance exhibitionism, and significantly influencing Road March titles (134). The disproportionate masking by professional women functions to achieve agency outside of the cult of respectability but to also transgress the daily suppression of their sexuality—to experience carefree feeling.[28]

Festive gatherings scatter hegemonic rules as well as ordinary community values with extraordinary licentiousness and sensual license. I center St. Croix and St. Kitts particularly, due to the unstructured performance art engaged on J'ouvert morning, before the crack of dawn. The lament from a Crucian CFF organizer in 1965 may still persist: "However, it can be extremely appalling at time when small children are permitted to dance during a festival event in a most vulgar and distasteful manner" (Brodhurst). In accordance with other urban sites, Carnival for children connotes release from parental control and gaining access to freedom in the streets (Ottenberg and Binkley 185). Unescorted, small clusters of young girls and women tend to be the first to hit the streets of Basseterre. This pattern suggests darkness as portending a rite of passage for young girls. Unsheltered or chaperoned, at the first hint of music blasting from the mobile sound systems, wining (the Caribbean version of twerking) pubescent girls initially dance together in frisky movements, performing a provocative dance dialect as a prelude to the Jump Up to come. St. Kittitian youth not only gather early but emerge as ethereal figures frolicking to the hypnotic pulse of the sonic environment as the trucks begin weaving through Basseterre in total darkness. Meanwhile, adult revelers meet up at 2 a.m., drinking and jamming at the various Mas camps until about 5 a.m., just before the sun begins to peep out and the full procession is truly under way. Kevin Birth quotes Peter van Koninsbruggen's thick description of J'ouvert from his seminal work, *Trinidad Carnival*: "There is no room for individual manoueuvring in the darkened streets; everyone is forced to follow the collective, steady rhythm coming from the nearest source of music. Whether they like it or not, everyone is borne on the rhythmick wave which runs through the crowd, back to back and belly to belly" (112). In conformity with J'ouvert in Trinidad, the debauchery commences "when the people want it to start" (Mason 89).

Typically, in St. Croix, the carnivalesque dancing explodes as crowds of people engulf at least three flatbed trucks, each carrying musical bands that not only pump up but pump out a volume of original songs onto the surrounding streets of St. Croix. People generally surge around the truck that is transporting their favorite band. The usual competing bands are The Stylee Band, Fusion Band, and Evalushan Band. The trucks also convey young women aplenty, performing animated unchoreographed dance movements, dangerously even atop the vehicles' roofs while avoiding low-hanging power lines. Revelers arrive before sunrise, eager to dance for miles. St. Croix's police have a highly visible presence. In 2007, thousands assembled in anticipation, until the authorities unceremoniously cancelled the road tramp, possibly in fear of retaliation or a spontaneous insurrection due to a police shooting spree in a housing project on Christmas Day.[29] Such reprisals never came. In 2012, on J'ouvert morning, people still narrated accounts about a disruption the year before due to all the fighting involving females. The exact cause of the five to eight brawls remained unknown and is, moreover, the novelty of a foreign nature to the older adult population (Mason 45). Violent incidents affect the flow of the rules and boundaries of play, resulting in the reinstatement of "grave consequences" (Abrahams, *Everyday* 105).

Describing nocturnal bliss within the framework of Caribbean social life, Nassauvian Cleveland Eneas reports:

> There was no electricity in Bain Town or over the hill, before the late '20s; there were no streetlights of any kind, and the nights were beautifully dark. In a simple (pastoral) community such as ours, when the night was dark, the stars were particularly brilliant. There was a delightful softness to the nights, especially when the moon was ripe; it is at such times that the moonlight could be enjoyed. All over our area children delighted themselves with the construction of "moonshine babies." (27)[30]

Moonlit nights seemingly signified a shadowy daylight as they allowed for extended time for the big "jump in" dance that took place on those nights. It is my belief that a "jump in" dance is a Bahamian creation, born out of the vestiges of African culture, which, according to Eneas, "lurked in the genes and generic memories of the descendants of Africans who were brought here" (27). Eneas is not essentializing the nature of the dance; mindful of local ancestry, he articulates the body politic pertaining to Bahamian decolonized subjects.

Regardless of place, one commonality is that these cultural productions are inaugurated or terminated in total darkness. In the case of Belize, this ludic genre commences about midmorning but does not draw a mass crowd until nightfall on Boxing Day as revelers congregate in downtown Dangriga and beyond.[31] Besides being metaphoric, Black bodies flow through the nightscape, which is endarkened and polysemous. Darkness captures the resonant ambience of social beings; whether masked or unmasked, bodies drift into darkness occasionally made eerie by the glimmer of firelight. When a social group gathers, it "celebrates itself" (Turner 16). In this immediate context, the Black interior inspires a collective joy, the spirit of freedom regained. These forms of aesthetic cultural representation come with their own propaganda—affirming while they subvert. According to Riggio, "Carnival in Trinidad offers any individual on the island an opportunity, in the local parlance to 'play yuhself,' to find the authentic link between the person and the disguise, which as often as not leaves the face painted but unmasked" (20).

When it comes to Carnival fetes, some proclaim that they give expression to "the darker side of human life," while others define these festivities as a "religious experience, the dance from dark to light."[32] Combined, these interpretations position Carnival as being archetypal, signifying a degree of symbolism. One reality is that, unlike Lenten Carnival, the Boxing Day cultural holiday is more secularized, being without the solemnity of a religious observation such as fasting.[33] After midnight on Boxing Day and with Christmas having passed into memory, individuals readily indulge in disorder as appropriate for their locales without the weight of "the battle between the forces of Lent and those of Carnival" (Harris 9). Harris, however, also reports a "blurring of distinctions between 'Christian' and 'pagan' festivals" (8). In the Anglicized Atlantic World, indeed, holiday Boxing Day fetes launch the Carnival season to come. For most, late December signals Carnival time and stirs reciprocal support networks into preparatory action. Related to Caribbean cultural flows in turn, locals emigrate and venture out, experiencing Carnival not just in Trinidad and Tobago, but in St. Thomas, Montreal, Miami, Notting Hill in London, and elsewhere.[34]

In the twenty-first century when postcolonial discourse invokes a political consciousness among neocolonial elites without regard to the subaltern masses, these resilient, reanimated traditions (re)form a sense of Africanity and Black pride. In keeping with past adaptations of their enslaved ancestors, the masses re-create new memories and narratives to frame "new reasoning for old practices" (Wilkie and Farnsworth 10). In counterbalance, it should be reiterated that the enslaved labor forces' day typically began at daybreak. Historian Waldemar Westergaard wrote, "At about four o'clock in the morning the negro driver, or bomba, would rouse the sleeping slaves by ringing a bell or blowing a *tuttue*, or conch shell" (55). Even under duress, daybreak at Carnival time in the Caribbean embraced political and symbolic acts to network and to insistently perpetuate a cultural identity and social alliances. Instead of compliance, the temporality of social life, rooted in temporal/historical contingencies, ruled their creation of resistance art.

It is in these regards that darkness recurs as an expressive trope. The phrase "in total darkness" speaks both literally and figuratively. As discussed, the nighttime is the right time to assemble and to achieve something like collective bliss (Ehrenreich 8). Folklorists like John Cowley widely substantiate the benighted orientation of these fetes: as Cowley writes, "The city was in total darkness at night in those days. When they came to some convenient spot the drummer put down the drum and sitting astride it proceeded to batte tambour" (*Carnival* 1). Also, as noted, total darkness connotes Boxing Day's obscurity, even invisibility, to many. Even though it appears on many calendars globally, many people fail to have even an exoteric understanding of the holiday. For other British postcolonial subjects, the holiday persists and is generally allied with Canada and Australia where the day includes other preoccupations. Few may associate it with Scandinavia as well, where it is also a public holiday. Elsewhere in the Commonwealth (as in the US), December 26 now is little more than the consummate day for consumerism. As one news outlet reported, "Foreign visitors [from Africa, China, and the Middle East] were at the forefront of the Boxing Day sales surge yesterday as they took advantage of deep price cuts."[35]

While the concept of people loving the cover of darkness may seem strange to outsiders, the following post appeared in 2013 on the Crucian Christmas Carnival Facebook page:

> Let's keep our traditions alive! The origin of the Ole Time Night Parade comes
> from the time of the enslaved Africans on St. Croix. During the Christmas time the
> Africans were allowed time off to "parade" from plantation to plantation. They did
> that in remembrance of a time in their homeland when they paraded from village
> to village highlighting their queens, kings, warriors and spirit protectors. These
> "parades" lasted well into the night time. We are trying to keep these traditions
> with the Night Parade that is THIS Saturday, December 7. PARTICIPATE! Use your
> last year costume and let's see the tradition continue. . . . You don't have to sign up,
> JUST COME. At the end of the parade we will be tramping with X6 and the World
> Famous XPress Band!

These kinds of nocturnal sonic events, leading up to Boxing Day fetes, are de rigueur in the ACW. For the remainder of the year, hardly a night descends without a well-attended splash of festive activities. Another comment to the same Facebook group supports the salience of this contention: "remembered those good old days when we went from house to house, ate all the Crucian foods, drinks, and desserts served by family and friends all ova deh place. All night into the early morning hours . . . den yoh just fall out! Ah yoh have a fabulous time . . . melt all the troubles away! LOL!"[36] Even mas camp activities often occur in the dead of night as people trek there to conduct the necessary creative groundwork.[37]

In conjunction with darkness, in this chapter, I have argued for an interpretive deconstruction of cultural performances mired in centuries of European hegemonic rule. On a daily basis, "the police and the night guard maintained a surveillance of urban slaves, especially after dark" (Johnson 56). The dominant ideology equated the tropic operation of total darkness with evil, and the nocturnal orientation of Boxing Day festivities still elicit civic hindrance and hegemonic control by the ruling class. To further contextualize, anthropologist Paul Bohannan explains that "the darkness had much more to do with the

European and American visitors to [Africa], and workers in it, than it had to do with Africans" (1). In the final analysis, the end result was temporal suppression, quashing celebrations. In effect, the Gombeys', Junkanoo/Jankunú, and J'ouvert embrace of nightfall during the holiest Christian season is a counterhegemonic strategy, not only to oppose the domination of Western imperialism, but to reify sociocultural repositories attesting to a communal aesthetic attained under the mystique of darkness. From an endogenous perspective, Ronald Simms said to Rosita Sands, "An to see the transition from night to day is one of the real points that interest people" (qtd. in "Conversation" 100). Thus, in spiritual unity, they become one with the darkness, determining the experience to be soothing and harmless. The next chapter will interrogate the temporal and spatial ideologies that advance nocturnal desire emanating from the back o' town.

CHAPTER SEVEN

From "Back o' Town"

Boxing Day parades and processions multivocally and dynamically dramatize the symbolic reclamation of spatialized seats of power and even valorize an alternative temporal proclivity. Fundamentally, there is an affective and onto-logical dimensionality attached to a strong sense of place. Place attachment sig-nifies the emotional bond between people and places, whereas a sense of place is multitudinal, engaging not only emotion but memory, imagination, and mean-ing. Drawing on Yi-Fu Tuan's theory regarding a sense of place and place attach-ment literature, Martin and Storr write that "places are known both abstractly and experientially" (27). Although increasingly rare, an emotional fidelity to place also denotes rootedness (Tuan 152). It emerges out of a cultural, social, and even historical awareness, demonstrating that this cognizance is congruent with local identity. An identification with a collective enables a primary social function to protect ideas of cultural heritage and implicitly communicate to the ruling class a steadfast commitment to remember past grievances (Fabre 61). Festivals allow a break from fixed units of time and structured spatial experi-ences derived from capitalist systems of production; therefore, time and space are open to manipulation and change. The main contention of this chapter is that time and its social structuring in the context of spatial inversion on Boxing Day serve to distinguish festive time from Western paradigms and everyday life.

Boxing Day functions as a powerful vehicle for celebrants to protect their African-enriched cultural worlds, drawing upon their kinesthetic imagination to both remember and reinvent embodied experiences. Although the term "her-itage" is contested by some, one definition invigorates this project: "heritage is that part of the past which we select in the present for contemporary purposes, whether they be economic or cultural (including political and social factors) and choose to bequeath to a future" (Ashworth and Graham 7). This definition upholds the very sentiment often maintained by festal tradition bearers, who communicate a phenomenal desire for social time and space. Relegated to the "back o' town," out of view, they experienced life as if dispossessed strangers, without landownership. Historically, the back o' town existed as communities where the servants of the ruling class or those who serviced the towns resided. It is mainly during Carnival and festive times that those groups gain socio-cultural capital to collectively materialize front and center on main street. For instance, in Nassau, Bay Street developed as a symbol of economic exploitation and political repression. It represented the temporary freedom of Black Bahamians to frolic and create "noise" at the epicenter of white power (Wood; E. Bethel). A culturally specific time-space continuum is fully operational regarding the functionality of thoroughfares like Bay Street as representational of a behavioral vortex occupying liminal ground, "open to appropriation by both official texts and hidden transcripts," even if only in total darkness on public holidays (Roach 66).

As a theater of the street, perambulation through the center of commerce functions as a form of "resistance art" (Innes et al. ix). Innes et al. go on to explain, "The claiming of public space in the use of the street is a statement of presence that is as much political as artistic." In her study *Parades and Power*, Susan Davis refers to the streets as "structured and contested terrain" (13). She documents some important aspects of nineteenth-century urban street use: "the propertied worried about how public spaces should be used and what public events communicated" (31). En masse, those marginalized and consigned to the back o' town, "Over-the-Hill," and other racialized enclaves circulate in the open, redefining themselves and free enterprise in opposition to the stakeholders. Despite regulations and other hegemonic demands, through the cultural production of resistance art, revelers enable a revitalization process that endeavors to negate or evade the "rules." All ultimatums regarding constraining time, suppressing violence, and/or honoring intrusive barricades fall apart. Additionally, it is a globalizing fallacy to equate back-o-town neighborhoods with "the ghetto."

At their most successful, fetes become a temporally complete social world in which people experience happiness and sensual pleasure for up to eight hours—and beyond (R. Sands, "Conversation" 103). While the fete experience concerns the self, it requires the masses to represent the aesthetic and cultural desire for recurrent forms of sociality. A large portion of their routine social life resonates during the Christmas season; besides being leisurely time-consuming fun, the season also can instigate somewhat of a mini-war. Boxing Day is the time when people, especially of lower economic status, can enact revenge for ills they experienced during the year. Playing mas, they could enact mischievous behavior while disguised for self-protection to escape identification. In Nassau, Eneas comments about how youth traditionalized agonistic play when various gangs from the east, from the west, from Bain Town and Grant's Town, and from several other sections of the island clashed. He reports that each group had its own percussion band with its own particular rhythm. As in a jousting exhibition, each entered Bay Street from a different point in the early part of the morning and, with resolve, tried to crash through the ranks of the other: "All of us are familiar with the song 'We're Rushing . . . Through the Crowd,' the lyrics of which tell the story of these encounters. It now reminds me of the jousting in the days of King Arthur, and sometimes it was just as bloody" (50). Alleyne-Dettmers analyzes how such artistic expressions invigorated society's underdogs, empowering the powerless ("Political" 335).

At this point, it would be useful to state that economic time and Carnival time are not synonymous, one being linear and the other reckoned to be cyclical in nature. Hegemonically, on the one hand, Western industrialized societies commodify time. Ehrenreich reports that, "In late-seventeenth-century England, an economist put forth the alarming estimate that each holiday cost the nation fifty thousand pounds, largely in lost labor time" (101). This fetishizing of time led to granting punctuality the highest priority; for instance, folklorist Susan Davis wrote, "Philadelphians who worked in mechanized mills were forced to learn punctual habits" (37). This advance escalated into the gold standard used by colonizers to restructure order to modernize their Other (Nanni 144). Consequently, when time was viewed as a continuous progression, discontinuous temporal reckoning ultimately had to be abandoned as primitive.[1] On the other hand, the cultural Other continues to perceive time with a more flexible adherence to schedules. In the ACW, cultural holidays provide a suitable platform to challenge the West's culture of time that is inconsistent with the Black majority culture's valorizing of endarkenment as resistance, thus reconstructing the political nature of time and space.

Essays in Adjaye's *Time in the Black Experience* offer several likely theories pertaining to time reckoning in Africa and the African diaspora. In this text, time is "defined and applied variously," yet commonalities abound (9). For instance, Fu-Kiau interrogates the Bantu-Kongo concept of time situated, linguistically speaking, as the "dams of time," which are both abstract and concrete.[2] At the abstract level, time has no beginning or end and exists on its own and flows by itself, on its own accord. At the concrete level, it is *dunga* (events) that make it "perceptible, providing the unending flow of time" (20–21). Likewise, regarding concrete time, my urban and rural folklore studies of African American reciprocal support networks discovered similar temporal distribution.[3] Both sacred and secular performance communities adhere to an annual calendar of events that can last a lifetime. Their cultural performances constitute the "everyday" for those who have ritualized social life into a repetitive annual cycle through an adherence to phenomena (Birth).

This transformation to time-consciousness transpired in Europe during the late Middle Ages.[4] In his chapter "From Prestige Clock to Urban Accessory,"

Gerhard Dohrn-van Rossum documents the diffusion of public clocks in the fourteenth and fifteenth centuries, beginning in Milan, Italy. He writes, "The introduction of public clocks was not only a technological but also a social innovation" (126), conferring prestige on the town as well as its ruling class (138). Of significance, the ability to track time introduced modern hour-reckoning and competing interests requiring specific clocktimes: merchants' time, church time, market time, and eventually work time.[5] Therefore, as Edward Muir notes, "Public clocks meant that not just ritual life but business negotiations and civic affairs could be structured according to an ethic of punctuality" (86). Technologically, to ensure punctuality, striking clocks alleviated the need for ringing bells, "measuring the passing of time audibly" (Schafer, *Tuning* 55). By the nineteenth century, working time and hourly wage emerged as the central themes in modern industrial society.[6] Monarchs, monks, and merchants imposed their political, social, and economic autonomy globally, especially to regulate the "work clock" (Aveni 93). However, in the Caribbean, because it is in the tropics, the experience of time was compounded by the length of the day year-round (Munro 17).

In considering the discretionary time of persons who are enslaved, Edward Long's racialized history mentions Jamaica's Code Noir, "Laws affecting Negroes and other Slaves in that Island." Annually, at their first session, justices would determine the number of holidays given enslaved persons at Christmas, Easter, and Whitsuntide (491). Moreover, the enslaved persons took umbrage at any encroachment on what they emphatically called "their own time." Regarding the internal economy of those enslaved in Jamaica and Louisiana, McDonald's findings appear to be applicable here. In the conclusion, he writes, "The probability that an independent economic system was present in every slave plantation community in the two regions, however, renders the bifurcation of the day into 'sunup to sundown' and 'sundown to sunup' inadequate to the complexity of slaves' lives, since a division also existed between laboring for the planter and laboring for themselves and their families, a prerogative they zealously asserted and defended" (167). By most British laws, which granted time off work for Saturday afternoons and every Sunday along with three days at Christmas, two at Easter, and two at Whitsuntide (Pentecost), most of the enslaved persons had approximately eighty-six days a year to devote to "their own time."

In conjunction with the entrenchment of colonial settler states in the Black Atlantic, an imposed time-consciousness added to the woes of those in bondage. Munro asserts that the sounding of bells and horns were crucial in the change to "clock-dependent time consciousness" (17). He stresses that "the slaves or their forebears had come from societies in which clocks were virtually absent, where the sense of time was 'task-oriented' and 'natural.'"[7] One single motive mainly drove the obsession toward reifying time-consciousness: the demand for order

(135). Abstract time limits transformed the natural reference system of daylight, setting a timeframe for actions not previously regulated (Dohrn-van Rossum 272–23). Furthering the colonizers' obsession, pocket watches served as a means of maintaining hierarchy: "as if the mastery and domination of people went hand in hand with the control of time." Time achieved linearity, which meant it could be allocated even for torture (Dohrn-van Rossum 275–82). Munro says that the rhythmic lash of whips resulted in time also being "lived as punishments" (18). Therefore, subjectively, under duress, even experiential time differed with respect to one's sensitivity to the duration of the lash.

Postemancipation, in the process of modernization, Western imperialism imposed a punctuality fetish mostly in conflict with indigenous cultures. Carrie Lunn, interviewed by Olga Jenkins in The Bahamas, recalled that her brother worked in the sisal industry as the timekeeper: "He kept the records of who came to work and what time they got there (Jenkins 16). Public clocks also are prominently displayed in metropoles worldwide, but the one in Basseterre, St. Kitts, speaks volumes. In Basseterre, "The centerpiece of the city's evocative Georgian architecture is its Circus, a diminutive roundabout modeled in proper Victorian patriotism after Piccadilly, in London. In the middle of the Circus stands the bright green bronze of the Berkeley Memorial Clock, an ornate, cast iron tower with four clock faces and more than a little architectural decoration."[8] The following description further defines its public dominance: "Landing at the pier, and emerging from the customs house, one comes at once to the 'Circus,' a small circular open space or plaza from which several street radiate, and surrounded by towering palms shading an ornamental fountain. About the Circus, and in the vicinity, are the best stores, shops, and business houses, and near at hand are the most interesting and attractive sights of St. Kitts's capital" (Verrill 50). Today, the Circus exists as a relic of the institution of slavery and colonialism, functioning as a locale of interest for tourists near the taxi stand and, during Carnival time, as a roundabout for revelers.

In writing about time in the Black experience, Joseph Adjaye notes "salient differences, conceptually and behaviorally, from those observed in the West" (9). Examining the interrelated processes of constructing the "primitive" in colonial Bengal, Prathama Banerjee engages the "politics of time," stating that "Time itself becomes the universal parameter of judgement—that is, of judging if a society, a people or an act is modern or 'primitive,' advanced or backward, historical or timeless, distant from or contemporary to the subject-author of knowledge" (4). For Banerjee, in accordance with Hegel, colonizers condemned African subjects into objects of their knowledge, accusing them of being ahistorical (7).[9] Although lacking control over the occurrence of public holidays, celebrants indigenized Boxing Day by utilizing the performance art constructs consistent with their own sense of time and/or place. Indigenous time-reckoning systems continue to subvert colonially imposed modernity. As in traditional West African festival performances, celebrants build community in the dark in adherence to a phenomenon calendar, while claiming their own historicity. Identifying time with phenomena, the King of Junkanoo, Percy "Vola" Francis, said to me that "It is a time when we can renew our spirit: renew, revive, and replenish."

In the twenty-first century, why has phenomena-based time orientation endured in the ACW as a constant? Locals have oriented themselves to a time-less temporal rhythm, unleashed through concrete events (Birth 214). Of course, adherents possess both an awareness of linear time and a strong partiality for the cyclical (or spiral) as well.[10] Therefore, they privilege multiple realities to accommodate the obligatory culture of time imposed on them. Quantum theorists argued that time and space are experience-centered even though "Western science has been dominated by a metaphysical vision of a solid reified reality" (Thuan and Ricard 114). Thus, time is deemed to be of two sorts: a physical abstraction and the subjective (based on events and actions). Muir argues that, in Europe, the rhythms of a calendrical system aided in a rational ordering of the rituals of work and the rituals of festival and contends: "The implicit message was that everyone should be doing the same thing at the same time, and if they did so, the community would be stronger for it" (63). Fundamentally, European liturgical calendars regulated life, and this ideational time regulated standardization in the building of empires.[11]

Consistent with phenomena-based time reckoning are musical rhythms since, as Munro notes, "Rhythm also plays a fundamental role in bonding societies and groups and in structuring the collective experience of time" (5). Therefore, people are invested in preserving Carnival time as unique to them. Wood underscores how Junkanoo musicians, between September and January, encounter a new reality, with their "everyday life-world" observing different routines until the period ends (37). Participants expend an inordinate amount of time in their shacks or Mas camps. For example, in mid-December 2014, Frederiksted's Simply Sophisticated Fun Troupe posted on its Facebook page: "SLEEP is for the WEAK therefore Mas Camp time is GRIND TIME! S/O to our Mas Camp committee. They've been working effortlessly over the past 2 weeks and despite having kids, families, jobs and personal lives to tend too, they still find time to assist at the Camp! They honestly define DEDICATION! They're truly loved & appreciated!" Another Facebook site for St. Kitts and Nevis stated: "We know it only too well: if we are to preserve culture we must continue to create it." Time is a subjective momentum embracing collective effervescence; and in the vernacular, Carnival time translates into Grind Time, being of participants' own making and remaking through personal sacrifice if need be.

Roast-A-Time is a prevalent vernacular expression in the US Virgin Islands and is synonymous with J'ouvert. It suits the phenomenon-based time orientation that invites Carnival to boisterously commence by daybreak. *The Dictionary of English Caribbean Usage* says the phrase means "enjoy yourself thoroughly; to have a very good time" (474). The intent is to vigorously Jump Up, to celebrate with great satisfaction. Engaging Boxing Day's key tropes, journalist Cherra Heyliger expressively wrote: "St. Croix country dance the tune of the day and night with dem boys and dem girls 'roastin a time' and 'killin ting pappy.' Such were the days and nights and the foreday morning" ("Christmas Spirit"). "Enthralled" best describes the total absorption of participants and spectators, especially since such peak experiences are consistent with Mihaly Csikszentmihalyi's being in "flow," and one of its characteristics is a loss of self-consciousness during play, a forgetfulness of other realities (40). Perhaps Roger Abrahams best articulates this paradox: "On the one hand, we have a sense of disjuncture between the *flow* of everyday experience; *an* experience, a *typical* experience that is reportable about ourselves as a means of playing out our having entered, individually, into life's recurrent problem situations; and a large-scale Experience in which we recognize that the progress and pattern of our activities are part of a much larger story that began long before we were born and will continue after our death" (*Everyday* 124; emphasis in original). Culturally speaking, festival time translates as "Let's jump and roast a time all over St. Croix," in maintenance of an optimal experience.[12]

Dusk to dawn or vice versa, Caribbean festive time introduces a heightened level in which celebrants shed their inhibitions, generally without much police intervention. Given the nighttime framing, these public displays seldom are experienced widely.[13] The US Virgin Island St. Croix has the only Boxing Day event tempered by a sometimes-intrusive police presence and penchant for order. Otherwise, marathoning triumphs: "To do what needs to be done takes time—not clock time, but spirit time" (Gottschild 8). For those enslaved in the Protestant Caribbean, as well as their descendants, the perpetuation of a collective identity and joy depended on reclaiming the night and streets, en masse. "Time out of time" is a catchphrase popularized by Alessandro Falassi, meaning a period of suspension when the clock stops. However, this expression also reveals an ethnocentric bias. Anthropologist Margaret Drewal, in her research on Yoruba culture, concurs: "There is no time-out-of-time, properly speaking" (47). Instead of time out of time, the proper concept is a time-after-time arrangement. CPT (Caribbean people's time) never oriented itself to sheer clockwork or what we might call time. Furthermore, Birth's preference is to promote a "now-for-now quality" in respect to "moments of time" that are both transitory and durable (216). Mark Smith's assertion regarding enslaved Africans' temporal quantification of time, argues that CPT (Colored People Time) is a form of resistance against "white bourgeois sensibilities," exemplifying an opposition to the authority of "planter-defined time" (130).[14] Fundamentally, time is nonexistent—therefore, forsaking the regulatory aspects of its management, a timeless now functions within the seamless flow of life, punctuated by the repetition of experiences.

For centuries, according to Birth, local authorities have attempted to impose mechanisms of control to undermine these festal rites through temporal regulations and rules. By law, in The Bahamas, officials establish the clock time for commencing festivities, even judging contestants based on punctuality. However, obstinately, the Junkanoo rush usually still runs hours beyond the contracted time. If the published start time is midnight, rushin' will not start for another hour or two. In actuality, the temporal lag is conducive to liming, talking, drinking, eating, arguing, and minding other people's business; therefore, the cultural production is not "all-consuming" (Mason 67). In an effort at reform, however, any civic ritual such as presenting awards or ribbon-cutting ceremonies is generally punctual in accordance with Western measured time.[15] Of course, there are always locals who are not enamored of many celebrants' disregard of authoritative rules and embrace of a popular cultural aesthetic. For instance, one Bahamian clerk said to me, "I am no Junkanoo freak," meaning that she eschews the phenomenon and the unruly practices it spawns, preferring what Mason calls "playing social"—behaving with more restraint (68).

Wood's dissertation describes the culture of time from an endogenous perspective. She explains, "it is more important for Junkanooers to participate in practice and to share the 'we-relationship' with other musicians than it is to arrive at the practice site on time" (117). This reliance on "social time" precipitates great laxity about arriving "on" time, as Dr. Offfff noted: "If I say, 'Hey man, practice Thursday eight o'clock!' you see eight o'clock you there long time, nobody show up yet, you know what I mean? But they comin', you know what I mean? But time as they come, come eleven o'clock it ain't start yet." While some troupes, such as the Valley Boys and Saxons, are known for their punctuality, it is not unheard of for the judges to resort to deducting points for tardiness at the Junkanoo parade. Junkanooers may fail to negotiate the transition to clock time even if it might result in a lusterless performance due to absenteeism by key masqueraders. Additionally, mishaps may occur to inadvertently prolong the parade. For instance, every group leader sized their costumes to bring in 2011, yet the Roots' costumes became entangled with a power line, resulting in lengthy gaps in the procession.

In St. Kitts, without such rules, vast throngs of festivalgoers must wait good-naturedly for an indeterminable period of time for the New Year adult parade. After all, spectators assemble not to be on time but "in" time to direct their gaze upon one another—to see and be seen. They play mas in the dark in the spirit of competition, as the sponsored bands vie for prize money and bragging rights.

Therefore, a similar time reckoning holds true as part of the preparation for Junkanoo in their workplaces, called shacks. In their paper "Enhancing Productivity, Joy, and Fulfillment: A Dialogue on the Festival in the Workplace," Roosevelt Finley and Michael Diggiss said, "Many of the No's [were] spoken about in the shack." Their paper articulates how, unlike in the business and corporate worlds, in the shack all are equal partners. Of the dozen or so vernacular rules listed, number seven states: "No time limit—just show up for work and forget time." In this manner, a sense of place is related to a sense of time (Ashworth and Graham 4). Spatialized time is a concept challenged by Henri Bergson as being measurable, quantifiable, and antithetical to inner time as a continuous flow, or duration.

In considering Bergson's concept of inner and outer time, Wood postulates inner time as qualitative time, saying, "Thus the actual experience of music takes place in inner time" (45). Constructing more of a dialectic, she concludes, "Dimensions of both inner and outer exist in all of the Junkanoo provinces of meaning, as people become involved in what they are doing and lose track of passing time" (45). Along with functionality and intensity, real duration privileges an endless flow of experience, instead of an intellectual representation of time. Without dichotomizing, the two kinds of time combine to produce knowledge that is both intellectual and intuitive. As a participant-observer, Wood writes about her subjective experience of *duree*:

> Time seems to be suspended as the group moves slowly along. The music electrifies the crowd, people begin to dance on the sides of the street and on the bleachers, forcing those around them to move also. The response of the crowd pushes the musicians to *rush hard* (beat louder, ring harder, dance more), which in turn pushes the crowd to a higher level of excitement—a circle of experience that continues until the group has passed that section of the crowd. Then there is calm until another group approaches. (48; her emphasis)

As a spectator along with the those without paid bleacher seating, she experienced their sense of *duree*, occupying a parallel space (back o' town on Shirley St.) where more disorder reigns, representing how Junkanoo used to be.[16]

Geologist Edward Soja theorized social being within visible spaces, coining the phrase "spatialized ontologies" as a construct to denote social production and spatial practices. This spatializing of social life also pertains to north Florida, where racial politics played a role in the Henry family's acquisition of their landholding and eventual family autonomy. Their December 26th Shooting Match emerged out of a crucible of social control with a hint of impending violence. According to George Henry, folks always ask how his family obtained the land. He explained:

I started searching back into some of the history with the older persons, who are passed and gone, such as Major Anderson. He is the one who told me what had happened. He said, "Now, Florida Knight and her sons were living on a white man's place. They were sharecroppers, not very far from that land she has now. And what had happened is that this white man had some boys. And these little white boys came over and they were going to beat my daddy up, and my daddy whipped both of them. And they went home crying and they told their daddy what had happened, and he came over." And [he] told my grandmother, who was Florida Knight: "Florida, you're gonna have to leave. I don't want no trouble. Your boy beat my boys." So here they had to leave, almost overnight, with no place to go. So I understand she took her oldest son by the name of John Anderson. And they went out in search for land. As a little boy I remember my grandmother talk about Willie Markham. And they went to him; they asked him if they could rent his place. He said I have a place off Centerville. So they proceeded to go ahead and buy this place. There was a 168 acres in all that they proceeded to buy, and they bought it all and lived on it. John Anderson had his house to the south. And my daddy had his house to the north. And the eldest son, Allen, had his house to the west. And it's a peculiar thing, their mother house was on a hill so that she look around off that hill and could see every house, all her sons' houses. And if she saw anything going wrong, you better believe that she was coming.

Owning the land in a transition from slave to serf to landowner eventually created a common ground for all celebrants. Land ownership signaled independence and became foundational for defining a newly inscribed collective identity and a third space that is timeless. The firing of guns on one's own property carries a hint of retribution, supporting a positive redefinition of self and the inauguration of a spatialized ontology in which social being (interacting with others) is as fundamental as geography. The soundscape created by a battery of ludic vibrations, generated by the shooting of shotguns in combination with the tradition of rhythmically beating drums, produces one grand noise that inverts an otherwise pejorative, exoteric social milieu. Descendant George Henry gave his emic perspective on their musicality:

I think it's unique to this kind of music. This is the kind of music that they like to hear. This is the kind of music that they like to dance behind. If you had any kind of music, they probably wouldn't pay any attention to it; but the drum beat has a certain connotation to it that inspires them to get out there and dance behind that drum. I mean the old and the young.

Their cultural production bespeaks a heritage steeped in shared knowledge and enduring values. For the Henrys, the annual Shooting Match operates on ceremonial if not hallowed ground, as these tradition bearers preserve not only land possession but control over its sonic waves, allocated to them by their ancestors as a space for endarkened, collective joy.

It is by happenstance, too, that Bermuda's Gombeys experienced a long history similar to that of the Mardi Gras Indians in New Orleans, as the official suppression of African Americans in the context of the racialization of space and the spatialization of race. George Lipsitz theorizes about the "hidden architecture of landscape" specifically pertaining to the prevention of equality due to a different spatial imaginary. For example, judged to be the most British of the isles, Bermuda has an economic relationship with the UK and exports little or nothing to Europe; instead, its Monetary Authority renders financial and nonfinancial services that are headquartered in Bermuda. For two centuries, an oligarchy called the Forty Thieves ruled the nation, maintaining a political system of economic peonage. These politicos primarily descended from the early merchant class, often with a family background of piracy. In 1964, this group of elite families founded the United Bermuda Party and continued to hold an unhealthy grasp over the majority Black community. Descendants of the original white settlers, they perpetuated a system of racial segregation in both government and social life. Front Street constituted their central domain, and Black Bermudians could not work there (Swan). In opposition, leaders of the Black Power movement created the BPC to end political, economic, and cultural oppression but stipulated that its aim was not to replace the "White Front Street with a Black Front crowd" (Swan 37). They also exposed a colonial system of education that, through vocational education, intended to produce a cheap labor force. Moreover, still a British overseas territory in the 1960s, Bermuda served as a Caribbean site from which to prolong Western hegemony elsewhere in the West Indies.

In Bermuda, traditionally, the Gombey crowds were purely nocturnal, though restricted. Then, demonstrating the temporal changes imposed over time and space, the Gombey parade was "held on Christmas Eve between 11 pm and 2 am" (L. Jackson 8). Nowadays, Gombeys must be "properly" credentialed, so each Boxing Day, troupes must obtain a highly regulated permit to be on the road and "do jobs" (community service) from about 8:00 a.m. to midnight (for the diehards).[17] Gombey troupes only then may claim deserted Front Street to perform their empowered and rebellious refusal to stay out of sight, in their place. While Bermuda enjoys a relatively high standard of living, that prosperity results in a socioeconomic divide as well. Hamilton is Bermuda's capital and the isle's only full-fledged city, where upscale shops and restaurants prosper. In accordance with folklorist Susan Davis's descriptions, the Gombeys "[understand] that group motion could convey a message or image to the city at large" (16). As its name suggests, Front Street literally abuts the sea across from

the downtown district, and like the freewheeling masqueraders of old, numerous bands commandeer neighborhood streets and alleys along unannounced
routes. As *Your Bermuda* reports, on this day "They dance when they wish," once
all sanctioned obstacles are removed (Rushe 70). Bermuda's street dancers personify the tension between being the nation's most iconic cultural representation and the division within the political economy symbolized by Front Street
as the high finance district.

According to Lipsitz, "The lived experience of race has a spatial dimension,
and the lived experience of space has a racial dimension" (11). Many of the
Gombey dancers reside back o' town (or in Bermudian parlance "Backatawn")
labeled the "Great Black Belt," located in Pembroke Parish in North Hamilton.[18]
Generationally, it is the most densely populated area of Bermuda and where
the largest percentage of Black Bermudians dwell (Swan 12). Most notoriously,
Pembroke Marsh surrounds the community; it is swarming with mosquitos,
discarded refuse, and other pollutants. Locals are called Pond Dogs due to their
proximity to this marshland, where the residents survive "the daily stench and
flies."[19] However, residents convert this moniker into a sign of pride, granting
it a positive self-definition and valuation. Backatawn is where several of the
Gombey troupes flourish, producing the scenario for multiple clashes throughout Boxing Day. They usually troop through hotels first, visit hospitals and nurs-
ing homes next, and then parade in a road march along Front Street anytime
they please, into the night in a patterned reclamation that exemplifies Roach's
"vortices of behavior," which are sites of memory (28).

On my first site visit to observe Boxing Day, I asked a Bermudian concierge
about the Gombeys, attempting to assess her perspective on their authenticity
(I had been perhaps a bit jaundiced by their upcoming early morning performance advertised on the hotel's calendar of daily events). Often in New Orleans,
I had noted that, if asked, hotel and restaurant workers and clerks would dis-
parage local street performers. Being from back o' town herself, however, this
concierge expressed righteous indignation at my question; and I soon understood why. Once the Gombeys arrived at the hotel, to my surprise the concierge
delighted in dancing along with them, giving expression to her own personal
identity. Traditionally, spectators may perform a kind of breakdown dance step
to the music when so moved. However, within troupes, women primarily function as "money pickers," carrying bags to collect money thrown at the dancers'
feet. Once outside, I asked to ride along with them and then observed the proceeds being divided among the performers. Through questioning, I learned that
the performers operated on a system of collective economics and these dancers represented a variety of bands. I noted that Gombeys hold cultural capital
without which these Pond Dogs would be defined as mere reprobates. On other
days, Bermudian officials are accomplished at concealing Pond Dogs from back

o' town along with their cultural performances, unless they are authorized. Yet, as Percy Vola said in our interview regarding Junkanoo, "No one is able to stomp it out—like cockroaches."

Boxing Day allows for flux and flow with as many as six distinct groups of Gombeys appearing and disappearing from Bermudian streets. Troupes from Warwick, lying in the heart of the island, and St. George from its extreme eastern end travel by vehicles to "snake up the road." Their "road mob beats" along with the intermittent sounds of whistles signal multiple arrivals. If occupying the same space, they compete to show off their dancing prowess. Accordingly, "Most Bermudians are still entranced by the Gombeys, and turn out in large crowds when the sound of the drum, whistle, and pounding feet are heard" (Zuill, *Story* 238). Onlookers assemble (some still wearing pajamas as is customary) to witness each challenge or to support their favorite troupe. Others complain on social media such as Places Gombey's Facebook page: "I wish they will go home. I have to make early time in the morning."[20] Clearly, all do not embrace the Gombeys nor their spatial imaginary.

Throughout the Black Atlantic, not only race but social class distinctions and colonialism created obstacles to unity.[21] Almost from the beginning of their arrival in the colony, Bermuda's Black people enjoyed a relatively unchallenged existence: "Bermuda's race relations and the nature of slavery were both shaped by the unusually early growth of black families and their close relationships with the colony's white families" (Bernhard 39). Bernhard emphasized that the words "slave" and "Negro" were not synonymous (41). The fact that they command a certain respect, however, does not mean that social group problems do not plague Black Bermudians and immigrant communities in these times. In her interview with me, Louise Jackson noted the low esteem granted the Gombeys, saying they were often ridiculed by blacks and white locals as recently as the 1950s. She reported that, as Gombeys approached a home, they would be shouted off lawns, or no one would move from the table to greet them. They did not want to identify with poor Black people who lived back o' town. So, they reviled them.

Gombeys recall when upper- and middle-class Black Bermudians led the condemnation. Until about 1959, old Bermudians condemned them; today, the Gombeys are mostly extolled as a reflection of their past. Some negative reactions survive, although diminished somewhat by the tradition's global standing based on their recognition by the Smithsonian Institution's Center for Folklife and Cultural Heritage, appearance on postage stamps, and inspiration of literature, theater, and the visual arts. Presently, Gombeys are viewed not only as enduring cultural icons but a national treasure. While the Gombeys are distinctively Bermudian, the following quote applies: "Junkanoo has developed from what people believed to be the work of idle minds, to a very spectacular art form and is beginning to affect and will affect our everyday life." Expressing the root causes of enduring hostilities as recently as Boxing Day 2012, community members weighed in with some indignant comments.

Whether Gombeys, Junkanoos, or J'ouvert, each performance community comprises players experiencing the intersectionality of classical models of oppression. In the case of The Bahamas, arriving after the American Revolutionary War with their enslaved Africans, loyalists introduced a great racial divide:

> As an index of the new pressures on space in downtown Nassau, and of the more rigorous concern for racial separation which came in with the Loyalists, most of these no longer lived in the yards of their owners or employers, but in two distinct areas just "over the hill" on either side of the southward-stretching grounds of the governor's house. Most of the old slaves and some of the freedmen seem to have clustered around the southern slopes of Society (later Fort Fincastle) Hill. But the area which caused the white establishment the most concern was the stretch of former bush 'behind the hospital' on West Hill Street later to be called Delaney Town. For here were not only many of the new slaves, but most of the Loyalist blacks who claimed their freedom. (Craton and Saunders 195)

Notably, residents of Delaney Town tended to have lighter complexions. The locale absorbed by Grant's Town gained the moniker "Over-the-Hill," positioned as its back o' town: "These Grant's Town Africans continued to sell their labor and skills in town and to cut firewood, grow provisions and fruits, and raise hogs and fowls for the Nassau market. But they also developed a vigorous internal social life and economy, with their own churches, meetinghouses, informal crossroads markets, and shops" (Craton and Saunders 10–11). More precisely, beyond being designated as chattel, the Black newcomers arrived with multiple differences related to class, culture, incentive, and destinies (Craton, "Loyalists" 44–68).

To suit its American neighbors, New Providence introduced numerous segregation policies symptomized by U.S. spatialized racism.[22] By law, people of color were settled beyond the city limits, and a curfew of sundown was imposed unless permission to be out was granted. In 1807, with the abolishment of the slave trade, the government of The Bahamas constructed Grant's Town to accommodate the influx of Africans who had never been enslaved. In an area unique to it, Grant's Town boasted an area named Conta Butta: "south of Grant's Town, which placed it in the area of heaviest black middle- and working-class settlement on the southwestern edges of the capital" (Adderley 124). A second suburb, known as Bain Town, emerged during the late 1830s. Considered a sister settlement to Grant's Town, liberated Africans comprised its early population (Adderley 162). With a strong allegiance to Bain Town, its lay historian Eneas stated, "Technically, it may be said that [Bain Town] is that area of the valley that was originally settled by Yorubas" (2).[23]

Eneas's description of Bain Town helps to humanize these marginalized spaces as vortices of behavior. Like alley life for African Americans in large northern cities, white elites dominated the street, but their workers occupied the "byways," with ephemeral names mainly of "the activities that took place in their vicinity" (Eneas 3).[24] Their "streets" amounted to pathways for pedestrian and animal traffic: "There was no need for sidewalks, and where they normally would have been, low-growing weeds, grass, and wildflowers grew. The side streets, narrower still, constituting mainly alleys and lanes, were more picturesque." The folklife within these domains occurred "back o' the yard," where there were other essentials such as a well, an outdoor oven, a kitchen, and an outhouse (4). The community also had a retail section or "main drag" with their more prominent citizens living near "the big road" (3). As experienced by Eneas, "With the setting of the sun, he put the hill between him and the town, and he took himself 'over the hill' to Bain Town to look after himself" (22). In the very least, at their leisure, they could maintain a viable spatial imaginary.

Growing up, Eneas's elders communicated to him that Bay Street belonged to him: "it was the only Main Street in the world that I could walk on without apology" (81). It is often said that, on Boxing Day, "all roads lead to Bay Street" (Hanna). With a flourish, Ives provides an enduring description of this center of Bahamian commerce: "Bay Street monopolizes nearly all the business of the city, and is its principal thoroughfare. It skirts the harbor, is shaded by rows of almond trees, stretches east and west for several miles beyond the limits of the city, and is made lively and attractive by trade and travel" (49). Moreover, this descriptive fervor extends to representing those from Over-the-Hill as well: "For several miles, during all parts of the day, Bay Street is thronged with people, almost exclusively colored. Many of them are women and children, merchants in a very small way, bearing their stock in trade upon their heads" (Ives 48). The wide socioeconomic gap between the affluence of Bay Street and the impoverished squalor of Over-the-Hill revealed a greater racial divide than in the United States. Even in 1959, unlike other British colonies in the Caribbean, the area lacked lower income housing, sewage, water, public transportation, roads, and museums (Lewis 337).

Gail Saunders speculates a great deal about what emancipation had meant for those people living in Over-the-Hill. She discerns that while judged the "lowest in the hierarchical social pyramid" and supposed to behave in accordance with their station, in reality, the inverse occurred and "something positive emerged" (*Bahamian* 79). Drawing on remarks from a presentation by Eneas, Bain Town's eminent historian, Saunders notes that "the people of Bain Town and Grant's Town were free men and never allowed anyone to forget that fact; they 'brooked no interference' from Up-town in any form." To historicize this militant attitude, Saunders also documents two rebellions in the nineteenth century that materialized in Grant's Town, "caused by outside interference." The outcome resulted in a magistrate's banning further interference by the police. Eventually known as the place where no one sleeps, Over-the-Hill developed into a tourist attraction for thrill seekers. Over-the-Hill produced a host of successful Junkanoos and future leaders—not only from Bain Town or Grant's Town but from Mason's Addition, Anderson Street, Market Street, Vesey Street, Hay Street, Fort Fincastle, McPherson Street, East Street, Meadow Street, Lewis Street, McCullough Corner, Chippingham, Nassau Street, King Street, Ross Corner, and other residential areas, where people had been condemned to live back o' town.[25]

Still, the seats of economic power, whether located on Front Street (in Bermuda) or Bay Street, incentivized the lower stratum to pivot to the center since, as symbolic sites for comprehensive change, these icons of capitalism are most germane to the stakeholders who oversee them as if they were sacred spaces. As a case in point, Bahamian Junkanoos fought an assortment of battles to tramp along Bay Street. Local cultural producer Arlene Ferguson contextualized the results best: "Within the context of her environment in every age, our people have manifested their spirit through Junkanoo, and have moved from the plantations to Bay Street in triumph. For two mornings each year, historic Bay Street becomes the site whereon we demonstrate our sovereignty of spirit, and celebrated the triumph of a proud heritage" (16). In the parlance of Junkanooers as well as the title of a popular recording, the paraders are "Gone ta Bay." Winston Saunders further describes the parade's evolution and spatial proclivities:

In times past, when Junkanooers wore sponge costumes, flour on their faces, threw firecrackers on each other, in the days of Jush the trumpeter, and Sweet Richard the dancer, this celebration was a spontaneous free-for-all. The rushin' was confined to Bay Street, and groups rushed opposite each other with the barest of costuming. A degree of sophistication was brought to bear on the parade, however, when the Masquerade Committee rule that those not fully costumed were prohibited from rushin'. Today, solid Junkanoo groups have been formed, and they work assiduously all year on Junkanoo designs to ensure the winning of prize money. This has had the effect of diluting somewhat the old spontaneity associated with everyone having a good street dance. Moreover, the cowbell sound has now become familiar with any Bahamian celebration, from welcoming heroes home to parading beauty queens through the streets of Nassau to creating the finale of a folklore show. (246)

Based on early maps, the downtown section dated back to 1788 along the waterfront, even then with Bay Street operating as Nassau's main boulevard (Craton and Saunders 195).

Bay Street officials regulated for centuries which fetes might gain access to this main artery, but negotiation patterns remain ambiguous.[26] Famed Junkanooer E. Clement Bethel laments: "At times the festival was viewed favorably by the government; at others, however, it was threatened with extinction. Whenever The Bahamas was prosperous and the people content, Junkanoo was accepted and even encouraged. When, on the other hand, the islands were beset with hardship, the parades were suppressed" (3). Literally and figuratively, Bay Street was for "identified" whites (Conchy Joes), and this merchant class held absolute power.[27] They even controlled the government to the extent to which they inhibited the raising of livestock just so they would profit from meat imported from Australia and New Zealand (Jenkins 123). To discourage competition from Chinese, Greek, Jewish, and Lebanese immigrants, the Immigrant Act of 1920 restricted all but first-class passengers from entering The Bahamas (Jenkins 214).

In other words, the Conchy Joes ruled with an ironclad absolutism, despite their own ignoble origin. The following quote explains their common birth: "I do not know whether the original inhabitants of this island, or those who succeeded the extermination of the pirates in 1718, were called Conchs; but there is a class of people, and many of the highest respectability, still distinguished by that name, which I suppose must have been derived from the employment of diving for conchs and for coral, from which they obtained subsistence; but I have often remarked, that those whose origin was traced back to them, appeared not to be very proud of the name or distinction" (Hart and Culmer 44). This group came to acquire great economic status as well as nicknames—the Bay Street Boys or, originally, the Bay Street Oligarchy—because these mercantile elites controlled Bay Street and the nation's wealth (Craton and Saunders 214). It is in this milieu that the ruling class known as "Conchy Joes" rose to power. In an interview with Olga Jenkins, resident Alfred Love contended: "A Conchy Joe is a Bahamian white. I guess you know your history. During your War of Independence, the Loyalists came. That's how the white people got in here. They came in through slavery. They were the slave masters and what not. Conchy Joe was in the dictionary some years ago" (Jenkins 75).[28] This merchant class exemplifies the spatialization of power with their exclusionary policies meant to restrict the presence of the black majority, triggering acts of economic, political, and cultural resistance.

Today, Bahamians project a more conciliatory narrative: one of solidarity, at least for the duration of the Junkanoo holiday performances. Accordingly, one informant insisted that Junkanoo was a Boxing Day festival in which all social classes and races engaged to "forget their differences and unite."[29] Another assertion recorded by Wood in 1991 was: "White, Black, rich and poor are in Junkanoo" (226). This insistence invokes a sense of organic nationalism, a wistful dream, while, in reality, colorism within major Junkanoo groups defies these pronouncements. Despite being reticent about the subject, a veteran Junkanooer, speaking only off the record, claimed "that middle-class people are flocking into Junkanoo now that it has become acceptable and are 'taking it over' and changing it" (Wood 226). In the past, white Junkanooers rushed while in disguise, possibly as acts of individual subversion, while others still racialized Junkanoo as "something only for Black, stupid people to do" (227). Storr quotes Glinton-Meicholas stating, "In this society, Junkanoo is the great leveler, where . . . the rich make merry with the poor, the magistrate dances with the felon he may later prosecute, and members of the Government make brief accord with parliamentarians in opposition" (302). A social caste divide still stereotypes two of the major groups, one known as "brown-skin" translated to mean pretty girls and the other still reduced to being "Black people from over-the hill."[30] The changes wrought by middle-class entrants principally amounted to contributing a visual aesthetic, leaving the aural production, or Junkanoo music, to the lower-class people from back o' town (Storr 232–33). Therefore, ambulating annually down Bay Street communicates more than a celebration of solidarity and even transcends notions of purely positive nostalgic memories and sentimentality (E. Bethel; Wisdom; Wood).[31]

St. Croix presents an opportunity to examine wealth inequalities between two cities on opposite coastlines: Frederiksted and Christiansted.[32] Frederiksted is the harbor town and Christiansted is the seat of island commerce. Frederiksted, on the west side of the island (historically called West End), is where the bulk of Africa-descended people reside, whereas Christiansted's population, on the northeastern shore, includes many mainland American immigrants. Ober viewed neither space as being "attractive close at hand" (324), while Bayley provides a more positive portrayal: "The sidewalks of Christiansted are still shaded with the arched galleries that front the merchants' buildings. Just walking around is a pleasure in this pretty town" (128). As for Frederiksted, where building structures predate Christiansted's, Bayley writes, "Instead of being rebuilt in stone, the town houses were constructed of less expensive wood. But in their own way these Victorian examples of ornamental lattice and band-saw work are handsome, too" (131).

Frederiksted requires some qualifying to acknowledge the "Fire Burn" of 1878 that resulted in its being rebuilt. One critical letter, published in the local newspaper on January 3, 1901, underscores all the pertinent tropes: "The Christmas and New Year Eves have been solemnized in West End [Frederiksted] by these entire nights hideous with tom-tom rattle and yelling. The dwellers in this town . . . could only lie helplessly awake till morning, forced to listen wide-eyed to an almost continuous roar of barbarous drumming and howling" (Nicholls, *Old-Time* 173). Nicholls expounds upon this letter, indicating that the celebrations' exuberance after the Fire Burn uprising on "the terrible night of 1st October 1878" earned Frederiksted the nickname Freedom City (173). That letter was an example of racialized spatialization, which even today underlies denigration of revelers as what the letter-writer called "satiated brute[s]."

Seemingly abandoned to ruin, many of Frederiksted's wooden edifices have now aged beyond repair. However, it is the lee for cruise ships, with a big pier built for lightering passengers to shore (Robinson 119). It is the harbor town, by default. The Christiansted harbor is ample but never dredged; therefore, with its open ocean way, cruise ships mostly dock briefly in Frederiksted, allowing passengers to disembark and to browse through waterfront shops, regaled by American jazz music, the iconic Mocko (Moko) Jumbies, and a host of vendors surrounding the pristine park gazebo near the Fort. Acknowledging a rivalry, *Islands Magazine* states: "Frederiksted natives claim they have better cooks, livelier politics and more important history, but Christiansted residents point to a pastel 18th-century streetscape with plentiful boutiques, art galleries and some nightlife" (Tappan 83). Since the island's transfer to the US, American immigrants, who are locally called "continentals," also transported racial tension. Others interpret the "Native/Continental divide," intersectionality, as one of social class because the Americans tend to be white and middle or upper class.[33]

As one might suspect, tales about these two cities and social class rivalries antedate the American presence. According to Varlack and Harrigan's *The Virgin Islands Story*, "There was also a dichotomy between the 'pretentious' townsfolk and the rest of the population who were usually and vulgarly referred to as 'country people' and 'cay people'" (105). The explanation continued:

> On the one hand, the usual color caste system propelled distinctions between "black" and "brown" that supported a bourgeois model of assimilation and social mobility. They achieved economically and formed a status group known variously as the "decent" people, "respectable" people, or the "elite." They lived in town, owned businesses, and held white-collar typed positions. Although not always highly educated or wealthy, they set the marker for "success." On the other hand, the "country" and the "cay" people constituted the working labor market.

As a matter of fact, by law, officials formalized residential apartheid in Christiansted, creating "Negro Quarters" (Rezende). The intent was to establish a "physical buffer, separating the rural plantation environment from the white commercial areas." Rather than segregation by custom, here the creation was by law. To complete the narrative, tellingly, *The Virgin Islands Story* resorts to rampant stereotypes, appealing to them as if authentically real: "maintaining the hazy, lazy, bolero tempo of the unsophisticated lives; loving and hating, fighting and quarrelling, sometimes even killing, marrying and dying—doing in fact all those things which human beings had been doing before the discovery and invention of government and law, of church or state" (Varlack and Harrigan 106). Inadvertently, this text acknowledges a communitarian outlook: "The cooperative efforts in the economic sphere were also social occasions."

Early on, the white newcomers to the island gained a significant advantage, unlike other immigrant groups. They advanced in accordance with the Conchy Joes of The Bahamas, except they were not native to the island.[34] An unpublished paper by Varlack and Harrigan describes the prevailing atmosphere:

> The appearance of expatriate white residents associated in one way or another with the growth of investment also created difficulties, introducing the classic pattern of association between social inequality and racial difference which portended a reversion to the social pattern of the early nineteenth century. Groups and factions which in effect, if not in intent, were socially exclusive with high visibility and conspicuous affluence (in relative terms, at least) represented an affront to local sentiment leading to the cry of a "return to slavery." While to some such rhetoric appeared intemperate, irrational, irresponsible, and purely destructive in character, the fact was indisputable that there were grounds for ill-will. The islanders had to deal with a subtle form of arrogance and responsible people talked about the creation of a society whose essential features would not differ greatly from those of Rhodesia as a distinct possibility. ("Social Change" 23)

By the 1960s, social inequality, racism, and economic exploitation along with rank impoverishment became quite ingrained.

As a recent development, quarterly Jump Ups occur in Christiansted, sponsored by the Christiansted Restaurant and Retailers Association (CRRA), intended to be a unifying gesture for all islanders. Billed as a "cultural street party," Mocko Jumbies (stilt walkers) oblige their iconic function to thrill white hotel guests, while the sound of steel pan music infuses the night air. The CRRA's website says that it is "a non-profit organization comprised of Christiansted merchants, restaurateurs, and business persons concerned with the safety, security and economic vitality of Christiansted town proper."[35] Given the CRRA's mission, one might conjecture the ghettoization of cruise ship passengers (by social class). They, too, have been mainly relegated to "the back o' town," due to its harbor site. However, on Boxing Day, with its nightly grand noise, the annual Crucian Festival Village convenes for nearly two weeks significantly devoid of a touristy presence. The Crucian Christmas Festival (CCF) masks many tensions that seethe underneath year-round.

Until 2002, Christiansted alternated with Frederiksted in hosting the annual CCF. After Christiansted hosted events in 2002, in keeping with established custom, Frederiksted presented the parade and activities the next year. Ostensibly, in 2004, the rationale for ending the reciprocity between cities was due to construction work on a recreation center and the renovation of Christiansted's

Times Square. Thereafter, Frederiksted became the default site for all subsequent festivities. Christiansted, with its high-end residential sections, had long complained about the loud music and voices traveling "up the hill."[36] Such sentiments intimated that the holiday parades function better on Frederiksted's narrower streets. Then, the treasurer of the CCF committee told the local paper that "Frederiksted has the optimum chances to bring the most revenue during the festival." Nicks further elaborated, "'We're in the red.' We are trying to make money."[37] Nonetheless, metaphorically speaking, given the economic disposition of attendees, nightly noise factors, and youthful demographics, the fiscal focus abetted social class, racial, and cultural discrimination. There appears to be something disingenuous about the rationales presented for the deterritorialization of the Christiansted CCF.

For the past ten years, the pre-Lenten Mardi Croix, organized by expatriate Louisianans, can be construed as another sanitizing approach to the CCF. At best, the organizers bowdlerize it by attempting to reproduce Carnival, based more on elite social class allegiances than traditionality and the spirit of the carnivalesque.[38] Given the island's Americanization, on the one hand, it is not far-fetched to condemn the move based on a preexisting white spatial imaginary and a commercialized impetus. In St. Kitts, on the other hand, its aficionados readily recognize that Boxing Day is Carnival at Christmastime. Advertised to begin at 4 a.m., J'ouvert begins freely in total darkness along multiple streets in Basseterre; but unlike elsewhere, on Boxing Day, the street scene supports few passive observers. The sun rises comparatively early in easterly St. Kitts, and it is this celestial force that signals festive time in company with a black spatial imaginary. The mobile sound trucks amble through the dark until the narrow hamlet's streets (the real Carnival stage) can hardly sustain the frolicking multitudes.

In what is considered a sibling rivalry, the two-island federation St. Kitts and Nevis engages in a half-century-old reciprocal exchange of festivities. Interestingly, Christmas and Boxing Day are "now celebrated more in St. Kitts. There, few except traders and churchgoers even *mention* Christmas. It is CARNIVAL time" (R. Williams 14). Whereas Nevisians host the annual Emancipation Day celebration, "Here in Nevis words like 'Culturama' and 'Carnival' were unknown in those days" and are "now part of Culturama where little mention is made of the abolition of slavery."[39] Actually, St. Kitts and Nevis residents consider their islands to be Ground Zero as relates to the festival arts, too. Historically reliant on transnational cultural flows, "Masquerades are indigenous to St. Kitts-Nevis. Wherever they appear throughout the Caribbean region, their roots could be traced to these islands."

Comprising St. Kitts's back o' town of the nine administrative parishes, St. Anne contains its capital, Sandy Point town, which is the second largest city but in the smallest parish. The origin of the Mocko Jumbie tradition is associated with this town, having a large ancestral Yoruba constituency (Lee). Also contributing to the festal year, the town is known for its Easterama during the Lenten season. The site of Brimstone Hill, Sylvester's Masquerade supplies another back o' town feature. Masqueraders do not descend for J'ouvert but offer an iconic presence on Christmas Day to entertain tourists visiting the island and during holiday parades. Therefore, these residents "have a profound appreciation of the seasonality" of their practices (Birth 215). In the ACW, preparation for festive time in December spans a period of at least two months, beginning with Guy Fawkes Day.

In Bermuda's history, enslaved persons provided just cause for slaveholders to fear them. Zuill's *The Story of Bermuda and Her People* notes that "Gombeys date back to at least the mid-eighteenth century, as is shown by the banning of their festivities after the trouble of 1761" (220). In accordance with past rebellious actions, unresolved political tensions continue to manifest symbolically through public displays of physical survival, purposeful visibility, and a refusal to be silenced or to stay in place. While not waging political warfare, the masses contest colonial discourse by strategically allocating time and space for a subject people, through the production of cultural knowledge and the exercise of antithetical power to persevere. Perhaps speaking for many in the ACW, one individual described the carnivalizing of Boxing Day and other fetes, which provide a world of self-actualization for the otherwise dispossessed:

we talkin' 'bout the people who live in these li'l clapboard houses, never had nothin' but Junkanoo, and that's what they's thrive off comin' Christmas 'cause they never, they'n know nothin' 'bout no Santa Claus and Christmas gifts. Just, that's me. I never knew 'bout no Santa Claus and Christmas gift growin' up in Kemp Road. Junkanoo was it. That's the reason why I'm so hook on it. I don't even go Christmas shopping. (qtd. in Wood 237)

By intentionality and design, then, these aesthetic modes serve as a means of guaranteeing mental health and physical survival to overcome the many obstacles that otherwise demean one's spirit. Accordingly, Boxing Day fetes serve incisively as cultural productions celebrating the outcome of political events that eventually led to independence and Black rule (Wisdom 7). They signify, foremost, that it is a time for a carnivalesque celebration, Carnival time.

From Carnivalesque to Ritualesque

I conclude with reflections and projections based on an accumulation of rel-evant data to produce an additional outpouring rather than a final summa-tion. I am intrigued by folklorist Jack Santino's argument problematizing the ritualesque within the carnivalesque ("Ritualesque"). While his ethnographic examples are of parades and political demonstrations intended "to effect social change," still his exploration compares well with the ACW's intra-island ten-sion regarding questions of marketization, national identity, and cultural reten-tion. As island communities fragment, some due to a push toward assimilation and others due to the pull of emigration, practitioners may no longer seek just the carnivalesque psychic release but the heuristic value of symbolic action, directed toward the enculturation of their youth in the face of continued mar-ginalization. As defined by Edward Muir, "ritual then is basically a social activity that is repetitive, standardized, a model or a mirror, and its meaning is inher-ently ambiguous" (6). Muir also interprets ritual to be dangerous because of the tendency to manipulate its meaning. In this instance, cultural tourism becomes the mechanism that imposes a threatening hermeneutics, relative to fear of the standardization of the festival art.

"Ritualized habits" is Kinser's term for New Orleans Black Indian groups' preparations for Mardi Gras (159). What stabilizes these performance commu-nities is a "we relationship" that incorporates multitasking as a quotidian part of their social life (Wood 117). Boxing Day festive gatherings function as commu-nity rituals, with each organized group of Gombeys or masqueraders devoted to a localized cultural identity, in addition to a national one.[1] Furthermore, in the process of playing mas, they affect transnational and cisgendered identities. The Gombeys, like the Mardi Gras Black Indians and the Garifuna, exhibit fixed disguises, whereas Bahamian Junkanooers display greater fluidity due to the-matics. Regarding Boxing Day, especially on J'ouvert morning, the spirit of the carnivalesque rules the mass crowd: "J'ouvert is about abandon, physicality and fear, a deliberately hellish counterpoint to pretty mas" (Mason 9). Because of the extended preparation required for each group's enactment, ritualized habits pertain more to the troupes' need to display virtuosity and creativity. *Trinidad Carnival's* editors Green and Scher specify: "Whatever the Carnivals may be in their many incarnations, they are the products of unique histories, manifestations of social tensions, barometers of cultural change, and crucibles for creating, discovering, and asserting identities" (9). Boxing Day fetes contain all of these ritualized elements indicative of "an all-year-round statement of identity" (Mason 7).

Although public display events on Boxing Day are generally execrated in conjunction with risqué carnivalesque behavior, constitutive violence, and social conflict, Santino helps to unpack the conflation needed to construct a paradoxical assessment. His study ritualizes protest movements as symbolic and instrumental. As a calendrical rite, Boxing Day festivities reconcile the "expressive symbolic acts" identified with the carnivalesque through "instrumental symbolic actions" pervasive in the ritualesque (Santino, "Ritualesque" 11). Martinez's "ritualism" regarding the Black Indians of New Orleans supports his contention that, under oppression, members of that group project a simulacrum that displays surface conformity with the hegemon while never relinquishing "their sacred beliefs and cherished traditions" (22). For many, the perpetuation and preservation of Gombeys, Junkanoos, and J'ouvert fulfill time-honored practices conducive to exhibiting cultural politics with the possibility for social change. In an instance of "Crowley's Law," the carnivalesque blends festive action with serious purpose for the lower classes "(and darker the skin)," guaranteeing the public display event is a political act beyond just a cultural one ("Sacred" 225).

In Joseph Adjaye's construction of rituals as an enduring aspect of African cultural landscapes, he reveals how Ghanaians derived from them the means to conceptualize and change their present and shape their future (*Boundaries*). In other words, social rituals help individuals escape the boundaries of self by promoting a sense of collective purpose and agency. In the ACW, the pervasive engagement of young people (as participants and spectators) cultivates a durable sociocultural affirmation and respect for oppositional aspects that do not adhere to mainstream tenets.[2] One spectator, who asked not to be named, insisted to me, "This is the Bermudian spirit. This is who we are. It's important that we keep this, pass it on to our children, because it's a unique part of our culture, a beautiful part of our culture." The celebrants participate in a form of social mnemonics enacted through constantly repeating festal rituals, politicizing Boxing Day by enculturating their children to pass on esoteric, shared knowledge, so that they might be compelled to preserve these cultural productions, ensuring continuity and the perpetuation of their commitment.[3]

Undoubtedly, through the preservation of Boxing Day and its traditions, practitioners and, to an extent, governmental officials alike partake in ritualizing the future. The Gombeys and the Garifuna often socialize their children to perform when toddlers. Elsewhere in the ACW, local schools and other cultural organizations participate in organizing children's parades, usually occurring prior to Boxing Day or New Year's Day. In The Bahamas, the Junior Junkanoo Parade is the chief program intended to conserve cultural heritage in both public and private schools.[4] Junkanooers believe that just as every child living on the island should learn to swim, children also need to know about their culture through Junkanoo. Besides boosting school spirit and self-pride, these events for children serve as both educational tools and apprenticeships. Their stated objective is "to assist students in research, planning, organizing, critical thinking, problem solving and role playing activities and stimulate the development of creativity."[5] In 1987, transculturalism by way of Trinidad shaped this development when members of the National Junkanoo Committee and other representatives first held its Kiddies Carnival. Having gone through this rite of passage, these young people, by the time they are teens, are committed performers, rushin' in the Senior Junkanoo Parade as musicians and dancers.

Although pre-Lenten Carnivals are well known globally, Boxing Day is less familiar outside the Commonwealth of Nations, perhaps because it receives less media attention and corporate support. Mummers in Philadelphia and Mardi Gras receive more international acclaim than the ritualized Boxing Day festivities in the AWC. While not under immediate threat, those Boxing Day events might suffer the same fate of Jamaica's—shifting to the pre-Lenten carnivalesque model in uniformity with highly affective transnational trends. For instance, in Wiregrass Country (a little-known southern US region), the Texan Juneteenth Emancipation Day celebration is now overdetermined in many locales instead of the communities' own historical, long-honored Twentieth of May tradition, which was the day freedom papers were delivered in their region (McGregory 2011). By so doing, Wiregrass African Americans lose sight of something of value unique to them in recognition of their own geopolitical diversity. Addressing the transnational flow of ideas, this chapter engages particular ritual moments in the ACW and the reciprocal support networks that generate tropological revision along with the mediation of cultural tourism.

Previous scholars have tended to enjoin a sacred connectivity between the origin of these end-of-the-year masquerades and African religious rites in the ACW. Perhaps Kenneth Bilby's discursive analysis should have the final word in debates over this sacred-secular dichotomy ("Surviving"). He uses diachronic and synchronic research methodologies to develop an etic interpretation, claiming that an irrefutable religious/spiritual foundation informs today's cultural production (216). I argue that dualistic modes of thinking should be rejected in order to destabilize interpretations of present-day cultural holidays and tourism and reveal their complexities. To do so requires an interpretation of ritualized acts, their context, and their tenacity, thus assessing the inherent power of the ritualesque to mediate a marketization move. Photographer Phyllis Galembo's anthropological posture seemingly verifies this argument. In an interview with the *Huffington Post*, she expressed an interest in affirming "how creative people are. I'm not talking about the costumes that come out of a box set here, but the things people make. It's wonderful to watch them put their personal touches on it."[6] In the same vein, cultural creativity applies to the refined negotiation between revitalization and capitalized misappropriation.

Prior scholars have also predicted a reduction in ritual density in contemporary life.[7] However, ritual is the only way to describe the repetitive and stylized nature of cultural productivity that occurs with cyclical regularity throughout the African diaspora, as made manifest in conformity with long-held calendrical proceedings. As a matter of fact, Errol Hill acknowledged that Canboulay was the "ritual beginning" of Carnival (*Trinidadian* 23–31). On November 5, Guy Fawkes Day is a signature holiday marking the commencement of countless politicized activities along with heralding the ritualesque start of preparations for Boxing Day. In the British overseas territory of Bermuda, on Guy Fawkes Day, no matter what the weather conditions, firework parties attract large crowds. It also traditionally alerted Gombey troupes, Junkanooers, and Mas camps to consolidate plans and begin rehearsing, so that their organization will be ready to entertain the masses. Regarding the considerable preparation for stages of ritualized play, James Fernandez noted, "There is planfulness in this playfulness" (22). In Nassau, the season begins in June for those constructing the larger costume pieces, with the musicians beginning to practice in September (Wood 36–37). Accordingly, ritual is a strategic form of cultural practice, which Gikandi defines as ritual rebellion, "a mode of resistance against the order of enslavement and the ideologies that informed it, including aesthetic ones" (255). Green and Scher suggest that indefinability is as an enduring factor of Carnival festivities everywhere, "to codify [an aversion to any exertion] once and for all" (9–10). Behind the scenes throughout the ACW, such ritual habits endure outside the gaze of the cultural tourism industrial complex.

To further contextualize these events, Craton and Saunders's *Islanders in the Stream* describes the delights of island life in Nassau in the nineteenth century:

> The even tenor of daily life was punctuated by the weekly parades at church, the
> arrival of boats with mail and tourists, and (as since slavery days) the annual cel-
> ebrations of the monarch's birthday, Guy Fawkes Day (celebrating at a great remove
> the preservation of James I from the Gunpowder Plot of 1605), the official opening
> of Parliament, and the Christmas and New Year's Junkanoo. Since 1834 had been

added to these the commemoration of Emancipation Day on August 1, including downtown parades by the friendly societies, a service and sermon. (83)

Since nineteenth-century middle-class Americans distrusted leisure, the first American tourists to the Caribbean tended to be elite, seeking health and pleasure (Aron 16). Nonetheless, no matter the social class, Americans would equate the revelry of local islanders with racialized hijinks and not forms of genuine artistic expression. By the 1930s, the surge in white tourism resulted in American-style apartheid segregating Black Bahamians from sites frequented by these visitors except as servants; even musicians were denied the ability to work in hotels (Jenkins 219).

In the ACW, the tourist season usually starts in mid-December and runs through Easter. Therefore, during the low season (summer months), each locale vies to attract tourists, especially from cruise ships. Each markets its national treasures to assist in the "selling" of their ports and airports without "selling out." In order to conduct a comparative analysis of the ACW's Boxing Day fetes with representations of their intangible cultural heritage outside of the peak tourist season, I returned to Bermuda twice (May 2009 and 2010) to observe its Bermuda Day Parade, which coincided with the US Memorial Day holiday and was when May 24th (Queen Victoria's birthday) occurs on the weekend. In addition, I visited Nassau twice to witness its Independence Day Rush on July 10 and then again to observe what was billed as the Summer Junkanoo Festival. To attract tourists, St. Croix's Christiansted implemented quarterly Jump Ups, whereas its "archrival" (Frederiksted) highlights its Sunset Jazz: Third Friday of each month. St. Kitts's sibling and rival Nevis celebrates Culturama in conjunction with Emancipation Day in August. Because the Garifuna's Settlement Day festivities (to commemorate its founding) happens in September, this site is the only one where I did not make another site visit.

The cultural tourism impetus shapes the calendar year in these islands. Without any viable alternative for economic development, they attempt to lure visitors for seasonal, national, and historical events. Yet, generally, as they occur during broad daylight, off-peak public display events specific to Boxing Day are decontextualized. Unlike the pre-Lenten Carnivals, for the most part, the AWC fetes are not the key attraction that the cultural purveyors robustly promote, except as glossy iconography to make the areas seem more exotic. Therefore, tourist bureaus schedule a scattering of Gombey troupes for public appearances as photo opportunities with the incentive of generating some revenue from passersby. For instance, up until his death in 2019, the legendary Junkanooer John "Chippie" Chipman, with his well-worn goatskin drum and straw hat, continued to perform at the Cruise Port as tourists disembarked in Nassau; and even today, the Mocko Jumbies dance at the quarterly Jump Ups in St. Croix,

and masqueraders compete for tourist dollars near the port in Basseterre. I concur with Scher's assessment that the "growing importance of culture makes the
host society in a tourist exchange a sort of perpetual performance site" ("Power"
161). Moreover, each atoll showcases the more respectable steelpan as the music
of choice at airports, the more exclusive resorts, and casinos, failing to show its
island's musical diversity.

    With roots in the eighteenth- and nineteenth-century Grand Tour, in which
aristocrats travelled to European destinations to experience high culture, cultural tourism in the Caribbean arose to promote leisure recreation and as a
human developmental tool. Writing in 1919, Verrill historicizes how "A dozen
years ago Bermuda was scarcely known to Americans at large, and only the fortunate few who had learned the secrets of is charms visited its shore. But once
the islands were discovered by the American public its rise to popularity and
fame was swift" (12). In 2015, Bermuda emerged as one of the ten most prosperous states in the world (Graci and Dodds 35), resulting in an enviably high standard of living. Bermuda owes its early surge in American tourism to its racial
segregation, too.[8] US segregation policies meant that African American tourists
in Bermuda were denied hotel accommodations, and they were given the nickname "longtails" by the Black Bermudians who housed them.[9] Moreover, due to
their migratory pattern, Bermuda's longtail birds are harbingers of spring and
are as iconic as the Gombeys.

    Tourism and cultural identity are inextricably linked, requiring a fine nego-
tiation between cultural producers and island tourist bureaucrats. While the
various manifestations of Carnival on Boxing Day in the ACW have always
entailed corporate sponsorship, television rights, and marketing schemes, those
festivities remain essentially local events, carried out by and for the enjoyment
of residents, with only some outside observers. However, ACW countries are
increasingly using elements of local culture as means to attract and generate
money from tourists. In pursuit of tourism, Bermudians enlist multiple ploys
to attract visitors, chiefly from docked cruise ships. For instance, Bermudian
tourism chiefly depends on optimal product placement to capitalize on the
intrinsic value of the Gombeys. Annually in September, the already-ritualized
annual Gombey Festival aspires not only to serve as cultural performances,
but to express an appreciation for the art form's longevity, experienced as col-
lectivized embodied memory. Hosted by the Department of Community and
Cultural Affairs (DCCA) recently, the festival is held at a site that may still be
in flux. Brimming with esoteric meaning, the annual Gombey Festival is not
the usual tourist attraction, nor were many visitors in evidence. Yet the DCCA
insists on the cultural production occurring at the Bermuda Botanical Garden
instead of the stadium for greater exposure to "our folk art tradition and cultural heritage."[10] Additionally, two evenings are being alloted for other extrane-

ous events, including a symposium to discuss the Gombeys' diasporic linkages. Also, rebranded, it is currently highlighted as the "International Gombey Festival Showcase!"

In May 2010, I traveled again to document another annual celebration, the Bermuda Day Holiday, which coincided with another benchmark—the island's four hundredth anniversary.[11] Since Bermuda remains a British territory, Bermuda Day on May 24 (formerly Empire Day, Victoria Day, Commonwealth Day, and Heritage Day) is a national holiday with a now highly diversified parade. In furtherance of the theater of the street, the parade historically perambulated from bleacher seating downtown on Front Street through the center of commerce before proceeding to the back o' town to celebrate. Since this parade's current purpose is to negotiate a privileged site for its diverse population, historically, the presence of Gombeys is minimized. Of late, tensions flared due to the addition of the Soca Passion Truck at the end of the procession, which caused a musical sensation when a throng of gyrating spectators created a spontaneous road march. This inclusion dismayed traditionalists, who contest the carnivalization of Bermudian traditions that contrast with their own perceived regimen of values. The Soca DJ, Jason R. Sukdeo (aka D'General), said, "Tradition has to start somewhere."[12] He also led the charge to transition the Bermuda Day festivities to a three-day weekend beginning on Friday instead of another recent move to Mondays. Commencing in June 2015, three Caribbean organizations united to create an innovative new ritualized event, named the Bermuda Heroes Weekend. The president of the West Indies Association, Chandrae Persad, said, "We are all trying to promote the carnival-type atmosphere here in Bermuda."

Of course, as part of the Caribbean cultural flow that characterizes the region, Bermudians are familiar with Carnival, and many go to the Carnival in Trinidad, the Crop Over in Barbados, and events like Reggae SunFest in Jamaica. However, such a Carnival in Bermuda had yet to happen. Now, a J'ouvert Celebration of Our Heroes takes place annually from 3 a.m. until 8 a.m. to watch the sun rise, as participants dutifully salute Bermuda's local leaders who inspire the nation. In this way, the organizers of J'ouvert managed to subvert the island traditionalists who had, in accordance with Santino's ritualesque theory, asserted "popular agency and challenge[d] the normative power structure" ("Ritualesque" 22). In carnivalizing an ontological space of their own, the new Bermudian immigrants ironically superimpose all of the Boxing Day tropes—total darkness, phenomenon timing, and sonorous soca party music—onto their event, so unlike the Gombeys.

By the late 1980s, The Bahamas had cornered the cruise ship market in the Caribbean, ranking fourth globally in total cruise bed nights (Cleare 232). To capitalize on the cultural tourism market, the focus shifted to entice Bahamian visiting friends and relatives (VFR). VFR tourists already compose the bulk of the Christmas vacation festivalgoers. Returning transnationals bring with them a sense of nostalgia; and each Junkanoo parade attracted approximately fifty thousand spectators—no small feat for an island with a population of about three hundred thousand.[13] Unlike the Bermuda Tourist Authority, Bahamas Ministry of Tourism's considerable attempts to boost tourism via Junkanoo culture have proven to be ephemeral. Many of these initiatives—National Junkanoo Museum, Junkanoo Summers, etc.—originated with the people who petitioned online for community-based support.[14] Bilby details how the secularization of Junkanoo contributed to its marketization, becoming "One of the main tourist attractions of Bahamas and is by far the most commercialized of the surviving variants of Jankunu" ("Surviving" 188). Junkanoo is stigmatized as commodified and secularized since "the close links with tourism, the cooptation by the state and the decreasing grassroots control characterizing the contemporary tradition all work against a sense of sacredness" (190). Equating regulation with retrograde limitation overdetermines governmental control. In reality, the official efforts to use it for cultural tourism have failed since typical travelers and cruise ship passengers are oblivious to it.

The much-extolled National Junkanoo Museum (also called Junkanoo Expo) at the cruise ship port of call, Prince George Wharf, is already defunct. Rather than intercede in the ritual "cycle of renewal and destruction," the museum reproduced it by annually discarding the old to make room for the latest champion pieces (K. Thompson, "Destroying" 502). Selah Portier started an online petition with the primary rationale printed in bold: "Our Authentic Bahamian **culture** is good enough to market on an international scale." Such measures intend to safeguard living cultural traditions, practices, and expressions. Intending to expose travelers to the Junkanoo tradition by displaying a curated collection of the usually discarded costumes of the most memorable annual Boxing Day winners, the effort now has only a few discarded artifacts to suggest the overreach of this endeavor.[15]

Ressa Mackey's thesis, "All That Glitters Is Not Junkanoo," is helpful in understanding the objectification of the festal arts through the lens of identity politics, nationalism, and the tourism industry. The first implication arises from the fact that the creation of the museum, for the sake of tourism, triggered the demise of a historic public market whose primary consumers were local Bahamians. In this case, it burned down in 2001 and newly reopened on Bay Street in 2011. Although economic necessity superseded its historical preservation on site, at least it maintains an indigenized mode regarding its strawmaking tradition without completely sanitizing local entrepreneurship. Another argument made by Mackey is that nostalgia also served as the impetus for this ingress into the exhibitionary genre. To support her theorizing, she writes, "the Bahamians are nostalgic for certain types of costumes and festival practices. I define nostalgia as a yearning for lost patterns of everyday life and the invention of a romanticized version of what can never be regained or recreated" (8). She indicts local adherents as being "nostalgic for the 'authentic' crépe-paper costumes of the past since these particular types of costumes allegedly signify a 'purer' and 'simpler' period in Junkanoos history" (8). However, the entire intentionality and design actually were the opposite: through a transmission of surrogation, it offers more of a pastiche or mashup of newer designs along with the old.

Finally, Mackey's thesis falsely interprets the root cause of this supposed nostalgic sentiment toward the "commodification of Junkanoo because it constitutes a significant break from the past that threatens the cultural integrity of their community." For example, she denigrates Junkanoos for refusing, in 1989, to redirect the processional away from Bay Street to the Sports Centre to oblige the large assemblage of spectators and performers for their safety and to become more lucrative by attracting greater tourist attention (3–4).[16] Reportedly, the Saxon Superstars and the Valley Boys rallied to the chant "Bay Street forever! Sports Centre never!" The critique negates the symbolic aspects of Junkanoo as a representation of hard-fought battles not to glorify the past but to retain a strategic coping mechanism. The Junkanoo community is suspicious of and resents a turn by the tourism industry to reify a transnational carnivalesque festival and seemingly nullify the historic, indigenous arts of The Bahamas. For now, the cultural tourism agenda acquiesces to the Junkanoo community in fulfillment of promoting greater international understanding so that tourists "experience this authentic celebration of national pride."[17] In this case, nostalgia harnesses the past to accummulate capital and to create hope for the future.

In a move on behalf of its own cultural tourism aspirations, Crucians indigenize quarterly Jump Ups and a monthly jazz concert. In homage to being a US possession, its enthusiasm for jazz is rationalized to countermand the prevalence of jazz festivals generally as a globalized phenomenon.[18] Likewise, the Frederiksted Economic Development Association (FEDA) feels heavily scrutinized for introducing Sunset Jazz by its harbor. Local critics of Sunset Jazz, like those who deride Carnival in Bermuda and The Bahamas, reject the emphasis on a musical import deemed external to Crucian culture, although its Adult Parade is indubitably influenced by Trinidad's Carnival. FEDA decided to routinely host a concert with a roster of local and international jazz artists. Jazz also appealed to the island's diverse communities, especially Latin American music fans. FEDA has since diversified even more by featuring local artists who play Quelbe Jazz Fusion, the Sounds of Motown, and the Big Band Era. As a result, Ross proclaimed Frederiksted as the cultural trendsetter, spreading calypso, jazz, and Latin music across the island. Predictably, given the island's dynamics, recently Christiansted introduced a monthly jazz concert, too. Whereas Christiansted's tourist efforts do attract tourists and assist its own economic development, Frederiksted may not be as fortunate since it is dependent on the cruise ship industry, and only a few ships dock at the port overnight.

Predominantly Black, Frederiksted's fate depends on ritualizing and mainstreaming, against the odds, its entry in the cultural tourism marketplace. VFR seeking ritualesque/carnivalesque moments over the long Christmas–Boxing Day holiday participate in a form of reciprocity. The T-shirts residents regularly sport often tell the story as they promote the Carnival of other islands, and many of these do not occur during the pre-Lenten season but take other springtime weekends for their fetes. For instance, St. Thomas (another US Virgin Island) ritualized its Carnival during an annual stretch in April. St. Croix's Department of Tourism readily promotes its CCF with advertising campaigns in east coast African American and Caribbean newspapers. These cultural exchanges depend on reciprocity, with each cultural production staking out calender dates for Carnival time usually with VFR.

Regarding St. Kitts and Nevis, reciprocity is the hallmark of these two linked islands' ritualized, festival moments: J'ouvert and Culturama, with each occurring at the same time each year. Revelers travel roundtrip by regularly scheduled ferries and even freight ships with standing-room only.[19] The long-standing cultural exchange between these twin island-nations demonstrates a nuclear familial relationship, whereas the other paired islands, Trinidad and Tobago, exhibit more of an extended family—a dynamic of city and country cousins with distinct ways of life. Commitment to the same Carnival pre-Lenten season limits any transnational ritualized festival interaction. Therefore, St. Kitts and Nevis engage in long-standing temporal arts that consume them both and provide greater continuity for VFR homecomings, a form of niche tourism. Nonetheless, as often with conjoined twins, Nevisians periodically strive to separate from St. Kitts.

Belize is known for its ecotourism, and horse racing is another ritualized Boxing Day tradition for its residents. Boxing Day traditions in Belize are not likely to be compromised by cultural tourism; sustainability turns more in the direction of ecotourism.[20] Besides the Boxing Day *Charikanari* in Dangriga, celebrants in Burrell Boom Village near the one-time capital Belize City engage in traditionalized horse races sponsored by the National Horse Racing Association.[21] A Kriol (creole) community, Burrell Boom is named after a Scottish lumberjack who built a log boom there in the 1700s to create a barrier to collect the floating logs. In keeping with the festival cycle of Boxing Day and New Year's Day events to come and in the more English tradition of Christmas sports' being synonymous with many sports, this village has an established history of horse racing dating back to the 1920s. Locals first gathered to race little bush ponies, drink, gamble, and boisterously cheer on the jockeys. As with the Florida Shooting Match, this sport generates income for the community and entertainment for the local attendees.

To attend the Shooting Match in Tallahassee, many adherents arrive from as far away as Hartford, Connecticut, and Washington, DC, sometimes accompanying friends home for a family reunion. Now around the city, I often hear people lament that they are no longer attending and miss the drums. In immense and lesser ways, all are beneficiaries; the Henry family is no longer just consumers but the sellers of their own goods and services, nor are they mere sufferers from the powers of the "global gaze." For once, they fit within the cultural borders of their own choosing, often while sharing their marginality with those from elsewhere, along with those who retain stark remembrances of not only the site but especially the convivial noise. Cross-culturally, the Yule season offers a time for visiting and parties. As befits transnational villagers, displaced Tallahasseeans also ritually return. Virginia Henry Barnes told me, "Whosoever was living in this town and left town and came back during the Christmas, they made sure that they go to George Henry's place on the 26th day of December. And it was just a meeting place, or a gathering place, and they had fun all the time." While appearing serendipitous, this seasonal festive gathering conforms structurally to Boxing Day celebrations in the ACW. It offers another kind of site, "nostalgic tourism," for those returnees seeking to relive personal past experiences (Russell 104).

Indeed, it is any perceived threat to their cultural inheritance that needs safeguarding and should not be simplified as sheer nostalgia for the past.[22] Therefore, I concur with Roger Abrahams that, "For those groups who have been relegated to the margins and whose memories of the past are saturated with the pain of displacement, exclusion, and oppression, the performance of tradition in the service of national belonging is potentially transformative, liberating, and even redemptive" (*Everyday* 147). Dialectically speaking, locals view their living cultural traditions as an industry, but not just for the sake of commodification but for each consummated ritualized moment, unleashing a cyclical spirit that lasts year-round. Accordingly, "The future needs the mas. When everybody is so passive in front of a computer screen or television screen or a movie screen looking at somebody else doing the stuff, you need people to get together to take the road. The greatest thrill to any artist is to affect and profoundly move other people" (Minshall, "Masman" 330). Given the mounting concerns impacting their ritual masquerade and festival moments, tradition bearers socialize their young to maintain their intangible heritage themselves. Boxing Day fetes are the anchor, ever vigilant against all threats to its mooring, self-imposing both continuity and change.

ACKNOWLEDGMENTS

This book took a long time to write and, given its historical and geographic reach, depended on the expertise of some amazing strangers. In July 2002, by serendipity, in a random conversation with a local Tallahasseean, I mentioned that I teach folklore at Florida State University. I will never know why he teasingly said, "I bet you might like to hear some drumming." Instead of being straightforward, he told me to wait until December 26 and then to drive over to what was then called Dave's Blues Club. Not even knowing the assigned hour, I arrived after noon. Instead of drumming, I encountered a cluster of men with shotguns setting up targets for a shooting match. Soon, others began to arrive, including a few elders I recognized from Greater Mount Pleasant Church, a few people I'd met at the Shriner's Club, and Wilbur Barnes. Barnes had a video camera and lived on the compound as a descendant of the family who arranged the first match circa 1911. He spent most of the day escorting me around and introducing me to people. Once the event gained momentum, the drumming shocked me because I'd only read about this type of fife and drum music and had no idea of its existence in the region. I probably was not the only one because the next year a vanload of African hand drummers and dancers showed up, creating an interesting dynamic from an ethnographic perspective.

Two of the foundational bass and snare drum musicians, Otis and Hunter Hill, were not strangers for long, assisting with research for my monograph *Downhome Gospel*. Their family also are landowners and have hosted a large annual Twentieth of May Emancipation Day celebration for generations. It was not until I developed a curiosity, for informational purposes, about Boxing Day that I noted an absence of publications on the subject. Once I located studies about the cultural holiday in the Caribbean, I viewed illustrations with the same military-style drums. Hooked after also receiving an assortment of VHS tapes from Wilbur Barnes, I started conducting formal interviews with Virginia Barnes, Henry Barnes, and the Hill brothers. This book's title I attribute to Glen Hurd; she was one of my "nontraditional" undergraduate students from Spanish Town, Jamaica. As soon as I mentioned Boxing Day, she proclaimed, "It's one grand noise!" I then committed to this study; and while on a sabbatical,

I travelled to Jamaica in 2003, expecting to write an article about the experience. While in Montego Bay, Ocho Rios, or the Blue Mountains, I anticipated that merely saying "Jonkonnu" to others would cause them to respond with enthusiasm, but I departed unfulfilled. With my appetite whetted nevertheless, I ultimately identified the appropriate Caribbean locales and developed a strategic ethnographic strategy for a larger study. Travel for the initial phase of the research was made possible by FSU's Department of English RACA fund. Further study and travel expenses were supported by a university-funded Summer COFRS grant and eventually another sabbatical.

I am also indebted to many others, including the staff at the Library of Congress, University of Miami, University of Florida, Florida Atlantic University, and Florida International University. Many thanks also go to librarians in The Bahamas Winifred Murphy and Dorcus Bowler; University of the Virgin Islands librarian Judith Rogers; St. Kitts's St. Christopher Heritage Society at the St. Kitts National Museum's Grace Challenger-Bird and Althea Spencer; and staff members at Dangriga's Gulisi Garifuna Museum. Folklorist Jan Rosenberg read an early version of parts of this book and gave me sound advice. While serving for years on the Florida Folklife Council, I found that fellow members provided rare opportunities to interface with others in the discipline: these included Peggy Bulger, Annette Fromm, Jose Fernandez, Gene Crook, Natalie Underberg-Goode, Amanda Hardeman, Tina Bucuvalas, and Teresa Hollingsworth. Camaraderie with another Caribbeanist in my department, Candace Ward, provided me with books and insights along the way. Other friends who are like family to me—Delia Poey, Virgil Suarez, Donna Marie Nudd, Terry Galloway, Carol Batker, and William Rollins—provided me succor. A core of graduate students enrolled in my African diaspora classes were supportive of my research: Lisa Griffin, Aron Myers, Alex Brickler, Cocoa Williams, Esther Spencer, Yolanda Franklin, Misha Rai, Oluwafunke Ogunye Olaosebikan, and many others over the years.

In the early stage of my career and until now, Craig Gill, director of the University Press of Mississippi, must as always be thanked for his patience. The careful, sustained, and substantive reading by anonymous readers immensely enriched this book. Also at the University Press of Mississippi, acquisitions editor Katie Keene nurtured the book through a long process, and I thank her for her professionalism. Lisa McMurty assisted in detecting many glitches in the manuscript, especially pertaining to complicated copyright issues. And in the final stages, Lynn Whittaker proved invaluable, for copyediting the text meticulously and certainly improving my style. Finally, thanks to all of those from other departments to whom I owe an immeasurable debt.

Special thanks to my son Dr. Keith Robinson and his spouse, Dr. Lauren Lira, in Fort Lauderdale, who housed me over countless summer months as both a kind of port of call and an informal writers' colony. Mostly, I appreciate their routinized lifestyle that allowed me to stay tethered to my work. My son Julian Robinson and his wife, Lia, offered me respite from time to time in Jacksonville and quality time with their son, Syrus, always curious about my progress on this project and urging its completion so that I could begin my current onomastic study. I dedicate this work to my grandchildren Kalli and Elijah with love and devotion. They lived with this book for so long that they cannot imagine a time when it didn't exist.

Last but not least, I am forever indebted to a multitude of people along the way spread across the circum-Caribbean Anglicized World. While I cannot name all of them in expressing my gratitude, in St. Croix Marsha Roberts stands out: although we had just met, she dedicated her entire day to transporting me across the isle gratis, suggesting contacts, and offering a camaraderie that continues to this day. In Bermuda, community photographer Wayne Gilbert volunteered to become my guide and key consultant over multiple visits. At other times, Gombey dancer Sheridan Castle was a perennial presence, and Carvel Van Putten ensured my success by being the consummate guide. It was also an unforeseen decency that the Honorable Louise Jackson surprised me on a Sunday morning by being prepared for a full-blown interview as an advocate and Gombey insider. In The Bahamas, my highlights include interviews with the King of Junkanoo (Percy "Vola" Francis), Arlene Nash Ferguson, "Fast" Eddie Dames, John "Chippie" Chipman, and Quinton Barabbas Woodside. In St. Kitts, on each visit Zack Nisbett was a docent guiding me through his museum and library or pausing as he conducted summer music institutes for children learning to play traditional instruments. Among the Garifuna, there was a bit of a language barrier, and most of those I spoke with on the street were Black expatriate retirees who had moved back to Dangriga after years of working in US. Belize has a huge immigrant population spread out across the US, with hopes of being singled out in the next census. The help of all these individuals was essential to my research and its presentation in this book.

NOTES

Introduction: Transmigration of the Spirit

1. Mark Connelly is one of the few exceptions. In his social history of Christmas, he explores the process of exporting Christmas globally. Yet he only remarks on the "English-speaking societies" in Australia, New Zealand, Canada, South Africa, and India, centering those stakeholders. Encyclopedia entries on the internet tend to be whimsical, repetitive, or just plain erroneous. For a preliminary idea, see the following example, which does mention Bahamian Junkanoo without specific mention of any of the others: http://content.time.com/time/world/article/0,8599,1868711,00.html (accessed November 10, 2020).

2. Cowley explains: "Among other 'Protestant' islands, St. Kitts-Nevis have their 'Christmas Sports' including mumming, Bermuda its 'Gombey' parades, while the Bahamas also use 'Jonkonnu' as the name for their Christmas festivities" (40). Ottley proposes aligning nineteenth-century Trinidadian postemancipation with the conversion of an "annual celebration of emancipation in August into the pre-Lenten carnival period" (68). His statement carries weight in suggesting a likelihood for those in the ACW that share the same 1838 emancipation date.

3. Junkanoos' or Junkanooers' participation in the parade is called "rushin." Wood particularizes the origin of the term (31–32).

4. Folklorist David Evans established that the fife and drum tradition was a far-reaching one; nevertheless, Otha Turner and his daughter receive the greatest recognition. Folklorist Alan Lomax shared personal experience narratives about recording the Young brothers in Mississippi (324–43).

5. I interviewed Jamaica-born Glen Hurd in my Florida State University office (June 6, 2003). I also interviewed the following Tallahasseeans in their homes: Virginia Henry Barnes and her grandson, Wilbur Barnes (June 6, 2003); George Henry (June 16, 2003); and brothers Otis and Hunter Hill (July 21, 2003).

6. In mapping the Trinidadian Carnival tradition, Suzanne Burke creates a table of overseas carnivals in the Caribbean and its diaspora that identifies over one hundred carnivals, including sixty in the US alone (109–110). The one misstep by Gikandi in his excellent theoretical analysis of slavery and cultural taste is positioning John Canoe as a "form of off-season carnival" (272).

7. Researching Brazilian Candomble, Rachel Harding positions it as connected to "Spirit, to a pre-slavery past, to ancestors, to community to ensure the formation of an alternative identity" (xvii).

8. In *The Development of Creole Society*, poet Kamau Brathwaite became among the first to theorize creolization from an endogenous perspective. Another classic study is *Caribbean Discourse* by Glissant and Dash. Hannerz enumerates variant applicable terms: "Anyway, here we are now, with hybridity, collage, mélange, hotchpotch, montage, synergy, bricolage,

creolization, mestizaje, mongrelization, syncretism, transculturation, third cultures and what
have you; some terms used perhaps only in passing as summary metaphors, others with claims
to more analytical status, and others again with more regional or thematic strongholds. Mostly
they seem to suggest a concern with cultural form, cultural products (and conspicuously often,
they relate to domains of fairly tangible cultural materials, such as language, music, art, ritual,
or cuisine); some appear more concerned with process than others" (324). See Charles Stewart,
Creolization: History, Ethnography, Theory, a collection that is interdisciplinary in scope. His
chapter "Syncretism and Its Synonyms: Reflections on Cultural Mixture" led me to adopt his
argument related to "cultural interpenetration." As with "hybridity," scholars tend to avoid
using "syncretism" as it is considered a pejorative term (40). I would argue that much of this
negative discourse arises from "armchair" theorists living abroad and lacking an ethnographic
perspective. Douglas B. Chambers's "Ethnicity in the Diaspora," further adds to the discourse,
describing a long-term process of African-derived cultural adaptation that I term "historical
creolization." A reprint, Abrahams (2011) has the last words on creolization in the conclusion
of Baron's *Creolization as Cultural Creativity* (285–305). Birth situates both creolization and
hybridity as reified concepts that negate the complexities of "ongoing processes" (3).

9. As a keyword, "creolization" addresses syncretic cultural forms, but has led to much
debate among linguists, folklorists, ethnomusicologists, etc. and remains much contested.

10. Although the term is contested, see Sidney Mintz and Richard Price. Also see Herskovits, *Acculturation,* a classic in African diaspora studies. As a relatively recent addition to this
literature, see Buisseret and Reinhardt, *Creolization in the Americas.* In spite of these discus-
sions, I find the term "transcultural," coined by the Cuban social historian Fernando Ortiz in
Cuban Counterpoint, the most appropriate.

11. Although a bit dated https://www.newsamericasnow.com/caribbean-christmas-unique-
traditions-from-across-the-region/ comprehensively elucidates "Caribbean Christmas" specified by island (accessed November 9, 2020). For greater specificity, see Scher "When."

12. "Mas" derives from French *le masque* (mask), a disguise that covers the face. "Jump Up"
is defined as dancing, belonging to the Carnival performance repertoire. Bilby conducted
interviews with residents of Cat Island in The Bahamas and documented two variants of "rushing"—one sacred and performed in church featuring only singing and percussive handclapping
and the other to the accompaniment of gombay drumming and fervent dancing. Temporal
fluidity enabled participants to move from the sacred world of the church directly into the
streets to dance Junkanoo (197).

13. See, for example, Featherstone and Palmié's "Creolization and Its Discontents," which
acknowledged "lending ostensible credence to Hannerz's (1987) assertion that the world is (or
perhaps has always been) in creolization" (434).

14. Discourse related to the very survival of folklore study (due to urbanization) informed
the rationale for organizing the American Folklore Society in 1889.

15. Peter Backeberg, "Freedom Movement: The Bermuda Gombeys," *The Bermudian,*
December 25, 2018, at https://www.thebermudian.com/culture/the-consummate-bermudian/
freedom-movement-the-bermuda-gombeys/ (accessed April 23, 2019).

16. The virtual extinction of Jonkonnu in Jamaica constitutes a real cultural loss. At the time
of the formation of the American Folklore Society, the possibility of such losses was the driving
reason for the study of folklife. For more detailed ethnographic studies of Jamaican Jonkonnu,
see Beckwith, "Christmas Mumming of Jamaica," in her *Jamaican Folklore.* Thirty years ago,
Sheila Barnett's essay, although outdated, deconstructed one intriguing Jonkonnu costume:
pitchy patchy. The most ethnographic rendering of Emancipation Day in Jamaica appears in a
blog, "Gela! Just me talking about the things that I observe as I go about the business of living,"
at http://veesgirl.blogspot.com/2006/08/emancipation-day.html.

17. I thank St. Vincentian Winston McKell, whom I met in St. Croix in 2013 during Christmas Carnival there, for sharing this custom. Also, see Michael Peters's news page about Nine Mornings: https://www.iwnsvg.com/2013/06/03/svgs-unique-tradition-turns-100-years/. The following websites include personal experience narratives about the festivities: https://www.bajanthings .com/nine-mornings-st-vincent-and-grenadines-christmas-tradition/ and http://discoversvg .com/index.php/en/whattodo/festivals-a-events/nine-mornings (accessed May 7, 2017).

18. "Barbados Crop Over Festival: History," at http://www.funbarbados.com/crop_over/ history.cfm (accessed April 30, 2014).

19. This tropological approach intends to answer Bilby's call to ascertain "deeper meanings" ("Masking" 10). In answering his own call, Bilby chose to illuminate "older variants of the tradition" from darkness (11). In contrast, my study constructs an interpretive analysis based on a deeper structural interpretation.

20. Quote by John Chippie Chipman, 26, published to honor her famous Junkanoo parents, at http://amasewa.tripod.com/Bahamian_sister_writers.html. According to Keith Wisdom, "Only in the Bahamas has Junkanoo thrived, becoming a national celebration" (23). His observation suggests that this celebration has belatedly become a national treasure.

Chapter 1: Christmas: Boxing Day Eve

1. Paradigmatically, most historians commence with the venerable festal rite, the Roman Saturnalia. See J. Barnett 57. Alexander Tille assigns most winter holiday customs as originating when the Germans adopted the Roman calendar (11). His point was to certify that the names of months, etc. had their origin beyond the world of the Aryan family of languages and nations and were borrowed from Egyptian and Syriac or some other Oriental languages. Another classic historical work, by W. F. Dawson, describes Christmas celebrations among early Christians as "resembling those of the Saturnalia" (17–18). Roy Christian is no exception (114). On the other hand, Clement Miles seemingly demotes Roman customs since they were "heavily overlaid with Greek ideas and practices" (167). In the US, Nissenbaum explains how the Puritans regarded Christmas, with their viewpoint being it was a "difficult holiday to Christianize" (8).

2. Robert Tallant established that European Carnivals date back to the Egyptians of Africa (85). Kimani Nehusi, too, traces the origin of Carnival via Ancient Egypt (Kemet). Folklorist Tristram Coffin in *The Book of Christmas Folklore* credits early Egyptians with introducing the ceremonial use of evergreen as a forerunner to Christmas trees as well (209). Alfred Hottes links the Christmas tree with Egypt because of its connection to the palm tree during the midwinter festival of the goddess Isis (155). While his title, *4000 Years of Christmas*, signals ancient provenience, Earl Count's quaint historical overview designates Mesopotamia as the holiday's root source: "Christmas began there, over four thousand years ago" (18). In their introduction, Roger Matthews and Cornelia Roemer, the editors of *Ancient Perspectives on Egypt*, acknowledge archeological evidence concluding that the Mesopotamians established trade with Egypt by the fourth millennium BCE (5–6).

3. See Timothy Freke and Peter Gandy's "Mother of God" in *The Jesus Mysteries: Was the "Original Jesus" a Pagan God?* (57–58). Then, concerning the Christ child, there is the matter of the commonly accepted biblical story of the parents' flight into Egypt; see Hervey 141. Although the scriptural chapter Matthew is the recorded source, the "infancy Gospels" are deemed noncanonical because they are located in Gnostic texts. For more, see Paul Perry, *Jesus in Egypt*, which traces the route of the Holy Family based on ethnographic interviews he conducted with Coptic Egyptian Christians to document their living legends.

4. Of course, these terminologies are linked to subjugation. In actuality, the Greeks conferred the name "Egypt" on the region known by the ancients as Kemet. Lawson provided full details regarding the centuries of continuity (22). Kevin McGeough added to discourse regarding Roman hegemony and the usurpation of Greek deities: "Because of this, it has often been assumed that Roman religion was entirely based on Greek religion, but in fact, only the mythological accounts were integrated in this manner" (180–81).

5. McGeough centered women as worshippers: "Most of the worshipers of this deity were women. These women would work themselves into ecstatic frenzies, and they ate raw flesh. Livy describes the Bacchanalia (the rites of worship of Bacchus) as wild and criminal" (190). I speculate that gender dynamics played a role in the moralizing by elites. For greater detail fully contextualizing the Julian calendar and inclusive of all the Roman festivals, see chapter 6 in E. O. James, *Seasonal Feasts and Festivals*.

6. Historians of Christmas customs commonly link the celebration with the emergence of the Christian church, linking pagan winter solstice cycles with the uncertain date of Christ's birth, which was previously observed on January 6 as the Feast of the Epiphany. See Roy Christian, *Old English Customs* (114). William Dawson showcases evidence pertinent to Constantine's role based on visual representations in the Catacombs (21–22). E. O. James further traces the development of the Christian liturgical calendar through Constantine (199).

7. Orlin explains: "Many hypotheses have been advanced concerning both the worship of Bacchus and the senatorial reaction, ranging from the ways in which this cult may have represented a social, economic, and/or political challenge to the Roman state to the senate's fear of allowing members of a religious group to swear allegiance to each other, or its desire to extend its control of religion over all of Italy" (64). Also, see Park McGinty's analysis, which also mentions the Bacchic cult's propensity towards "dramatic often dangerous rites" (6).

8. Goldberg draws on Hutton's accounts from churchwardens to reconstruct the perpetuation of pagan-derived seasonal customs (232). According to Tille, "When the Roman missionaries under Augustine, sent by Pope Gregory to Great Britain, settled down in Canterbury, they found there a St. Martin's Church, as Bede states, of Roman origin a church which, after some medieval reconstructions, still exists, and is not the least interesting of the antiquities of Canterbury" (31). William Dawson contends that the Anglo-Saxons worshipped both Christ and Thor "side by side" for 150 years (25).

9. Additionally, James counters that the Teutonic and Celtic Yuletide calendars did not privilege the winter solstice, based on the influential Roman Catholic Church (292). See Michael Harrison's delineation of the Church's propensity to appropriate pagan festivals rather "than to abolish them altogether" (11). William Auld further explicates the Germanic Yule festival influence (41–47).

10. Michael Harrison provides even greater depth about the holiday's spelling variants: "This word is found spelt in various ways in olden times: Crystmasse, Cristmes, Cristmas, Crestenmes, Crestenmas, Cristmas, Cristynmes, Crismas, Kyrsomas, Xtemas, Cristemesse, Cristemesse, Cristemasse, Crystenmas, Crystynmas, Chrystmas, Chrystemes, Chystemasse, Chrystymesse, Christenmas, Christmass, and Christmes are only *some* of the variant spelling to be encountered in old manuscripts and printed books" (16; his emphasis). In conclusion, he states, "The name, though, is thoroughly English, no matter how it is spelt" (16). Auld, too, calls it "distinctly English," but he goes as far as to attribute the word to "the medieval custom of celebrating Mass at midnight on Christmas Eve" (47).

11. In South Africa, Boxing Day was renamed Day of Goodwill in 1994, set aside as a public holiday to continue the Christmas spirit. It is also recognized as St. Stephen's Day in many European countries. In the Netherlands, Latvia, Lithuania, Austria, Germany, Scandinavia, and

Poland, December 26 is celebrated as Second Christmas Day. For more details about the calendrical holiday, see http://www.calendarpedia.com/when-is/boxing-day.html and http://www.snopes.com/holidays/christmas/boxingday.asp (accessed July 16, 2003).

12. According to the liturgical calendar of the Catholic Church, most saints have holy days designated as feast days. Customarily, on these days, the patron saints are to be remembered in a special way. The Catholic Church in England dates back to medieval times (circa 600 CE) and became officially established when Christians gained effective control of Britain. In practice, Christina Hole relates: "At Drayton Beauchamp the villagers used to go to the Rectory on Boxing Day to receive as much bread, cheese and ale as they could consume from the Rector. This custom was known as Stephening; the gift was looked on as a right and according to local tradition, when one clergyman refused to admit them, the people broke a hole through the roof and completely cleared both larder and cellar" (25). *Brand's Popular Antiquities*, being encyclopedic, uses several authorities to document the custom's evolution into a money box proffered to servants "that they too might be enabled to pay the priest for his masses" (Brand et al. 116). Over time, the working class resisted the custom, by holding on to their cash money (117). Evidently, by 1840, many Christmas customs had declined: "Christmas had shrunk. It had lost in spiritual content and emotional appeal" (Pimlott 83). With secularization, the working-class enthusiasm for Boxing Day underwent immense transformations.

13. John and Miles Hadfield devote a chapter to Boxing Day and date the holiday by Samuel Johnson's usage in his *Dictionary*, which quotes John Gay's *Trivia* of 1716 and also refers to the supposedly first written account of the hyphenated "Christmas-box" (117). Dyer singles out the Roman *Paganalia* as a possible source (493). Accordingly, on December 26, he relates the custom of parishioners arriving at the rectory to eat and drink excessively as "Stephening." Brand's *Popular Antiquities*, too, cites the *Paganalia* as a predecessor for the Christmas Box (116).

14. An online Catholic dictionary avers that the derivation of the word in Old English is *Cristes Maesse*, the Mass of Christ: http://www.newadvent.org/cathen/03724b.htm (accessed May 23, 2013).

15. Harrison goes so far as to comment, "In Britain, for instance, the names of rivers show that the people of these islands once spoke a language allied to the tongues still spoken in North Africa" (9).

16. W. F. Dawson, too, credits the Crusades as having "a vast influence upon our literary tastes, as well as upon the national manners and festivities of Christmastide" (59). He goes on to identify some theatrical representations; however, in a theoretical sense, the medieval period was rife with examples of transnational cultural flows. In *Ancient Egypt, the Light of the World*, Gerald Massey says that his "earlier books were met in England with truly orthodox conspiracy of silence" (1). Craton's *Empire, Enslavement, and Freedom in the Caribbean* historicizes how the Crusaders "established a presence that lasted 200 years and changed Western Europe forever" (10).

17. Michael Harrison strongly supports the rise of Byzantium's influence and renewal of the Saturnalia: "I feel, then that we may attribute the revival of the *Saturnalia* at the end of the fifteenth century to this spreading of Byzantine influence over Europe" (65). Auld dates the word "Christmas" as being "no older than the twelfth century" (47). Also, in *Going Dutch in Beijing: How to Behave Properly When Far Away from Home*, travel writer Mark McCrum allocates several pages to explain the baksheesh custom, which adheres throughout the Arab world as well as Pakistan and India. Later usage seems to equate baksheesh more with bribery than tipping. For instance, by the time of Franklin Delano Roosevelt's presidency, he proposed to mollify Palestinians with a "little baksheesh" diplomacy; see Medoff.

18. George Long identifies blackened faces as a part of disguising (232). Also, see http://www.wickham-morris.org.uk/main_history.html (accessed September 20, 2013).

19. For example, Fernand Braudel, a leader of the French Annales school of social history, links the Crusades to Westerners' discovery of cane sugar, saying, "Sugar conquers the world": "Cane was in Egypt by the tenth century and sugar was already being produced by an advanced process. The Crusaders met it in Syria" (224). Sugar is unsurpassed as the ingredient of which feasts are made and, ironically, the crop was almost singularly responsible for the African slave trade in Caribbean.

20. Via *All Empires*, an online history community, "Crusade in the Middle East: The Impact of the Holy Land Crusades on Europe," November 1, 2006; revised at http://www.allempires .com/article/index.php?q=crusades_impact_europe (accessed November 28, 2015).

21. Roy Christian surmises that popular assumptions link Charles Dickens and Prince Albert as the originators of modern Christmas—trees and all (114). The general disdain by chroniclers of the tipping practice signifies its possible foreign origin. The Chambers website reports the boxophobic sentiment: "This custom of Christmas-boxes, or the bestowing of certain expected gratuities at the Christmas season, was formerly, and even yet to a certain extent continues to be, a great nuisance," at http://www.thebookofdays.com/months/dec/26.htm (accessed June 26, 2013).

22. Neil Armstrong recounts the significance of attractions and entertainment such as visits to museums and galleries and circuses on Boxing Day (130–31). Connelly emphasizes it as "a form of protest, for the pantomime often managed to make political points under the cover of its comedy and grotesquery" (44).

23. Michelle Cliff writes in *Abeng*: "Last Boxing Day, Joshua had made a feast for the family by buying two kids, slaughtering them with a machete, and building an enormous fire in the backyard, stewing the pieces of lesh and sharp splintery bones into curried goat. Miss Mattie had given him a length of English tweed which she would make into his first long-pants—the feast was in return for this" (115–16). An observation in *Christmas Past* by Weightman and Humphries further suggests the far-reaching move during the Victorian period toward distinguishing "between celebrations at home and in public, indoors and outdoors" (50).

24. Actually, the entire period from mid-December to January 1 is universally quite festive. Wherever Boxing Day exists, however, many local residents erect a barrier between the sacred and profane. When it falls on a Sunday, observances are postponed until Monday. The same recognition of dichotomy led folklorist Daniel Crowley to dissect the sacred components of pre-Lenten Carnivals in "The Sacred and the Profane in African and African-Derived Carnivals." Yet, in self-contradiction, Christmas Day can abound with festive behaviors, too. Historian James Barnett presents American Christmas as cultic and centering on certain rites: "For instance, most persons look forward to unusual indulgence in holiday food and drink, and eating and drinking to excess is considered a virtue at this one time of the year" (137). With Boxing Day as a public holiday in the Anglicized African World, it offers other sites worthy of interrogation and photography: see *Telegraph Magazine*'s "Hidden Meaning," in which photojournalist Phyllis Galembo mentions that, in Ghana, "For a week from Boxing Day clusters of outlandish figures march together through the streets all over the country, in costumes that have taken up to a year to create" (34).

25. See Robert Dirks, Eugene Genovese, and Judith Bettelheim, who writes, "To be sure, these occasions assumed the character of ritualized freedom, or at least ritualized unrestraint" (45). A 1905 dissertation, "The Bahama Islands" by James Martin Wright, contains more details: "Christmas Day and the two following days were allowed as holidays," adding that the presence of plantation managers as overseers were required to keep order (452). Roach thoroughly examines "gestures of deference" within a paternalistic system, "permitting a season of misrule" (273–79).

26. In *Merry Christmas! Celebrating America's Greatest Holiday*, Karal Marling thoroughly documents visual representations of enslaved Africans and African Americans relevant to

Christmas in the US, including the use of "Christmas gif!" (256). Kane's *The Southern Christmas Book* provides the most extensive relevant treatment. For instance, based on the account of a Princeton student tutoring in Colonial Virginia, Kane cites a succession of house servants appearing with Christmas greetings, requiring payment: "Next the slave who did Mr. Fithian's clothes sent a message for 'a Christmas Box' or a small gift, and to him the tutor passed on a bit [coin]" (19). Perhaps, Dirks interpreted this level of participation best: "In a way, it was as much a white saturnalia as it was a black one" ("Black Saturnalia" 5). Nissenbaum's Pulitzer Prize-winning history of American yuletide traditions includes ample documentation of Christmas in the antebellum South (258–300).

27. Historian Guion Johnson relies on primary and secondary resources to substantiate this tradition along with John Canoe in North Carolina (552–53). See also "Antebellum North Carolina," at http://www.cfhi.net/JohnKuneringatChristmas.php (accessed July 7, 2013).

28. See http://content.time.com/time/world/article/0,8599,1868711,00.html (accessed July 7, 2013). John and Miles Hadfield report "families [being] reunited—perhaps for this one day in the year, and they tend to sit and talk and relax" (74). See Belisario's *Sketches of Character* excerpts in Abrahams and Szwed, *After Africa* (259–63). Bettelheim's dissertation also delineates "the gumbay" in Belisario's sketches.

29. Simon Lee's "Carnival at Christmas in St. Kitts," https://www.caribbean-beat.com/issue-112/carnival-christmas#axzz6pJm8fwIJ, highlights the creolization process, crediting "creolized Mummies" from the rural area of East Anglia, a region in the United Kingdom (accessed April 25, 2015). Coffin and Cohen's anthology includes "Christmas Masking in Boston," collected by the renowned folklorist William W. Newell. His informant disclosed a family history in which the mother, born in 1752, described the rudiments of masking and asserted: "At this time Christmas was not kept" (205).

Chapter 2: "Military Drums Remain": Gombeys, John Canoe, and The 26th

1. See Hedrick and Stephens (14). Relative to Jamaica, Mervyn Alleyne specifies three drum types of different dimensions and contours that begin with the "gumb" prefix (109). Their demarcation, significantly, depends on oral transmission that lends itself to variant spellings when written: *gumbi* (or gumby), *gumba* (or gumbah), and *gumbe* (or gumbay). Gombey (or goombay) stipulates the drum music indigenized in Bermuda to accompany its masquerading tradition on Boxing Day. Moreover, popularized in the 1950s, Bahamian musicians released recordings that they called goombay (the primary instrument for this style of music) to show that their songs remained rooted in the local tradition—Junkanoo.

2. See Bilby, "Africa's Creole Drum," which fills a void regarding eighteenth-century Jamaican Maroon returnees to Sierra Leone and the trans-African creolization of the *gumbe*, which is square or rectangular (137–77).

3. It is gratifying that John Cowley confirms this mapping of the region: "For the purpose of this investigation, the circum Caribbean provides geographical scope and includes Guyana in South America, Belize in Central America, and the island of Bermuda, situated north of the Caribbean Sea, in the Atlantic Ocean" (*Carnival* 41). Likewise, Glissant offers a holistic territorialization of what some call the "Mediterranean of the Americas" (81). Roach contributes his elaborate interrogation of the circum-Atlantic as a European invention. While Boxing Day is an official holiday in Guyana, there is no evidence that it accommodates any festal customs to celebrate it.

4. Furthermore, Ward's introductory essay, "The Place of the American South in Atlantic and Other Worlds," defines the Atlantic World with particularity along with interrogating the

role of transnationalism (9–36). In the context of Carnival characteristics, Nehusi extends consideration by proposing that the Caribbean Sea is the "defining geographical phenomenon of the region" ("Origins" 3).

5. In 1919, with a degree of representative wonder, zoologist A. Hyatt Verrill wrote: "And speaking of 'discovering' Bermuda it may be of interest to note that islands were repeatedly discovered, and usually by accident, which is scarcely to be wondered at when we consider what a mere speck they form in the waste of waters of the North Atlantic; the wonder is that they were ever discovered at all" (13).

6. The ubiquity of Bermuda Triangle legends resurfaced April 23, 2016, when the boat of two youths missing since July from Florida was discovered. For example, see these comments from Twitter: "the bermuda triangle conspiracy always fascinated me but now that they found this boat there I'm a believer"; "The world's biggest mysteries:—who killed Kennedy—bermuda triangle—Gwen's carpool appearance"; "Where do you wanna go this summer? the Bermuda Triangle"; "The stories behind the Bermuda Triangle are mind blowing"; and "Life is full of mysteries like what's up with the bermuda triangle or why do i know all of the lyrics to Daylight by Maroon 5." See a sample website: http://thoughtcatalog.com/tj-farhadi/2016/04/5-true-terrifying-ghost-stories-from-the-bermuda-triangle/?utm_content=buffera767f&utm_medium=social&utm_source=twitter.com&utm_campaign=buffer (accessed April 23, 2016).

7. More succinctly, published in 1826, Cotter sketched an eyewitness account of his own: "Some most Caliban looking negroes have just been dancing on the lawn; for in this season of general festivity, they are all permitted to indulge in the wildest mirth and revelry" (89–90). In addition, he mentions "Gombey parties" and pinpoints Hamilton and Hearne Bay as the most renowned for festive gatherings.

8. In the literature, almost as a taunt, this *Bermuda Gazette* passage is often quoted by today's *BerNews*; see https://bernews.com/2010/12/the-beat-goes-on-for-our-gombeys/ and https://bernews.com/2011/09/photos-videos-bermuda-gombey-festival/ (accessed October 28, 2020).

9. The redistribution of wealth continues as one of the mainstays. From Ireland, historically, Henry Glassie deduces the same response from an interviewee: "So, anyway, then they had to go around for the money. Coorse, we all give a little to it" (6). By the 1960s, thirty years had elapsed, and mumming was defunct, so Glassie obtained substantial rhymes from nonmumming interviewees (14–17). Accordingly, for them, mumming reflected a pastime, not a way of life as in the Caribbean.

10. Heather Kopelson published an entire article positing the pair historically occupying a once-uninhabited land: "It began the multicontinental habitation of an Atlantic island: Bermuda was one of the few places Europeans settled that did not have an indigenous population" (273).

11. See VanSpanckeren, in which she delineates the speculations of numerous scholars regarding this group's affinity toward American Indian costuming (59). Kinser, in his chapter "Wildmen," also engages New Orleans's Mardi Gras Indians "commonly considered the most 'folkloric' phenomenon in Gulf Coast Carnival" (159). Harris conducted ethnographic research to witness Trinidadian Carnival, noting that Indians wore the most popular costume (188).

12. Kinser rather caustically attributes the turn by Mardi Gras Indians to claim a Native heritage to the 1960s Black Power movement (161). He argues the lack of visibility ("written accounts of whites," 163) prior to 1880 as why their familial claims of Native origin are untenable. Crowley, in "The Traditional Masques of Carnival," uncovers a host of masque traditions historically popular in Trinidad, identifying many variants of the Indian characters. Roach approaches the argument most theoretically (192–202).

13. Along with citing the decorous use of paint, flowers, and ribbons, Tucker privileges early dancers' Africanity: "At first they danced the traditional dance mimes of Africa" (88).

14. See Carly's twitter: https://threadreaderapp.com/thread/1040974013957373954.html. She is a proponent of the Gombey tradition and wrote an unobtainable master's thesis, "Exploring Performative Culture: The Mediation of the Bermuda Gombey Image and the Disparity from Its Cultural Significance," about their upholding the suppressed historical meaning that underlies their dances, speaking to freedom, rebellion, and subversion. Also, a short YouTube video has surfaced of a 1959 Gombey crowd's appearance at https://www.youtube.com/watch?v=J7nvVtF2EWA&feature=youtu.be.

15. With Gombey identified as an African word for the rhythm played on hand drums made from goat skin and a hollowed-out tree trunk, Tucker's subtitle, "Today and Yesterday, 1503–1980," does not address the evolution of drum instruments. Neville Hall identifies "Goombay drumming" in rural sectors of the Dutch West Indies and invests it with ritual significance, entertainment value, and artistry (119).

16. See *Memoir of Mrs. Virginia Hamill Biddle*, at https://www.loc.gov/item/mfdipbib001684/, for another mention of Charles Norford's role: "They were led by Charles Norford, otherwise known as Shaky Bean, getting his nickname from the dexterity with which he performed his parts. It was he who had brought them from St. Kitts in 1922 and was active in keeping the Gombie dances alive." Richardson devotes a chapter, "To Bermuda and Santo Doming, and Back Again," to explicating these "extraisland livelihood outlets." Louise Jackson speaks to the "West Indian Influence" too (19). At the Annual Gombey Festival in 2012, there were special performances by the visiting Kittitian Moko Jumbie (Stiltwalkers), another African-derived Christmas Sport. In 2009, during Bermuda Day holiday weekend, the St. Kitts and Nevis prime minister, Dr. Denzil Douglas, conducted a well-attended forum in which this transmigrant community revealed an uncommon interest in their homeland. Christopher Famous utilizes his journey back to St. Kitts to describe the island's root genealogy. He estimates that Kittitians and Nevisians compose between 50 and 60 percent of Bermudian births along with surnames; see http://bermudasun.bm/Content/OPINION/Opinion/Article/There-is-much-to-learn-from-our-St-Kitts-and-Nevis-roots/4/135/74152 (accessed April 27, 2016). Bettelheim's 1979 dissertation attributes the modern-day metamorphosis to "immigrants from the West Indies" (223). Matheson remarks how contemporary masqueraders' costumes no longer capture the decorative "effort or expense" in St. Kitts. Therefore, apparently, in Bermuda, tradition-bearers never schematized their approach to masking.

17. Alisha Warner's commentary in the Kawahley-Lathan video documentary *Behind the Mask* proclaims an earlier affiliation with the Lady Di Gombey Girls established by her mother. Also, see *National Geographic*'s https://www.nationalgeographic.com/travel/article/gombeys-behind-the-mask-in-bermuda (accessed September 11, 2019). I personally witnessed female masqueraders along with males on the streets of Basseterre in St. Kitts.

18. For example, a fracas was reported in the news during Boxing Day road march in December 2012; see https://bernews.com/2012/12/police-called-to-altercation-between-gombeys/ (accessed February 25, 2013). Another local publication posted a video and photo gallery of more recent Boxing Day appearances; see http://bernews.com/2016/12/video-gombeys-celebrate-boxing-day-2/ (accessed July 19, 2017).

19. I draw on E. Clement Bethel's inferences, too, that indicate a long history of trade "between the islands and coastal colonies" (5).

20. Originally, the corridor extended to Jacksonville; however, it is significant to note an extensive five-hundred-year migration pattern of Africans into the region via the Spaniards. The quote is from http://staugustine.com/opinions/2010-02-21/

gullahgeechee-corridor-step-closer-st-augustine#.UQwkY7bpxhE (accessed February 1, 2013; site discontinued). See also http://hiddenhistorymiami.com/the-spanish-kings-edict.html.

21. Craton's "Loyalists" article speaks to the significantly different backgrounds of Black immigrants to The Bahamas, many of whom emigrated directly from St. Augustine (45). His interrogation offers insight into cultural diffusion via the US mainland (61–65). See also Warner, *Free Men in an Age of Servitude*. Also, Landers reports Carnival to be a mainstay in St. Augustine, Florida (94).

22. This quote is an example of the disinformation about John Canoe that typifies websites; see http://www.serenitypoint.com/news/tag/john-canoe/ (accessed February 22, 2013). On another site, while comprehensive, a derisive tone dominates; see https://bahamianology .com/a-problem-with-history-what-are-we-really-celebrating-at-john-canoe/ (accessed October 29, 2020).

23. Of the discussants, E. Clement Bethel offers the most in-depth theory about the derivation of the festival's name and meaning (10–16, 22–23). Elizabeth Fenn's evaluation indicates that "Jonkonnu also spread to the North American continent, although it did so in a surprising and mysterious geographical fashion" (130; drawings, 131). Nissenbaum mentions in passing that Edenton is "near the Virginia line" (285), which could suggest such masquerades were more widespread and go undocumented. As relates to the US, the fact of the matter is that so-called Negro Spirituals existed simultaneously with John Canoe, without attracting widespread reportage, until a union officer, Higginson, wrote them down for publication in the *Atlantic Monthly*. The same can be said for African American folktales' being disregarded prior to Joel Chandler Harris's appropriation.

24. W. J. Gardner details another variant of John Connu's history in Jamaica (184). Orlando Patterson, too, engages Long's account as well as referencing and analyzing other pertinent sources (232–48).

25. MacMillan recorded additional songs, describing performers, dances, and instrumentation as well. Also, see the website of the Cape Fear Historical Institute, at http://www.cfhi.net/ JohnKuneringatChristmas.php (accessed July 27, 2013).

26. Even Harriet Jacobs's despicable slaveowner, Dr. Norcom, years later wrote about the "John Koonahs" in a letter to his daughter, according to Nissenbaum (288).

27. Fenn associates the demise of Kooners in Wilmington with the race riot of 1898 (134). White youth appropriated the tradition thereafter; see photo on 135.

28. Kaapse Klopse, called the Coon Carnival under apartheid, is a minstrel festival celebrated on January 2 (Second New Year) in Cape Town, South Africa, adding to the mystique about the common derogatory usage of the terminology by descendants of enslaved Africans. See Denis Martin.

29. Drawing the same conclusion, Bilby footnotes his supposition that these celebrations compose a Junkanoo complex, "springing from a common root tradition" via Jamaica ("Surviving" 193). Fabre delineates the same transcultural flow from Jamaica but indicates its arrival in North America to be "most mysterious" (54). In contrast, Gikandi presents a plethora of questions regarding the scanty presence of John Canoe in the United States (272).

30. Part of MacMillan's discourse cites only two towns where "John Kuners" performed: Wilmington and Hillsboro, accompanied by a footnote mentioning Edenton where Harriet Jacobs's text proves otherwise (55). He also specifies that its termination coincided with African American ministerial interference to evade negative stereotyping by whites (57). However, Roach's thesis regarding the intercultural circulation of circum-Atlantic memory further guides my speculation via his assessment that "this world resembled a vortex in which commodities and cultural practices changed hands many times" (4).

31. Smithsonian Folkways issued an album featuring a Junkanoo Band recorded in Key West: http://www.folkways.si.edu/junkanoo-band/key-west/caribbean-world/music/album/smithsonian (accessed February 15, 2017). Rosita Sands downplays a Key West connection to John Canoe as known in North Carolina, before indicating the need for more research ("Musical" 150). Moreover, she notes that Junkanoo musicians generally perform year-round on special occasions for dancing purposes (153).

32. See Dennis Folly for a comprehensive history of African American Christmas observances from slavery to freedom and beyond.

33. Also, see Restad who notes that in the North the ritual shooting occurs on New Year's Eve, whereas in the South shooting marked Christmas Day (25). In addition, Restad devotes a chapter, "Christmas in the Slave South," to the expressive cultural experience of enslaved Africans (75–90). Piersen situates them within an African aesthetic ("Festive Style and Creation" 257). In addition, see the recent publication by Karal Marling, who reads Christmas's visual and material culture as texts; but, while interesting, the interrogation of African Americans reinscribes the often stereotypical "Black Christmas" pictorials and how they were representational to others (256). In that book, when Marling is speaking more globally in the chapter "Somebody Else's Christmas," the material culture of the diverse peoples themselves are centered (243–83). The introduction to Kennedy's *Life, Liberty, and the Mummers* attributes the New Year's Shooters in Philadelphia to Swedish and German immigrants (1). Still, Moore and Johnson note that in Jamaica the firing of guns was a "creole custom" Victorian elites opposed, preferring more "civilized" and less noisy conventions (159).

34. According to Karal Marling, "Dixie Christmas was an outdoor-celebration, with holly, mistletoe, and roses everywhere, practical jokes, hunting, fireworks, and the shooting of guns to announce the coming of the big day" (256). Walter Robbins adds a few notes not specific to the South in "Christmas Shooting Rounds in America and Their Background." Reports indicate that, in this same vicinity of the South, "People too poor to afford firecrackers for Christmas celebrations substituted forest fires" (qtd. in McGregory 95).

35. If the term "turkey shoot" enters one's vocabulary today, it tends to be as a metaphor, meaning being in a direct firing lane. Turkeys are very easy to shoot. They are large and move slowly. Despite the fact that they are birds, turkeys don't fly very well. Turkeys are not very intelligent animals. On modern turkey farms, the birds sometimes forget to drink and die of dehydration, despite the fact that a water supply is tied to their bodies, and they sometimes die of heart attacks when scared by loud noises. Today, usually some kind of target is substituted for actually shooting live turkeys and is awarded as the grand prize. In Tallahassee, other cuts of meat are won. For another interesting context, read about a fundraiser in Maine and the history of the turkey as "game" at http://www.crabcoll.com/journal/turkeyshoot.html (accessed July 11, 2009). In Zürich, the custom dates back to the seventeenth century, when all the boys were required to practice their shooting during the summer holidays. Shooting at a mark as a test of skill began with archery, long before the advent of firearms (c. 1300). Firearms were first used in warfare and later in sport shooting (hunting), and because of the shadowy early history of firearms, it is not known when target shooting began. The early history of the sport is largely that of shooting with rifles.

36. On the one hand, researchers acted to substantiate the purity of Western cultural practice, negating any evidence of African provenance. On the other hand, scholars like Herskovits challenged tabula rasa theories that cast aspersion upon the retention of any African cultural connections within African American folklife. Yet, his view about the role of cultural reinterpretation dismissed the homogeneous/heterogeneous binary as does Roach's surrogation.

37. From Jamaican setts to Bermudian troupes, bands, etc., Abrahams noted a lack of a nationalistic identification: "Rather, community identification was achieved through significant

movement together through an improvised value space, a togetherness that can be transported anyplace" ("Afro-Caribbean Culture" 99).

38. See Stewart, "Syncretism." Gerstin makes a "case for a greater homogeneity of African point of origin than previously thought" (31). Even more influential, the term "global moderni-ties" illustrates globalization as hybridization. Olwig better defines the processes of hetero-genization "which occur as global culture is incorporated into local contexts of life" (*Global Culture* 5).

39. Routinely, musicologists associate African American fife and drum music with the state of Mississippi, where they identify folklorist Alan Lomax as locating this music's survival in 1942. David Evans contributed further to this scholarship. Although Evans furnished details of other localities where the fife and drum tradition survived such as in Fayette County, Ten-nessee, and Talbot County, Georgia, there is no mention of the tradition being long-lived in a relatively metropolitan area like Florida's state capital. However, the fife and drum corps there coexists with African-style hand drumming as throughout the Caribbean.

40. Shaw accomplishes the yeoman's task for me by historicizing the blues fife and drum tradition as a survival of British military field music.

41. For more about the last well-known fife player, see http://www.othaturner.com (accessed September 18, 2003).

42. George Henry, interviewed at his home on June 16, 2003, in Tallahassee.

Chapter 3: Junkanoo/Jankunú

1. Here, I will not rehash debates regarding origin—other scholars concur that the ubiq-uitous question is now subsumed by comprehending the creolization or surrogation process. Bahamian scholars authenticate Junkanoo as representational of items of unabashed African provenience. See Saunders, *Slavery* 88–93; Craton, "Loyalists" 61. Kenneth Bilby credits liter-ary theorists with centering "Jankunu" as a significant, autonomous African-inspired cultural manifestation ("Masking" 2). Additionally, he enumerates a core of interdisciplinary scholar-ship conducted about the festivals (3).

2. As relates to Sayles, see Craton ("Loyalists" 56–64). New Providence originally was named Sayles's island for its colonizer (Saunders and Cartwright 3).

3. See Craton, *History* 56. Also, Craton and Saunders attest to a well-known practice by Bermudians and Jamaicans "of dumping their most troublesome slaves on unsuspecting neigh-bors" (139).

4. See "Arawak Tribe of the Bahamas (the first tribe encountered by Christopher Columbus in the Americas)," at http://originalpeople.org/arawak-tribe-of-the-bahamas-the-first-tribe-encountered-by-christopher-columbus-in-the-americas/ (accessed May 3, 2016). Robert Curry's self-published text offers some lore of his own.

5. E. Clement Bethel relies on a host of other sources, mentioning Bartolome de Las Casas's search in 1516 that after three years only identified eleven survivors, who were summarily removed (3).

6. For a more comprehensive analysis of the Lucayan peoples, see Craton and Saunders (38–47). Howard, in *Black Seminoles in the Bahamas*, presents an ethnographic study docu-menting the influx of this fugitive group during the First Seminole War to Andros Island. Known by locals as "Fish Fry"; for its origin, see https://www.bahamas.com/plan-your-trip/restaurants/fish-fry-arawak-cay (accessed May 3, 2016). A fish fry is a Bahamian version of a seafood festival, sort of a tasty Bahamian backyard experience.

7. Gail Saunders in *Family* explained the Cay's origin as "a man-made island which was built by the Government of The Bahamas in the late 1960s. On the island is a base which receives fresh water barged in from Andros Island" (33). Hunter's *The Bahamas* elaborates that, in 1969, the enlargement of the harbor of Nassau was completed and the artificial island of Arawak Cay was formed (101).

8. See Adderley, which contrasts Bahama's diversified slave-based economy (including salt production) with Trinidad's sugar-dominated economy (61).

9. Folklorist Joyce Jackson recently conducted ethnographic research about rushin' on Andros Island, privileging a comparative analysis with Easter Rock in Louisiana (89–123). From an endogenous perspective, Turner's *Overcoming Self-Negation* comprehensively addresses tension within the Junkanoo and church divide in the Bahamas.

10. Rosita Sands, in "Carnival," goes as far as to assert The Bahamas is "the only known place where a full-scale Junkanoo celebration still exists" (80).

11. Additionally, in *Race Relations*, Johnson, drawing on documents from the Farquharson plantation, presents the probable source for Saunders's "grand dance" quote. Johnson also provides a full rendering of activities surrounding Christmas Day but also as a precursor to the bank holiday, reporting the evening of December 26 was the actual date for the slaves' grand dance and, assaying the "total darkness" trope, says it "lasted until almost daylight the next day" (134).

12. In addition, Martha Beckwith is among the early researchers who usually projected a Eurocentric etymology for the festival's name ("Jamaica Folklore" 7). Still, Louise Jackson in an interview with me (May 2009) recalled being told of a Senegal connection. Based on the observation of a visitor to Bermuda knowledgeable about Yoff, she suggested Senegal had a cultural affinity with the Gombeys. Yoff is a small island off the coast and near Goree, the notorious site of slave barracoons in Senegal. Andrew Burke specifies a direct association with the Lebu (Lebou) people in *The Gambia and Senegal*, writing: "Despite, or because of, their relatively small population (they number a few thousand, whereas the Wolof are counted in millions) they have remained culturally intact" (242). Identified as Muslims with a difference, the Lebu experienced their own creolization process howbeit in syncretism with African, Muslim, and European cultural resources. They also are noted as maintaining a vital spirit of independence. Traditional Wolof instruments include a small drum held under the arm, which can be pressed against the body to produce different pitches. The goatskin drumhead is hit by a wooden stick with a curved end. Although with little religious significance, Christmas is observed. To read more, see http://www.everyculture.com/wc/Rwanda-to-Syria/Wolof.html#b#ixzz2YU34S190 (accessed August 15, 2014). Bilby lists other scholars who have attested to a West African origin ("Masking" 7).

13. Keith Wisdom's dissertation was the first bountiful study of the Junkanoo Festival, followed by the dissertation of E. Clement Bethel. They theorize as they historicize. Later, Bethel's daughter published her father's dissertation with addendums of her own.

14. The Street Nuisance Act curtailed the temporal orientation of Junkanoo by issuing restraints and banning the custom of randomized festive gatherings throughout late December (Mackey 24). Rommen acknowledges the act's impact as well (*Funky Nassau* 75).

15. E. Clement Bethel supplies detailed descriptions, too, of the "grotesque masqueraders" along with speculation about the origin of the "store-bought" wire masks—whether from Germany or Japan (42).

16. In addition to costume descriptions, Wisdom includes a repertoire of popular songs endemic of the period (38). Rather than an overview, E. Clement Bethel includes an extensive

history of Junkanoo's growth spurt during Prohibition: "During the 1920s, the masqueraders became more concerned with the visual aspect of the parade than before and they had both the means and the incentive to see to its development" (49).

17. See Jenkins for oral histories regarding the rioting (160–68). Additionally, Jenkins presents an emic perspective of Junkanoo itself (89).

18. For greater detail, see Wisdom (60–61). Wood further delineates the history of this level of participation (93–98).

19. Quote from Katherine Beneby, in "Junkanoo: Hidden Treasure of the Bahamas," *Bahamas Weekly*, at http://www.thebahamasweekly.com/publish/a-taste/Junkanoo_Hidden_Treasure_of_the_Bahamas35433.shtml (accessed July 2, 2014).

20. See Wisdom (56–60) for more details. Wood historicizes an assortment of the 1980 favorites (81–89).

21. Just as Wisdom acknowledges that the "Junkanoo step" described by Bethel became obsolete, ever-evolving, the same applies to Wisdom's dynamic assessment (67–68). For instance, based on personal observation on Boxing Day 2011, Percy "Vola" Francis no longer danced, but appeared majestically as Neptune on a splendid float as part of the group's finale.

22. On his behalf, the daughter of E. Clement Bethel posthumously published the definitive endogenous text on Bahamian Junkanoo (E. Bethel). Other local authors extend his findings. In *Bahamian Memories: Island Voices of the Twentieth Century*, Jenkins furnishes a hybrid text filled with personal experience narratives from a contingent of islanders along with her own interpretive threads. Pinterest pages abound as well such as Inez Samantha C's page: https://www.pinterest.com/bahamasweets/junkanoo-nassau-bahamas-past-and-present/ (accessed July 2, 2014).

23. Interviewed at the Prince George Dock Centre, where he entertained disembarking tourists on weekdays in Nassau, Chipman informed me that he had traveled all around the world (July 10, 2009). In 2014, Lifebuoy Street was renamed in his honor with a Junkanoo rush out following the ceremony. Also, a Smithsonian website features a taped interview with John Chipman: http://www.folkways.si.edu/bahamian-junkanoo-parade/caribbean-world/music/video/smithsonian (accessed February 27, 2017).

24. Cassidy's *Jamaica Talk* identifies a more detailed rendering, differentiating the bass drum as the *goombah,* while the higher-pitched small drum is called the *gumbi.* Cassidy delineates a range of other endogenous musical instruments as well as other relevant vernacular terms (267–68). Gardner's history provides an apt description as well (183).

25. Given the ephemeral nature of the World Wide Web, several websites I accessed in my research are now defunct.

26. See the blog "Bahamian Musicians: An Oral Narrative History of the Lives of Some Influential Bahamian Musicians," at http://bahamianartists.blogspot.com/2015_04_01_archive.html (accessed August 6, 2015). Roach situates traditionalized inventions showcased here as a part of the "transmission of surrogacy" (29).

27. See http://www.tribune242.com/news/2014/oct/17/junkanoo-brings-happiness-costs-18m-unwaged-labour/. Nicolette Bethel's Microsoft PowerPoint reports the results of a survey, "Violence on the Street," which assessed the opinions of spectators. See http://ufdcimages.uflib.ufl.edu/AA/00/01/23/79/00001/ViolenceSymposium2011_ViolenceontheStreet.pdf.

28. Most recently, the tallest height may be up to fifteen feet, according to Beneby.

29. See Besson and Olwig's *Caribbean Narratives of Belonging: Fields of Relations, Sites of Identity,* which sought to "redirect attention to aspects of Caribbean life that have received relatively little attention" (1). Eneas's book will inform future interpretations, especially as related to combating the stigma of living in back-o-town.

30. See Bob Nevil's editorial that castigates the Ministry of Tourism because "we can only draw 20 % of our tourists off the cruise ships," while offering three worthwhile suggestions, at https://www.bahamaslocal.com/newsitem/84215/Fixing_our_downtown_and_tourism_prod uct.html (accessed July 2, 2014).

31. This contentious ongoing dispute remains unresolved with consideration being given to taking the claim to the International Judicial Court.

32. See Karen Judd, "Creolisation and Its Discontents" (147–57) and Shoman (140–42).

33. Dorothy Franzone's dissertation contains the full historical background. Also, see https://www.theroot.com/how-do-i-find-my-garifuna-ancestors-1790897076 (accessed July 9, 2013), which speaks popularly about the Garifuna's past.

34. For greater insights regarding the migration patterns of Black Caribs and Garifuna as ethnic groups, see Nancie Gonzalez's *Sojourners of the Caribbean*.

35. See Lita Hunter Krohn, "All a we mek Belize!," *Amandala*, November 11, 2011, at http://amandala.com.bz/news/all-a-we-mek-belize/ (accessed March 16, 2013).

36. Bolland provides more in-depth insights about the Christmas season among loggers, though little about it suggests that Afro-Belizeans were celebrating any event in the Christian calendar ("Timber" 49).

37. See http://www.lameca.org/publications-numeriques/dossiers-et-articles/ as a Garifuna language website (accessed July 16, 2013).

38. See Servio-Mariano (85). The Garifuna language gives evidence of an intangible heritage as supported by receiving, in 2001, one of UNESCO's Masterpiece of the Oral and Intangibles Heritage of Humanity awards.

39. Kerns and Dirks single out Thomas Young's publication in which he reported observing John Canoe "among the Caribs" in the 1840s (5). Franzone's review of the literature reports the tendency of researchers to negate any mention connecting the Garifuna's wanáragua to Africa (203).

40. See Belize's Wanaragua dancers at http://www.youtube.com/watch?v=j1y87f2E6Ag (accessed October 10, 2013). Bilby relegates the Boxing Day Charikanari to a footnote ("Surviving" 205).

41. Whipple differentiates further the African-oriented drumming found in Belize from the more complex rhythms in Haiti or Cuba (40–41).

42. See http://www.lameca.org/dossiers/garifuna_music/eng/p2.htm (accessed July 23, 2013). E. Clement Bethel has a section on "Belize and St. Vincent" (21–22). Also, see Edward Conzemius's typically biased description of the wanaragua (192–93). For an endogenous focus on the drums, see http://www.belize.com/music-drums (accessed September 13, 2014).

43. See Cowley, who writes that "Only in Belize, however, can the term be shown to have been in use in the 1820s, where it was said to have been 'recently introduced from Jamaica' in a Methodist Missionary Society document, dated 1829" ("Music" 176).

44. See Oliver Greene, based on an interview with a preeminent Garifuna scholar (200). Green additionally offers a detailed discussion concerning the origin of Wanaragua as an artistic expression (207–210). To add to the discourse, Jamaica was a former seat of government of British Honduras, which included a monopoly over their mail route, meaning a long history of shipping and trade with potentially cultural exchanges among workers (Judd, "In the Name" 139).

45. Due to surrogacy, these festive gatherings have transformed over time and space, for Solien provides yet another thick description in which only two actors portray males and another is a female impersonator; the group members cavort together in a sexualized manner and are "thought to be clowns" (306).

46. I have yet to locate any comparative studies or ethnographic studies privileging *Chari-kanari* and European charivaris comprehensively. Regarding charivaris, see Susan Crane's chapter "Wild Doubles in Charivari and Interlude," in which she recuperates the material culture and performances by elite courtiers in "costumed events, more closely allied to theater" (140). In addition, charivari involved malicious, hostile, and more "iconoclastic revelry" identi-fied as "Rough Music," the beginning of folk justice.

47. In "Playing with the Future," Cameron and Jordan identify the role of "playing with fear," discussing how children "play with their fear of masks, approaching and taunting them, then screaming and running away when chased" to learn how to negotiate their fear (242–43).

48. This expressive development also conforms to Louis T. Moore's descriptive representation of Wilmington's John Kuners: "As the groups approached with their 'outlandish,' fantastic, or fear-some masks, the youngsters in awe, astonishment, and fear would run and hide behind their moth-ers, or those of the household slaves who were not participating in the revels" (74). In the context of Mardi Gras, Marcia Gaudet speaks of masked marauders frightening small children (154).

49. Hurd's thick description basically matches that of MacMillan related to fin de siècle "John Kuner" in Wilmington, North Carolina (53–57).

50. See http://www.belizeanjourneys.com/features/wanaragua/newsletter.html (accessed July 16, 2013). Also, Conzemius provides an early condescending ethnographic study, which describes the "John Canoe dance" on Christmas and New Year's (192–93).

51. See Keith Wisdom for more descriptive passages (22). Shoman added that it was custom-ary in the nineteenth century for the Garifuna to travel as far as Belize Town to dance and mas-querade house-to-house and to collect offerings (166). Today, based on participant-observation, on Boxing Day, visits occur from midmorning to dusk, when two masquerade troupes take their antics to opposite ends of the main street, causing much crowd anticipation for when they might clash. These appearances in yards, at the gates, and in front of homes come from prior special requests as well as spontaneous interactions.

Chapter 4: J'ouvert

1. Patricia Alleyne-Dettmers's "Political Dramas" provides the most exhaustive interrogation of J'ouvert in all its glory and offers a few correctives that still pertain (326–38).

2. According to *Michael Anthony*, "Jour Ouvert (sic) was already essentially what it is today: an old-mask jamboree, reflecting the mood of the people, and a show-window for satire and wit, for picong, for irreverent remarks, all mainly through apt disguise and the little placard. This of course drew its characteristics from the bitterness and guile of the ex-slaves who were anxious to come out onto the streets and hurl cutting remarks at their former masters." Other texts include glossaries defining cultural constructs with in-depth specificity; see the Balliger dissertation and Sloat's two edited volumes.

3. Writing about Nassauvian Junkanoo, Wood's chapter "This Ain't Carnival, This Junkanoo" discloses that by the 1990s Junkanooers already were bemoaning Trinidadian influence, dating back to cultural contact from the 1950s. According to Nurse, "Almost every major city in North America and England has a Caribbean-style carnival that is in large part modeled after the one found in Trinidad" (80). Alleyne-Dettmers analyzes the transportability of Trinidadian Carnival and its extensions ("Ancestral" 208). Regarding glocalization, also see Sarah Fernan-dez's publications.

4. As a matter of fact, this island outproduced even the much-larger Jamaica in growing "the highest quality sugar in the West Indies," according to Zazek (18).

5. "Kamina" refers to "the piece of land which is cultivated at the same time by a group of [enslaved Africans]. It refers both to the field and the work that is performed on it" (C. G. A. Oldendorp qtd. in Tyson and Highfield xii).

6. Thurlow Weed describes the particulars regarding a rebellion in St. John, which was being planned for Christmas but rushed to commence in November 1733 instead (Weed et al. 167–68). Documenting Christmas rebellions in the US, Nissenbaum reports that one-third of recorded revolts occurred during this holiday and, in 1856, almost every slave state reported one (291).

7. Ober not only denigrates the island, but glibly deems Frederiksted to be more exciting overall due to this insurrection, somehow linking that event to the grounding of the US frigate *Monongahela*, which was caught in a tsunami with the tidal wave sweeping it a mile inland and striking Frederiksted (324). As he expressed it: "Rather the better appearing of the two towns is Frederiksted.... Perhaps nothing more exciting ever took place here, except the negro insurrection of 1878, for the event was caused and accompanied by a tidal wave 60 feet high, which left the old 'tub' standing erect among the dwellings of the town." On the other end of the spectrum, Weed also is an apt primary source for details about the all-consuming nature of Christmas holiday gatherings by enslaved persons. John Knox writes a dramatic account of the 1848 rebellion (113).

8. According to Dookhan, King Frederik VI approved a plan by von Scholten to divide freed and enslaved Africans into two classes. It created a social stratification based on "superior education, mental capacity, good conduct, situation in life, or from other considerations" (146).

9. Kinser records that by the 1820s, during the winter season, "The English colonies developed festivals more during the twelve days from Christmas to Epiphany" (68). In their *Twelve Days of Christmas*, John and Miles Hadfield found it "remarkable how quickly the Twelfth Night celebrations have vanished (among the British)" (168).

10. See Kate Melone, "Compliments of the Season: The Joy of Crucian Holidays," *The Croixer*, vol. 2, issue 2, Dec. 22–28, 1994. However, a traveler named Fuller devotes an entire racially biased chapter to the phenomenon and "black magic"; but he also avers that "There are always races the day after Christmas on St. Croix" (53). Schrader, in *Notes*, has a chapter outlining horse racing as a Crucian folk cultural tradition.

11. See Cheyenne Harty, "Crucian Christmas." Wayne James does contextualize the ban as "supposedly an attempt to check the spread of a cholera outbreak" and confine gombay dancing and drumming to the rural sectors (Part II, 1).

12. Harty cites local columnist Wayne James as the source for this reference. The article also mentions the Labor Riots of 1878 as being of significance in the revitalization of African drum dances (2). Gikandi identifies how these thick descriptions by white planters were not endorsements of their music, musical instruments, or dancing. Rather, the noisy cultural performances of enslaved persons were antithetical to planters' "culture of taste" (255).

13. Willocks briefly summarizes St. Croix's Christmas festival (22).

14. See Harty (1). On page 7 of the same article, Harty attempts to reconstruct the era: "It was 1952. Bouffants and shirts made of newly invented nylon were in style. So was the limbo. But a young disc jockey named Ron de Lugo [the future first delegate nominated to serve in the US House of Representatives] suggested that the Virgin Island government get hip to something else." More recently, attending Crop Over in her native Barbados, pop singer Rihanna grabbed similar media attention, which called attention to her "raunchy" costume and/or dancing; see https://www.washingtonpost.com/news/act-four/wp/2015/08/07/rihanna-and-the-liberation-of-carnival/ and https://www.youtube.com/watch?v=2qKWG70c0Oo (accessed August 11, 2015).

15. Guilbault's chapter "Independence, Innovation, and Authenticity" focuses on calypso music's evolution post-Independence in Trinidad, which certainly was influential elsewhere, especially as relates to juried competition.

16. Pelzer historicizes the first parade, names key committee members, and describes other established customs, while also noting the inverse of the foreday morning trope: the first parade "turned out to be the last night parade, in part due to the convenience a daylight parade would provide for our [tourist guests]" (4).

17. Platt explains epiphany as the ways in which invisible gods were made visible to their worshippers (10). She adds, "Epiphanies played a crucial role within this system by providing *cognitive reliability,* not only for the gods' existence, but also for the traditions of representation by which they were known to their worshippers" (12). "In the Christian tradition," she continues, "the very possibility of Christ's representation is dependent upon a notion of incarnation that does not apply to Graeco-Roman polytheism. . . . Christ's form can be visualized and envisioned because of his very corporeality most dramatically emphasized in the tactile epiphany offered to (but not necessarily taken by) Doubting Thomas" (20–21). The issues of Christ's divine mortal status, his visibility to mortal worshippers, and his depiction in image form thus all hinge upon a theological tradition focused on correct interpretation of a master-text and the desire to define religious orthodoxy. One might argue that Christian narratives appropriated, subverted, and transformed Greek religious traditions in ways that were fundamental both to the forging of a distinctive group identity and successful evangelism within the Hellenized world of antiquity. As Margaret Mitchell pointed out in "Epiphanic Evolutions in Earliest Christianity," the Gospel's account of Christ's entry to Jerusalem and Crucifixion is in many ways a conscious inversion of Greek epiphanic conventions (22). In contrast to Christianity's scriptural mission to shape and determine a normative faith, Graeco-Roman polytheism was neither a religion of the book nor committed to defining a commonly held credo. Moreover, just as Christian epiphanic conventions exist in a complicated yet necessary relationship with pagan tradition, so the self-conscious, even playful treatment of epiphany we find in Greek imperial authors such as Plutarch exists in an informed and complex dialogue with the epiphanic conventions and concerns of earlier Hellenic culture (23). Also, Kinser recognizes the relevance of the Epiphany in the West Indies and its lack of relevance to Mardi Gras in Louisiana. Nevertheless, he adds that "January 6 was mainly the occasion for the upper classes to give an especially sumptuous ball" (59). Jean Muteba Rahier devotes his book to the study of Afro-Ecuadorian Three Kings festivals.

18. Occasionally, due to the calendar, when Boxing Day is on a Sunday, the Adult Parade and Village Closing occurs on a Saturday as in 1999–2000 when it took place January 8. This information is garnered from the St. Croix Festival Committee Village Entertainment Schedule since the first Saturday was on January 8.

19. Oliver briefly historicizes the Crucian Christmas season to center women and cultural events (38–39). Signaling their institutionalization by the CCF, Wayne James authoritatively situates J'ouvert celebrations as "preced[ing] Carnival parades" with the "tramps bring[ing] them to a climatic close" (Part II, 3); however, with the ascendancy of the Village, the tramps mark the season's opener. On the sixtieth anniversary celebration, I observed two J'ouvert events, two road tramps, and two Carnival parades within ten days, not counting activities in Christiansted.

20. Scher marks the transition to allocating costume making to Mas camps in Trinidad (*Carnival* 104). He also indicates a plan to simulate Mas camps for walking tours in West Indian Brooklyn, home to a large diasporic Carnival (111). For more information regarding the Trinidadian influence in the creation of Mas camps, which drive the Carnival process,

see Jeffrey Chock's "The Mas I Know." More contemporary troupes there are reportedly being outsourced now to Asia and Latin America for mass production. See http://www.discovertnt.com/articles/Trinidad/The-Birth-Evolution-of-Trinidad-Carnival/109/3/32#axzz48eJDqjrG (accessed May 14, 2016). Alleyne-Dettmers examines Mas camps relative to Carnival in Notting Hill London, assessing the roles of the creative artists (Mas men and women) who design the costumes based on theme and the mass engineers who decide feasibility, etc. ("Ancestral Voices" 202). She also describes these sites as a "social free-for-all along with the division of labor there" ("Jump!" 293–303). A key consultant, Ena McKell, who masquerades in both St. Croix and Trinidad informed me it cost her $1500 to play mas in Trinidad, complete with facilities for a lunch break of complementary food and drinks (interviewed in Frederiksted, January 1, 2013).

21. Using digital ethnography, I have found Facebook to be indispensable in communicating with Boxing Day-related social groups such as https://www.facebook.com/USVIFestivals (accessed November 21, 2013).

22. From Facebook: "Please be advised that the Crucian Christmas Carnival has received a significant amount of booth applications this year to operate a booth in the Frederiksted Carnival village. The Crucian Christmas Carnival village has limited booth space. Therefore, for those of you who haven't paid for his/her booth space or have a down payment pending, I urge you to pay in full today at the meeting in order to secure your booth space for the 2013–2014 Crucian Christmas Carnival village. Remember today is the deadline to pay in full."

23. Ferguson further attests to the glee when, through the grapevine, junkanoos hear that "The shack is open! The message goes forth, passed on at funerals, weddings, on the job, in church, at ball games, everywhere (28). In 2011, the day after Boxing Day, I felt thrilled when allowed to watch proceedings in preparation for the New Year's Day parade.

24. This trend updates previous research centering the mumming tradition such as Nicholls, *Jumbies*. However, Ray Allen documents a similar shift in Brooklyn among revelers (266). Alleyne-Dettmers is probably the most reliable source regarding the trendification of casual wear ("Jump!" 53).

25. C. R. Ottley situates steelbands as the grandson of African drums (67). Guilbault extensively documents the development of steel pan (the people's instrument) and calypso (the voice of the people) (39–63).

26. Replaced by soca, steelband music is no longer the music of J'ouvert. It is relegated to school band units who primarily highlight children's parades and community events. With a move into respectability, steel pan also signals touristy safe spaces, performing in hotel lobbies and entertaining diners at upscale restaurants.

27. In *American Speech*, Cassidy examines the etymology for "hipsaw" describing a seductive dance as "shaking, twisting, and winding," and includes lyrics to a song to illustrate its use *in situ* (46). Max Harris elaborates with a self-reflexive description of the dancing along with a glib definition (197).

28. See https://www.youtube.com/watch?v=zhmkKYoTVLc, a YouTube video accompanied by this caption (accessed September 4, 2013).

29. See *St. Croix Daily News* at https://stcroixsource.com/2004/11/29/me-son-crucian-christmas-festival-has-begun/ (accessed October 31, 2020).

30. See Schrader, who extols Frank Charles as "the maestro of the Crucian scratch band" (*Notes* 71).

31. Given calypso's widespread longevity, publications are plentiful. See Guilbault; John Cowley; Donald Hill. In *The Trinidad Carnival*, Errol Hill discusses in detail calypso's start in 1933 as short skits performed in the calypso tents.

32. Balliger notes how the press centers calypso and asks, "Who's really listening?" (128).

33. Mason examines its roots as derivative of West African derision songs, as well as indigenous Amerindian, South American, and British traditional folk songs (20–21).

34. Harrigan and Varlack report that "The first English settlement was made without royal authority in St. Kitts in 1624" (3).

35. Charles Kingsley's travelogue declared St. Kitts, with its majestic Mount Misery, "what a West Indian island" should appear to be, informing readers of its "worthy" nickname—Mother of the Antilles. He added that it captured Columbus's imagination, as he envisioned "a giant St. Christopher bearing on his shoulder the infant Christ, and so gave a name to the whole island" (24). Matheson historicizes the island's naming as well.

36. Klein, "Uncovering the Secrets of St. Kitts." The following blog offers an interesting array of historical information: https://www.thedailybeast.com/uncovering-the-secrets-of-st-kitts (updated July 12, 2017).

37. A major exhibit on "Sugar at the University of Michigan" comprehensively delineated the harsh reality for laborers into the twenty-first century, stating that at one time the enslaved African population in the "sugar colonies" was ten times that of Europeans. See https://lsa. umich.edu/daas/engagement/gallerydaas/currentexhibition.html (accessed November 19, 2019).

38. The rapid closure of St. Kitts's sugar industry in 2005 shocked all of the laborers. One study exposes the plight of former female sugar workers; see Clarke and Barker.

39. See Alleyne-Dettmers's "Political Dramas" for more details regarding these ole mas characters relative to Trinidad (328–29) and her "Moko Jumbie" for a description of the ritual of "washing and cleansing" by caking on the mud of J'ouvert (263).

40. Balliger engages the "body" politics of soca as "a new paradigm of cultural politics in the context of globalization" (146). See Manuel et al.'s "Trinidad, Calypso, and Carnival" chapter for an overview of the rise of soca (183–211).

41. Mosimba is an obvious pseudonym. Although I've been unable to determine the author's birth name, the text credibly fills multiple gaps with great specificity.

42. Balliger's "Noisy Spaces" also centers the Road March as "probably the most accurate in terms of popularity" (121). Also, see Kevin Birth, "to achieve a party that never ends" (*Bacchanalian* 156). Manuel et al. explicate the democratizing role of audience enthusiasm in selecting the winning J'ouvert Road March (204). Guilbault legitimates how audiences exercise agency (14).

43. For more details, including interviews, see Mosimba's *History of St. Kitts.*

44. For a comprehensive reading of the conflict, see https://www.facebook.com/SKNTimes/posts/recently-named-a-recipient-of-the-queens-new-year-honour-in-st-kitts-and-nevis-w/189397834477403/.

45. Meanwhile, in Brooklyn, New York, two factions continue to coexist on Labor Day weekend. See Ray Allen, who documents the acrimonious tension resulting in an antagonistic breach over traditionality. The Carnival on Eastern Parkway still launches J'ouvert on island time, CPT (Caribbean People's Time)

46. For more about Christmas sports in St. Kitts and Nisbett's role in its survival, see https://www.myvuenews.com/the-survival-of-the-christmas-sport/ (accessed November 10, 2020).

47. Also see interview in Mosimba (58–61). Matheson also references these characters as mummies/mummers; therefore, apparently, these more Eurocentric aesthetic models disappeared.

48. See Lee, "Carnival at Christmas in St. Kitts." This site provides a large aggregate of ethnographic particulars.

49. Of interest to this study, Cape Town, South Africa, boasts a long New Year's tradition engaging blackface minstrelsy called Coon Carnival. See Denis Martin.

50. See pictures on Facebook of Xtreme Jouvert (SKN) as well as on the official site for Sugar Mas, at https://www.facebook.com/SKNCarnival/?hc_ref=NEWSFEED (accessed April 25, 2015). Since Carnival is a dynamic process, we can expect new trends to launch with glocality via Trinidad and Tobago; for instance, there is the use of "wet down" meaning watershowers from all directions to cool off from the heat along the parade route. At this writing, "Monday wear" is the latest incarnation. It is an added expense as some elect to hire designers for what is a highly bedazzled bikini to outfit Monday Carnival.

51. Guilbault cites Shalini Puri's term "marginal migration," which conveys intraregional cultural and economic exchanges (11).

Chapter 5: "One Grand Noise"

1. For an excellent reading of the culture of taste in the global eighteenth century, see Simon Gikandi, who is especially nuanced regarding Enlightenment discourse (42).

2. Arguably, Stravinsky's musical compositions were influenced by African "primitivism" and jazz, in the same sense of Picasso's visual African art period; also, allowances should be made for the dissonance in Russian folk soundscapes. Besides polyrhythm as a constructive element, the use of timbre is particularly significant: "Stravinsky's handling of the instruments of the orchestra is new and unique: his accented chords in the strings often sound percussive, while the actual percussion is really inexhaustible in its expressive function" (Stravinsky, "Forward" x). Likewise, in the chapter "Stravinsky as Modernist" in *The Cambridge Companion to Stravinsky*, his "Ebony Concerto" is deemed to be tantamount to Picasso's art in the same period (27). As a reminder of Western sensibility to affect, consider the audience's oppositional reception to Stravinsky, whose "The Rite of Spring" concert debut elicited rage, vehemence, recklessness, anger, disturbance, and riotous chaos. In 2013, to commemorate the Paris Riot, see the following report: "The tumult began not long after the ballet's opening notes—a meandering and eerily high-pitched bassoon solo that elicited laughter and derision from many in the audience. The jeers became louder as the orchestra progressed into more cacophonous territory, with its pounding percussion and jarring rhythms escalating in tandem with the tensions inside the recently opened Théâtre des Champs-Élysées." At https://www.theverge. com/2013/5/29/4375736/igor-stravinsky-rite-of-spring-100-anniversary-paris-riot. On National Public Radio, esteemed conductor Gustavo Dudamel declared, "Stravinsky is the father of Heavy Metal." See https://www.npr.org/sections/deceptivecadence/2012/09/28/161964987/ gustavo-dudamel-on-the-magic-of-stravinskys-crazy-music. In actuality, Stravinsky knowingly discovered his affinity with American jazz music elements before the 1920s, a musical style from which US popular music evolved. Incorporating the affective sonic ecology of Stravinsky's ballet composition furthers comprehension of how colonizers leveraged the Afrocentric soundscape of Caribbean cultural flows to reify a hierarchy of dualistic polar oppositions. Stravinsky produced a concertized soundscape that apparently infuriated listeners because of its pejorative association with a primal mania and a cognitive dissonance that coincided with the rise of scientific racism. Therefore, Stravinsky's frequent African-like polyrhythmic percussive sounds disrupted the classical–romantic aesthetics of concert music and ballet choreography, perceived to be heavenly compared to the hellish sonority of people conceived as others.

3. As relates to The Bahamas, see Rosanne Adderley, whose study explores a large population of liberated Africans from illegal slave ships and captured by the British. She explains they "established their own cultural practices or institutions, distinct if not necessarily separate, from the wider black community" (2). The Bahamas received six thousand of the documented forty thousand African immigrants. See Rommen's "Home Sweet Home" for details about

drumming patterns and transcription of the musical lines. Recently, Rommen identified a performance aesthetic shift toward the bass drum privileging the fast beat, deviating from the slow
beat pattern of the early twentieth century (*Funky* 160–61). Rosita Sands judges the Junkanoo
beat to be "very African in sound," the quintessence of its appeal ("Musical" 144). Bohannon
speaks to the "artistic achievement" of polyrhythm in conjunction with African dancing (142).

4. Furthermore, Timothy McCartney concludes that the goatskin drum and the cowbell are
fundamental to all their music (31).

5. Sacred–secular dichotomies are not traditionally upheld in West Africa, but with Christianity in Nassau, religious leaders excoriated the popular use of the tunes of standard hymns,
such as singing "Neely, your rum so sweet" to the tune of "Jesus, Your Name's So Sweet."

6. Quote appears in the St. Croix Christmas Festival program of 1961–1962 authored by
Charles H. Emanuel. Purportedly, the bamboula dance event garners its name from the boula
drum. Boula means "to beat," according to McDaniel (82). Willocks stresses some interesting propositions regarding the dance's history, purportedly by Catholic nuns dancing the
Bamboula sacree, and when secularized, "The *Bamboula* was a choir in motion. People sang as
they danced. They organized functions and protests by using the *Bamboula*. The *Bamboula* was
accompanied only by a percussion instrument, namely, the drum" (15). Breberton mentions a
range of traditional dances in the British and French West Indies ("The British" 106).

7. A. C. Carmichael authored a detailed account of domestic life in the Caribbean that also
notates Christmas food allotments distributed to enslaved persons, mentioning ox as another
common provision (193). Her thick descriptions repetitively confirm the requisite nighttime
nature of holiday festivities, extending until sunrise.

8. Bettelheim reports that, in Jamaica by the 1950s, the *Daily Gleaner*, spearheaded by its
chief editor, used competition to revitalize the Jonkonnu festival ("Festival Arts" 42).

9. Andy Hamilton applauds recent ethnomusicologists and anthropologists for determining that many African languages do not have a term for music, unlike post-Enlightenment
Europeans (50).

10. In *Popular Culture in Early Modern Europe*, Peter Burke labels the descriptions acquired
from foreign visitors as "an elusive quarry" (65–88). See Mary Louise Pratt's *Imperial Eyes:
Travel Writing and Transculturation*, billed as the seminal work in the study of travel literature.
Roach reconciles "literate observers" and their Eurocentric notions of rude noise with a failure
to legitimize their subjects' "incorporated memory" (62).

11. See Kenneth Bilby, "Africa's Creole Drum," which fills a void regarding eighteenth-
century Jamaican Maroon returnees to Sierra Leone and the trans-African creolization of the
gumbe, which is square or rectangular (137–77).

12. Perhaps, more metaphorically, Kamau Brathwaite evokes Roach's theoretical principle, in
his own "bridges of sound" line as allegorized in his poem "Jah."

13. Rifting off of Pratt's "imperial gaze" and "the seeing-man" construct, Hill introduces "the
hearing-man," the travelers who supplemented their texts by inscribing native soundscapes (4).

14. Attali theorizes noise as a "simulacrum of murder": "noise had always been experienced
as destruction, disorder, dirt, pollution, an aggression against the code-structuring message"
(27).

15. In *Funky Nassau*, Rommen relies on this Ferguson quote as an example of attempts to
"describe the ineffable dimensions of the festival [and] its great value for Bahamian identity"
(128).

16. See Franzone for a more detailed analysis of soul based on Garifuna, St. Vincentian,
Yoruba, and Dahomean cultures, finding significant overlap.

17. Wood reinforces the similarities of West African music ensembles and Junkanoo music
in her section on polyrhythms (347–50). She also draws from Ghanaian ethnomusicologist

Nketia. Interestingly, Alan Lomax most thoroughly articulates the formation of the Delta blues and frequently addresses African retentions, writing, "Most black African music—in Africa and in the New World—is highly rhythmic, group-performed, and sanguine in tone" (277). His use of the word "sanguine" connotes a commitment to a full-bodied expression of one grand noise.

18. *The Drummer's Path* by Sule Wilson speaks to stick technique and African drums along with supplying an illustration of drumsticks—African, Native, and Euro-American (75–78).

19. Tricia Rose's *Black Noise* addresses the manipulation of sound using technology, stating, "they deliberately work in the red" (75). For Carnival 2018, apparently with new technologies, there was a move to discard sound trucks. See http://www.panonthenet.com/tnt/2018/articles/who-needs-big-trucks-and-big-speakers-for-carnival.htm (accessed August 7, 2019).

20. This speculation is based on an overview, "Trinidad, Calypso, and Carnival," in *Caribbean Currents*. Also, "Time Out or Time In?" by Riggio discusses Trinidad Carnival's long appropriation of discarded objects for musical use and the "controversial use of the big truck" (20).

21. As relates to linguistics, see Palmié, "Is There a Model in the Muddle?" (191–92). Harewood establishes the degree to which scholars unabashedly subscribe to African retentions in the Caribbean. It has become a much-maligned and taboo ideological position, but Africanness claims should not be viewed as a denial of the implicit pluralisms inherent in the colonial experience but can be perceived as a coping strategy that centers surrogacy as a process to maintain an ethnic cultural stance, paying homage to their ancestors' refusal to assimilate. Researching the settlements of liberated African immigrants, contraband from the then-illegal slave trade, historian Rosanne Adderley explains: "That is, claims of Africanness just as much as claims of Indianness are evidence of a collective rejection of the largely negative experience of the New World and a casting of cultural and geographic allegiances elsewhere" (223). Such discourse opens up a dialectic that privileges an African pulsating musical rhythm and dance complex. Furthermore, Storr writes to decenter the work ethic espoused by sociologist Max Weber by way of extolling Junkanoo artists: "Another significant lesson that Bahamians learn from Junkanoo is to trust in their own creativity" ("Weber's Spirit" 303). Adderley concludes that "Africans and their descendants simultaneously and over long periods of time could and did negotiate a dialectical experience of simultaneously remaining African and becoming African American" (236). In so doing, they relied on their cultural equipage to deal with the unique situations presented by sociopolitical change.

22. This testament to Africanisms is in keeping with the conceptualizing of the African diaspora by other folklorists, anthropologists, archaeologists, musicologists, etc. Archaeologists Wilkie and Farnsworth "consider the mechanisms through which people think that they are maintaining cultural links with their past" (6). They entitled one chapter "The Many African Origins of Bahamian" as a preface to an archaeological study of a plantation there. Similarly, Rosalyn Howard writes, "Despite these ongoing debates, there is a strong consensus that some elements of contemporary cultural practices and belief systems found among peoples of African descent in various areas of the diaspora appear to have evolved from the legacies of African cultures" ("Yoruba" 159). Intent on righting a wrong in his dissertation, calypsonian Hollis Liverpool centers the "noble contributions" of African peoples. Also, see Hedrick and Stephens (27). Allahar relentlessly scrutinizes what he considers essentialism in the Caribbean.

23. Interestingly, along the way, one of the first arbiters of the Caribbean festival arts, Judith Bettelheim, differentiates between African- and English-influenced troupes ("Jamaican Jonkonnu" 82–83). Fundamentally, her interrogation reveals the one-time coexistence of two "dichotomous underlying influences," "with the animal characters of horsehead and cowhead [appearing] to be the most direct legacies of an African heritage." In 1976, although viewed as rural, "To the contemporary Jamaican, the horse head and cowhead are African symbols,

powerful, wild, and scary" (84). Along with articulating the genealogies of performance and the kinesthetic imagination as features of memory, Joseph Roach enters the discursive fray regarding the nature and extent of Africanism by centering performance as the compelling evidence for retention (22–23).

24. See Martin Munro, *Different Drummers*, which contributes to the field of aural history and engages Africanized culture. More exactly, Scher insists, "it seems possible to negotiate an anthropology that is both anti-essentialist and sensitive to the role that 'essentialisms' play, without condemnation" ("Carnival" 5). In his conclusion to "Flows, Boundaries, and Hybrids," Hannerz writes, "We need to have a sense of which words, and ideas, and interest, are ours, and which are theirs" (15).

25. The Maroons of Jamaica were notorious for their use of drumming as part of their early warning "espionage system"; see Mavis Campbell (40). The travel writing of Janet Schaw proves to be contradictory. Seemingly unperturbed about "the beautiful sights" gleaned from viewing a procession of enslaved holiday revelers and offering how they idolized their master as a "Buccra God," yet she writes, "It is necessary however to keep a look out during this season of unbounded freedom; and every man on the Island is in arms and patrols go all round the different plantations as well as keep guard in the town. They are an excellent disciplined Militia and make very military appearance [in Antigua]" (Schaw et al. 107–108). See also "Drums and Power" by Cullen Rath; while specific to South Carolina, it directly uses fear as the motivating factor to ban African drumming.

26. Also, Nketia's "The Intensity Factor in African Music" states, "it seems essential in African music practice to consider not only the modes of communication that can be established through music itself, but also the ways of presenting music as an event that provides an integrated aural, kinesics, and visual experience that stimulates particular modes of response and interaction" (56). Munro establishes the role of catharsis "through the rhythmic intensity of the dance and the drum" (20).

27. For instance, Bohannan enlists reciprocity as an important "allocative principle" (219).

28. Archaeologists Wilkie and Farnsworth, too, credit initial searches for Africanisms, "establishing that enslaved Africans reconstructed aspects of their traditional lifestyles and beliefs despite the restraints of enslavement" (3).

29. In addition, see Anton Allahar, referencing Kimani Nehusi in Henke and Réno: "the street parade segment of the celebration is symbolic of the Africans' reclaiming their physical, spiritual and cultural freedom" (40).

30. Abrahams, in the context of agricultural ceremonies, privileges the processions held by English elite stakeholders, but does state, "Moreover, those slaves who had come from agricultural areas of Africa would have held on to harvest ceremonies of their own" (*Singing the Master* 55). In his book published in 1888, Powles substantiates the ubiquity of the cultural practice: "The darkies are fond of processions, and never miss an opportunity of getting one up" (147).

31. Also, see Williams-Mysers's documentation of the Pinkster Carnival in Albany, New York, as an African religious holiday. Dewulf centers Pinkster as an Atlantic Creole production.

32. Dance scholar Gottschild further explicates this propensity as a "democracy of structure": "Even in line dances there may be a shifting circle of onlookers surrounding the performers" (9).

33. In devising her articulation of performance praxis as relates to play, Dikobe recognizes it as "an engaging participatory, transformational process that is often, but not always, competitive" (15). Yet, on Boxing Day in particular and in most ancillary events during the holiday in the Caribbean Anglicized World, competition rules. Julian Gerstin, in "Tangled Roots," specifies the Congo–Angola area as the region likely to champion "challenge/display" dancing, highlighting a men's competitive display event sighted in The Bahamas (22). Guilbault

theorizes about the politics of musical aesthetics and its articulation through calypso competitions (72–89).

34. In the context of Junkanoo, Wood reports the camps were "a compound-like area that houses several small shacks, or an area in which a well-known Junkanooer lives and where several other Junkanooers from the same group work on costumes or music. A camp can also be a following of a particular performer, especially in the case of drummers" (243).

35. Bashi describes a "culture of reciprocity" as central hubs in transmigrant social networks (83). In my prior research, I categorized this propensity as "reciprocal support networks."

36. Studying Port of Spain, Trinidad, Balliger addresses "Word, Sound, Power: Music in Everyday Spaces," even adopting "sonic mapping" to convey the quotidian location of various forms of musics (103).

37. The term was coined by Murray Schafer in *The New Soundscape*. While a defining moment, his study fails to consider the functionality of sound. Moreover, informed by a Westernized ethos, his tendency is still to study environments in relation to qualitative studies of "noisy and unpleasant places." Franzone speaks to ethos as an aesthetic communal bedrock within the African diaspora in response to colonization (303–304).

38. Of course, some aggregate residents view noise with displeasure and discord as well. Peter Bailey, in "Breaking the Sound Barrier," addresses the dialectic of noise and silence (26).

39. There is a certain reflexivity and consciousness grounded in the subversion and alternative identity connected to hip hop's "new noize." Nelson and Gonzales's *Bring the Noise* serves as an introduction to this new music: "Air electric, buzzin' wit da hum of new noize; steady beat shaking da ground like an earthquake in da jungle" (xvi). Tricia Rose titled her first hip hop study *Black Noise*, as it was among the first to theorize hip hop culture's transgressive power relationships. She stated, "for many young people they are the primary cultural, sonic, and linguistic windows on the world," which is apropos to my interrogation (19). DJ Kool Herc, a Jamaican immigrant, is credited for rap music's genesis in the mid- to late 1970s. The sound systems he used "produced powerful bass frequencies and also played clear treble tones" (Rose 52). Therefore, hip hop culture's godfather introduced island sonic waves into the US mainland.

40. Indeed, together with the Lord of Misrule, "the waits" were bands of poor amateur musicians who played street music. See Weightman Humphries's *Christmas Past*, which explains, "The illegitimate excess of the poorer people were in drinking, and filling the streets with noise" (53; see photo on 52).

41. Additionally, see *Neither Led nor Driven* by Moore and Johnson, who fault missionaries in the islands with the deliberate "effort to replace one culture with another" (195).

42. R. Murray Schafer uses the term "earwitness" to differentiate soundscapes from a landscape: "A soundscape consists of events *heard* not objects *seen*" ("Soundscapes" 6; his emphasis). In *Tuning of the World*, Schafer's glossary defines earwitness: "One who testifies or can testify to what he or she has heard" (272).

43. Most read Carnival as "organized cultural resistance," according to Liverpool (xx).

44. While adding depth to my study, Nechvatal's argument is dependent on social position as a practicing artist and theorist engaging Western philosophical considerations.

Chapter 6: Foreday Morning

1. Annually, in August, Barbados's Crop Over Festival features the Foreday Morning Jam, described as a night till morning "jump-up" of music, revelry, and mas with thousands of people frolicking behind music and/or percussion trucks. Colorz Entertainment is a top-rated Barbados promoter of Crop Over and assures participants they will have an enjoyable

on-the-road jump-up experience. Also, African American blues music discographies reveal the same vernacular usage, such as James Cotton's "Fore Day Blues" and Ida Cox's "Fore Day Creep."

2. Henriquez's ethnography introduced me to the vernacular term "bashment" (another name for dancehall music) and the prominence of base culture's hard-core sound systems booming out of doors through the night.

3. For one glaring example, see Matt Ridley, "Is the Enlightenment Dimming?," at http://www.rationaloptimist.com/blog/endarkenment/ (accessed June 9, 2019), which describes current reactionary populist defenders of the Enlightenment era. "Endarkenment," deriving from "endarkened," is based on grammatical rules specifying the "-ment" to denote a product. For example, see Ridley's sentence: "Or maybe the entire world is heading into a great endarkenment, in which an atmosphere of illiberal orthodoxy threatens the achievement of recent centuries." The "-ment" suffix also alludes to "new things," while the "-ed" suffix in "endarkened" expresses a completed action, as implied by my usage. Nonetheless, I assume that neoconservative ideologies in opposition to political correctness and dependent on enlightenment philosophy are incapable of perceiving endarkenment as a positive. Allowing for nonbinary thought is beyond Western dichotomous thinking. Then, there is also "sacred endarkenment" as affiliated with Wicca and other New Age forms of spirituality. However, at least the belief system is formulated on pre-Enlightenment-era "paganism," which includes "decolonizing time" among its list of spiritual endarkenment practices.

4. Regarding temporality, Junkanoo shares this one commonality with Trinidadian Carnival and J'ouvert, beginning at 2 a.m. See Balliger, "Noisy Spaces," 121. Additionally, Rosita Sands reports finding the same commonality in Key West, Florida, where traditionally on New Year's Day a low-scale festive gathering occurred in the wee hours when unmasked Junkanoo musicians appeared playing from a truck bed ("Musical" 153).

5. See "Junkanoo Spirit," at http://amasewa.tripod.com/Junkanoo-Soulsite-index.html (accessed October 25, 2017).

6. Ghosts, witches, and other supernatural beings populate African American folklore as memorates—personal experience narrative. Throughout the Caribbean, the jab-jab, jumbies, and soucouyants nightly occupy the cultural imaginary. More theoretically, Schafer provides an appendix and reports on an "International Sound Preference Survey" in which 10 percent of the Jamaicans surveyed responded to night sounds as unpleasant, with none for the Canadians and Swiss (*Tuning* 268–69).

7. In *Jumbies*, Nicholls suggests duppies and Mocko Jumbies are synonymous. I would differ based on a few admittedly etic technicalities. Although in the oral tradition, the terms may be used interchangeably to denote spirits in general, jumbies as part of a festival art equate with ancestral spirits, which are distinct entities. Furthermore, Nicholls refers to an African derivation of the term, leading to an assessment equating these spirits with animism—a long-debunked association. See Vincent Brown, who discusses the Jamaican plantocracy's penchant to exact awe by terrorizing enslaved persons, making use of "the relationship between dead bodies, haunting spirits, and political authority" (24). Errol Hill explains why the Carnival figures from folklore (soucouyant, diablesse, loup garou, etc.) emit "weird noises" and are "nocturnal beings" unable to face the light of day (*Trinidadian*). Also, "J'ouvert" allegedly derives from the soucouyant (vampiric hag) avoidance of the crack of dawn; see Alleyne-Dettmers ("Political" 328).

8. See David Scott's *Conscripts of Modernity*, which notes that, by the mid-nineteenth century, "an aggressive and openly derogatory racialism" contributed to the outlawing of funerals, with bleak consequences for both owners and enslaved persons (387). By happenstance, Rashford mentions duppies in the context of plants that attract them as well as those with a "generic

term in their compound names" (63). Gardner's description of Jamaican wakes mentions that they removed any fear of trouble-causing duppies or ghosts. Orlando Patterson discusses spirit beliefs in Jamaica as well as the derivation of "duppy" (202–207).

9. Bessie Pullen-Burry's description typifies Eurocentric response to Caribbean funerary customs (150–53). Pullen-Burry witnessed Nine-Night, which is similar to a wake and allows time for the spirit of the deceased to move on before burial. Nightly, it features a lively party. For more contemporary details, see Wardle, who, in two chapters, creates an in-depth depiction and interpretation of this period of bereavement (138–76). See also Rev. Joseph J. Williams, *Whisperings of the Caribbean: Reflections of a Missionary*, which quotes Gardner: "In 1831, night funerals were prohibited by law, owners permitting them were liable to a penalty of fifty pounds, and slaves attending them, to a whipping of thirty-nine lashes. In the early part of the century they were very frequent. The scenes presented on these occasions were wild in the extreme, though rarely witnessed by white people, and only then by stealth. One or more negroes played upon the goomba, and another, at intervals, blew a horn made of conch shell; another took the solo part of a recitative of a wild funeral wail, usually having reference to the return of the departed to Africa; while a party sitting in a circle, gave the chorus. These melancholy dirges were often protracted through the night the coffin not being laid in the grave till the morning star arose. Food consisting of pork, yam, rum, etc., was placed in the coffin, for the use of the departed in his long journey across the blue waters to the fatherland. In later years it became common to use more expedition at the grave, and when the funeral was over, and a few dirges sung, to return to the house and spend the night in feasting, often accompanied with dancing" (234–35). Franzone describes "Ninth Night" rites among the Garifuna as being inclusive with a full complement of music and dancing, the role of women, and the finale featuring late night storytelling to socialize children, functioning as African griots might (195, 300). Gonzáles also describes Garifuna burial rites (ch. 4). Sörgel adds to the discourse related to Nine-Night funerary customs, ancestral forces, and dancing (51–52).

10. Alleyne-Dettmers also analyzes the Mocko Jumbies' origins, nomenclature, sculptural iconography, etc. ("Moko Jumbie" 262–87). Rashford restricts the term "Jumbie" to the eastern Caribbean, which would include St. Croix and St. Kitts. He further identifies Rev. J Scoles as a source for their being "associated with danger and death" (63). Franzone enhances the discussion by noting, "the Garinagu of Belize call [them] 'guibida'" and set a "jombee table" for the ancestors at Christmas (261).

11. This interpretation suits the need to differentiate Mocko Jumbies from duppies or evil spirits since, as with ancestral forces, they defend primarily family members during time of crisis. See Cowley, *Carnival*. Beckwith includes a photograph of two masked stilt dancers (supposedly called John Canoe) performing at Christmas in Belize City, marching up the street to the accompaniment of a fife and drum band; the picture had been given to her by a British ex-judge from Belize (*Black Roadways* 32). Nicholls is the Crucian authority regarding the Mocko Jumbies' masquerade genre, and he provides a full etymology and its relationship to Mumbo Jumbo ("African Arts" 51–53).

12. Moore and Johnson include an in-depth listing of "signs that the duppies were close by" (37).

13. Similarly, out of curiosity, Charles Kingsley's travelogue includes a description after attending a "Jumby-dance amongst the Africans on the estate that very night" (242). His thick description contains the expected disapprobation related to sights, sounds, and smells.

14. Bonham C. Richardson, in *Igniting the Caribbean's Past Fire*, describes Caribbean sugarcane fire as environmental, biological, and social phenomena. According to Michael Anthony, "Following the Carnival Proclamation of 1884 which banned the canboulay, Carnival was not permitted to begin before six a.m. on Carnival Monday and it ended at midnight on Carnival

Tuesday" (16). Zazek dissects the catastrophes that challenged colonizers' reports on the risk of fire. Matheson, too, makes mention of crop-over festivities in St. Kitts.

15. Long's *Folklore Calendar* documents Bonfire Night's transitioning into a jolly carnival, along with explicit "Reference to the Carnival at Lewes, Sussex" (204–207). Daniel Crowley ethnographically describes an observance in Abros, The Bahamas, in which one reply to the significance of Guy Fawkes Day was "Burning a guy is like John Canoe" ("Guy Fawkes" 14–115). Craton and Saunders's chapter "Nassau and the First Tourists" lists it among holiday celebrations (83). More recently, the *Guardian* reported on the 2013 celebratory event; see http://www .theguardian.com/uk-news/davehillblog/2013/nov/05/bonfire-night-london-2013 (accessed October 25, 2017). Also, politicized groups appropriate a mask of the legendary figure as an iconic meme, popularized by the *V Is for Vendetta* graphic novel franchise.

16. In "Crucian Myths and Customs Were Sporting Fun," Heyliger notes that Guy Fawkes Day (November 5) is the date that often signals (like the US Thanksgiving) the start of the holiday season. Packwood describes how "Bermudians celebrated that day by building bonfires, setting off fire squibs, serpents, crackers, plus burnt 'The Guy' in effigy. This gave Blacks a time to handle and hide gun powder. . . . not surprisingly after the Conspiracy of 1761, a proclamation was issued forbidding Guy Fawkes Day for that year" (94).

17. When they tune drums during Junkanoo, drummers now also use sternos to maintain the heat. Wood provides a lengthy description of the process (257–60).

18. For elemental features, see J. D. Elder, "Cannes Brûlées" (48–52). Sands's conversation with Ronald Simms describes how the "jumping dance" involves fire and "raw, unadulterated" Junkanoo music (104).

19. During a site visit to The Bahamas, anthropologist Powles actually "arranged for the sergeant of police to have one get up for his benefit," and goes on to provide a thick description of drumming, chanting, and dance (148). He concludes, "It was, in short, a savage African dance in European dress."

20. See Frank Roberts's Huffpost article: http://www.huffingtonpost.com/frank-leon-roberts/ lee-daniels-double-consci_b_3767252.html (accessed October 25, 2017). Roberts overtly reinscribes Frantz Fanon's distinction in *Black Skin, White Mask* about being Black among one's own versus the sense of inferiority felt while being Black under the white gaze (110).

21. Edwards's text includes a trickster tale cycle of prose narratives such as "B'Bouki an' B'Rabby" (equivalent to African American Brer Rabbit folktales), with the night as a major leitmotif (67). Historian W. J. Gardner also describes moonlit nights as ripe for festivities in postemancipation Jamaica (383–84).

22. See Young and Harris's "Demonizing the Night in Medieval Europe: A Temporal Monstrosity," which situates the night as a metaphor for evil, dividing day and light from night and darkness. Vincent Brown wrote that, in the eighteenth century, judges sent to rural areas invoked "the power of light and darkness to pronounce death sentences by donning a black cap" (29). Therefore, darkness became synonymous with evil, death, and blackness.

23. LIME (an acronym for Landline, Internet, Mobile, Entertainment) is a communications provider owned by the UK-based Cable & Wireless Communications. Cellular companies sponsor many Carnival troupes, and their logo is a constant presence. Sponsorship means the acquisition of T-shirts, limitless beverages both alcoholic and water, etc.

24. The term "deep play" derives from Clifford Geertz's usage in his study of Balinese cockfighting. Franco's chapter delineates the domination of women's participation in Trinidad's Carnival and efforts to suppress them. Also, see *Walking Raddy: The Baby Dolls of New Orleans*, edited by Kim Vaz-Deville.

25. Wood also devotes space to discussing the discrimination faced by women who perform in the back line (222). Some of the resentment might also stem from the hard work and past experiences with women who "have no desire to get involved in the pasting of their costume" (224).

26. With the emergence of new media, especially YouTube, the possibility for exploration of Christmas masquerades worldwide has grown. For example, see https://www.youtube .com/watch?v=5TvOzd7HP6k (accessed August 4, 2014). On the New Year's Day Cape Town Coon Carnival in South Africa, see Denis Martin and the video at https://www.youtube .com/watch?v=8IDx5toJf8s (accessed August 4, 2014), which reveals a rarified parade tradition engaging subversive blackface minstrelsy. In a conversation with me, Dr. Christopher Okonkwo alluded to having witnessed cross-dressing by youth in his Nigerian hometown on Boxing Day. In a *Slate* exposé, "Scare Tactics: Why Are Liberian Soldiers Wearing Fright Wigs?," Mark Scheffler writes that cross-dressing was a military strategy to induce paralyzing fear, saying, "The cross-dressing 'dual identity' isn't just a source of battlefield bravado, though. Cross-dressing has deep historical roots in West African rites-of-passage rituals involving 'medicine men' who would recommend wearing masks, talismans, and bush attire as a means of obtaining mystical powers"; http://www.slate.com/articles/news_and_politics/the_gist/2003/08/ scare_tactics.html (accessed June 29, 2016). Bolich's *Transgender History and Geography* offers a comprehensive interrogation of gender variances in traditional African societies, unrelated to ritual as well as anatomy.

27. See https://www.vice.com/en_ca/article/xw7wxz/we-asked-the-women-of-pretty-mas -about-the-true-essence-of-trini-carnival (accessed June 18, 2019). This site gives voice to the Trinidadian women of Pretty Mas. Regarding inclusivity, this Vice website engages issues related to intersectionality in terms of colorism and body type: https://www.vice.com/en_ca/ article/d3exdm/i-want-to-celebrate-freedom-for-all-bodies-at-carnival (accessed June 18, 2019).

28. As pertains to Carnival, Mason meticulously examines the emergence of women-centered mas since the 1980s (134–36). Formerly, when masculinity prevailed, according to Matheson, St. Kittitians generated the transnational cultural flow that influenced not only Bermudian Gombeys but possibly festival in the Dominican Republic as well.

29. 9. The violent event that precipitated this response involved two police culprits later charged with killing two men and wounding four. See https://www.policeone.com/officer -shootings/articles/1645356-US-Virgin-Islands-police-officer-arrested-for-shootingbiblio -spree/ (accessed June 26, 2017).

30. Harlem Renaissance writer Claude McKay, in his autobiographical article "Boyhood in Jamaica," later published along with short stories in *My Green Hills of Jamaica*, comprehensively describes how, on moonlit nights, the childhood custom was to outline their bodies with pieces of broken crockery and says the practice was of African origin (10).

31. For confirmation, see Dirks, "Evolution" (92). Also confirmed by my own participant-observation in Dangriga on December 26, 2013.

32. See http://www.tntisland.com/jouvert.html (accessed September 23, 2013) and https:// www.discovertnt.com/articles/Trinidad/The-Birth-Evolution-of-Trinidad-Carnival/109/3/ 32#axzz6prKQmg34 (accessed July 5, 2012).

33. The intent here is not to debate the spirituality quotient inherent in such fetes. However, Kilby's "Surviving" furnishes a clearer, more thorough idea of a scholarly argument that supports masking as a dialectical extension of religious culture.

34. Mason discusses exporting Carnival (161–66).

35. The following site confirms the globalizing shift from centuries-old Boxing Day customs to late capitalism's allure: http://www.dailymail.co.uk/news/article-2078597/Boxing-Day-sales -Record-numbers-shops-open-8o-push-grab-shoppers.html (accessed July 5, 2012).

36. The quote is from a Facebook page (no longer available) I found about upcoming fetes in St. Croix.

37. See Sands, "Conversation."

Chapter 7: From "Back o' Town"

1. Walts's dissertation breaks down the bifurcation of time, positioning "traditional time (qualitative, concrete, local, imprecise, organic time—also referred to as 'primitive' time) against modern time (quantitative, abstract, uniform, exact, mechanical time)." Nanni presents the hegemonic response that positioned Western time as one of the measures of civilization, with African time signifying "evidence of a state of immature cultural development" (136–37).

2. Michael Stausberg historicizes time in the context of religion and contends there is a basic absence of abstract time in traditional cultures.

3. Munro speaks of the temporal conflict regarding the rhythmic ordering of African-based and Christian festivals in the Caribbean, identifying the interdependence of time and culture (18). Generally, this temporal orientation signifies a phenomenon-based reality: "the same time next year."

4. Dohrn-van Rossum's *History of the Hour: Clocks and Modern Temporal Orders* presents the first sustained and reliable treatment of how mechanical clocks functioned in cities and dispels myths about the role of merchants. Rather than hypothesize, he maintains, "Still, the question remains open whether merchants or commercial practice made special use of the new timekeeping devices and/or their product, the new hour-reckoning, for their own purposes" (227). Aventi attributes the demands for church time as the key to "timekeeping in our culture" (92). In a nutshell, Landes argues, "The clock did not create an interest in time measurement; the interest in time measurement led to the invention of the clock" (58). Nanni's nuanced analysis attributes race-consciousness to the move toward "temporal asceticism" by first colonizing the leisure time activities of British workers (46–47).

5. See the seminal study of time during the Middle Ages by Jacques Le Goff, *Time Work and Culture*. He argues that merchant and church time were in competition, while Walts analyzes the commodification of time as a status symbol and Nanni's research focuses on the forging of European temporal identities and its interlocking relationship with colonialism.

6. Also see Mavis E. Mate, "Work and Leisure" (290). The invention of mechanical clocks made it easier to calculate time by the hour and even by the minute. According to Mate, clocks can be documented all over Europe, including southern England, from the second quarter of the fourteenth century although it may have been another hundred years before most towns had one. As towns acquired their own clocks, the urban day came to be regulated by the bell. Goods could not be sold in the market before and after certain hours. Town gates opened and shut a specific time rather than at sunrise or sunset. Finally, the length of the working day was set down by local and national authorities. In addition, Nanni writes that colonizers developed a racialized sense of superiority, whereas McDonald addresses various holiday scenarios prevalent in Louisiana (52–53). N. A. T. Hall extols the use of "free" time as conducive to cultures' building distinctly their own (122).

7. Nanni devotes a chapter to African time and colonial discourse, writing, "In turn, the apparent lack of temporal knowledge among Africans would help Europeans justify the need for the redemptive civilizing influences of Christianity and civilisation whose moral material

virtues were encoded in their culture of the clock and the Sabbath" (125). Additionally, he addresses the Western taxonomy created to reflect the colonizers' "evolutionist worldview" of Bushman-time, Hottentot-time, and Kaffir-time (135–40).

8. This website provides a visual image of the Circus as well as the quoted description: http://www.geographia.com/stkitts-nevis/knpnto2.htm (accessed October 4, 2010).

9. Gupta, too, examines the profound impact of Western colonialism's domination in representations of time over Indian subjects (192).

10. For Glissant, "rhythmic plainsong" is the idea that since the tropics lack seasonal changes as in Europe, there is "another rhythm . . . another notion of time" (161).

11. Carlo Cipolla's short book *Clocks and Culture, 1300–1700* elaborates on the Chinese Mandarins' response to Western clocks. He surmises that, since they were eager to trade with the Chinese for its silk and tea, the invention of the clock answered the European traders' lack of exportable goods. While the intricacy of clocks enchanted Asians, still they preferred their seasonal time reckoning and resisted living by ordered time.

12. See Heyliger, "Xmas on St. Croix" (6). One of Heyliger's older articles, it lists by name a host of revelers, details musical forms, and describes masquerade traditions, stating that "Masquerades coming out" was the watchword. The phrase "anytime is Trinidad time," an expression from a calypso song, captures a shared knowledge regarding clock time and phenomenon time (Birth 33).

13. In comparison, on New Year's Day, the Philadelphia Mummers Parade currently is organized to launch at 11 a.m., lasting six and a half hours, and in no way approximating the timetable of similar festivities in the ACW. Turning parading into a science, officials even predict that each band will follow at twelve- or thirteen-minute intervals. Timewise, not even New Orleans Mardi Gras compares, with its earliest parade scheduled for 8 a.m. The Black Indians do not step off until usually 1:00 p.m. but are subject to police harassment toward women and children alike. In Louisiana, Kinser reports a segregation pattern even during Festive Time: "Down to the 1830s, at least, holiday meant for both whites and blacks, above all else, music and dancing. They were conveniently physical, wordless ways of forgetting the reasons people had for hating each other in a slave-based world, and a world of sharp political and economic competition between Creoles and Anglo-Americans. The timing of holiday, however, insured that slaves and free men rarely danced at the same places. Slaves danced throughout the year on Sundays in some places also on Saturdays. The Christmas holidays and the days before Lent provided a little extra festive time. White festivities were more concentrated in the cool, clement winter season and above all in the period from New Year's Day to Ash Wednesday" (60). Also, see Robert Tallant's *Mardi Gras*. Roach addresses the intolerable harassment by police there (192).

14. Nanni proposes that the same could be said for Australian Aboriginal mission laborers and their contestation of time, by redeploying temporal consciousness as a "negotiation tool" (115).

15. Nanni notes a change in the discursive dynamics caused by an inversion in which Westerners perceive tardiness as exotic and more favorable (234). I observed the induction into the National Junkanoo Legends Circle at the 2010 Independence Day Anniversary people's rush. Although it commenced at 2 a.m., the actual rushin' was a couple of hours later.

16. Thompson locates the viewers on Shirley Street as a site "longtime Junkanooers would not perform on because it lacked the prestige of Bay Street" ("Shine" fn. 103). Ives explains, "Sherley [sic] street runs next south of and parallel with Bay Street and is the second street in extent and importance" (50). Based on my personal observation on this poorly lit street, Boxing Day Junkanooers become more alive before the mobs of people who eschewed purchasing bleacher seating appeared and order was enforced on Bay Street. Afterwards, when I would

mention Shirley as my street preference, locals would warn me of its dangers. Nevertheless, I'll never forget how, when walking with the crowd, a group of passing young men protectively said to the swarm of people, "Watch out for mama," guarding me from inadvertent harm by the exhilarated throng.

17. Lipsitz's article is a response to a similar imposition in New Orleans although "those assembled posed no threat to civic order and the Indians had never needed a permit before though their organizations have been parading every St. Joseph's Day for more than a century" (10). Coinciding with my site visit in 2010 to observe Boxing Day along with the debacle of Boxing Day occurring on Sunday (meaning no petitions would be granted until Monday), a Nor'easter ravaged the US Northeast and also affected the Gombeys due to the towering head-dress that is worn. After hours of trying to obtain information, I finally heard a rumor that the children of one troupe would perform instead. Therefore, all was not lost; plus, on Sunday I did make rounds with Places troupe, who rationalized that no permit would be needed. I gained a sense of these leaders' mastery in negotiating boundaries to their advantage.

18. To historicize the wealth of business leaders, see Juanae Baker, "Legacy, History & Con-tributions of 'Backatawn,'" *Bernews*, February 9, 2015; at http://bernews.com/2015/02/legacy -history-contributions-of-backatawn/ (accessed July 22, 2016). She notes how "Affectionately known as Backatawn, the North Hamilton area has been the hub of black activity and business in the City of Hamilton for many years."

19. Regarding insights into the plight of back-o-town businesses in Bermuda, see http:// ourac.royalgazette.com/news/article/20181220/drive-to-boost-business-in-back-of-town-shops (accessed July 30, 2015).

20. For Places Gombey, see https://www.facebook.com/search/top?q=places%20gombey (accessed July 14, 2016).

21. Gail Saunders, in *Social Life in the Bahamas, 1880s–1920s*, correctly identifies a three-tier system, stating, "The institution of slavery left an indelible mark on Caribbean society. Post-emancipation society was divided into three major tiers or classes. At the top of the social pyramid was the white or upper class, in an intermediate position was the coloured and black middle class and at the bottom, the black masses comprising the former slaves, Liber-ated Africans and their descendants" (3). Powrie also deconstructs the social class divide that hindered the colored cult of respectability in Trinidad from participating in Carnival except as an eventual "periodic safety valve" (226).

22. According to Whittington Johnson's *Post-Emancipation*, "Most governors of the Bahamas did not condone white Bahamians who displayed color prejudice against their nonwhite brethren. One of those governors, William Colebrooke, believed that color prejudice was an American import, a legacy of the American Loyalists who had settled in the Bahamas after the American Revolution" (124). Craton states, straightforwardly, "The most obnoxious effect of the flood of American tourists and investors, traceable since the 1920s or even earlier . . . was the substitution of American patterns of racism and residential apartheid for the relaxed and pragmatic Bahamian tradition of coexistence and interdepen-dence" (*History* 80).

23. In *Bahamian Society*, relying on Eneas, Gail Saunders specifies that because Conta Butta was settled by the Congos, the Yorubas deemed them to be socially inferior (78). Additionally, see Whittington Johnson, *Post-Emancipation*. Back-o-town included Fox Hill, which contained a series of neighborhoods—called "towns"—bearing the names of African clans (tribes) or of prominent inhabitants: Congo Town, Nango (Yoruba) Town, Joshua Town, and Burnside Town (W. Johnson 53). Regarding the residents, called Fox Hillians, see the official Fox Hill site: http://www.bahamas.com/vendor/fox-hill#zoom=14&lat=25.02059&lon=-77.29362&layers

=00BoT (accessed August 29, 2016). Craton and Saunders mention an additional locale: "The inland Blue Hill Ridge was the favorite location for African apprentices working in town" (10). Nicolette Bethel's dissertation devotes a chapter to Fox Hill, establishing that it was no longer the "illegitimate child of the city" (Nassau), but suburban (100). Howard, in "Yoruba," adds to this discourse regarding back o' town in The Bahamas (167).

24. See Borchert's *Alley Life in Washington*; and Frankel and Goldstein's *In the Alleys*.

25. For instance, in 1997, medical doctor Philip W. Thompson AKA "Slimy" was an honoree of a National Junkanoo Legends Circle Award, and he was raised in the heart of Market Street, another predominantly Junkanoo stronghold. According to an unpublished award banquet program, Sammy Thompson was first introduced to Junkanoo as a dancer in 1973. After participating as a dancer in a couple of groups, in 1976, at the age of nineteen, he created his own group, the Music Makers. That year his group won and then became the first unit to win three consecutive Boxing Day parade prizes. This group is credited with introducing the very fine fringe pasting, brass section, and off-the-shoulders dancers. Lee furnishes more details about the role of de facto segregation in the maintaining the Bay Street oligarchy (23–26).

26. See S. Davis (31). In 1954, officials banned the parade for the first time on Bay Street due to "misconduct and rowdyism by participants," but reestablished it the next year due to the tenacity of the Masquerade Committee (Wood 61).

27. According to Gail Saunders, "Whites in Barbados were called 'Red legs,' and in the Bahamas, they became known as 'Conchy Joes'" (*Social Life* 4). See also Martin and Storr, "Demystifying Bay Street."

28. Jenkins's interviewees also mention miscegenation and insinuate that several Conchy Joe members were mixed race: "*At one point, I asked [George Leopold Roberts] whether a family to whom he was referring was black or white. His green eyes twinkled as he gave me a lecture on families in the Bahamas and the mixing of the races. One of his conclusions was, 'When they try to explain his white and black business, they can't'*" (78; italics in original). This ruling class extended something like noblesse oblige, allowing for some exceptionalism while wielding much social, economic, and political control (Jenkins 75–81). For a nuanced interrogation of The Bahamas' white minority, see Johnson and Watson. Gordon Lewis situates The Bahamas and Bermuda as outliers: granted greater autonomy by London, members of their ruling class were "not mere agents of the imperial centre" (340). A dissertation by Maria Lee with an interest in investigating the political capital of Black Bahamians diagnoses the origin of this mercantile elite.

29. In *Bahamian Society After Emancipation*, Gail Saunders writes, "Although underprivi-leged blacks were the originators and main participants of the Junkanoo festival, coloured and even some whites joined the parade spontaneously. Later in the 1930s, when the festival was seen as a tourist attraction by the white elite, the coloured middle class became more actively involved in it and it began to take on greater respectability" (3).

30. Wood goes on to historicize the racial–social class divide, with the emergence of the Valley Boys in 1958 comprising a "watershed": "for the first-time . . . Junkanoo saw the serious involvement of the middle-class of The Bahamas" (231–40). Ironically, the social class divide also draws hierarchical distinctions between musical sections, with the brass section group leaders professing to be the real musicians. Moreover, they are paid participants in Junkanoo (Wood 241). According to Bettelheim's dissertation, the Valley Boys' name locates their neigh-borhood "east of over the hill" (215).

31. Such complexities elude those critics such as Mackey who merely point out the urgency by Junkanoos to maintain authenticity as a rationale for the fetishizing of Bay Street, without

regard to symbolic and other extratextual meanings (3). One of Rosita Sands's interviewees attested: "You know what make Bay Street so valuable? The sounds come together! You see those buildings keep the sounds in" ("Conversation" 106).

32. Published in 1920, at about the time of the US purchase, Franck's depiction of St. Croix's two towns Christiansted and Frederiksted as rivals captures the relationship today. Moreover, his vituperative comments add to the disdain regarding Africa-descended people: "These names being too much for the negro tongue, the towns are known locally as 'Boss End' (either a corruption of the French *Bassin* or an acknowledgement that the 'bosses' of island always lived in the capital) and 'West End'" (324).

33. This divide is the focus of a forum, "Continentals look down at us Cruzans," *St. Croix Source*, January 27, 2010.

34. Karen Judd's *White Minority in the Caribbean* reports that only three British West Indian colonies had sufficiently large and politically well-organized white minorities to ensure the uninterrupted continuation of self-legislation after the emancipation of their slave majorities in the 1830s: Bermuda, Barbados, and the Bahamas (71).

35. See http://www.gotostcroix.com/events/jump-up-in-christiansted/ (accessed March 11, 2010).

36. Neighborhoods such as American Hill and Hungry Hill designated elevated spaces where affluent whites live. Historically, in Christiansted, free Blacks lived and owned homes in Free Gut, established by the Danish and comprising its back o' town.

37. See *St. Croix Source,* at https://stcroixsource.com/2005/09/09/crucian-christmas-festival-set-frederiksted-again-706/ (accessed September 16, 2013). Moreover, that July, the Senate questioned Nicks about shortfalls of $57,000 from 2003–2005; see https://visourcearchives.com/content/2005/07/22/senate-questions-christmas-festival-finances/ (accessed December 6, 2013).

38. See http://www.gotostcroix.com/events/mardi-croix/ (accessed July 17, 2015).

39. Olwig presents the most sustained mention of Culturama dating back to its inception in 1974 ("Global Culture" 188–92).

Conclusion: From Carnivalesque to Ritualesque

1. Gerald Creed, by way of quoting folklorists Dorothy Noyes and Henry Glassie, formulates community ritual beyond the archetypal: "they are usually symbolic commentaries on the very nature of community relations," and he also interprets the mumming season in Bulgaria (17). Nurse speaks to Carnival as a "ritual negotiation of cultural identity" (663).

2. Lyndon Phillip explores the role by which youth indulge their "diasporic sensibilities" during Carnival in Toronto. Anita Waters discusses "social memory" as contributing to national identity in the Caribbean.

3. Owain Johnston-Barnes quotes an unnamed spectator in Bermuda's *Royal Gazette*, at http://www.royalgazette.com/news/article/20171226/gombeys-dance-on-boxing-day (accessed April 23, 2019). Relative to Trinidadian "kiddie's carnival," Mason effusively affirms, "The bands may continue to get bigger, the noise will get louder and crowds will swell, but the spirit will continue. Right now it looks as though Trinidadians will play mas until the end of time" (119). Wood describes her family's ritual of attending Junkanoo from childhood into her teens, when her father drove her to the best vantage point and left her to experience the celebration (8). Especially seminal to this argument, see Ottenberg and Binkley's anthology, which explores the world of play by African children who engage in masked dancing with such Christmas

memories, instilling a "commemorative function of human desire for immortality of the community" (155). Therefore, those children "play important roles" that potentiate them (197). However, in greater detail, Alleyne-Dettmers promotes the elevated role of children as a part of "setting the stage for Carnival" there ("Moko Jumbie").

4. See "Junior Junkanoo Parade Rules and Regulations," at https://www.bahamas.gov.bs/wps/wcm/connect/ff5d177c-f2e9-4bcb-a8fa-22ba19c344a1/Junior+Junkanoo+Rules+and+Regulations.pdf?MOD=AJPERES&CONVERT_TO=url&CACHEID=ff5d177c-f2e9-4bcb-a8fa-22ba19c344a1 (accessed February 4, 2017).

5. See statement at http://www.bahamas.co.uk/about-the-bahamas/junkanoo/junior-junkanoo (accessed December 12, 2014). A member of the management committee confirmed to me the future orientation of the kiddie parade: "The senior parade just has an ongoing life and so it is very important that we keep this junior parade active and encouraged."

6. For visual anthropology, see http://www.huffingtonpost.com/entry/phyllis-galembo-maske-photos_us_576306afe4bodf4d586fa6ae (accessed July 18, 2015).

7. The blog at http://pancocojams.blogspot.com/2012/02/jonkanoo-gombey-new-orleans-indians.html (accessed July 18, 2015) offers comparative videos of the festival arts in the circum-Atlantic rim.

8. This sentiment is relevant to other isles, too; see Rosemary Jones, *Bermuda Five Centuries* (134).

9. Interview with Bermudian Wayne Gilbert by phone (April 2009). By explaining that the longtails are one of the birds native to Bermuda along with their breeding pattern upon their migratory return from March to September, Tucker concretizes their metaphorical meaning (16, 21).

10. See Johnston-Barnes's *Royal Gazette* news report, "Gombey Festival Returns Next Week," at https://www.royalgazette.com/other/news/article/20191007/gombey-festival-returns-next-week/ (accessed November 5, 2020).

11. See Terry Tucker for mention of commemorative ceremonies marking Bermuda's tercenary as well as three hundred and fiftieth anniversary, with the latter in 1959 being accompanied by substantial political unrest and the voluntary end to segregation.

12. Quoted from http://www.royalgazette.com/article/20150605/NEWS/150609800 (accessed January 16, 2017; site discontinued). Also, see http://communityandculture.bm/events/national-heroes-day/ and http://bernews.com/tag/national-heroes-day/ (both accessed January 16, 2017). A Facebook page legitimates Bermuda Carnival's addition to the island's ritual calendar of events and reveals that promotion begins six months in advance; see https://www.facebook.com/bermudacarnival/ (accessed January 16, 2017). Max Harris highlights the commodification by commercial and government sponsors that "joined forces to appropriate, tame, and prettify" Trinidadian Carnival, which may assist in explaining the recent nascent developments in Bermuda and The Bahamas (192). A staff writer's *Nassau Guardian* article captures the island's reception to Bahamas Carnival, although the 2020 event was postponed due to Covid; see https://thenassauguardian.com/organizers-say-big-changes-coming-to-carnival/ and https://www.carnivalbahamas.com/. Without a doubt, only time will demonstrate the outcome.

13. Department of Statistics, "Population and Growth Rate for Census Years 1838 to 2000," The Commonwealth of The Bahamas. In The Bahamas, tourism generates 74 percent of household income and 58 percent of government revenue, according to Graci and Dodds (35). Strachan wrote that he views The Bahamas as an ideal subject on which to base his study of island paradise. With cultural specificity, Scher's *Carnival* devotes an entire chapter to returning transnationals and the Carnival in Trinidad and Tobago, in which he demarcates the importance and the art of nostalgia.

14. See the online petition for cultural survival at https://www.change.org/p/the-bahamas
-government-s-ministry-of-youth-sports-culture-protect-the-cultural-identity-of-the-bahamas
(accessed July 26, 2016).

15. See Thompson, who explains that costumes are discarded due to a "belief that the costumes are no longer meaningful outside of their communal creation and public performance"
(500). Ferguson's Educultural Museum and the Junkanoo World Museum & Arts Centre still
coexist although travel books and online travel sites tend to confuse the three, based on recent
reviews by tourists on websites such as TripAdvisor. See, for example, a comment by a tourist at
https://www.tripadvisor.com/Attraction_Review-g147416-d149335-Reviews-Junkanoo_Expo_
Museum-Nassau_New_Providence_Island_Bahamas.html#review_378762760 (accessed July
25, 2016). Junkanoo World Museum has an active Facebook page, which can be attributed to
the organizational skill of Barabbas, its founder, with whom I spent a full day; see https://www
.facebook.com/barabbasandthetribe242 (accessed July 25, 2016). The museum has a neighborly
vibe and hosts regular educational workshops; in terms of performance, Barabbas's Junkanoo
group is well traveled. In May 2020, there is news of a groundbreaking ceremony to revive
the old Junkanoo Museum; meanwhile, tourist guides ceaselessly promote it. See http://www
.thebahamasweekly.com/publish/news/Bahamian_cultural_icons_contribute_to_ground
breaking_junkanoo_museum_plans65581.shtml.

16. 6. Mackey cites the following news reports: Gladstone Thurston, "Junkanoo Move to
Boost PLP Carnival at Sports Centre?," *The Tribune*, October 10, 1989; and MaryAnn Burrows,
"Saxons and Valley Boys Will Defy Move to Have Junkanoo at Sports Centre," *The Tribune*,
October 10, 1989. Thompson, in *Eye for the Tropics*, concurs that, while costumes demand
construction elsewhere, "Bay Street is a fundamental part of Junkanoo, and despite the government's numerous attempts to relocate the parade to a more tourist-friendly locale, Junkanoo
remains on Bay Street to this today" (147). Nicolette Bethel's dissertation delineates concrete
rationales for the failure to secure a tourist base (59).

17. For example, see the following website affiliated with International Culinary Tourism:
https://www.trubahamianfoodtours.com/bahamas-special-events-and-festivals/junkanoo/
(accessed May 4, 2017). This site reports the best vantage points for viewing Junkanoo, realisti-
cally portrays its temporal orientation, and provides details about what to eat and drink as well
as viewing options that may require the use of portable toilets. Of course, out of necessity for
its industry, the site also conveys other "opportunities to witness this rhythmic parade throughout the year."

18. The blog "Cottontail on Jazz," at http://cottontailonjazz.blogspot.com/, introduces Jimmy
Hamilton as a jazzman who performed with the great Duke Ellington and the likelihood that
indeed St. Croix enthusiastically embraced jazz as a part of its culture thanks in part to the
Buccaneer as a well-established venue.

19. Traveling on one of the island's freighters to Nevis for Culturama after signing a
manifest that would create a record of all passengers, I found it difficult not to remember the
disaster that precipitated this form of registration: the sinking of *Christena*, a ferry boat. Also
traveling on Emancipation Day to Nevis, that boat carried twice as many passengers as recom-
mended, and a pilot error caused the death of all aboard. There was no manifest on that boat to
register the deceased. See http://www.numa.net/2012/10/the-christena-a-sad-caribbean-saga/
(accessed November 18, 2017).

20. Tourism Master Plan for Hopkins, Belize, 2010. Mick told me that in Hopkins there
have been quite a few projects, including the Tourism Master Plan from 2010, in which
the consultants show up and produce the document, and the community never sees it. See

Teunesha Evertse, "Practitioners' Perceptions on Community Involvement in Land Use Planning in Belize." Thesis. Vancouver Island University, 2015.

21. Citing Richard Hadel, Franzone fills in a long-standing gap by reporting that, at one time, Jankunu troupes annually traveled from Dangriga to Belize City, trooping throughout the urban center (295).

22. See Hafstein's "Intangible Heritage," in which he coins the term "folklorization" to describe the role of modernization in which social institutions engage in their own forms of "safeguarding" (124). He warns about the consequences of the "dangers of success" when local culture is popularized by another form of exploitation—those institutions destined to reframe it.

BIBLIOGRAPHY

Archives Consulted

Bahamas-Nassau

Nassau Public Library

Belize-Dangriga

Gulisi Garifuna Museum

Bermuda-Hamilton

Bermuda National Library

St. Croix-Frederiksted

Estate Whim Plantation Museum
University of the Virgin Islands Library

St. Kitts-Basseterre

The International House Museum and Edgar Challenger Library
The National Archives
St. Christopher Heritage Society (SCHS)

Books, Articles, and Other Sources

Abrahams, Roger D. "About Face: Rethinking Creolization." *Creolization as Cultural Creativity*, edited by Robert Baron and Ana C. Cara, UP of Mississippi, 2011, pp. 285–305.

Abrahams, Roger D. "Afro–Caribbean Culture and the South: Music with Movement." *The South and the Caribbean: Essays and Commentaries*, edited by Bonham C. Richardson et al., UP of Mississippi, 2001, pp. 97–116.

Abrahams, Roger D. "Christmas Mummings on Nevis." *North Carolina Folklore*, vol. 21, 1973, pp. 120–31.

Abrahams, Roger D. *Everyday Life: A Poetics of Vernacular Practices*. U of Pennsylvania P, 2005.

Abrahams, Roger D. *The Man of Words in the West Indies: Performance and the Emergence of Creole Culture*. Johns Hopkins UP, 1983.

Abrahams, Roger D. "Play in the Face of Death: Transgression and Inversion in a West Indian Wake." *The Many Faces of Play*, edited by Association for the Anthropological Study of Play and Kendall Blanchard, Human Kinetics Publishers, 1986, pp. 29–45.

Abrahams, Roger D. "Questions of Criolian Contagion." *Journal of American Folklore*, vol. 116, no. 459, 2003, pp. 73–87.

Abrahams, Roger D. *Singing the Master: The Emergence of African American Culture in the Plantation South*. Penguin, 1992.

Abrahams, Roger, and John Szwed, editors. *After Africa*. Yale UP, 1983.

Aching, Gerald. *Masking and Power: Carnival and Popular Culture in the Caribbean*. U of Minnesota P, 2002.

Adderley, Rosanne Marion. *"New Negroes from Africa": Slave Trade Abolition and Free African Settlement in the Nineteenth-Century Caribbean*. Indiana UP, 2006.

Adjaye, Joseph K. *Boundaries of Self and Other in Ghanaian Popular Culture*. Praeger, 2004.

Adjaye, Joseph K., editor. *Time in the Black Experience*. Greenwood Press, 1994.

Albury, Paul. *The Story of the Bahamas*. Macmillan, 1975.

Aldred, Cyril. *The Egyptians*. Thames and Hudson, 1987.

Alexander, Elizabeth. *The Black Interior: Essays*. Graywolf Press, 2004.

Allahar, Anton. "'Racing' Caribbean Political Culture: Afrocentrism, Black Nationalism and Fanonism." *Modern Political Culture in the Caribbean*, edited by Holger Henke and Fred Réno, U of the West Indies P, 2003, pp. 21–58.

Allen, Ray. "J'ouvert in Brooklyn Carnival: Revitalizing Steel Pan and Ole Mas Traditions." *Western Folklore*, vol. 58, 1999, pp. 255–77.

Alleyne, Mervyn. *Root of Jamaican Culture*. Pluto Press, 1988.

Alleyne-Dettmers, Patricia T. "Ancestral Voices, Trevini—A Case Study of Meta-Masking in the Notting Hill Carnival." *Journal of Material Culture*, 1998, pp. 201–221.

Alleyne-Dettmers, Patricia T. "Jump! Jump and Play Mas!" Diss. U of Pennsylvania, 1993.

Alleyne-Dettmers, Patricia T. "The Moko Jumbie: Elevating the Children." Sloat, *Caribbean Dance*, pp. 262–87.

Alleyne-Dettmers, Patricia T. "Political Dramas in the Jour Ouvert Parade in Trinidad Carnival." *Caribbean Studies*, vol. 28, 1995, pp. 326–38.

Alleyne-Dettmers, Patricia T. "The Relocation of Trinidad Carnival in Notting Hill, London and The Politics of Diasporisation." *Globalisation, Diaspora and Caribbean Popular Culture*, edited by Christine G. T. Ho and Keith Nurse, Ian Randle Publishers, 2005, pp. 65–77.

Allsopp, Jeannette. *Dictionary of Caribbean English Usage*. U of the West Indies P, 2003.

Anthony, Michael. *Parade of the Carnivals of Trinidad, 1839–1989*. Circle, 1989.

Armitage, David, and M. J. Braddick. *The British Atlantic World, 1500–1800*. Palgrave Macmillan, 2002.

Armstrong, Douglas V. *Creole Transformation from Slavery to Freedom: Historical Archaeology of the East End Community, St. John, Virgin Islands*. UP of Florida, 2003.

Armstrong, Irene. *Robert Skeoch—Cruzan Planter*. 1971.

Armstrong, Neil. *Christmas in Nineteenth-Century England*. Manchester UP, 2010.

Aron, Cindy. *Working at Play: A History of Vacations in the United States*. Oxford UP, 2001.

Ashworth, G. J., and B. J. Graham. *Senses of Place: Senses of Time*. Ashgate, 2005.

Atiya, Aziz Suryal. *Crusade, Commerce, and Culture*. Indiana UP, 1962.

Attali, Jacques. *Noise: The Political Economy of Music*. U of Minnesota P, 1985.

Auld, William Muir. *Christmas Traditions*. Macmillan, 1931.

Aveni, Anthony F. *Empires of Time: Calendars, Clocks, and Cultures*. Basic Books, 1989.

Backeberg, Peter. "Freedom Movement: The Bermuda Gombeys." *The Bermudian*, 25 Dec. 2018, https://www.thebermudian.com/culture/the-consummate-bermudian/freedom-movement -the-bermuda-gombeys/.

Bailey, Peter. "Breaking the Sound Barrier." *Hearing History: A Reader*, edited by Mark Smith, U of Georgia P, 2004, pp. 23–35.

Baker, Houston A. *Blues, Ideology, and Afro-American Literature: A Vernacular Theory*. U of Chicago P, 1984.

Baker, Juanae. "Legacy, History & Contributions of 'Backatawn.'" *Bernews*, 9 Feb. 2015.

Bakhtin, Mikhail. *Rabelais and His World*. Translated by Hélène Iswolsky, Indiana UP, 1984.

Balliger, Robin. "Noisy Spaces: Popular Music Consumption, Social Fragmentation, and the Cultural Politics of Globalization in Trinidad." Diss. Stanford U, 2000.

Banerjee, Prathama. *Politics of Time: "Primitives" and History-Writing in a Colonial Society.* Oxford UP, 2006.

Barnett, James. *The American Christmas: A Study in National Culture.* Macmillan, 1954.

Barnett, Sheila. "Jonkonnu: Pitchy Patchy." *Jamaica Journal,* vol. 43, 1979, pp. 18–32.

Barrett, Leonard E. *Soul-Force: African Heritage in Afro-American Religion.* Anchor Press, 1974.

Bashi, Vilna. *Survival of the Knitted: Immigrant Social Networks in a Stratified World.* Stanford UP, 2007.

Bastian, Darren. "Perspective on the Future of Junkanoo." *Junkanoo and Religion: Christianity and Cultural Identity in The Bahamas—Papers Presented at the Junkanoo Symposium, March 2002,* edited by Jessica Minnis, Media Enterprises, 2003.

Bayley, Robert. *The Sunny Caribbees: An Informal Guide to the West Indies.* Duell, Sloan, Pearce, 1967.

Beckford, William. *A Descriptive Account of the Island of Jamaica.* London, 1790.

Beckles, Hillary. "'War Dances': Slave Leisure and Anti-Slavery in the British-Colonised Caribbean." *Working Slavery, Pricing Freedom: Perspectives from the Caribbean, Africa and the African Diaspora,* edited by Verena Shepherd, Palgrave, 2002.

Beckwith, Martha. *Black Roadways: A Study of Jamaica Folk Life.* U of North Carolina P, 1929.

Beckwith, Martha. *Jamaica Folk-Lore.* American Folklore Society, 1928.

Beckwith, Martha, and Helen Roberts. *Christmas Mummings in Jamaica.* Vassar College, 1923.

Beneby, Katherine. "Junkanoo: Hidden Treasure of the Bahamas." *Bahamas Weekly,* 13 June 2014.

Bergson, Henri. *Matter and Memory.* Translated by Nancy Margaret Paul and W. Scott Palmer, S. Sonnenschein, 1919.

Berlin, Ira. *From Creole to African: Atlantic Creoles and the Origins of African-American Society in Mainland North America.* Institute of Early American History and Culture, 1996.

Bermuda. Fodor's Travel Publications, 2003.

Bernhard, Virginia. *Slaves and Slaveholders in Bermuda.* U Missouri P, 1999.

Besson, Jean, and Karen Fog Olwig. *Caribbean Narratives of Belonging: Fields of Relations, Sites of Identity.* Macmillan Caribbean, 2005.

Bethel, E. Clement. *Junkanoo: Festival of the Bahamas.* Edited and expanded by Nicolette Bethel. Macmillan Caribbean, 1991.

Bethel, Nicolette. "Navigations: The Fluidity of Identity in the Post-Colonial Bahamas." Diss. U of Cambridge, 2000.

Bethel, Nicolette. "Navigations: Insularity versus Cosmopolitanism in the Bahamas—Formality and Informality in an Archipelagic Nation." *Social Identities: Journal for the Study of Race, Nation and Culture,* vol. 8, 2002, pp. 237–53.

Bethel, Nicolette. "Violence on the Street." University of the Bahamas. 4 Nov. 2011. Presentation.

Bettelheim, Judith. "Jamaican Jonkonnu and Related Caribbean Festivals." *Africa and the Caribbean: The Legacies of a Link,* edited by Margaret Crahan and Franklin Knight, Johns Hopkins UP, 1979, pp. 80–100.

Bettelheim, Judith. "The Afro-Jamaican Jonkonnu Festival: Playing the Forces and Operating the Cloth." Diss. Yale U, 1979.

Bettelheim, Judith. "The Jonkonnu Festival in Jamaica." *The Journal of Ethnic Studies,* vol. 13, 1985, pp. 85–105.

Bettelheim, Judith. "The Jonkonnu Festival: Its Relation to Caribbean and African Masquerades." *Jamaica Journal,* vol. 10, 1976, pp. 21–27.

Bettelheim, Judith. "Jonkonnu and Other Christmas Masquerades." *Caribbean Festival Arts: Each and Every Bit of Difference*, edited by John W. Nunley and Judith Bettelheim, U of Washington P, 1988.

Bildhauer, Bettina, and Robert Mills. *The Monstrous Middle Ages*. U of Toronto P, 2003.

Bilby, Kenneth. "Africa's Creole Drum: The Gumbe as Vector and Signifier of Trans-Atlantic Creolization." *Creolization as Cultural Creativity*, edited by Robert Baron and Ana C. Cara, UP of Mississippi, 2011, pp. 137–77.

Bilby, Kenneth. "Masking the Spirit in the South Atlantic World: Jankunu's Partially Hidden History." Presented at the Ninth Annual Gilder Lehrman Center International Conference at Yale University, 2007.

Bilby, Kenneth. "Surviving Secularization: Masking the Spirit in the Jankunu (John Canoe) Festivals of the Caribbean." *NWIG: New West Indian Guide*, vol. 84, 2010, pp. 179–223.

Binkley, David. *Playful Performers: African Children's Masquerades*. Taylor & Francis, 2017.

Birth, Kevin K. *Bacchanalian Sentiments: Musical Experiences and Political Counterpoints in Trinidad*. Duke UP, 2008.

Bleeker, C. J. *Egyptian Festivals: Enactments of Religious Renewal*. E. J. Brill, 1967.

Bleeker, C. J. *The Rainbow: A Collection of Studies in the Science of Religion*. Brill, 1975.

Bohannan, Paul. *Africa and Africans*. Natural History Press, 1964.

Bolich, Gregory. *Transgender History and Geography: Crossdressing in Context*. Vol. 3. Psyche's Press, 2007.

Bolland, O. Nigel. *Colonialism and Resistance in Belize: Essays in Historical Sociology*. Cubola Productions, 2003.

Bolland, N. O. "Creolization and Creole Societies: A Cultural Nationalist View of Caribbean Social History." *Caribbean Q*, vol. 44, 1998, pp. 1–32.

Bolland, N. O. "Timber Extraction and the Shaping of Enslaved People's Culture." *Slavery without Sugar: Diversity in Caribbean Economy and Society Since the 17th Century*, edited by Verene Shepherd, UP of Florida, 2002.

Bolton, Carrington. "Gombay, a Festal Rite of Bermudian Negroes." *Journal of American Folklore*, vol. 3, 1890, pp. 222–26.

Borchert, James. *Alley Life in Washington: Family, Community, Religion, and Folklife in the City, 1850–1970*. U of Illinois P, 1980.

Bowe, Ruth M. L. "Grants Town and the Historical Development of 'Over-The-Hill.'" *The International Journal of Bahamian Studies*, vol. 3, 1982, pp. 22–27.

Brand, John, et al. *Brand's Popular Antiquities of Great Britain: Faiths and Folklore; A Dictionary of National Beliefs, Superstitions and Popular Customs, Past and Current, with Their Classical and Foreign Analogues, Described and Illustrated*. Reeves and Turner, 1905.

Brasch, Rudolph. *Strange Customs, How Did They Begin? The Origins of the Unusual and Occult Customs, Superstitions, and Traditions*. McKay, 1976.

Brathwaite, Kamau. *The Development of Creole Society in Jamaica, 1770–1820*. Clarendon, 1971.

Braudel, Fernand. *The Structures of Everyday Life: The Limits of the Possible*. U of California P, 1981.

Breasted, James Henry. *The Empire in a History of Egypt: From the Earliest Times to the Persian Conquest*. Cambridge UP, 2016.

Brent, Linda (Harriet Jacobs). *Incidents in the Life of a Slave Girl*. Harvest Books, 1973.

Brereton, Bridget. "'All Ah We Is Not One': Historical and Ethnic Narratives in Pluralist Trinidad." *The Global South*, vol. 4, 2010, pp. 218–38.

Brereton, Bridget. "The British and French West Indies." *The Modern Caribbean*, edited by Franklin W. Knight and Colin A. Palmer, U of North Carolina P, 1989, pp. 85–110.

Brereton, Bridget, and Kevin A. Yelvington. *The Colonial Caribbean in Transition: Essays on Postemancipation Social and Cultural History.* U of the West Indies P, 1999.

Bridenbaugh, Carl. *Vexed and Troubled Englishmen, 1590–1642.* Oxford UP, 1968.

Brodhurst, Roy. "Christmas Festival a Lasting Tradition." *Crucian Christmas Festival Program Book*, 1965.

Brown, Karen McCarthy. *Mama Lola.* U of California P, 1991.

Brown, Vincent. *The Reaper's Garden: Death and Power in the World of Atlantic Slavery.* Harvard UP, 2008.

Buisseret, David, and Steven G. Reinhardt, editors. *Creolization in the Americas.* Texas A&M UP, 2000.

Burgess, Carla. "The Legends of John Kunner and Old Buck." *UNC Sea Grant College Program*, 1992, pp. 13–17.

Burke, Andrew. *The Gambia & Senegal.* Lonely Planet, 2002.

Burke, Peter. *Popular Culture in Early Modern Europe.* New York UP, 1978.

Burke, Suzanne. 2012. "Policing the 'People's Festival': State Policy and the Trinidad Carnival Complex." Innes et al.

Burnard, Trevor. *Mastery, Tyranny, and Desire.* U of North Carolina P, 2004.

Burton, Richard D. E. *Afro-Creole: Power, Opposition, and Play in the Caribbean.* Cornell UP, 1997.

Cambridge Companion to Stravinsky. Cambridge UP, 2003.

Cameron, Elizabeth, and Manuel Jordan. "Playing with the Future: Children and Rituals in North-Western Province, Zambia." *Playful Performers*, edited by David Binkley, Taylor & Francis, 2017.

Campbell, Mavis Christine. *The Maroons of Jamaica, 1655–1796: A History of Resistance, Collaboration & Betrayal.* Bergin & Garvey, 1988.

Campbell, R. J. *The Story of Christmas.* Macmillan, 1934.

Carey, Daniel, and Lynn M. Festa. *The Postcolonial Enlightenment: Eighteenth-Century Colonialism and Postcolonial Theory.* Oxford UP, 2009.

Carmichael, A. C. *Domestic Manners and Social Condition of the White, Coloured, and Negro Population of the West Indies.* Negro Universities P, 1969.

Carroll, Anthony. *The History of Junkanoo, Part One: My Way All the Way.* AuthorHouse, 2007.

Cartey, Wilfred. *The West Indies: Islands in the Sun.* Thomas Nelson & Sons, 1967.

Cartwright, Keith. *Sacral Grooves/Limbo Gateways: Travels in Deep Southern Time, Circum-Caribbean Space, Afro-Creole Authority.* U of Georgia P, 2013.

Cassidy, Frederic. "'Hipsaw' and 'John Canoe.'" *American Speech*, vol. 41, 1966, pp. 45–51.

Cassidy, Frederic. *Jamaica Talk: Three Hundred Years of the English Language in Jamaica.* U of the West Indies P, 2007.

Casson, Lionel. *Everyday Life in Ancient Egypt.* Johns Hopkins UP, 2001.

Chambers, Douglas B. "Ethnicity in the Diaspora: The Slave-Trade and the Creation of African 'Nations' in the Americas." *Slavery & Abolition*, vol. 22, no. 3, 2001, pp. 25–39.

Chambers, William. "December 26." *Chambers' Book of Days*, http://www.thebookofdays.com/months/dec/26.htm.

Chipman, Donna L. M. *Bahamian Cultural Dynasty: With "Chippie," the Honourable John Arthur "Chippie" Chipman, MBE, OMA, King of the Goombay/Junkanoo Drums and Godfather of Culture.* PMT Atlantean, 2001.

Chock, Jeffery. "The Mas I Know." Innes et al., pp. 93–106.

Christian, Roy. *Old English Customs.* Drake Publishers, 1973.

Cipolla, Carlo M. *Clocks and Culture, 1300–1700.* Norton, 2003.

Clarke, E. A. "The John Canoe Festival in Jamaica." *Folklore*, vol. 38, 1927, pp. 72–75.

Clarke, Joyelle, and David Barker. "Sugar, Land, and Female Livelihood in Transition in St. Kitts." *Dialogue and Universalism*, vol. 3, 2012, pp. 1–26.

Cleare, Angela. *History of Tourism in the Bahamas.* Xlibris, 2007.

Cliff, Michelle. *Abeng.* Plume, 1995.

Coffin, Tristram. *The Book of Christmas Folklore.* Seabury, 1973.

Coffin, Tristram Potter, and Hennig Cohen. *Folklore in America: Tales, Songs, Superstitions, Proverbs, Riddles, Games, Folk Drama and Folk Festivals.* Doubleday, 1966.

Collier, Gordon, and Ulrich Fleischmann, editors. *A Pepper Pot of Cultures: Aspects of Creolization in the Caribbean.* Rodopi, 2003. Special double issue of *Matatu: Journal for African Culture and Society,* nos. 27 and 28, 2003.

Collins, John. *West African Pop Roots.* Temple UP, 1992.

Connelly, Mark. *Christmas: A Social History.* I. B. Tauris, 1999.

Conzemius, Eduard. "Ethnographic Notes on the Black Carib (Garif)." *American Anthropologist*, vol. 30, 1928, pp. 183–205.

Cooper, Carolyn. *Sound Clash: Jamaican Dancehall Culture at Large.* Palgrave Macmillan, 2004.

Coronil, Fernando. "Can Postcoloniality Be Decolonized? Imperial Banality and Postcolonial Power." *Postcolonialism: Critical Concepts in Literary and Cultural Studies,* edited by Diana Brydon, vol. 1, Routledge, 2000, pp. 191–206.

Cotter, Richard. *Sketches of Bermuda.* London, 1826.

Count, Earl W. *4000 Years of Christmas.* H. Schuman, 1948.

Cowley, John. *Carnival, Canboulay, and Calypso: Traditions in the Making.* Cambridge UP, 1996.

Cowley, John. "Music & Migration: Aspects of Black Music in the British Caribbean, the United States, and Britain, Before the Independence of Jamaica and Trinidad & Tobago." Thesis. U of Warwick, 1992.

Crane, Susan. *The Performance of Self: Ritual, Clothing, and Identity during the Hundred Years War.* U of Pennsylvania P, 2002.

Craton, Michael. "Decoding Pitchy-Patchy: The Roots, Branches, and Essence of Junkanoo." *Slavery & Abolition*, vol. 16, 1995, pp. 14–44.

Craton, Michael. *Empire, Enslavement, and Freedom in the Caribbean.* Ian Randle Publishers / Markus Wiener Publishers, 1997.

Craton, Michael. *A History of the Bahamas.* Collins, 1962.

Craton, Michael. "Loyalists Mainly to Themselves: The 'Black Loyalist' Diaspora to the Bahamas, 1783-c.1820." *Working Slavery, Pricing Freedom: Perspectives from the Caribbean, Africa, and the African Diaspora,* edited by Verene Shepherd, UP of Florida, 2002.

Craton, Michael, and Gail Saunders. *Islanders in the Stream: A History of the Bahamian People.* U of Georgia P, 1992.

Creed, Gerald W. *Masquerade and Postsocialism: Ritual and Cultural Dispossession in Bulgaria.* Indiana UP, 2011.

Crippen, T. G. *Christmas and Christmas Lore.* Gale Research Co., 1971.

Crowley, Daniel. "Carnivals, Carnival, and Carnivalization, or How to Make a Living without Actually Working." *Western Folklore*, vol. 58, 1999, pp. 213–22.

Crowley, Daniel. "Guy Fawkes Day at Fresh Creek, Andros Island, Bahamas." *Man*, vol. 58, no. 1, 1958, pp. 14–15.

Crowley, Daniel. "The Sacred and the Profane in African and African-Derived Carnivals." *Western Folklore*, vol. 58, 1999, pp. 223–28.

Crowley, Daniel. "The Traditional Masques of Carnival." *Caribbean Quarterly*, vol. 4, no. 3–4, 1956, pp. 194–223, http://www.jstor.org/stable/40652635.

Csikszentmihalyi, Mihaly. *Flow: The Psychology of Optimal Experience*. Harper & Row, 1990.

Culmer, Jack, editor. *Letters from the Bahama Islands, Written in 1823*. Providence Press, 1967.

Curry, Robert. *Bahamian Lore*. Paris, 1929.

Curtis, Debra. *Pleasures and Perils: Girls' Sexuality in a Caribbean Consumer Culture*. Rutgers UP, 2009.

da Matta, Roberto. *Carnivals, Rogues, and Heroes: An Interpretation of the Brazilian Dilemma*. U of Notre Dame P, 1991.

Davis, Fred. *Yearning for Yesterday: A Sociology of Nostalgia*. Free Press, 1979.

Davis, Jim. "Boxing Day." *The Performing Century: Nineteenth-Century Theatre's History*, edited by Tracy Davis and Peter Holland, Palgrave Macmillan, 2007, pp. 13–31.

Davis, Susan G. *Parades and Power: Street Theatre in Nineteenth-Century Philadelphia*. Temple UP, 1986.

Dawe, Kevin, editor. *Island Musics*. Berg, 2004.

Dawson, Ashley. *Mongrel Nation: Diasporic Culture and the Making of Postcolonial Britain*. U of Michigan P, 2007.

Dawson, William Francis. *Christmas: Its Origin and Associations, Together with Its Historical Events and Festive Celebrations During Nineteen Centuries*. Gale Research Co., 1968.

Dewulf, Jeroen. "Pinkster: An Atlantic Creole Festival in a Dutch-American Context." *Journal of American Folklore*, vol. 126, no. 501, 2013, pp. 245–71, 357.

Diawara, Manthia. *In Search of Africa*. Harvard UP, 1998.

Dikobe, Maude. "Doing She Own Thing: Gender, Performance, and Subversion in Trinidad Calypso." Diss. U of California, Berkeley, 2003.

Dillard, Cynthia. *On Spiritual Strivings: Transforming an African American Woman's Academic Life*. State U of New York P, 2006.

Dirks, Robert. *The Black Saturnalia: Conflict and Its Ritual Expression on British West Indian Slave Plantations*. U of Florida P, 1987.

Dirks, Robert. "The Evolution of a Playful Ritual: The Garifuna's John Canoe in Comparative Perspective." *Forms of Play of Native North Americans*, edited by Edward Norbeck and Claire R. Farrer, West Pub. Co., 1979, pp. 89–109.

Dohrn-van Rossum, Gerhard. *History of the Hour: Clocks and Modern Temporal Orders*. U of Chicago P, 1996.

Dookhan, Isaac. *A History of the Virgin Islands of the United States*. Caribbean Universities P for the College of the Virgin Islands, 1974.

Drake-Carnell, F. J. *Old English Customs and Ceremonies*. Scribner, 1938.

Drewal, Margaret. *Yoruba Ritual: Performers, Play, Agency*. Indiana UP, 1992.

Du Bois, W. E. B. *The Gift of Black Folk: The Negroes in the Making of America*. Stratford Co., 1924.

Dyer, T. F. Thiselton. *British Popular Customs, Present and Past: Illustrating the Social and Domestic Manners of the People*. Singing Tree Press, 1968.

Edmonson, Munro. "Carnival in New Orleans." *Caribbean Quarterly*, vol. 4, 1956, pp. 233–45.

Edwards, Bryan. "The History, Civil and Commercial, of the British Colonies in the West Indies." Abrahams and Szwed, pp. 147–49.

Edwards, Charles Lincoln. *Bahama Songs and Stories: A Contribution to Folk-Lore*. American Folk-Lore Society, 1895.

Ehrenreich, Barbara. *Dancing in the Streets: A History of Collective Joy*. Metropolitan Books, 2007.

Ellis, Simon P. *Graeco-Roman Egypt*. Shire Publications, 1992.

Emanuel, Charles. *St. Croix Christmas Festival Program Book*, 1961.

Emmer, Pieter C. *The Dutch Slave Trade, 1500–1850*. Berghahn Books, 2006.

Eneas, Cleveland W. *Bain Town*. Timpaul Pub. Co., 1976.

Eriksen, Thomas Hylland. "Liming: The Art of Doing Nothing." *Folk*, vol. 32, 1990, pp. 23–43.

Evans, David. "Black Fife and Drum Music." *Mississippi Registry*, vol. 6, 1972, pp. 94–107.

Fabre, Geneviève. "Festive Moments in Antebellum African American Culture." *The Black Columbiad: Defining Moments in African American Literature and Culture*, edited by Werner Sollors and Maria Diedrich, Harvard UP, 1994, pp. 52–63.

Falke, Stefan, and Laura Anderson. *Moko Jumbies: The Dancing Spirits of Trinidad*. Pointed Leaf, 2004.

Falassi, Alessandro. *Time Out of Time: Essays on the Festival*. U of New Mexico P, 1987.

Famous, Christopher. "There Is Much to Learn from Our St. Kitts and Nevis Roots." http:// bermudasun.bm/Content/OPINION/Opinion/Article/There-is-much-to-learn-from-9our -St-Kitts-and-Nevis-roots/4/135/74152.

Fanon, Frantz. *Black Skin, White Mask*. Translated by Charles Lam Markmann. Grove Weidenfeld, 1967.

Featherstone, Mike, editor. *Global Culture: Nationalism, Globalization, and Modernity*. A *Theory, Culture & Society* Special Issue. Sage, 1990.

Fenn, Elizabeth A. "'A Perfect Equality Seemed to Reign': Slave Society and Jonkonnu." *North Carolina Historical Review*, vol. 65, 1988, pp. 127–53.

Ferguson, Arlene Nash. *I Come to Get Me!: An Inside Look at the Junkanoo Festival*. Doongalik Studios, 2000.

Fernandez, James W. *Bwiti: An Ethnography of the Religious Imagination in Africa*. Princeton UP, 1982.

Fernandez, Sarah Elizabeth. "Contemporary Carnival (Carnaval) in Asturias." *The Dynamics of Changing Rituals: The Transformation of Religious Rituals within Their Social and Cultural Context*, edited by Jens Kreinath et al., Peter Lang, 2004, pp. 21–39.

Fernandez, Sarah Elizabeth. *Persuasions and Performances: The Play of Tropes in Culture*. Indiana UP, 1986.

Fernandez, Sarah Elizabeth. "A Theory of Cultural Glocality." Diss. U of North Florida, 2009.

Firestone, Melvin. "Christmas Mumming and Symbolic Interactionism." *Ethos*, vol. 6, 1978, pp. 92–113.

Fithian, Philip Vickers. *Journal & Letters of Philip Vickers Fithian 1773–1774: A Plantation Tutor of the Old Dominion*, edited by Hunter Dickinson Farish, Colonial Williamsburg, Inc., 1957.

Fleming, Carrol, editor. *Virgin Islands Holiday Cooking*. U of the Virgin Islands, n.d., https:// dloc.com/UF00096202/00001/2x.

Folly, Dennis. "'Christmas Gif'!': Afro-American Celebration of Christmas." *International Folklore Review*, vol. 3, pp. 120–30.

Francis, Dale. *The Quelbe Commentary, 1672–2012: Anthropology in Virgin Islands Music*. iUniverse, 2014.

Franck, Harry Alverson. *Roaming through the West Indies*. Blue Ribbon Books, 1920.

Frank, Priscilla. "For 30 Years, This Photographer Has Documented Disguises Around the World." *HuffPost*, 17 June 2016, https://www.huffpost.com/entry/phyllis-galembo-maske -photos_n_576306afe4b0df4d586fa6ae.

Franco, Pamela. "The Invention of Traditional Mas and the Politics of Gender." Green and Scher, pp. 25–47.

Frankel, Godfrey, and Laura Goldstein. *In the Alleys: Kids in the Shadow of the Capitol.* Smithsonian Institution Press, 1995.

Franzone, Dorothy. "A Critical and Cultural Analysis of an African People in the Americas: Africanisms in the Garifuna Culture of Belize." Temple U, 1995.

Freke, Timothy, and Peter Gandy. *The Jesus Mysteries: Was the "Original Jesus" a Pagan God?* Harmony Books, 2000.

Fu-Kiau, K. K. Bunseki. "Ntangu-Tandu-Kolo: The Bantu-Kongo Concept of Time." *Time in the Black Experience,* edited by Joseph Adjaye, Greenwood Press, 1994, pp. 17–35.

Galembo, Phyllis. "Hidden Meaning." *Telegraph Magazine,* 9 Oct. 2010, pp. 32–36, http://www.galembo.com/press/Telegraph-Maske.pdf.

Gant-Britton, Elizabeth. "Exploring Color Coding in the Twentieth Century." *Into Darkness Peering: Race and Color in the Fantastic,* edited by Elisabeth Anne Leonard, Greenwood Press, 1997.

Gardner, W. J. *A History of Jamaica from Its Discovery by Christopher Columbus to the Year 1872, Including an Account of Its Trade and Agriculture; Sketches of the Manners, Habits, and Customs of All Classes of Its Inhabitants; and a Narrative of the Progress of Religion and Education in the Island.* F. Cass, 1971.

Gaudet, Marcia. "Christmas Bonfires in South Louisiana: Tradition and Innovation." *Mardi Gras, Gumbo, and Zydeco: Readings in Louisiana Culture,* edited by James McDonald, UP of Mississippi, 2011, pp. 59–70.

Gaudet, Marcia. "'Mardi Gras, Chic-a-la-Pie': Reasserting Creole Identity through Festive Play." *Journal of American Folklore,* vol. 114, pp. 154–72.

Gaudet, Marcia G., and James C. McDonald. *Mardi Gras, Gumbo, and Zydeco: Readings in Louisiana Culture.* UP of Mississippi, 2003.

Geertz, Clifford. *The Interpretation of Cultures.* Basic Books, 1973.

Genovese, Eugene. *Roll, Jordan, Roll: The World the Slaves Made.* Vintage, 1976.

Gerstin, Julian. "Tangled Roots." *Making Caribbean Dance: Continuity and Creativity in Island Cultures,* edited by Susanna Sloat, UP of Florida, 2010, pp. 11–34.

Gikandi, Simon. *Slavery and the Culture of Taste.* Princeton UP, 2011.

Glassie, Henry H. *All Silver and No Brass: An Irish Christmas Mumming.* U of Pennsylvania P, 1983.

Glissant, Édouard. "Creolization in the Making of the Americas." *Caribbean Quarterly,* vol. 54, 2008, pp. 81–89.

Glissant, Édouard, and J. Michael Dash. *Caribbean Discourse: Selected Essays.* UP of Virginia, 1989.

Gmelch, George, and Sharon Gmelch. *The Parish behind God's Back: The Changing Culture of Rural Barbados.* U of Michigan P, 1977.

Godet, T. L. *Bermuda from the Earliest Period to the Present Time.* London, 1860.

Golby, John, and A. W. Purdue. *The Making of the Modern Christmas.* Sutton, 2000.

Goldberg, P. J. P. *Medieval England: A Social History, 1250–1550.* Arnold, 2004.

González, Nancie L. Solien. *Sojourners of the Caribbean: Ethnogenesis and Ethnohistory of the Garifuna.* U of Illinois P, 1988.

Goodenough, Erwin Ramsdell, and Jacob Neusner. *Jewish Symbols in the Greco-Roman Period.* Princeton UP, 1988.

Goodman, Steve. *Sonic Warfare: Sound, Affect, and the Ecology of Fear.* MIT P, 2012.

Gottlieb, Karla Lewis. *The Mother of Us All: A History of Queen Nanny, Leader of the Winward Jamaican Maroons.* Africa World Press, 2000.

Gottschild, Brenda Dixon. "Crossroads, Continuities, and Contradictions: The Afro-Euro-Caribbean Triangle." Sloat, *Caribbean Dance*, pp. 3–10.

Graci, Sonya, and Rachel Dodds. *Sustainable Tourism in Island Destinations*. Earthscan, 2010.

Green, Garth L., and Philip W. Scher. *Trinidad Carnival: The Cultural Politics of a Transnational Festival*. Indiana UP, 2007.

Greene, Oliver. "Music Behind the Mask: Men, Social Commentary, and Identity in Wanaragua (John Canoe)." *The Garifuna Music Reader*, edited by Oliver Greene, Cognella, 2018, pp. 120–61.

Green-Pedersen, Svend. "The History of the Danish Negro Slave Trade, 1733–1807." *Revue Française D'histoire D'outre-Mer*, vol. 62, 1975, pp. 196–220.

Griaule, Marcel. *Conversations with Ogotemmêli: An Introduction to Dogon Religious Ideas*. International African Institute / Oxford UP, 1970.

Guilbault, Jocelyne. *Governing Sound: The Cultural Politics of Trinidad's Carnival Musics*. U of Chicago P, 2007.

Gupta, Akhil. "The Reincarnation of Souls and the Rebirth of Commodities: Representations of Time in 'East' and 'West.'" *Cultural Critique*, vol. 22, 1992, pp. 187–211.

Hadfield, John, and Miles Hadfield. *The Twelve Days of Christmas*. Little, Brown, 1962.

Hafstein, Valdimar T. "Intangible Heritage as a Festival; or, Folklorization Revisited." *The Journal of American Folklore*, vol. 131, no. 520, 2018, pp. 127–49. JSTOR, www.jstor.org/stable/10.5406/jamerfolk.131.520.0127.

Hall, Douglas. *In Miserable Slavery: Thomas Thistlewood in Jamaica, 1750–86*. U of the West Indies P, 1989.

Hall, Kim F. *Things of Darkness: Economies of Race and Gender in Early Modern England*. Cornell UP, 1995.

Hall, N. A. T. *Slave Society in the Danish West Indies: St. Thomas, St. John, and St. Croix*. U of the West Indies P, 1992.

Hamilton, Andy. "The Sound of Music." *Sounds and Perception: New Philosophical Essays*, edited by M. Nudds and C. O'Callaghan, Oxford UP, 2006.

Hanna, Dennis. *Oou Oou Junkanoo*. 2000.

Hannerz, Ulf. "Cosmopolitans and Locals in World Culture." *Global Culture: Nationalism, Globalization, and Modernity*, edited by Mike Featherstone, Sage, 1990, pp. 237–51.

Hannerz, Ulf. "Flows, Boundaries, and Hybridity." *Readings in Globalization: Key Concepts and Major Debates*, edited by George Ritzer and Zeynep Atalay, Wiley, 2010, pp. 324–25.

Hannerz, Ulf. "'Nigerian Kung Fu, Mahhattan Fatwa' and 'The Local and the Global': Continuity and Change." *Transnational Studies Reader: Intersections and Innovations*, edited by Sanjeev Khagram and Peggy Levitt, Routledge, 2008, pp. 235–50.

Hannerz, Ulf. "Notes on the Global Ecumene." *Public Culture*, vol. 1. no. 2, 1989, pp. 66–75.

Hannerz, Ulf. "The World in Creolization." *Africa*, vol. 57. no. 4, 1987, pp. 546–59.

Harding, Rachel. *A Refuge in Thunder: Candomblé and Alternative Spaces of Blackness*. Indiana UP, 2003.

Harewood, Susan. "Masquerade as Methodology . . . or, Why Cultural Studies Should Return to the Caribbean." *Globalizing Cultural Studies: Ethnographic Interventions in Theory, Method, and Policy*, edited by Aisha Durham et al., Peter Lang, 2007, pp. 61–77.

Harris, Max. *Carnival and Other Christian Festivals: Folk Theology and Folk Performance*. U of Texas P, 2010.

Harrison, Faye. "Commentary: Building on a Rehistoricized Anthropology of the Afro-Atlantic." *Afro-Atlantic Dialogues: Anthropology in the Diaspora*, edited by Kevin Yelvington, School of American Research Press, 2006, pp. 381–89.

Harrison, Michael. *The Story of Christmas: Its Growth and Development from the Earliest Times.* Odhams Press, 1951.

Hart, (Miss), and Jack Culmer. *Letters from the Bahama Islands: Written in 1823-4.* Providence Press, 1967.

Harty, Cheyenne. "Crucian Christmas Festival Celebrates 50." *St. Croix Avis,* 15–16 Dec. 2002, p. 2.

Hayward, Walter Brownell. *Bermuda Past and Present: A Descriptive and Historical Account of the Somers Islands.* Dodd, Mead, 1910.

Hazzard-Donald, Katrina. "Dancing Under the Lash: Sociocultural Disruption, Continuity, and Synthesis." *African Dance: An Artistic, Historical and Philosophical Inquiry,* edited by Kariamu Welsh Asante, Africa World Press, 1996, pp. 104–130.

Hedrick, Basil Calvin, and Jeanette E. Stephens. *In the Days of Yesterday and in the Days of Today: An Overview of Bahamian Folk Music.* University Museum / Southern Illinois U, 1976.

Heid, Stefan. "The Romanness of Roman Christianity." *A Companion to Roman Religion,* edited by Jörg Rüpke, Blackwell Pub., 2007, pp. 406–426.

Hendy, David. *Noise: A Human History of Sound and Listening.* Profile Books, 2013.

Henriques, Julian. *Sonic Bodies: Reggae Sound Systems, Performance Techniques, and Ways of Knowing.* Bloomsbury Publishing, 2011.

Hernandez, Deborah. "Amalgamating Musics: Popular Music and Cultural Hybridity in the Americas." *Musical Migrations: Transnationalism and Cultural Hybridity in Latin/o America,* edited by Frances R. Aparicio and Cándida Frances Jáquez, Palgrave Macmillan, 2003, pp. 13–32.

Herskovits, Melville. *Acculturation.* J. J. Augustin, 1938.

Herskovits, Melville. *The Myth of the Negro Past.* Harper and Row, 1941.

Hervey, Thomas Kibble. *The Book of Christmas.* Boston, 1888.

Heuman, Gad. *The Caribbean: A Brief History.* Bloomsbury, 2013.

Heyliger, Cherra. "Christmas Spirit." *The Avis,* 28–29 Dec. 2003.

Heyliger, Cherra. "Crucian Myths and Customs Were Sporting Fun." *The Avis,* 30 Dec. 1989.

Heyliger, Cherra. "Origins of Our Festival." *The Avis,* 8–9 Jan. 2006.

Heyliger, Cherra. "Xmas on St. Croix." *The St. Croix Avis,* 23 Dec. 1986.

Hill, Donald. *Calypso Calaloo: Early Carnival Music in Trinidad.* UP of Florida, 1993,

Hill, Donald. *The Impact of Migration on the Metropolitan and Folk Society of Carriacou, Grenada.* Anthropological Papers of the American Museum of Natural History, 1977.

Hill, Edwin C. *Black Soundscapes, White Stages: The Meaning of Francophone Sound in the Black Atlantic.* Johns Hopkins UP, 2013.

Hill, Errol. *The Jamaican Stage, 1655–1900: Profile of a Colonial Theatre.* U of Massachusetts P, 1992.

Hill, Errol. *The Trinidad Carnival: Mandate for a National Theatre.* U of Texas P, 1972.

Ho, Ro. "Arawak Tribe of the Bahamas (The First Tribe Encountered by Christopher Columbus in the Americas)." Originalpeople.org, 15 Nov. 2012, originalpeople.org/arawak-tribe-of-the -bahamas-the-first-tribe-encountered-by-christopher-columbus-in-the-americas/.

Hole, Christina. *English Custom & Usage.* Batsford, 1950.

hooks, bell. *Black Looks: Race and Representation.* South End, 1993.

Horrox, Rosemary, and W. M. Ormrod. *A Social History of England, 1200–1500.* Cambridge UP, 2006.

Hottes, Alfred. *1001 Christmas Facts and Fancies.* A. T. Delamare, 1946.

Howard, Rosalyn. *Black Seminoles in the Bahamas.* UP of Florida, 2002.

Howard, Rosalyn. "Yoruba in the British Caribbean: A Comparative Perspective of Trinidad
    and the Bahamas." *The Yoruba Diaspora in the Americas*, edited by T. Falola and M. Childs,
    Indiana UP, 2004, pp. 157–76.

Hudson, Mark. *Our Grandmothers' Drums*. Secker & Warburg, 1989.

Huell, Jade. "Performing Nostalgia: Body, Memory, and Aesthetics of Past-Home." Diss.
    Louisiana State U, 2012.

Hunter, George. *The Bahamas*. Batsford, 1975.

Hurston, Zora Neale. "Dance Songs and Tales from the Bahamas." *Journal of American Folklore*,
    vol. 43, July–Sept. 1930, pp. 294–312.

Hutton, Ronald. *The Pagan Religions of the Ancient British Isles: Their Nature and Legacy*.
    B. Blackwell, 1991.

Hymes, Dell. *Pidginization and Creolization of Languages*. Cambridge UP, 1971.

Innes, Christopher, et al., editors. *Carnival: Theory and Practice*. Africa World Press, 2013.

Isaac, Tania. "Helen, Heaven, and I: In Search of a Dialogue." *Making Caribbean Dance:
    Continuity and Creativity in Island Cultures*, edited by Suzanna Sloat, UP of Florida, 2010,
    pp. 247–64.

Ives, Charles. *The Isles of Summer, or, Nassau and the Bahamas*. New Haven,1880.

Jackson, John J. *Bermuda*. David & Charles, 1988.

Jackson, Joyce. "Rockin' and Rushin' for Christ." *Caribbean and Southern: Transnational
    Perspectives on the U.S. South*, edited by Helen Regis, U of Georgia P, 2006, pp. 89–123.

Jackson, Louise A. *The Bermuda Gombey: Bermuda's Unique Dance Heritage*. 1987.

James, E. O. *Seasonal Feasts and Festivals*. Barnes & Noble, 1961.

James, Wayne. Review. *St. Croix Avis*.

Jarvis, Michael J. "Maritime Masters and Seafaring Slaves in Bermuda, 1680–1783." *The William
    and Mary Quarterly*, vol. 59, 2002, pp. 585–622.

Jenkins, Olga Culmer. *Bahamian Memories: Island Voices of the Twentieth Century*. UP of
    Florida, 2000.

Jones, Rosemary. *Bermuda: Five Centuries*. Panatel VDS Limited, 2004.

Johnson, Guion Griffis. *Ante-Bellum North Carolina: A Social History*. U of North Carolina P,
    1937.

Johnson, Howard. "Slave Life and Leisure in Nassau, Bahamas, 1783–1838." *Slavery and
    Abolition*, vol. 16, 1995, pp. 45–64.

Johnson, Howard, and Karl S. Watson, editors. *The White Minority in the Caribbean*. Ian Randle
    Publishers, 1998.

Johnson, Michele A., and Brian L. Moore. *Neither Led nor Driven: Contesting British Cultural
    Imperialism in Jamaica, 1865–1920*. U of the West Indies P, 2004.

Johnson, Sara. "Cinquillo Consciousness: The Formation of a Pan-Caribbean Musical
    Aesthetic." *Music, Writing, and Cultural Unity in the Caribbean*, edited by Timothy Reiss,
    Africa World Press, 2005.

Johnson, Walter. "Time and Revolution in African America: Temporality and the History of
    Atlantic Slavery." *A New Imperial History: Culture, Identity, and Modernity in Britain and
    the Empire, 1660–1840*, edited by Kathleen Wilson, Cambridge UP, 2004.

Johnson, Whittington Bernard. *Post-Emancipation Race Relations in the Bahamas*. UP of
    Florida, 2006.

Johnson, Whittington Bernard. *Race Relations in the Bahamas, 1784–1834: The Nonviolent
    Transformation from a Slave to a Free Society*. U of Arkansas P, 2000.

Johnston-Barnes, Owain. "Gombeys Dance on Boxing Day." *The Royal Gazette*, 26 Dec. 2017.

Johnston-Barnes, Owain. "Gombey Festival Returns Next Week." *The Royal Gazette*, 7 Oct. 2019.

Joyner, Charles. *Down by the Riverside*. U of Illinois P, 1984.

Judd, Karen. "Creolisation and Its Discontents." Johnson and Watson, pp. 147–57.

Judd, Karen. "In the Name of the People: Populist Ideology and Expatriate Power in Belize." Johnson and Watson, pp. 133–46.

Kane, Harnett T. *The Southern Christmas Book: The Full Story from Earliest Times to Present: People, Customs, Conviviality, Carols, Cooking.* D. McKay Co., 1958.

Karenga, Maulana. *Kwanzaa: Origin, Concepts, Practice.* Kawaida, 1977.

Karp, Ivan. *Museum Frictions: Public Cultures/Global Transformations.* Duke UP, 2006.

Kawaley-Lathan, Adrian. *Behind the Mask: Bermuda Gombeys, Past, Present and Future.* Department of Community and Cultural Affairs, 2008. Documentary.

Kearney, M. "The Local and the Global: The Anthropology of Globalization and Transnationalism." *Annual Review of Anthropology,* vol. 24, 1995, pp. 547–65.

Kelley, Robin D. G. *Race Rebels: Culture, Politics, and the Black Working Class.* Free Press, 1994.

Kennedy, E. A. *Life, Liberty, and the Mummers.* Temple UP, 2007.

Kennedy-Fraser, Marjory, and David Kennedy. *David Kennedy, the Scottish Singer.* Paisley, 1887.

Kerns, Virginia, and Robert Dirks. "John Canoe." *National Studies,* vol. 3, no. 6, 1975, pp. 1–15.

Kingsley, Charles. *At Last: A Christmas in the West Indies.* Macmillan and Co., 1910.

Kinser, Sam. *Carnival, American Style: Mardi Gras at New Orleans and Mobile.* U of Chicago P, 1990.

Klein, Debra. "Uncovering the Secrets of St. Kitts," http://www.thedailybeast.com/articles/2014/06/21/uncovering-the-secrets-of-st-kitts.html.

Knepper, Wendy. "Colonization, Creolization, and Globalization: The Art and Ruses of Bricolage." *Small Axe,* vol. 10, 2006, pp. 70–86.

Knox, John P. *A Historical Account of St. Thomas, W.I., with Its Rise and Progress in Commerce and Incidental Notices of St. Croix and St. Johns.* Negro Universities P, 1970.

Kokole, Omari. "Time, Language, and the Oral Tradition: An African Perspective." *Time in the Black Experience,* edited by Joseph Adjaye, Greenwood Press, 1994, pp. 35–54.

Kopelson, Heather Miyano. "'One Indian and a Negroe, the First Thes Ilands Ever Had': Imagining the Archive in Early Bermuda." *Early American Studies: An Interdisciplinary Journal,* vol. 11, 2013, pp. 272–313.

Kuper, Adam. "The English Christmas and the Family." *Unwrapping Christmas,* edited by Daniel Miller, Clarendon, 1993, pp. 157–75.

La'da, Csaba. "Encounters with Ancient Egypt: The Hellenistic Greek Experience." *Encounters with Ancient Egypt: Ancient Perspectives on Egypt,* edited by R. Matthews and C. Roemer, UCL, 2003, pp. 157–69.

Landers, Jane. *Black Society in Spanish Florida.* U of Illinois P, 1999.

Landes, David S. *Revolution in Time: Clocks and the Making of the Modern World.* Belknap Press of Harvard UP, 1983.

Lawson, J. C. *Modern Greek Folklore and Ancient Greek Religion: A Study in Survivals.* Cambridge UP, 1910.

Lee, Maria. "Black Bahamas: Political Constructions of Bahamian National Identity." Thesis. U of Richmond, 2012.

Lee, Simon. "Carnival at Christmas in St. Kitts," http://caribbean-beat.com/issue-112/carnival-christmas#axzz4QTeycJhF.

Le Goff, Jacques. *Time Work, and Culture in the Middle Ages.* Translated by Arthur Goldhammer, U of Chicago P, 1980.

Lesko, Leonard. "Ancient Egyptian Cosmogonies and Cosmology." *Religion in Ancient Egypt: Gods, Myths, and Personal Practice,* edited by Byron E. Shafer et al., Cornell UP, 1991, pp. 88–122.

Leslie, Charles. *A New and Exact Account of Jamaica.* 3rd ed. Edinburgh, 1740.

Leu, Lorraine. "'Raise Yuh Hand, Jump Up and Get on Bad!': New Developments in Soca Music in Trinidad." *Latin American Music Review,* vol. 21, 2000, pp. 45–58.

Levarie, Siegmund. "Noise." *Critical Inquiry,* vol. 4, no. 1, Autumn 1977, pp. 21–31.

Levitt, Peggy. *The Transnational Villagers.* U of California P, 2001.

Lewis, Gordon. *The Growth of the Modern West Indies.* M[onthly] R[eview] Press, 1968.

Lightbourne, Ronald. "Gombeys, Bands, and Troubadours." *Bermuda Connections Cultural Resource Guide for Teachers,* Smithsonian Center for Folklife and Cultural Heritage, 2001, pp. 261–78.

Lipsitz, George. "The Racialization of Space and the Spatialization of Race: Theorizing the Hidden Architecture of Landscape." *Landscape Journal,* vol. 26, 2007, pp. 10–23.

Lisle, Andria. "'Nothing Fail But a Try': A Tribute to Otha Turner and Bernice Turner Pratcher." *Living Blues,* vol. 34, no. 168, 2003, pp. 130–33.

Liverpool, Hollis Urban. "Origins of Rituals and Customs in the Trinidad Carnival: African or European?" *TDR,* vol. 42, no. 3, Fall 1998, pp. 24–37.

Liverpool, Hollis Urban. "Rituals of Power and Rebellion: The Carnival Tradition in Trinidad and Tobago." Diss. U of Michigan, 1993.

Lloyd, Susette Harriet. *Sketches of Bermuda.* London, 1835.

Lomax, Alan. *The Land Where the Blues Began.* Delta, 1993.

Lomax, Alan, et al., editors. *Deep River of Song: Bahamas 1935.* Rounder Records, 1999.

Long, Edward. *The History of Jamaica.* Arno Press, 1972.

Long, George. *The Folklore Calendar.* Gale Research Co., 1970.

Longstreet, Augustus Baldwin. *Georgia Scenes.* Sagamore Press, 1957.

Lougheed, Vivien, and Carol O'Donnell. *Adventure Guide to Belize.* Hunter Publishing, 2003.

MacAloon, John J. *Rite, Drama, Festival, Spectacle: Rehearsals toward a Theory of Cultural Performance.* Institute for the Study of Human Issues, 1984.

Mackey, Ressa Ann. "All That Glitters Is Not Junkanoo: The National Junkanoo Museum and the Politics of Tourism and Identity." Thesis. Florida State U, 2009.

MacMillan, Dougald. "John Kuners." *Journal of American Folklore,* vol. 151, 1926, pp. 53–57.

Maehler, Herwig. "Roman Poets on Egypt." *Ancient Perspectives on Egypt,* edited by Roger Matthews and Cornelia Roemer, UCL Press / Institute of Archaeology, 2003, pp. 203–215.

Magnus, Kellie. "The Wrongs and Rights of Jamaica Carnival," https://www.caribbean-beat.com/issue-132/word-mouth-marchapril-2015#axzz6qG2J3xdh.

Manning, Frank. "Carnival and the West Indian Diaspora." *Round Table,* 1983, pp. 186–96.

Manuel, Peter, et al. *Caribbean Currents: Caribbean Music from Rumba to Reggae.* Temple UP, 1995.

Marling, Karal. *Merry Christmas! Celebrating America's Greatest Holiday.* Harvard UP, 2000.

Marsden, Peter. *An Account of the Island of Jamaica; with Reflections on the Treatment, Occupation, and Provisions of the Slaves.* Newcastle, 1788.

Martin, Denis. *Coon Carnival: New Year in Cape Town, Past to Present.* David Philip, 1999.

Martin, Nona, and Virgil Storr. "Demystifying Bay Street: Black Tuesday and the Radicalization of Bahamian Politics in the 1960s." *Journal of Caribbean History,* vol. 43, 2009, pp. 37–50.

Martin, Nona, and Virgil Storr. "Whose Bay Street? Competing Narratives of Nassau's City Centre." *Island Studies Journal,* vol. 4, 2009, pp. 25–42.

Martinez, Maurice. "Delight in Repetition: The Black Indians." *Wavelength,* vol. 16, 1982, pp. 21–26.

Mason, Peter. *Bacchanal!: The Carnival Culture of Trinidad.* Latin America Bureau, 1998.

Massey, Gerald. *Ancient Egypt, the Light of the World: A Work of Reclamation and Restitution in Twelve Books.* T. F. Unwin, 1907.

Mate, Mavis. "Work and Leisure." *A Social History of England, 1200–1500,* edited by Rosemary Horrox and W. Mark Ormond, Cambridge UP, 2006, pp. 282–92.

Matheson, Donald. *The Folklore of St. Christopher's Island.* Creole Graphics, 1985.

Matory, James L. *Black Atlantic Religion: Tradition, Transnationalism, and Matriarchy in the Afro-Brazilian Candomblé.* Princeton UP, 2005.

Matory, James L. "The 'New World' Surrounds an Ocean: Theorizing the Live Dialogue between African and African American Cultures." *Afro-Atlantic Dialogues: Anthropology in the Diaspora,* edited by Kevin Yelvington, School of American Research Press, 2006, pp. 151–92.

Matthews, Roger, and Cornelia Roemer, editors. *Ancient Perspectives on Egypt.* UCL Press, 2003.

Maxwell, Clarence. "Enslaved Merchants, Enslaved Merchant-Mariners, and the Bermuda Conspiracy of 1761." *Early American Studies,* vol. 7, 2009, pp. 140–78.

Maxwell, Clarence. "'The Horrid Villainy': Sarah Bassett and the Poisoning Conspiracies in Bermuda, 1727–1730." *Slavery and Abolition,* vol. 21, 2000, pp. 48–74.

McCartney, Donald M. *Bahamian Culture and Factors Which Impact upon It: A Compilation of Two Essays.* Dorrance, 2004.

McCartney, Timothy O. *Ten, Ten, the Bible Ten: Obeah in the Bahamas.* Timpaul, 1976.

McCrum, Mark. *Going Dutch in Beijing: How to Behave Properly When Far Away from Home.* Henry Holt and Co., 2008.

McDaniel, Lorna. *The Big Drum Ritual of Carriacou: Praisesongs in Rememory of Flight.* UP of Florida, 1998.

McDonald, Roderick A. *The Economy and Material Culture of Slaves: Goods and Chattels on the Sugar Plantations of Jamaica and Louisiana.* Louisiana State UP, 1993.

McGeough, Kevin M. *The Romans: An Introduction.* Oxford UP, 2009.

McGinty, Park. *Interpretation and Dionysos: Method in the Study of a God.* Mouton, 1978.

McGregory, Jerrilyn. *Wiregrass Country.* UP of Mississippi, 1997.

McKay, Claude. *My Green Hills of Jamaica.* U of Exeter P, 1922.

McKoy, Henry. "Do You Remember When?" 1905, https://digital.lib.ecu.edu/17026.

Medoff, Rafael. *Baksheesh Diplomacy: Secret Negotiations between American Jewish Leaders and Arab Officials on the Eve of World War II.* Lexington Books, 2001.

Miles, Clement A. *Christmas in Ritual and Tradition, Christian and Pagan.* T. F. Unwin, 1912.

Miller, Daniel. "Christmas in Trinidad." *Unwrapping Christmas,* edited by Daniel Miller, Clarendon, 1993, pp. 134–56.

Miller, Paul B. "Africanity and Continuum in Sacred and Popular Trinidadian Musical Forms." *Music, Writing, and Cultural Unity in the Caribbean,* edited by Timothy Riess, Africa World, 2005.

Mills, Frank, et al. *Christmas Sports in St. Kitts-Nevis: Our Neglected Cultural Tradition.* F. L. Mills and S. B. Jones-Hendrickson, 1984.

Minnis, Jessica, editor. *Junkanoo and Religion: Christianity and Cultural Identity in the Bahamas—Papers Presented at the Junkanoo Symposium, March 2002.* Media Enterprises, 2003.

Minshall, Peter. "Masman/Artist." Innes et al.

Minshall, Peter. "'To Play Mas.'" *Caribbean Quarterly,* vol. 45, no. 2–3, 1999, pp. 30–35, http://www.jstor.org/stable/40654077.

Mintz, Sidney W., and Richard Price. *An Anthropological Approach to the Afro-American Past.* Institute for the Study of Human Issues, 1976.

Mitchell, Margaret. "Epiphanic Evolutions." *Earliest Christinity: Illinois Classical Studies,* vol. 29, 2004, pp. 183–204.

Molton, Fred. "The Case of Blackness." *Criticism,* vol. 50, 2008, pp. 177–218.

Monteith, Kathleen E. A., and Glen Richards, editors. *Jamaica in Slavery and Freedom: History, Heritage and Culture.* U of the West Indies P, 2002.

Moore, Brian, and Michele Johnson. "Celebrating Christmas in Jamaica, 1865–1920: From Creole Carnival to 'Civilized' Convention." *Jamaica in Slavery and Freedom: History, Heritage and Culture,* edited by Kathleen E. A. Monteith and Glen Richards, U of the West Indies P, 2002, pp. 144–78.

Moore, Louis T. *Stories Old and New of the Cape Fear Region.* Wilmington, 1956.

Moreno, Jairo. "Bauzá-Gillespie-Latin/Jazz: Difference, Modernity, and the Black Caribbean." *The South Atlantic Quarterly,* 2004, pp. 81–99.

Morley, David. "Where the Global Meets the Local." *Screen,* vol. 32, 1991, pp. 1–15.

Mosimba. *The History of St. Kitts and Nevis Carnival.* Xlibris, 2011.

Moss, Valeria Mosely. *Reminiscing: Memories of Old Nassau.* Media, 2001.

Muir, Edward. *Ritual in Early Modern Europe.* Cambridge UP, 1997.

Munro, Martin. *Different Drummers: Rhythm and Race in the Americas.* U of California P, 2010.

Mwakikagile, Godfrey. *Belize and Its Identity.* Africa World, 2010.

Nanni, Giordano. *The Colonisation of Time: Ritual, Routine, and Resistance in the British Empire.* Manchester UP, 2012.

Nechvatal, Joseph. "Immersion into Noise." Open Humanities Press, 2011, http://dx.doi.org/10.3998/ohp.9618970.0001.001.

Nehusi, Kimani S. K. "Migration, Transmission, and Maintenance." *Museum International,* vol. 56, 2004, pp. 78–83.

Nehusi, Kimani S. K. "The Origins of Carnival: Notes from a Preliminary Investigation." *Ah Come Back Home: Perspectives on the Trinidad and Tobago Carnival,* edited by Ian Isidore Smart and Kimani S. K. Nehusi, Original World Press, 2000, pp. 77–104.

Nelson, Havelock, and Michael A. Gonzales. *Bring the Noise: A Guide to Rap Music and Hip-Hop Culture.* Harmony Books, 1991.

Nettleford, Rex. *Mirror, Mirror: Identity, Race, and Protest in Jamaica.* W. Collins and Sangster, 1970.

Nketia, J. H. Kwabena. "The Intensity Factor in African Music." *Performance in Contemporary African Arts,* edited by Ruth Stone, Folklore Institute, 1988, pp. 53–86.

Nevil, Bob. "Fixing Our Downtown." *The National Guardian,* 23 Oct. 2013.

Newton, Margaret. *Glimpses of Life in Bermuda and the Tropics.* Digby and Long, 1897.

Nicholls, Robert. *The Jumbies' Playing Ground: Old World Influence on Afro-Creole Masquerades in the Eastern Caribbean.* UP of Mississippi, 2012.

Nicholls, Robert. "The Mocko Jumbie of the U.S. Virgin Islands: History and Antecedents." *African Arts,* vol. 32, 1999, p. 48.

Nicholls, Robert. *Old-Time Masquerading in the U.S. Virgin Islands.* Virgin Islands Humanities Council, 1998.

Nissenbaum, Stephen. *The Battle for Christmas.* Alfred A. Knopf, 1996.

Noel, James. *Black Religion and the Imagination of Matter in the Atlantic World.* Palgrave, 2009.

Nunley, John, and Judith Bethlehem, editors. *Caribbean Festival Arts: Each and Every Bit of Difference.* U of Washington P, 1988.

Nurse, Keith. "Globalization and Trinidad Carnival: Diaspora, Hybridity and Identity in Global Culture." *Cultural Studies,* vol. 13, 1999, pp. 661–90.

Ober, Frederick A. *A Guide to the West Indies and Bermudas.* Dodd, Mead, 1908.

Oliver, M. Cynthia. *Queen of the Virgins: Pageantry and Black Womanhood in the Caribbean.* UP of Mississippi, 2009.

Oliver, M. Cynthia. "Winin' Yo' Wais': The Changing Tastes of Dance on the U.S. Virgin Island of St. Croix." Sloat, *Caribbean Dance*, pp. 199–220.

Olwig, Karen. "Cultural Sites: Sustaining a Home in a Deterritorialized World." *Siting Culture: The Shifting Anthropological Object*, edited by Kirsten Hastrup and Karen Olwig, Routledge, 1997, pp. 17–38.

Olwig, Karen Fog. *Global Culture, Island Identity: Continuity and Change in the Afro-Caribbean Community of Nevis*. Harwood Academic, 1993.

"Origins of Boxing Day." *Jamaica Gleaner*, 21 Feb. 2000.

Orlin, Eric. "Urban Religion in the Middle and Late Republic." *A Companion to Roman Religion*, edited by Jörg Rüpke, Wiley, 2011, pp. 58–70.

Ortiz, Fernando. *Cuban Counterpoint: Tobacco and Sugar*. 1947. Translated by Harriet De Onís et al., Duke UP, 1995.

Ottenberg, Simon, and David Aaron Binkley. *Playful Performers: African Children's Masquerades*. Transaction Publishers, 2006.

Ottley, Carlton Robert. *The Trinidad Callaloo: Life in Trinidad from 1851–1900*. Crusoe Publishing House, 1978.

Ownby, Ted. *Subduing Satan: Religion, Recreation, and Manhood in the Rural South, 1865–1920*. U of North Carolina P, 1990.

Packwood, Cyril Outerbridge. *Chained on the Rock: Slavery in Bermuda*. E. Torres, 1975.

Palacio, Joseph O., editor. *The Garifuna: A Nation across Border: Essays in Social Anthropology*. Cubola Productions, 2005.

Palmer, Robert. *Deep Blues*. Penguin, 1982.

Palmié, Stephan. "Creolization and Its Discontents." *Annual Review of Anthropology*, vol. 35, 2006, pp. 433–56.

Palmié, Stephan. "Is There a Model in the Muddle? 'Creolization' in African American History and Anthropology." *Creolization and Diaspora: Historical, Ethnographic, and Theoretical Perspectives*, edited by C. Stewart, Left Shore Press, 2007, pp. 178–200.

Parsons, Alan. *A Winter in Paradise*. A. M. Philpot, 1926.

Parsons, Elsie Clews. "Spirituals and Other Folklore from the Bahamas." *Journal of American Folklore*, vol. 41, 1928, pp. 453–524.

Patterson, Orlando. *The Sociology of Slavery: An Analysis of the Origins, Development, and Structure of Negro Slave Society in Jamaica*. Fairleigh Dickinson UP, 1967.

Pelzer, Jon Stuart. "Three Kings Day on St. Croix." *Caribbean Impressions*, 1991, pp. 3–10.

Pernet, Henry. *Ritual Masks: Deceptions and Revelations*. U of South Carolina P, 1992.

Perrotte, Tony, editor. *Belize*. APA Publications, 1995.

Perry, Paul. *Jesus in Egypt: Discovering the Secrets of Christ's Childhood Years*. Ballantine Books, 2003.

Peters, Michael. "SVG's Unique Tradition Turns 100 Years." iWitness News, 3 June 2013.

Phillip, Lyndon. "Reading Caribana 1997: Black Youth, Puff Daddy, and Diaspora Transformations." Green and Scher, pp. 102–35.

Piersen, William. "African-American Festive Style." *Signifyin(g), Sanctifyin', & Slam Dunking: A Reader in African American Expressive Culture*, edited by Gena Caponi, U of Massachusetts P, 1999, pp. 417–33.

Piersen, William. "African American Festive Style and the Creation of American Culture." *Riot and Revelry in Early America*, edited by Dennis Pencak, Penn State UP, 2002, pp. 255–72.

Pimlott, J. A. R. *The Englishman's Christmas*. Harvester, 1978.

Poitier, Khashan. "Social and Community News." *The Nassau Guardian*, 16 Aug. 2002, n.p.

Pope, Pauline. "Cruzan Slavery: An Ethnohistorical Study of Differential Responses to Slavery in the Danish West Indies." Diss. U of California, Davis, 1969.

Powles, L. D. The Land of the Pink Pearl; or, Recollections of Life in the Bahamas. London, 1888.

Powrie, Barbara E. "The Changing Attitude of the Coloured Middle Class Towards Carnival." Caribbean Quarterly, vol. 4, no. 3–4, 1956, pp. 224–32, http://www.jstor.org/stable/40652636.

Pratt, Mary Louise. Imperial Eyes: Travel Writing and Transculturation. Routledge, 1992.

Pullen-Burry, Bessie. Ethiopia in Exile: Jamaica Revisited. T. F. Unwin, 1905.

Rahier, Jean Muteba. Kings for Three Days: The Play of Race and Gender in an Afro-Ecuadorian Festival. U of Illinois P, 2013.

Rashford, John. "Plants, Spirits and the Meaning of 'John' in Jamaica." Jamaica Journal, vol. 17, no. 2, 1984, pp. 62–70.

Rath, Richard Cullen. "Drums and Power: Ways of Creolizing Music in Coastal South Carolina and Georgia, 1730–1790." Buisseret and Reinhardt, pp. 99–130.

Ray, R. Celeste. Southern Heritage on Display: Public Ritual and Ethnic Diversity within Southern Regionalism. U of Alabama P, 2003.

Regis, Louis. The Political Calypso True Opposition in Trinidad and Tobago, 1962–1987. UP of Florida, 1998.

Reid, Ira De A. "The John Canoe Festival: A New World Africanism." Phylon, vol. 3, no. 4, 1942, pp. 345–46, 349–70.

Restad, Penne. Christmas in America: A History. Oxford, 1995.

Rezende, Elizabeth. "Renovating the Barracks' Ruins." The Virgin Islands Daily News, 16 Feb. 2017, http://www.virginislandsdailynews.com/news/renovating-the-barracks-ruins/article_bob7c43f-ee1c-58f2-896d-96b5465bfbb7.html.

Rice, Michael. Egypt's Making: The Origins of Ancient Egypt, 5000–2000 BC. Routledge, 1990.

Richardson, Bonham C. Caribbean Migrants: Environment and Human Survival on St. Kitts and Nevis. U of Tennessee P, 1983.

Richardson, Bonham C. Igniting the Caribbean's Past Fire in British West Indian History. U of North Carolina P, 2004.

Riggio, Milla Cozart. Carnival Culture in Action: The Trinidad Experience. Routledge, 2004.

Rigoglioso, Marguerite. The Cult of Divine Birth in Ancient Greece. Palgrave Macmillan, 2009.

Ritzer, George. The Globalization of Nothing. Pine Forge Press, 2004.

Rivera, Eulalie. Growing Up on St. Croix: Recollections of a Crucian Girlhood, Including a Selection of Best-Loved Virgin Islands Spirituals, a Description of a Tea Meeting, and Some of the Games We Played. Antilles Graphic, 1987.

Roach, Joseph R. Cities of the Dead: Circum-Atlantic Performance. Columbia UP, 1996.

Roberts, Frank. "Lee Daniels's Double Consciousness." The Feminist Wire, 20 Aug. 2013.

Robertson, Roland. "Glocalization: Time-Space and Homogeneity-Heterogeneity." Global Modernities, edited by Roland Robertson, Sage Publications, 1995, pp. 25–44.

Robbins, Walter L. "Christmas Shooting Rounds in America and Their Background." Journal of American Folklore, vol. 86, no. 339, pp. 48–52.

Robinson, Bill. Where the Trade Winds Blow: A Yachting Guide to Southern Waters of FL, the Bahamas . . . etc. Scribner's, 1963.

Robinson, M., and D. Picard. Tourism, Culture and Sustainable Development. Division of Cultural Policies and Intercultural Dialogue, Culture Sector, UNESCO, 2006.

Rohlehr, Gordon. "The Calypsonian as Artist: Freedom and Responsibility." Small Axe, 2001, pp. 1–26.

Rohlehr, Gordon. "The State of Calypso Today." Trinidad and Tobago Review, 1997, pp. 10–12.

Roll, Susan K. Toward the Origins of Christmas. Kok Pharos Pub. House, 1995.

Rolle, Rashad. "Junkanoo Brings Happiness But Costs $10m in Unwaged Labour." *The Tribune*, 20 Oct. 2014.

Rommen, Timothy. *Funky Nassau: Roots, Routes, and Representation in Bahamian Popular Music*. U of California P, 2011.

Rommen, Timothy. "Home Sweet Home: Junkanoo as National Discourse in Bahamas." *Black Music Research Journal*, vol. 19, 1999, pp. 71–92.

Rose, Tricia. *Black Noise: Rap Music and Black Culture in Contemporary America*. Wesleyan UP, 1994.

Roy, Christian. *Old English Customs*. Drake Publishers, 1973.

Runciman, Steven. *A History of the Crusades*. Cambridge UP, 1951.

Rushe, George. *Your Bermuda: All You Need to Know about Our Island Home*. 1995.

Russel, David. "Nostalgic Tourism." *Journal of Travel & Tourism Marketing*, vol. 25, 2008, pp. 103–116.

Rylander, Amalia. "The Belizean Garifuna Identity: Migratory and Transnational Space and Its Effects on the Home Community." Thesis. U of Tromsø, 2010.

Ryman, Cheryl. "Jonkonnu: A Neo-African Form." *Jamaica Journal,* vol. 17, no. 1, 1984, pp. 13–23 and vol. 17, no. 2, 1984, pp. 50–61.

Ryman, Cheryl. "When Jamaica Dances." *Making Caribbean Dance: Continuity and Creativity in Island Cultures,* edited by Susanna Sloat, UP of Florida, 2010, pp. 97–131.

Said, Edward. *Musical Elaborations*. Columbia UP, 1991.

Salzman, Michele Renee. "Religious Koine and Religious Dissent." *A Companion to Roman Religion*, edited by Jörg Rüpke, Blackwell Pub., 2007, pp. 109–126.

Samuels, Shepard. "In the Caribbean, It's Jonkonnu!" *Wavelength,* vol. 16, 1982, pp. 16–18.

Samuelson, Sue. *Christmas: An Annotated Bibliography*. Garland, 1982.

Sands, Kirkley. *Early Bahamian Slave Spirituality: The Genesis of Bahamian Cultural Identity*. Nassau Guardian Limited, 2008.

Sands, Kirkley. "Junkanoo in Historical Perspective." Minnis, pp. 10–19.

Sands, Kirkley. "Theological Implications of Junkanoo." Minnis, pp. 69–74.

Sands, Rosita. "Carnival Celebrations in Africa and the New World: Junkanoo and the Black Indians of Mardi Gras." *Black Music Research Journal*, vol. 11, 1991, pp. 75–92.

Sands, Rosita. "Conversation with Maureen 'Bahama Mama' Duvalier and Ronald Simms: Junkanoo Past, Present, and Future." *The Black Perspective in Music*, vol. 17, 1989, pp. 93–108.

Sands, Rosita. "The Musical Culture of Junkanoo." *Wooster Review*, vol. 9, 1989, pp. 143–53.

Sandys, William. *Christmastide: Its History, Festivals and Carols*. Norwood, PA, 1860.

Santino, Jack. "The Carnivalesque and the Ritualesque." *Journal of American Folklore*, vol. 124, 2011, pp. 61–73.

Santino, Jack. "The Ritualesque: Festival, Politics, and Popular Culture." *Western Folklore*, vol. 68, no. 1, 2009, pp. 9–26.

Saunders, Gail. *The Bahamas: A Family of Islands*. Macmillan, 1993.

Saunders, Gail. *Bahamian Loyalists and Their Slaves*. Macmillan Caribbean, 1983.

Saunders, Gail. *Bahamian Society after Emancipation*. Ian Randle Publishers, 2003.

Saunders, Gail. *Social Life in the Bahamas, 1880s-1920s*. Rosebud, 1996.

Saunders, Gail, and Donald Cartwright. *Historic Nassau*. Macmillan Caribbean, 1980.

Saunders, Winston. "The Cultural Arts in the Bahamas." *Modern Bahamian Society*, edited by Dean Collinwood and Steve Dodge, Caribbean Books, 1989.

Schafer, R. Murray. *The New Soundscape: A Handbook for the Modern Music Teacher*. BMI Canada, 1969.

Schafer, R. Murray. "Soundscapes and Earwitness." *Hearing History: A Reader,* edited by Mark Smith, U of Georgia P, 2004.

Schafer, R. Murray. *The Tuning of the World: Toward a Theory of Soundscape Design.* U of Pennsylvania P, 1980.

Schaw, Janet, et al. *Journal of a Lady of Quality; Being the Narrative of a Journey from Scotland to the West Indies, North Carolina, and Portugal, in the Years 1774 to 1776.* Yale UP, 1921.

Schechner, Richard. *The Future of Ritual.* Routledge, 1993.

Scheffler, Mark. "Scare Tactics: Why Are Liberian Soldiers Wearing Fright Wigs?" *Slate,* 1 Aug. 2003.

Scher, Philip W. *Carnival and the Formation of a Caribbean Transnation.* UP of Florida, 2003.

Scher, Philip W. "The Power and Pitfalls of Carnival as Cultural Heritage." Innes et al.

Scher, Philip W. "When 'Natives' Become Tourist of Themselves: Returning Transnationals and the Carnival in Trinidad and Tobago." Green and Scher.

Schrader, Richard A. *Kallaloo: A Collection of Crucian Stories.* 1991.

Schrader, Richard A. *Notes of a Crucian Son.* 1989.

Schrader, Richard A. *St. Croix in Another Time.* 1990.

Schuerkens, Ulrike. "Social Transformations between Global Forces and Local Life-Worlds: Introduction." *Current Sociology,* vol. 5, 2003, pp. 195–208.

Scott, David. *Conscripts of Modernity: The Tragedy of Colonial Enlightenment.* Duke UP, 2004.

Scott, Michael. *Tom Cringle's Log.* New York, 1895.

Segrave, Kerry. *Tipping: An American Social History of Gratuities.* McFarland & Company, 2009.

Shafer, Byron E., et al. *Religion in Ancient Egypt: Gods, Myths, and Personal Practice.* Cornell UP, 1991.

Shepherd, Verene. *Working Slavery, Pricing Freedom: Perspectives from the Caribbean, Africa, and the African Diaspora.* Palgrave, 2002.

Shoman, Assad. *[13] Chapters of a History of Belize.* Angelus Press, 1994.

Showerman, Grant. *Rome and the Romans: A Survey and Interpretation.* Macmillan Co., 1931.

Silverman, David. "Divinity and Deities in Ancient Egypt." *Religion in Ancient Egypt: Gods, Myths, and Personal Practice,* edited by Byron Shafer, Cornell UP, 1991, pp. 7–87.

Sloane, Hans, et al. *A Voyage to the Islands Madera, Barbados, Nieves, S. Christophers and Jamaica, with the Natural History . . . of the Last of Those Islands: To Which Is Prefix'd an Introduction, Wherein Is an Account of the Inhabitants, Air, Waters, Diseases, Trade, &C. . . . ; Illustrated with the Figures of the Things Describ'd.* London, 1707.

Sloat, Susanna, editor. *Caribbean Dance from Abakuá to Zouk: How Movement Shapes Identity.* UP of Florida, 2002.

Sloat, Susanna, editor. *Making Caribbean Dance: Continuity and Creativity in Island Cultures.* UP of Florida, 2010.

Smith, M. G. *The Plural Society in the British West Indies.* U of California P, 1965.

Smith, Mark M. *Mastered by the Clock: Time, Slavery, and Freedom in the American South.* U of North Carolina P, 1997.

Smith, Mark Michael, editor. *Hearing History: A Reader.* U of Georgia P, 2004.

Smith, Richard. "Gombey Dancers Lend a Primitive Touch." *The Bermudian,* vol. 17–18, 1946, n.p.

Smith, Theophus Harold. *Conjuring Culture: Biblical Formations of Black America.* Oxford UP, 1994.

Smithsonian Folklife Festival, 2001. Smithsonian Institution, 2001.

Soja, Edward. "Reassertions Towards a Spatialized Ontology." *Postmodern Geographies: Reassertion of Space in Critical Social Theory,* Verso, 1989, pp. 118–37.

Solien, Nancie. "West Indian Characteristics of the Black Carib." *Southwestern Journal of Anthropology*, vol. 15, Autumn 1959, pp. 300–307.

Sörgel, Sabine. "Dancing Postcolonialism: The National Dance Theatre Company of Jamaica." 2007. Transcript.

Southern, Eileen. *Black Americans: A History*. W. W. Norton, 1971.

Spicer, Dorothy Gladys. *Yearbook of English Festivals*. H. W. Wilson Co., 1954.

Sprung, James. "'Jonkonnu' or 'John Kunering' or 'John Kooner' at Christmas." Cape Fear Historical Institute, 2006, http://www.cfhi.net/JohnKuneringatChristmas.php.

Staff Writer. "Crucian Christmas Festival Set for Frederiksted Again." *St. Croix Source*, 9 Sept. 2005, n.p.

Stark, James H. *Stark's History and Guide to the Bahama Islands*. Boston, 1891.

Stausberg, Micheal. "Approaches to the Study of 'Time' in the History of Religions." *Temenos*, vols. 39–40, 2004, pp. 247–68.

Steber, Bill. "Interview: Bernice Turner Pratcher." *Living Blues*, vol. 34, no. 168, p. 135.

Steelman, Bennett L. "John Kuners." 2006, http://ncpedia.org/john-kuners.

Stern, Robin. *Say It in Crucian: A Complete Guide to Today's Crucian for Speakers of Standard English*. Antilles, 2008.

Stewart, Charles. *Creolization: History, Ethnography, Theory*. Left Coast Press, 2007.

Stewart, Charles. "Syncretism and Its Synonym: Reflections on Cultural Mixture." *Diacritics*, vol. 29, 1999, pp. 40–62.

Stone, Michael. "Garifuna Song, Groove Locale, and 'World-Music' Mediation." *Globalization, Cultural Identities, and Media Representations*, edited by Natascha Gentz and Stefan Kramer, State U of New York P, 2012.

Storr, Virgil Henry. "Weber's Spirit of Capitalism and the Bahamas' Junkanoo Ethic." *The Review of Austrian Economics*, vol. 19, 2006, pp. 209–309.

Stravinsky, Igor. *The Rite of Spring*. Dover Publications, 2000.

Strode, Hudson. *The Story of Bermuda*. Harrison Smith & Robert Haas, 1932.

Strouhal, Evžen, and Werner Forman. *Life of the Ancient Egyptians*. U of Oklahoma P, 1992.

Stuckey, Sterling. *Slave Culture: Nationalist Theory and the Foundations of Black America*. Oxford UP, 1987.

Stuempfle, Stephen. *The Steelband Movement: The Forging of a National Art in Trinidad and Tobago*. U of Pennsylvania P, 1995.

Suárez, Juan Antonio. *Pop Modernism: Noise and the Reinvention of the Everyday*. U of Illinois P, 2007.

Swan, Quito. *Black Power in Bermuda: The Struggle for Decolonization*. Palgrave Macmillan, 2009.

Tallant, Robert. *Mardi Gras*. Doubleday, 1948.

Tapper, Joan. "Magical History Tour." *Islands Magazine*, Sept.-Oct. 2006, pp. 78–85.

Taylor, Douglas MacRae. *The Black Carib of British Honduras*. Johnson Reprint Corp., 1963.

Terborg-Penn, Rosalyn, and Andrea Benton Rushing, editors. *Women in Africa and the African Diaspora: A Reader*. Howard UP, 1996.

Thomas, Deborah A. *Modern Blackness: Nationalism, Globalization, and the Politics of Culture in Jamaica*. Duke UP, 2004.

Thomas, Nicholas, and Krista A. Thompson. *An Eye for the Tropics: Tourism, Photography, and Framing the Caribbean Picturesque*. Duke UP, 2007.

Thomas, Tamika. "Boxing Day: Not Sure about Origins, But It's a VI Holiday." *St. Thomas Source*, 23 Dec. 2003.

Thomas-Hope, Elizabeth. "Globalization and the Development of a Caribbean Migration Culture." *Caribbean Migration: Globalised Identities,* edited by Mary Chamberlain, Routledge, 1998, pp. 188–202.

Thompson, E. P. "The Moral Economy of the English Crowd in the 18th Century." *Past & Present,* vol. 50, 1971, pp. 76–136.

Thompson, Krista A. "Destroying While Preserving Junkanoo: The Junkanoo Museum in the Bahamas." *Museum Frictions: Public Cultures/Global Transformations,* edited by Ivan Karp, Duke UP, 2006, pp. 500–503.

Thompson, Krista A. *Shine: The Visual Economy of Light in African Diasporic Aesthetic Practice.* 2015.

Thomson, P. A. B. *Belize: A Concise History.* Macmillan, 2004.

Thrall, William Flint, et al. *A Handbook to Literature.* Macmillan, 1992.

Thuan, Trinh Xuan, and Matthieu Ricard. *The Quantum and the Lotus: A Journey to the Frontiers Where Science and Buddhism Meet.* Crown, 2009.

Thuersam, Bernhard. "'Jonkonnu' or 'John Kunering' at Christmas." Cape Fear Historical Institute, 2006, http://www.cfhi.net/JohnKuneringatChristmas.php.

Thurland, Karen C. *The Neighborhoods of Christiansted: St. Croix, 1910–1960.* Author House, 2009.

Tille, Alexander. *Yule and Christmas: Their Place in the Germanic Year.* London, 1899.

Toner, J. P. *Leisure and Ancient Rome.* Polity Press, 1995.

Tsuji, Teruyuki. "The 'Other Half': The Articulation of Carnival in Nineteenth-Century Trinidad." Innes et al.

Tuan, Y. F. "Place: An Experiential Perspective." *Geographical Review,* vol. 65, 1975, pp. 151–65.

Tucker, Terry. *Bermuda: Today and Yesterday, 1503–1973.* R. Hale, 1975.

Turner, Carlton. *Overcoming Self-Negation: The Church and Junkanoo in Contemporary Bahamian Society.* Pickwick, 2020.

Turner, Samuel P. "Maritime Insights from St. Augustine's British Period: From St. Augustine's British Documentary Records." *Escriban,* vol. 47, 2010, pp. 1–21.

Tyerman, Christopher. *The Invention of the Crusades.* U of Toronto P, 1998.

Tyson, George F., and Arnold R. Highfield. *The Kamina Folk: Slavery and Slave Life in the Danish West Indies.* Virgin Islands Humanities Council, 1994.

Van Deburg, William L. *Hoodlums: Black Villains and Social Bandits in American Life.* U of Chicago P, 2004.

VanSpanckeren, Kathryn. "The Mardi Gras Indian Song Cycle: A Heroic Tradition in Southern Heritage on Display." *MELUS,* vol. 16, 1989–90, pp. 41–56.

Van Stipriaan, Alex. "The Ever-Changing Face of Watramama in Suriname: A Water Goddess in Creolization Since the Seventeenth Century." *Sacred Waters: Arts for Mami Wata and Other Divinities in Africa and the Diaspora,* edited by Henry Drewal, Indiana UP, 2008, pp. 525–48.

Varlack, Pearl, and Norwell Harrigan. "Social Change in the British Virgin Islands." Keynote address delivered at the BVI Mental Health Association Symposium of Social Change, Tortola, BVI, 20–22 May 1982.

Varlack, Pearl, and Norwell Harrigan. *The Virgin Islands Story.* Caribbean UP, 1975.

Vas-Deville, Kim, editor. *Walking Raddy: The Baby Dolls of New Orleans.* UP of Mississippi, 2018.

Verrill, A. Hyatt. *The Book of the West Indies.* E. P. Dutton, 1919.

Walts, Dawn Simmons. "Time's Reckoning: Time, Value, and the Mercantile Class in Late Medieval English Literature." 2007.

Walser, Richard. "His Worship the John Kuner." *North Carolina Folklore Journal*, vol. 19, 1971, pp. 160–72.

Ward, Brian, et al. *The American South and the Atlantic World*. UP of Florida, 2013.

Wardle, Huon. *An Ethnography of Cosmopolitanism in Kingston, Jamaica*. E. Mellen Press, 2000.

Warner, Lee H. *Free Men in an Age of Servitude: Three Generations of a Black Family*. UP of Kentucky, 1992.

Warner-Lewis, Maureen. *Central Africa in the Caribbean: Transcending Time, Transforming Cultures*. U of the West Indies P, 2003.

Waters, Anita. "Presenting the Past: The Construction of National History in a Jamaican Tourist Site." *Modern Political Culture in the Caribbean*, edited by Holger Henke and Fred Réno, U of the West Indies P, 2003, pp. 148–80.

Weaver, D. B. "Mass Tourism and Alternative Tourism in the Caribbean." *Tourism and the Less Developed World: Issues and Case Studies*, edited by David Harrison, Halsted, 1992, pp. 161–74.

Weed, Thurlow, et al. *Life of Thurlow Weed Including His Autobiography and a Memoir*. Boston, 1883.

Weightman, Gavin, and Stephen Humphries. *Christmas Past*. Sidgwick & Jackson, 1987.

Westergaard, Waldemar. *The Slave and the Planter*. Reprint. Bondmen and Freemen.

Whelan, Yvonne. "Mapping Meanings." *Senses of Place: Senses of Time*, edited by G. J. Ashworth and B. J. Graham, Ashgate, 2005, pp. 61–72.

Wheelock, Stefan M. *Barbaric Culture and Black Critique: Black Antislavery Writers, Religion, and the Slaveholding Atlantic*. U of Virginia P, 2016.

Whipple, Emory Clark. "Music of the Black Caribs of British Honduras." Thesis. U of Texas at Austin, 1971.

Whittingham, Ferdinand. *Bermuda: A Colony, a Fortress, a Prison*. Longmans Brown Green, 1857.

Wilkie, Laurie A., and Paul Farnsworth. *Sampling Many Pots: An Archaeology of Memory and Tradition at a Bahamian Plantation*. UP of Florida, 2005.

Williams, Joseph. *Whisperings of the Caribbean: Reflections of a Missionary*. Benziger, 1925.

Williams, Rolston. "Christmases Past in Nevis." Saint Kitts and Nevis, s.l., 1985.

Williams-Mysers, A. "Pinkster Carnival: Africanisms in the Hudson River Valley." *Afro-Americans in New York Life and History*, vol. 9, no. 1, 1985, p. 7.

Willocks, Harold. *The Umbilical Cord: The History of the United States Virgin Islands from Pre-Columbian Era to the Present*. 1995.

Wilson, Sule Greg. *The Drummer's Path: Moving the Spirit with Ritual and Traditional Drumming*. Destiny Books, 1992.

Wisdom, Keith Gordon. "Bahamian Junkanoo: An Act in a Modern Social Drama." Diss. U of Georgia, 1985.

Wood, Vivian Nina Michelle. "Rushin' Hard and Runnin' Hot: Experiencing the Music of the Junkanoo Parade in Nassau, Bahamas." Diss. Indiana U, 1995.

Wright, R. Little. *Revels in Jamaica, 1682–1838: Plays and Players of a Century, Tumblers and Conjurors, Musical Refugees and Solitary Showmen, Dinners, Balls and Cockfights, Darky Mummers and Other Memories of High Times and Merry Hearts*. Dodd, Mead, 1937.

Yelvington, Kevin A. *Afro-Atlantic Dialogues: Anthropology in the Diaspora*. School of American Research P, 2006.

Young, Deborah, and Simon Harris. "Demonizing the Night in Medieval Europe: A Temporal Monstrosity?" *The Monstrous Middle Ages*, edited by Bettina Bildhauer and Robert Mills, U of Toronto P, 2003, pp. 134–54.

Young, Thomas. *Narrative of a Residence on the Mosquito Shore: With an Account of Truxillo, and the Adjacent Islands of Bonacca and Roatan; and a Vocabulary of the Mosquitian Language.* London, 1847.

Zazek, Natalie. *Settler Society in the English Leeward Islands, 1670–1776.* Cambridge UP, 2010.

Zuill, William. *Bermuda Journey: A Leisurely Guidebook.* Bermuda Book Stores, 1946.

Zuill, William. *The Story of Bermuda and Her People.* Macmillan, 1973.

INDEX

ABOUT THE AUTHOR

Credit: Virgil Suarez

Jerrilyn McGregory is a full professor of folklore in the Department of English at Florida State University. She is author of *Wiregrass Country* and *Downhome Gospel: African American Spiritual Activism in Wiregrass Country.*